In-D
Interv

In-Depth Interviewing: Researching people

Victor Minichiello
Rosalie Aroni
Eric Timewell
Loris Alexander

Lincoln School of Health Sciences
La Trobe University

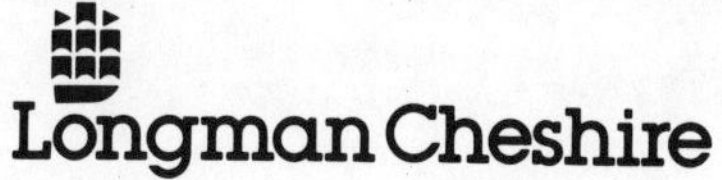

Longman Cheshire Pty Limited
Longman House
Kings Gardens
95 Coventry Street
Melbourne 3205 Australia

Offices in Sydney, Brisbane, Adelaide and Perth. Associated companies, branches and representatives throughout the world.

First published 1990
Reprinted 1991

Set in 10/11 Times Roman
Printed in Hong Kong

National Library of Australia
Cataloguing-in-Publication data

In-depth interviewing: researching people.
ISBN 0 582 71272 6.
1. Interviewing. I. Minichiello, Victor.
158.39

Contents

Preface

In-depth interviewing provides a discussion of the use of in-depth interviewing as a method for understanding people. The book is written for undergraduate and postgraduate social science and health science students who are studying research methods; for researchers who want a thorough exposition of the value of in-depth interviewing; and for clinical practitioners who wish to hone their skills.

This book was written at the request of our students who kept threatening to publish our lecture notes because they were unable to find an adequate Australian text. In some texts, in-depth interviewing is treated superficially as one among many research methods. In other texts, it is discussed as one of a number of ways of doing qualitative research and given second place to participant observation. A third type of book is the 'learned monograph' which attempts to put forward original and methodologically critical ideas but does not aid the novice and often uses jargon understood only by the initiated. Finally, there are manuals which provide prescriptive guidelines for the doing of 'good' in-depth interviewing. We believe that the intrinsic nature of in-depth interviewing does not lend itself to the manual or prescriptive text approach.

Therefore we have concentrated on one method—in-depth interviewing—by providing a systematic account of it. The book, written by a multi-disciplinary team, goes beyond simply providing a description of collecting data by this method. It shows the reader the relationship between theory and research; the connections between data collection, analysis and report writing; and the field strategies one might develop in order to cope with the social and political context of the research.

We hope that the book will stimulate interest in learning more about this method and its use in research. We do not, however, argue that this is the only way to collect and analyse data. We have written this book with the hope that the decision to use in-depth interviewing will emerge from an informed choice about the suitability of this method in relation to the research question being asked. If it is not regarded as suitable, we encourage the reader to consider learning and using other methods.

We would also like to caution the reader, especially the novice researcher, against making sweeping generalisations about how to evaluate research. Good research should be examined in terms of whether the researcher has conducted systematic and disciplined quality work. The exercise of comparing qualitative and quantitative methods and trying to determine which of these is better, more reliable and scientific has proved to be the fruitless chase of the 1970 and 80s. There is a growing appreciation that both approaches are legitimate tools of research and yield useful knowledge about people and their social world. Concepts such as sampling, reliability, and validity take on different meanings and purposes depending on the underlying premises of the approach used. Readers should not fall into the trap of using the criteria of one approach to judge another. Each method should be judged in the context of the conceptual and methodological principles which underpin it.

For students

The text was not written to be read like a novel. Some chapters contain more complex material than others. Digesting the information involves hard work and persistence. For this reason, we suggest that the student reads the book in the following way. First, skim the entire book to obtain a general understanding and appreciation of the scope, uses and issues surrounding the method. Do not get held up by difficult details but come back to them. Do not panic if you find chapters 2 and 3 difficult to grasp at first. The material presented here is a summation of many complex philosophical debates.

Second, reread the book, this time reading each chapter carefully and taking notes. Underline key issues and summarise these in your own words. Then you might wish to study selected chapters that pertain to your research project (for example, life histories, clinical in-depth interviewing). As with other research books, you may find that what you get from this book at one phase of your research project will change as you move from one phase to another.

Of course, as our own teachers have told us, learning how to do research ultimately rests on the experience of trial and error in the field. However, even this type of apprenticeship works more efficiently when the apprentice has a firm foundation. This book will provide you with that foundation so that you can confidently enter the field with a level of competence.

You will notice that we have highlighted words which are explained in a glossary at the end of each chapter. This will allow you to quickly check on new terms and their meanings. Students often complain about how jargon interferes with learning. However, jargon is a necessary evil because it enables the author to be more specific in defining the real world. Unfortunately, this specialised usage is not part of everyone's vocabulary. If the student wishes to participate in more advanced discourse then it is necessary to learn the language. The glossaries are there to be used as a means of understanding and demystifying the subject matter.

For the instructor

This text is not intended to be all things to all people. The aim of the book is to act as a guide rather than to be seen as a 'cookbook'. It does not cover all the special circumstances that may arise from the doing of in-depth interviewing. We believe that it would be inappropriate, if not impossible, to provide a recipe because each project will inevitably lead to different circumstances. We invite instructors to draw on their own research experience and knowledge to provide more detailed guidelines and illustrations to help students. We also would hope that instructors would take a critical approach and further discuss the definitions provided in the glossaries. Drawing on our own experience, we have found that the most useful and easily understood examples are those drawn from the disciplines in which the student is engaged. It is for this reason that we have purposely *not* set assignments at the end of each chapter.

Acknowledgements

The ideas for this book have evolved over a number of years through conversations with students and colleagues. The participants of the Australian Consortium for Social and Political Research Inc. summer programmes 1987–90 pointed to the need for such a book and provided us with the impetus for writing a textbook for teaching purposes. We are grateful for the support and encouragement given to us by our students and colleagues at the Lincoln School of Health Sciences, La Trobe University and for their thought-provoking discussions and constructive comments. In addition, we would like to thank Felicity Allen, Heather Gardner, Reverend David Hodges, Brigid McCoppin, Celia Ohlsen, Peter Otteson, Alison Page and Sue Stevenson who offered many useful ideas, criticism, comments and editorial assistance. We are grateful to Ron Harper at Longman Cheshire. He has proved a most patient and encouraging publisher. Our thanks to Carlo Golin for his graphic illustrations. Needless to say, only we are responsible for any weaknesses the book may have.

We owe a great deal to a number of people who have helped us in the preparation of this book. Carol Greene, Maggie Leek, Carol Nahal and Connie Purves deserve special mention for completing the onerous task of typing the manuscript and deciphering our handwriting. Our appreciation goes to Rita Calafiore, Margaret Green and Susan Inglis who provided invaluable assistance and time throughout the production of the manuscript. Their help considerably eased our work.

VM, RA, ET and LA
Lincoln School of Health Sciences
La Trobe University

For Claudie, Benni,
the Rechter family,
and to the memory of
the late
Carl Reinganum

Chapter 1
Introduction

There are a large number of research methods texts and manuals available on the market. So why would anyone want to add to their number? And why a book dealing with only one specific research method such as **in-depth interviewing?** This text was written because of our concerns regarding frequent misapprehensions about the use of in-depth interviewing as a method for understanding people.

The following quotation drawn from a conversation with one of our students illustrates the first misapprehension.

> I always thought that in-depth interviewing would be really easy until I got there. I bungled the first two interviews completely. It was only after I reread my lecture notes and spoke to people who had done it before that I had some idea of what to do next. (Undergraduate student at La Trobe University commenting on qualitative research methods assignment, 1989).

Most people assume that in-depth interviewing is not difficult to carry out because they have been exposed to journalistic interviewing. However, the interview is a far more complex and involved procedure when used as a social science research tool. Media presentations which rely on interviewing follow a pattern of interrogation rather than conversation. In-depth interviewing when used in social science research gives access to knowledge—a knowledge of meanings and interpretations that individuals give to their lives and events.

Secondly, we discovered an imbalance in research texts which are currently available in Australia. The large majority of these books have been written about what has come to be known as **quantitative research,** that is, those methods based on **positivist** understandings of social reality. Such understandings rely on looking for the causes of social phenomena apart from the subjective states of individuals (More detailed explanations can be found in chapters 2 and 3). In opposition to this, what is often labelled **qualitative research** was simply glossed over as being an alternative way of collecting data. This relatively minor mention gave the reader an indication of the low esteem in which such methods were held by authors and by implication, how readers should view this approach.

Apparently, qualitative methods did not conform to the canons of scientific method as described in such texts. In-depth interviewing as a qualitative research method is either not mentioned at all or it is briefly discussed in single paragraphs only. More recently, it has been presented in the context of 'asking questions' in chapters of books which deal predominantly with survey-style research (de Vaus 1985; Kidder and Judd 1986; Polgar and Thomas 1988). Such chapters focus largely on questionnaires and refer to interviewing as a complementary activity. However, when they use the term *interviewing* they are usually referring to structured interviews used in survey research. In-depth interviewing is called **unstructured interviewing** and is presented as an alternative to standardised or **structured interviewing**. These descriptions were usually restricted to less than a page of text in books of three hundred or more pages.

In the 1960s and 1970s, there was a change in the way that social science was thought of by many of its practitioners. The writing of this book is tied to these theoretical and methodological shifts which also became apparent in the social and health sciences in Australia. The perspective taken by these academics and researchers was the **anti-positivist approach** (also known as the **interpretivist, symbolic interactionist** or **social action** approaches). Irrespective of label, these perspectives followed the writings of certain German philosophers at the end of the nineteenth century who saw social reality as the product of meaningful social interaction. Holding such views binds one to understanding social phenomena from the actor's perspective. This led to the use of alternative methods.

As Bryman points out,

> The pivotal point for much of the controversy was the appropriateness of a natural science model to the social sciences . . . Much of the argument levelled against the orthodoxy of quantitative research derived from the growing influence of phenomenological ideas which gained considerable following in the 1960s . . . Research methods were required which reflected and capitalized upon the special character of people as objects of inquiry.

> A qualitative research strategy in which participant observation and unstructured interviewing were seen as the central data-gathering planks, was proposed (1988: 2–3).

Changes in Research Methods Teaching

The teaching of research methods occurred in tandem with the publication of texts. In reviewing research methods courses offered to undergraduate students in Britain between 1960–80, Wakeford (1981) notes that 'methods' often meant teaching students about survey research. While some mention of **participant observation** and unstructured interviewing was included in the curriculum, the emphasis was on drilling competence in quantitative techniques. Students in these courses were taught about the principles of sampling, how to conduct surveys, how to calculate means, significance tests and so on. What was often omitted from the curriculum was the development of a broader understanding of research and the relationship between theory and method; how research questions develop in the social and political context in which the researcher lives and works; and how the research questions to be asked influence the choice of method. The Australian scene was no different.

During the 1970s and 1980s, just as there had been change in the type of texts published, so there was an attendant change in curriculum and teaching practices. It is a chicken-and-egg argument as to which situation came first. More courses in Australian tertiary institutions included discussions of qualitative methods and integration of methods. Courses were being oriented to research *practice* rather than simply *methods*, and students were beginning to examine research practices not just in terms of the ethics of the individual researcher but in relation to the political and social context of the research process itself.

In the US, Britain and Australia there were a number of texts produced which dealt with two areas—qualitative research methods *in toto* (Bogdan and Biklen 1982; Lofland and Lofland 1984; Miles and Huberman 1984; Schwartz and Jacobs 1979; Strauss 1987; Bogdan and Taylor 1975) and accounts of the experience of social research in progress (Bell and Newby 1977; Bell and Encel 1978; Bell and Roberts 1984; Shaffir et al. 1980). Most of the former centred on participant observation as the preferred and most useful model of doing qualitative research. In-depth interviewing was included in these texts as a second choice and its unique and special features were not highlighted. The latter texts provided a realistic account of doing social research which contrasted with the sanitised process described in traditional texts. This mission of showing social research realistically, with all its difficulties was important and useful for intending researchers. However, when in-depth interviewing was discussed, it was mostly in terms of difficulties and failures. We felt that the advantages of using in-depth interviewing needed specific clarification.

This book provides social and health researchers with not only possible recipes for using in-depth interviewing but also a political legitimation for its use. After all, if you can point to a textbook in the area, then the method *must* really be worthwhile and acceptable within the scientific domain! Researchers who use in-depth interviewing have been, and often still are confronted with queries regarding the legitimacy of their data-gathering method and mode of analysis. Such challenges are usually framed within arguments which rely on distinguishing between quantitative and qualitative research strategies and subsequently categorising qualitative ones as being inadequate and unscientific. Such categorisations have been based on examining the technical adequacy of these methods. However, since the 1970s, this debate has also incorporated philosophical issues. The relative advantages and disadvantages of these two styles of research have been debated in terms of being based on different epistemological assumptions, that is, of what should pass as warrantable knowledge about the social world (Bryman 1988).

Let us point out at this stage that we regard in-depth interviewing as a method which can be categorised as a *qualitative* research method because it is drawn from that tradition. Although we recognise the inadequate and frequently inappropriate use of the terms *quantitative* and *qualitative* to describe and label methodologies (Bryman 1988), they are the ones that are most frequently used in the other texts. It is important for the reader to be aware of such usage for two reasons. First, so that there is less confusion in interpreting the jargon and secondly, so that the reader is aware of the underlying assumptions made when referring to in-depth interviewing as a *qualitative* method. To this end, we feel it is necessary to provide the reader with a brief account of the traditionally ascribed characteristics of quantitative and qualitative research.

Understanding Qualitative and Quantitative Research

Qualitative research attempts to capture people's meanings, definitions and descriptions of events. In contrast, quantitative research aims to count and measure things (Berg 1989). As shown in Figure 1.1, the characteristics distinguishing qualitative and quantitative approaches to research can be divided into two major categories. These are: (1) conceptual—the nature of the phenomena studied; and (2) methodological—the handling of data (Parse 1985).

	Qualitative	Quantitative
Conceptual	• Concerned with understanding human behaviour from informant's perspective. • Assumes dynamic and negotiated reality.	• Concerned with discovering facts about social phenomena. • Assumes a fixed and measurable reality.
Methodological	• Data are collected through participant observation, unstructured interviews. • Data are analysed by themes from descriptions by informants. • Data are reported in the language of the informant.	• Data are collected through measuring things. • Data are analysed through numerical comparisons and statistical inferences. • Data are reported through statistical analyses.

Figure 1.1 Traditional characteristics of qualitative and quantitative research approaches.

Researchers adopt a given method because they have been trained to believe that their preferred method is superior to or more scientific than others (Banks 1979; Goodwin and Goodwin 1984). However, a number of scholars have argued that whether researchers choose to use qualitative or quantitative methods is a matter of training, ideology and the research question asked (Denzin 1989; Sieber 1973; Strauss 1987). While there can be no doubt that training influences our methodological practice, this argument loses sight of the inter-relationship between theory and method. As chapters 2 and 3 will go on to discuss, the choice of method is also influenced by the assumptions that the researcher makes about science, people and the social world. In turn, the method used will influence what the researcher will see.

Conceptual

A major distinguishing characteristic between qualitative and quantitative approaches is the way in which the research phenomenon is identified for enquiry. Qualitative researchers challenge the assumption that human beings can be studied by a social scientist in the same way as a natural scientist would study things. They argue that human behaviour is different in kind from the actions of inanimate objects. People are uniquely conscious of their own behaviour. Smith et al explain,

> . . .inanimate objects do not react differently because a theory has been advanced or a prediction made, but human beings can alter their behaviour precisely because social scientists have proffered a theory or made a prediction (1976: 59).

For this reason, qualitative researchers seek to uncover the thoughts, perceptions and feelings experienced by informants. They are most interested in studying how people attach meaning to and organise their lives, and how this in turn influences their actions.

Qualitative methods, such as in-depth interviewing and participant observation, are said to allow the researcher to gain access to the motives, meanings, actions and reactions of people *in the context* of their daily lives. This methodological approach without relying on the predetermined and fixed application of the predictive and prescriptive requirements of the quantitative methodologies facilitates an understanding of the informants' perceptions. The focus of qualitative research is not to reveal causal relationships, but rather to discover the nature of phenomena as humanly experienced. It is a deliberate move away from quantification and testing of **hypotheses**. As chapters 2 and 3 will show, in-depth interviewing is more than a specific data-collection technique.

Quantitative researchers are said to take a different view of the role informants play in the research process. Informants are usually treated as *subjects* who supply data that have been preordered by the researcher. Many quantitative researchers argue that informants hold a blurry understanding of their social world. It is up to social scientists to provide accurate accounts of 'what is really going on out there' by using the tools of science. The researcher borrows familiar lay concepts, such as *family support*, *caregiving*, *discrimination*, gives them precise definitions, and develops measurement procedures that allow him or her to uncover regularities among the subject's observable characteristics. Of particular interest to the quantitative researcher are explanations that offer causes.

Social facts, it is argued, can only be explained by other social facts and in terms which are quite different from those employed by the informants themselves. The individual's interpretations of his or her situation stand outside the analysis or they play only a very small part in it.

As Babbie comments,

> One of the chief goals of the scientist, social or other, is to explain why things are the way they are. Typically, we do that by specifying the causes for the way things are: some things are caused by other things (1979: 423).

Methodological

Another way to distinguish between qualitative and quantitative research is in terms of the notation system used to handle the data. Qualitative researchers are not primarily concerned with assigning numbers to their observations or transcripts. Data from participant observation, unstructured interviews and oral accounts are studied for themes in the natural language of the participants. The classification system used to code the data is not usually numerical. The data are transformed by using the language of scientific knowledge to make the participants' descriptions and experiences of their social world accessible to those who have not participated in it. The handling of data in quantitative studies, by contrast, is predominantly through statistical analyses, where the data are produced by counting and measuring. These are assigned numerical scores.

Three Examples of In-depth Interviewing

Having described the characteristics of qualitative and quantitative approaches, we now turn our attention to presenting three studies which illustrate in-depth interviewing as a form of qualitative research. These studies provide illustrations which help us to better understand the nature and purpose of qualitative research.

As stated previously, a primary focus of in-depth interviewing is to understand the significance of human experiences as described from the actor's perspective and interpreted by the researcher. This requires that the researcher has personal interaction with the individuals and their context so that he or she can hear people's language and observe behaviour *in situ*. Face-to-face interaction and careful observation enable the researcher to discover contradictions and ambivalences within what 'on the surface' may seem to be a simple reality (Reinharz and Rowles 1988). For example, many gerontology studies report that caregivers often discussed giving care to a parent who is 'like a child' (Day 1985). However, Bowers' (1987) study shows that caregivers do not really perform these tasks in ways which would reinforce this description of their parents. Rather, these tasks are performed in a manner which protects the parent's self-image and is not a threat to the biological parent-child relationship.

Studies using in-depth interviewing attempt to tap into people's experiences by presenting analyses based on empirically and theoretically grounded descriptions. The aim is to understand the interpretations people attach to their situations. In the words of Clifford Geertz,

> Believing, with Max Weber, that man is an animal suspended in webs of significance he himself has spun, I take culture to be those webs, and the analysis of it to be therefore not an experimental science in search of law but an interpretative one in search of meaning (1973: 5).

For example, the authors of the studies described below state the purpose of their research in the following ways.

> In order to understand the invisible aspects of care-giving and the associated stress, it is necessary to understand the world of care-giving from the perspective of the care-givers . . . grounding a study in the experiential world of the subjects can indicate where researchers have incorporated assumptions that are inconsistent with that world and, consequently, how those theories need to be altered (Bowers 1987: 22).

> To address the issue of what physicians actually tell patients and how they arrive at that decision, this study focusses on a single episode in breast cancer treatment—the event of telling the patient for the first time that she has cancer. This study is a participant observation and interview account of the episode, framed from the physicians' perspective (Taylor 1988: 110).

> This study aims to conduct a comprehensive analysis of the complex human issues surrounding the admission history of older people who have moved from their homes to a nursing home. The decision-making process is studied in terms of a negotiation process that takes place between the aged person, their families and professionals from the point of view of both the older person and their next-of-kin. Specific attention is given to people's perceptions of the situation they find themselves in and how this influences their actions. The analysis aims to be sensitive to the informant's subjective interpretations and makes use of their own words to develop categories of decision-making processes (Minichiello et al. 1988: 3).

The accounts derived from the interviews are studied for themes. These themes are reported in the language of the researcher. This represents a shift in discourse from the original text; from the informant's language to the language of the researcher.

All three articles report their data in a narrative as opposed to a numerical format. Each report contains illustrations derived from quotes from informants, field-note excerpts from the researcher's note book or from case studies. Sometimes these illustrative data are used to give a sense of reality to the account and portray the viewpoint of the informant, as the case studies reported in the Minichiello study (see Appendix A). Or the illustrative data can be used to give credibility to and evidence for the author's theoretical argument, as in the Bowers (1987) study.

The three studies reported here are examples of theory-building studies. They are selected for discussion because many researchers equate excellence with conceptualisation research. However, because researchers may have different purposes in mind not all qualitative studies result in theory building. The main point to remember here is that while authors may use identical data-gathering techniques, they may be researching and writing with different ends in mind. It is important for the reader to understand that evaluation of the quality and usefulness of a study should be placed within the context of the author's purpose. We discuss this issue in more detail in chapters 9 and 10.

Analytical induction and **theoretical sampling** are two essential features underlying qualitative studies (Rose 1982). More will be said on these topics later. Suffice to say, these two processes aid the researcher in building, expanding and testing **propositions** while collecting data. Analytical induction requires that every interview substantiates the proposition developed. If an interview does not confirm the proposition, the researcher revises his or her explanation. Analysis and data collection are conducted concurrently allowing the research question to evolve in response to emerging conceptual insights. A common feature of qualitative studies is that the initial research question is often revised during the research process, moving from a very general to a very focussed question. For this reason, sampling decisions are dependent on analysis of the incoming data in relation to the developing theory. Sampling is guided by the search for contrasts which are needed to clarify the analysis and achieve the saturation of emergent categories (Glaser and Strauss 1967). The aim is not to strive for a representative sample but to identify purposive cases that represent specific types of a given phenomenon. This sampling strategy allows the researcher to study the range of types rather than determine their distribution or frequency (Trost 1986). For example, once the typology of decision-making situations was constructed, Minichiello et al. searched for nursing home residents who were classified as being in one of four categories. Residents with different characteristics (for example, marital status, living arrangement) were selected to test and expand the explanations being offered to account for why residents varied in their involvement in decision making.

Two of the three studies show how in-depth interviewing, as a data-gathering technique, can be used with other methods. While the Bowers (1987) study relied solely on in-depth interviews, the Taylor and Minichiello ct al. studies combined in-depth interviews with other data collection techniques, such as participant observation and questionnaires. It is important for readers to realise that the world of qualitative methodology extends beyond the in-depth interviewing technique. Methods should be selected and utilised according to the research question. Sometimes this means relying solely on one method; at other times a **multi-method approach** is useful (Jick 1979). The multi-methods approach could involve the use of participant observation, survey questionnaires, in-depth interviewing and the content analysis of documents. The integration of a multi-method approach is referred to as **triangulation** (Denzin 1989). This involves combining different methods in the same study to highlight different dimensions of the same phenomena, to compensate for shortcomings of each method or to validate the findings by examining them from several vantage points (Reinharz and Rowles 1988). Chapter 9 discusses the utility and legitimacy of using a multi-method approach.

Study Number 1

Intergenerational caregiving: adult caregivers and their ageing parents by Barbara Bowers. This study was published in *Advances in Nursing Research* 1987, 9(2), 20–31. The focus of Bowers' investigation is to understand the world of caregiving from the perspective of the caregivers. While there has been much research conducted on family caregiving in the past decade, Bowers notes that most studies have focussed on describing caregiving in terms of which tasks are being performed by whom, how often, and with what consequences for the person receiving care as well as the person giving care. This information has been largely collected by administering a questionnaire which asks people to report on the specific tasks involved in providing care. The tasks were often defined in terms of activities of daily living, such as bathing, transporting, grooming, preparing meals, giving financial assistance, etc. This information provided a rich data base of the characteristics of those in need of care and their caregivers; the content of caregiving; and the impact of caregiving on caregivers. An underlying assumption behind these studies is that caregiving is solely a task activity. However, Bowers argues that caregiving is an activity which includes plans and decisions made by caregivers, and that while these are not observable tasks, they may have important consequences for the lives of caregivers. In an attempt to reconceptualise caregiving as a purpose activity, Bowers undertook a study which focussed on the caregivers' experiences and the strategies used to provide care for frail parents. The aim of the study was to discover a conceptual model of different types of caregiving based on the purpose for providing such care.

In-depth interviews with a sample of sixty caregivers were conducted. Most of the interviews were carried out in the homes of the informants and were taped, transcribed and coded by the researcher. Bowers ensured that the sample included caregivers who found themselves in different types of situations. She included pairs of parents and offspring living together and those living in separate residences, as well as caregivers who were providing support to parents with different levels of cognitive and physical impairment. This sampling strategy (known as theoretical sampling, see chapter 9) allowed her to examine the caregiving role as it is experienced in a number of situations, and to compare and contrast how adults in different situations were providing care to their parents. The interviews were carried out in the form of a conversation (see chapter 5). That is, the researcher allowed the questions to arise as she was talking with her informant. Earlier questions centred around understanding 'How does one become a caregiver?', 'What is most stressful about being a caregiver?' and 'What is it like to be a caregiver of one's parent'? As Bowers gained a better understanding of the topic, she paid more attention to the consequences of failed caregiving and strategies for providing invisible caregiving.

Bowers' analysis centres around identifying and describing the characteristics of different categories of family caregiving based on purpose, and the caregiving work involved in each of these categories. Five categories of caregiving are discussed. Bowers documents the features surrounding different types of caregiving activities and provides support for her findings with case excerpts from her analysis file. The five categories of caregiving are: anticipatory, preventative, supervisory, instrumental and protective care. Each of these are highlighted with case studies. For example, the following case excerpt is used to illustrate an example of protecting the parent from awareness of the situation.

> A 57-year-old woman, Anne, described how her elderly mother took great pride in having dinner prepared for her each night when Anne came home from work. The mother's ability to cook was seriously affected by her mild cognitive as well as sensory impairment. This meant that Anne was frequently given meals she described as inedible (for example, salt was substituted for sugar). Rather than confront her mother with the situation, she ate what was put in front of her (1987: 27).

The study demonstrates how in-depth interviewing can be used to generate data which provide an understanding of how families care for their elderly relatives. The findings of this study have implications for health professionals. While health professionals often think of caregiving in terms of the 'hands-on' tasks which maintain the person's physical integrity and health status, family members place greater emphasis on emotional well-being and protection of parental identity. Successful intervention is partly dependent on it being congruent with the experiences of clients. Lack of an adequate assessment of family caregiving experience may preclude effective intervention.

Study Number 2

Telling bad news: physicians and the disclosure of undesirable information by Kathryn Taylor. This study was published in *Sociology of Health and Illness* 1988, 10(2), 109–132. Taylor provides an account of how physicians deliver 'bad news' to patients who have been diagnosed as having breast cancer. The purpose of the paper is to describe how physicians organise the event of telling patients their diagnosis and the strategies developed for routinising the task.

The research is based on observation of 118 events of surgeon disclosure to women who had breast cancer, and in-depth interviews with seventeen surgeons. While the observations of the patient/client interaction allowed her to see and hear how physicians stage the event of telling the patient for the first time that she had cancer, the interviews provided further information on physicians' rationale for their disclosure tactics. It also gave the researcher the opportunity to test out whether the conclusions she had reached from the observations were consistent with the physician's account.

Taylor conducted the study over four years in a breast cancer clinic at a general hospital in Canada. She remained in the room while surgeons talked to their patients. She explains,

> I sat facing the doctor, so that the patient had her back to me. In this way I was able to observe the physicians' facial expressions and gestures, and could clearly hear the conversation. I was introduced to each patient, and all women were asked if they preferred that I leave the room—none did. I made brief notes during the event, and dictated the details immediately after.

Taylor presents data which illustrate that the disclosure contains three phases designed to facilitate the surgeons' task of initiating 'a status change in women they did not know, from healthy female to breast-cancer patient with a life-threatening illness requiring immediate, but not always effective surgical intervention' (1988: 115). The three phases discussed are preamble, confrontation and diffusion. In each of these stages, the physician uses a number of strategies to reduce the impact of the disclosure and maintain control over a situation they see as stressful. However, Taylor illustrates that while each surgeon developed a predictable, rigid approach in order to routinise the disclosure process, how the event was staged varied in relation to whether the surgeon was an *experimenter* or *therapist*. Taylor labelled surgeons as *experimenters* if they emphasised the scientific-experimental approach to treatment. In contrast, the *therapists* were those surgeons who operated on the individuality of each case and saw their primary responsibility as recommending a particular treatment for each patient.

Taylor combined her participant observation and interview data to show the different approaches and strategies used by experimenters and therapists to disclose the bad news. Excerpts from her observation of surgeon/patient interaction are used to reconstruct situations which typify the disclosure policies. The following episode of a doctor-patient interaction is used to illustrate the experimenter's disclosure policy.

> *Experimenter*: Enormous strides have been made in cancer research. We are making terrific headway. You know, if you had had this diagnosis a few years ago, there would not have been a whole lot that could have been done. We now have techniques for conquering all sorts of problems we could not have touched, even ten years ago . . .
> *Patient*: Did you get my report back?
> *Experimenter*: Yes, as a matter of fact, I have the [pathology] report here somewhere on my desk. Let me see [*reaching over to pick up a slip of paper from a pile*]. Ah yes, it says, 'infiltrating and intraductal lobular carcinoma, well encapsulated in . . .'.
> *Patient*: You mean—it is—I've got cancer?
> *Experimenter*: Yes.
> *Patient*: Are you sure?
> *Experimenter*: Yes, I went down and checked in the lab and . . .
> *Patient*: Am I going to die?
> *Experimenter*: We have a lot of tools to fight with. Let's talk about the options. You see there is no real 'best therapy' as I am sure you are aware. As a matter of fact in the latest issue of the Journal [*New England Journal of Medicine*], there was an interesting article this week . . .
> *Patient*: You mean I am going to die? [*Patient cries and shakes*].
> *Experimenter*: Now listen, I was saying there is a lot we can do. We have to make some serious decisions. Pull yourself together . . . please.
> *Patient*: You mean I am going to die . . . my God . . . my kids . . . what

was that you were saying about surgery? I know I don't have to lose my breast . . . right? . . . right? . . . Oh my God.

Experimenter: We really don't know which surgery is best. We do not have any real answers. We are collecting data to help us with these questions. Let me tell you about this clinical trial . . .

Patient: Doctor, I am asking YOU what you think is best for me. For God's sake you are a doctor . . . I don't want my breast off . . . but then . . . I want to live . . . I've got three kids you know . . .

Experimenter: You know many women have breast disease. Why I was reading somewhere that the new figures show one out of every 11 women in North America will have some trouble during her lifetime. A lot of them will do well . . . and of course, some won't. But as they know, unfortunately, medicine has not always been considered an exact science . . . All those women who develop breast cancer now have a unique opportunity to help us get scientific answers to very old questions . . . to help their daughters somewhere down the road. YOU can really help us get more accurate information about the disease, and help us test the ammunition we are now using. We can't be sure of anything, until we have hard proof, and you can be very important in helping us do that. Entering a clinical trial, is one positive step patients can take in a very unfortunate situation.

After presenting this illustration, the author conducted an analysis of how the surgeon introduced the topic, arranged the discussion, handled stressful confrontation with the patient and diffused the impact of the diagnosis. A comparison between the strategies used by experimenters is contrasted with those used by therapists. For example, while experimenters gave exact and detailed information, whether the patients wished it or not, the therapists defined their role as selecting and interpreting information in a manner they thought the patient wanted to hear it. The author draws the readers' attention to ways of improving the doctor-patient communication and highlights the role of medical education training to teach physicians what and how to tell their patients bad news.

Study Number 3

A typology of decision-making situations for entry to nursing homes by Victor Minichiello, Loris Alexander and Deirdre Jones. The results of this research are presented in Appendix A. The study presents a framework which explains the older person's participation in the decision-making process. The authors note that the older person's control over the decision to enter a nursing home is an important topic of study because it can cushion the effects of institutional living. While there have been a number of studies which have addressed the issues of personal autonomy, patient responsibility, and competence of aged persons to participate in decision making, few researchers have examined how residents and their next-of-kin account for why some older people participate in the decision and others do not. The aim of this study is to develop a framework which sheds light on the question of why older people vary in their involvement in decisions to enter a nursing home.

Data for this study consisted largely of in-depth interviews with ninety residents in eight nursing homes in Sydney and their next-of-kin. This approach was selected because the authors thought that as the issues surrounding the institutional decision are not well understood, the level of data needed to make a significant contribution had to move beyond a survey approach. The in-depth interview technique can give a rich understanding of the meanings that the actions have to the actor involved and describe those meanings in personally and culturally appropriate terms. A questionnaire design would not have been suited to picking up these factors because the researcher is forced to design in advance the variables that affect people's experiences. This information was not available in the literature. The authors could not have predicted in advance the important elements in the decision-making process. A questionnaire using closed-ended questions was used after the qualitative data were collected. Data collected from the questionnaire were used to verify generalisations derived from the qualitative data. For example, the residents' stories suggested that those who had not participated in the decision-making process were less happy than those residents who had had some involvement. Their answers to the questionnaire substantiated this finding. Residents who had little or no involvement in the decision-making process had a lower score on the subjective well-being scale. These findings, derived from different methods, add support to the claim that the residents' involvement in the admission decision is an important determinant of well-being after entering the home.

Their report is organised around presenting a discussion of the factors which place the residents in different decision-making situations. Each of the different types of decision-making categories were discussed separately. Case studies were used to examine the ways in which social and personal situations affected participation and how this influenced outlook after admission to the nursing home.

The results show that while it is true that people with similar socio-structural attributes (for example, marital status, family support) tend to exhibit common patterns of behaviour, these factors only set a broad boundary for possible action. For example, while many of the fully involved residents were never married, and had limited family support available to them, others were married and had family support available to them but chose not to use it. Individuals may assign different meanings to their situational factors (such as family support) and act on the basis of the meanings they have assigned to them. What placed an elderly person in a certain decision-making situation was not solely determined by their social attributes but by how people were giving meaning to their situation through interaction with family members and health professionals. Perceptions of managing/not managing, entitlements and obligations played a crucial role in determining involvement in the decision-making process. By listening to how residents perceived their situations and the meanings they attached to these, and comparing and contrasting the ways the four decision-making groups differed from each other, the researchers were able to explain why some people were involved in the decision-making process and others were not. This analysis provides some interesting insights into the decision-making process of entry into nursing homes.

Chapter Overview

The chapters in this book have followed traditional divisions of subject matter not because we believe that that is how the research process occurs but simply for ease of writing about such processes in a digestible manner. Thus, chapters 2 and 3 examine how we conceive understanding other human beings, and how we perceive and define science when we wish to understand people as individuals or as members of groups. Chapter 4 covers the preparation work involved in doing a research project using in-depth interviewing. This aspect of research is very rarely examined in the literature and it is most often at this stage that research falls down.

Chapter 5 outlines in-depth interviewing as a social science method which is used to understand people. It provides an account of how in-depth interviewing has been done by workers in the field and highlights some of the advantages and the problems encountered in employing this method. Chapter 6 outlines some of the skills and strategies employed in asking questions. Chapters 7 and 8 provide the reader with discussions of two distinct models of in-depth interviewing—the life history and the clinical interview.

Chapter 9 considers the pragmatic and methodological issues that confront researchers in the field. Chapter 10 follows on by raising the political and ethical concerns that the researcher might encounter in doing in-depth interviewing.

Chapter 11 documents and formalises some of the ways in which data organisation and analysis can be approached by researchers using in-depth interviewing. Chapter 12 offers the reader suggestions for making sense of and interpreting the data, and for the encapsulation of the research project in a written form for dissemination purposes.

We have also included a final report of an in-depth interviewing study in the appendix so that readers can examine what such a report might look like and be able to recognise similar reports in reviews of literature. They are also given some idea of how to proceed when writing up their own study. In addition, a glossary and a list of references is included at the conclusion of each chapter.

Glossary

Analytical induction method A method used to make inferences from some specific observations to a more general rule. Used in constructing propositions or theory from data.

Anti-positivism An approach that holds that social reality is consciously and actively created by individuals who mean to do things and who attribute meanings to the behaviour of others.

Hypothesis A statement of the predicted relationship between two or more variables.

In-depth interviews Repeated face-to-face encounters between the researcher and informants directed toward understanding informants' perspectives on their lives, experiences or situations as expressed in their own words.

Interpretivist See *antipositivist.*

Multi-method See *triangulation.*

Participant observation Studying people by participating in social interactions with them in order to observe and understand them.

Positivism A doctrine in the philosophy of science. It is characterised by the insistence that sciences can only deal with observable entities known directly to experience. The positivist aims to construct general laws on theories which express relationships between phenomena.

Proposition A statement or assertion of the relationship between concepts. In philosophy, a proposition can be a true-or-false sentence which is expressed in a given statement.

Qualitative research design Allows the researcher to observe, discover, describe the themes and underlying dimensions of social life using non-numerical data.

Quantitative research design Allows the researcher to measure the magnitude, size or extent of a phenomenon using numerical data.

Social action approach An approach to sociology which emphasises how actors perceive a social situation. It emphasises conscious orientation and purposive action. It is argued that actors are thinking beings, who make choices and control their own actions through thought. Other terms used to define this approach are *interpretivist* or *anti-positivist*.

Structured interviews Refers to interviews in which the questions and the answer categories have been predetermined.

Symbolic interaction A sociological perspective that emphasises the centrality of meaning in interaction. It is the study of the self–society relationship as a process of symbolic communication between people.

Theoretical sampling Sampling directed by the evolving theory.

Triangulation The combination of different techniques for collecting data in the study of the same phenomenon.

Unstructured interviews Refers to interviews in which neither the questions nor the answer categories are predetermined. They rely on social interaction between the researcher and informant to elicit information.

References

Babbie, E.R. 1979. *The Practice of Social Research.* Second edition. Belmont, California: Wadsworth.

Banks, F. 1979. 'Sociological theories, methods and research techniques—a personal viewpoint.' *Sociological Review* 27: 561–578.

Bell, C. & Newby, H. 1977. *Doing Sociological Research.* Sydney: Allen and Unwin.

Bell, C. & Encel, S. 1978. *Inside the Whale: Ten Personal Accounts of Social Research.* Oxford: Pergamon.
Bell, C. & Roberts, H. 1984. *Social Researching: Politics, Problems, Practice.* London: Routledge & Kegan Paul.
Berg, B. 1989. *Qualitative Research Methods for the Social Sciences.* Boston: Allyn and Bacon.
Bogdan, R. & Biklen, S. 1982. *Qualitative Research for Education.* Boston: Allyn and Bacon.
Bogdan, R. & Taylor, S. 1975. *Introduction to Qualitative Research Methods.* New York: Wiley.
Bowers, B. 1987. 'Intergenerational caregiving: adult caregivers and their ageing parents.' *Advances in Nursing Research* 9: 20–31.
Bryman, A. 1988. *Quantity and Quality in Social Research.* London: Unwin Hyman.
Day, A. 1985. *We Can Manage: Expectations About Care and Varieties of Family Support Among People 75 Years of Age and Over.* Melbourne: Institute of Family Studies.
Denzin, N. 1989. *The Research Act: A Theoretical Introduction to Sociological methods.* Third edition. Englewood Cliffs, New Jersey: Prentice-Hall.
de Vaus, D. 1985. *Surveys in Social Research.* Sydney: Allen and Unwin.
Geertz, C. 1973. *The Interpretation of Culture.* New York: Basic.
Glaser, B & Strauss, A. 1967. *The Discovery of Grounded Theory.* Chicago: Aldine.
Goodwin, L. & Goodwin, W. 1984. 'Qualitative vs quantitative research or qualitative and quantitative research?' *Nursing Research.* 33: 378–379.
Jick, T. 1979. 'Mixing qualitative and quantitative methods: triangulation in action.' *Administration Science Quarterly.* 24: 6002–6011.
Kidder, L. & Judd, C. 1986. *Research Methods in Social Relations.* New York: CBS Publishing Japan.
Lofland, J. & Lofland, L. 1984. *Analysing Social Settings: A Guide to Qualitative Observations and Analysis.* Second edition. Belmont, California: Wadsworth.
Miles, M. & Huberman, M. 1984. *Qualitative Data Analysis.* Beverly Hills, California: Sage.
Minichiello, V., Alexander, L. & Jones, D. 1988. 'Australian literature in social gerontology: a content analysis of trends since 1980.' *Lincoln Papers in Gerontology* No. 1. Melbourne: La Trobe University.
Parse, R. 1985. *Nursing Research: Qualitative Methods.* Bowie, Maryland: Brady.
Polgar, S. & Thomas, S. 1988. *Introduction to Research in the Health Sciences.* Melbourne: Churchill Livingstone.
Reinharz, S. & Rowles, G. 1988. *Qualitative Gerontology.* New York: Springer.
Rose, G. 1982. *Deciphering Sociological Research.* London: Macmillan.
Schwartz, H. & Jacobs, J. 1979. *Qualitative Sociology: A Method to the Madness.* New York: Free Press.
Shaffir, W., Stebbins, R. & Turowetz, A. 1980. *Fieldwork Experiences:*

Qualitative Approaches to Social Research. New York: St Martin's Press.

Sieber, S. 1973. 'The integration of fieldwork and survey methods.' *American Journal of Sociology* 78: 1335–1359.

Smith, B., Johnson, K., Paulsen, D. & Shocket, F. 1976. *Political Research Methods: Foundations and Techniques.* Boston: Houghton.

Strauss, A. 1987. *Qualitative Analysis for Social Scientists.* Cambridge: Cambridge University Press.

Taylor, K. 1988. 'Telling bad news: physicians and the disclosure of undesirable information.' *Sociology of Health and Illness* 10: 109–132.

Trost, J. 1986. 'Statistically non-representative stratified sampling: a sampling technique for qualitative studies.' *Qualitative Sociology* 9: 54–57.

Wakeford, J. 1981. 'From methods to practice: a critical note on the teaching of research practice to undergraduates.' *Sociology* 15: 505–12.

Chapter 2
Being Scientific

Why should a book on in-depth interviewing start off with a chapter on being scientific? Why not just begin by describing how to do in-depth interviews? Well, there are several reasons, all interrelated. It is in fact controversial as to whether in-depth interviews are a good way to investigate how people are and what they think. Some researchers think that there is something inherently second-rate about interviews, and that we should try to find better—more scientific—ways to investigate people. We, on the other hand, believe that in-depth interviews are definitively the best way of getting to know how someone thinks; and part of the reason why we think this has to do with what we think is 'scientific'. So the disagreement about in-depth interviews depends in turn on a disagreement on how to be scientific. It also depends on a related disagreement about how to understand a human mind; that is the problem we address in the next chapter, *Understanding People*.

Next, even when researchers agree that in-depth interviews are a good thing, they often disagree on how to conduct them. Most of these disputes over detail, we discuss in the how-to-do-it chapters later in the book, but sometimes these local disputes turn out really to be about the larger issues of how to conduct an interview 'scientifically'. And that depends of course on what you mean by being *scientific*.

Finally, many of these disputes turn out to be expressions of anxiety about professionalism. Will my research technique look professional to my clients and colleagues? Well, it will look professional if it looks scientific, and it will look scientific if we are clear about *being* scientific in the first place.

Legitimising Professional Practice

No doubt there are many reasons why people should want to know how to be scientific. But this is a book about in-depth interviewing, and our particular interest is in: (a) doing it well, and (b) persuading others that we can do it well.

Part of learning to do this is learning to do it scientifically, and part of learning to do it scientifically is learning to understand what it means to be scientific. Nor is this just our particular problem. It is a problem which haunts many workers in many fields.

Professional workers depend on the legitimacy of their work. Not only do they expect to be paid for their work which they believe unqualified others should not be paid for, but also they expect a measure of respect from their clients for their experience, expertise and professional knowledge. Further, they expect the State to license them and guarantee their standard of professional education; and to penalise charlatans and quacks pretending to the same status. In short, they expect to be treated as legitimate and their opponents as illegitimate. And usually their claims to legitimacy come down to a claim that their practice is based on science whereas the practice of others is somehow unscientific. And of course this claim in turn depends on knowing what it means for a practice to be based on science. 'What is this thing called science?', as the title of a famous book on the subject puts it.

Definitions of Science

There have been many attempts to define just what science is. Obviously there are many *topics* (biology, economics) which we count as scientific, just as there are many (theology, art, sport) which we understand not to be part of science. It may be more convention than anything else that we regard some of these topics or fields of activity as scientific and some not, but if it is just a matter of convention, then, like most conventions, it lacks intrinsic interest.

But few people have thought that these matters were simply a matter of convention. And their interest has been *motivated*—motivated by a desire to *understand*, *discover*, *exclude* and *control*. These words will make a litany in our account of just what this thing called science is.

People have not just had an idle interest in what science was; they have wanted to exclude certain topics and fields of interest as non-science, and certain practitioners as non-scientists, possibly deluded, possibly impostors. So part of the motive for trying to define science has been to exclude competitors. Someone who believes that science can be separated off from non-science is said to be a **demarcationist**.

Another motivation has been to define science in order to discover more of it. If we can define science, then the hope might be that the definition will help us to *make* more science, that is, to make further discoveries. And perhaps to find entirely new sciences, new fields of discovery.

Notice that there are two logically distinct tasks implied in all this. The first is to define what science is—for that we would need what has been called a **logic of justification**. This is to allow us to recognise a piece of knowledge as scientific when we come across it.

A quite different task is to know how to find such a piece of knowledge. For this we need a **logic of discovery**. It seems pretty clear that if there are such logics, we need a logic of justification first—to find an elephant in the jungle, you first need to know roughly what one looks like. Otherwise you'd never know whether your plan for discovering one had worked or not. So a method of justification seems logically prior to a method of discovery.

People who have thought about these problems have wanted the logics ideally to produce guaranteed solutions; outcomes where we can be sure that what we think *is* science is science, and the method of discovering science *does* discover it. A technique or procedure for producing guaranteed results is called an **algorithm**. So what people have ideally wanted is first, an algorithm of justifying science, and second, an algorithm for finding it, that is, an algorithm for its **methodology**.

This desire to find a guaranteed path to truth arose historically as part of the general movement of thought known as **positivism**. The positivists, especially the French philosopher Comte, thought that the special form of knowledge which distinguished modern societies was scientific knowledge, and its special priesthood was scientists. The positivists' ambition therefore was even wider than that of the aspirants to professional dominance which we have been discussing; they wanted scientists to rule not just the professions but to dominate the whole of society's thought and action: science was to be the modern religion.

And it was the positivists who first emphasised the role of discrete and distinct steps on the path to knowledge as constituting the modern and best way of knowing things. So the programme of wanting an algorithm for science has often been part of a very much larger and more ambitious programme for directing the whole of modern society. But wanting is not the same as having.

It is common too for positivists to be hostile to supposing the existence of things which can neither be seen nor heard, like nineteenth-century children. While we sympathise with this attitude to some extent (as with nineteenth-century parents), it is an attitude inimical to most science. Atoms and viruses are things which cannot be seen or heard, though we may see traces of them in electron photographs. We know that they exist because the theories about them are true, or anyway some are. In that sense, atoms and viruses are theoretical entities. In a similar way, a belief is also a theoretical entity—we only know of its existence by inference from a person's actions and remarks.

Positivists have made many attempts to get around the existence of theoretical entities, either by denying the theories, or by saying that the theories were *just a manner of speaking*. The manner of speaking disguises, according to them, the fact that theoretical entities are just terms which summarise a lot of non-theoretical entities, to wit, facts. Notice that this idea depends on the existence of facts. This may seem a very uncontroversial assumption to you, but later on we are going to see that, paradoxically, *facts do not exist*. Before you throw the book into the waste-paper basket, we hasten to add that we do not quite mean that facts do not exist, but that they aren't the sort of things positivists would like them to be. Indeed, facts turn out to be theoretical entities themselves. Wait and see what we mean.

Jargon

While we are on the topic of theoretical entities, we might mention in passing the existence of jargon. To many people who are not scientists or professionals, one of the leading characteristics of science is its use of terms which seem to have a meaning private to the in-crowd. This gives the impression that people who do not understand the terms are in the out-crowd and fated to stay there.

No doubt jargon has often been used to gull outsiders in this way, but we should remember that jargon has a very useful role to play in science, as in all ways of life. Every group has words which summarise the matters that interest it, and often these matters are described in theories which need training to understand and apply them fully. Usually, then, jargon words will be words for theoretical entities. Asking us to jettison jargon amounts to asking us to do *without theory*, and so without understanding. The price is too high.

Critics

There have been many criticisms of such attempts to define science. As we have hinted, there is a motive behind many of these attempts at definition, and it is rarely pure. Defining science has often had in the back of its mind the idea of smiting one's enemies; getting them sacked from their jobs, or denied Commonwealth medical benefit payments, for instance. Some critics have even gone so far as to say that such motives are all there is to attempts to define science; that the motive is completely impure. These critics hold that such attempts are simply power grabs with a light gloss of rationalisation applied for the sake of public appearances. Power is to be neatly grabbed without the effort of having to shoot your opponents or put them in prison. It's simpler and cheaper *to define them as illegitimate*. More technically, these critics have argued that science has no real philosophical justification, only an ideology.

Not all critics have been so harsh. They might allow science some, or even a large, measure of legitimacy in its own right, but they do not believe that the motives of the would-be definers are so pure for all that. They argue that the definers are over-zealous in the interests of the orthodox in-group. Science might, according to these critics, be loosely defined, but not so strictly as to soothe the anxieties of those of us who want to hang on to our jobs and our prejudices.

Yet other critics have argued that science is so various that there can be no definition which does justice to all its parts. No definition can be **topic-neutral. Topic-neutrality** is the desired aim of fitting a definition to all parts of science, regardless of subject matter. Both the logic of justification and the logic of discovery might been seen as attempting to find topic-neutral algorithms. See how our jargon grows.

There does seem to be a set of problems lying in the path of these critics who argue that there cannot be a topic-neutral definition of science. Their attitude seems to imply that each topic in science has to remain fixed. For if Science Version One developed over time into Science Version Two, then the topics covered would necessarily shift to some extent; that is implied by the idea of discovery itself. But if such a change takes place, then there is no guarantee that the would-be Science Version Two is indeed any such thing. The legitimacy of Version One does not rub off on Version Two. So rigid opponents of topic-neutrality are left with a dismal choice between legitimacy and flaky new discoveries. Most people would prefer to sidestep that choice and find a definition of science with at least some measure of topic-neutrality.

Finally, other critics have said that most definitions of science are only good for **natural science**, that is, for the sciences of nature rather than the sciences of humanity. That is a subject we are going to leave for later.

You will have noticed that the most far-reaching of these criticisms is the one which is hardest to answer. How do you persuade someone that your motives are pure? One way to deal with these **sceptics** is to try and find a justification for science, and if we fail then, happily or unhappily, we must admit that these critics might be right. If, on the other hand, we find a justification, then their power-grab theory will look just that much less plausible. If we are to grab power, it will be because science legitimates our power-grab, not vice versa.

Foundations

So what definitions have been proposed? As you will see, they are, not surprisingly, the same ones that professionals put on their job applications. Here, science itself is making a job application, either on behalf of itself or on behalf of its many interested supporters.

Easily the most common definition of science is that it is the activity carried out by—wait for it—scientists. On the face of it, it is easy to find scientists, because they are in science departments in universities and big businesses, and by the proposed definition, science is just what they are doing there. This definition proposes minor problems like this one: is having a cup of tea science when a scientist has one? But it seems to have the major virtue of defining something problematic in terms of something already known. Similar solutions have been proposed in recent years for the problem of defining the concept of art.

This major virtue turns out, unfortunately, to be dubious. What happens when disputes arise as to who is a legitimate scientist, and who is not? If both are doing science and both claim to be scientists, who is to say that they are wrong? Well, what actually happens in real scientific life is that rival claimants calumniate one another, alter the minutes of meetings, spread rumours about one another's strange personal and political habits, and generally attack one another's general claims to credibility; and hence their particular claim to know what they are doing as a scientist.

And we can see that this kind of dirty argument can occur precisely because the clean argument is unsound. Specifically, the clean argument leads either to a logical regress or to a logical circle. Science is what the scientist does; and we know that the scientist is legitimate because he or she is a scientist! Or because everybody believes, or all his or her supporters believe, that he or she is a real scientist; or some other equally dubious reason.

You will have noticed that these problems arise for the definition of science when it is asked to do the real work of deciding *what is* good science versus bad; *who is* a good scientist versus a bad one or a charlatan. And when these problems arise, it becomes plain that defining science is not just a matter of settling a dispute over word usage. It leads us to wonder how we know that a scientist is a scientist and how we know that a piece of science is real science. In other words, these problems of defining science become problems of **epistemology**, the philosophy of knowledge; and of resting our claims to knowledge on sound foundations. And we could restate the question we have been discussing here as: is there any sound foundation for scientific knowledge?

Similar problems arise for claims that a good scientist is one with years of experience. Ten years of experience may simply be one year of experience ten times over (a thought which is apt to trouble many a professional in mid-career), and that one year may have been worthless. (Student readers will easily see that a claim to years of *training* might be even more dubious.) And if there are disputes about the value of the one year's experience (or training), who is to settle them?

Probably the most common defence put forward in such disputes by actual scientists is one known as **intuitionism**. When assessing the value of a painting, critics and artists can claim to know, as an aspect of connoisseurship, what it is worth, even though they may ultimately be unable to say exactly what it is about the painting which is of value. Similarly, scientists, or science critics, claim to know by intuition whether a piece of scientific work is valuable. *Intuition* here implies that real knowledge has been gained, but that no reason for it need, or indeed can, be given. Of course, the parallel with art criticism gives the game away: disputes between rival intuitionists could never be discussed because there would never be anything actually to be said besides name-calling one's opponents. This extreme defence is so hard to maintain that we would not bother to discuss it if it were not so popular among working scientists. Notice also that, since no reason is given to justify one's intuition, there can be no question of classifying the reason as of a particular type. And if this is so then there seems to be no chance of marking science off from religion, art, ideology, or any other branch of human intellectual activity. Marking off science from other such forms of activity, you will recall, was one of our original aims. It is not surprising, therefore, that demarcationists have usually come down in favour of defining science in term of its underlying *logic*.

Foundations in Logic

If science is to be founded on logic, there is a 2000-year precedent for doing so in the work of Aristotle. Aristotle tried to found our knowledge of the world in general on the particular kind of logic called **induction**. The (famous) idea here is that we make discoveries by collecting all the *facts* we can, and from those facts make a *generalisation*. The clichés which hold that (a) you have to know the facts, and (b) you can or can't generalise from them, thus have a long history.

Aristotle pointed out that this kind of reasoning is topic-neutral. It depends for its persuasiveness on the underlying logical *form* of the reasoning. So if we reason,

Tram A is green
Tram B is green
Tram C is green
Tram D is green

∴ All trams are green

Then, we likewise are prepared to reason,

Cancer A is caused by depression
Cancer B is caused by depression
Cancer C is caused by depression
Cancer D is caused by depression

∴ All cancer is caused by depression

Because the underlying form is the same,

This X is B
This X is B
This X is B
This X is B

∴ All Xs are B

The name of this particular underlying form of reasoning is, of course, *induction*. And as you can see, the conclusion of inductive reasoning is *never* guaranteed by the premises. To make the result come out true for sure, we have to add another hidden premise:

There are no other Xs which are not B.

But to know that this hidden premise was true would amount to already knowing the conclusion anyway, regardless of the reasoning. Statistical reasoning is of this kind; it moves from the facts about samples to inferring the facts about populations. It too is prone to the uncertainties of the problem of induction, and only really escapes them when it is dealing with artificially delimited populations which allow the researcher to add in something like the extra hidden premise described above. But then it is just those delimited cases which are of limited scientific interest.

This underlying difficulty with induction in all its forms is known as the **problem of induction**, and no satisfactory solution to the problem has ever really been found. So that to base science on induction would be to found it on something too shaky to bear it.

Deduction

Theorists of science have accordingly turned to the other main form of logic known as **deduction**. The underlying form here goes,

All Xs are B
This is an X

∴ This is B

An example of this pattern might be,

All cancer is caused by depression
This is a cancer

∴ This is caused by depression

Notice that the elements of deduction are the same as the elements of induction, namely *singular* statements (the *facts*) and a *universal* statement (the *generalisation*). Notice also that deduction too is topic-neutral. What differs in deduction is therefore not the scope of the reasoning or its elements but the *order* of the elements: truth flows from the generalisation as, one of the premises, to one of the singular statements, which is the conclusion.

This order is a logical order; it has to do with the flow of truth from one statement to another. It does not necessarily have anything to do with the sequence *in time* in which these truths might be discovered. For instance, we might start our investigation by collecting a lot of individual data, and in that sense our logic of discovery might be a kind of induction. But it does not follow that our scientific conclusion would follow on the basis of induction. That would be to confuse the logic of justification with the logic of discovery. If our logic of justification is inductive, then that is only to say that truth flows from singular statements to a universal statement, not that the scientist's activity followed the same steps one at a time.

Notice also that there is no problem of deduction corresponding to the problem of induction: no dummy assumptions have to be made on the quiet to make the reasoning come out right. If the premises of the deduction are true, then the conclusion will certainly be true.

But how do we know that the premises, especially the universal generalisation of the deduction, are true? Surely finding out for sure that, for instance, all cancer is caused by depression would be a difficult, if not impossible, task. We could decide to take the rationalist path favoured by Newton and other seventeenth-century intellectuals, and make deductions only from generalisations which are known to be transparently and certainly true. But this path leads to boredom or cheating: if the premise is indeed necessarily true then the conclusion always lacks interest, and if not then the conclusion only seems necessarily to follow.

This impasse has led in this century to a brilliant adaptation of **deductivism** by a thinker called Popper. If we have the reasoning,

All Xs are B
This is an X
―――――――――
∴ This is B

we can proceed without knowing that the universal statement of the two premises is true. Instead we can assume it to be true for argument's sake. In other words, we can treat it as a **hypothesis**. This temporarily evades the problem of how we can know the universal to be true. Then on this basis, we can **predict** that the conclusion will follow. (Notice that prediction here does not imply something that will necessarily unfold in the future: we can make predictions about what we expect to find in ancient records equally well). Then if our prediction agrees with what is actually found in experience to occur, our hypothesis is confirmed. But this confirmation does not show our hypothesis to be true. Truth in deductions does not, so to speak, flow uphill.

But falsehood does flow uphill. If we follow the hypothetical reasoning outlined in the last paragraph, but we find that in fact the prediction is false,

This is not B

then we can go back and conclude that the universal statement of our hypothesis is false;

This is an X
This is not B
―――――――――
∴ It is untrue that all Xs are B

This has led Popper (1968) to argue that science is indeed based on deduction, but based on it in this indirect way. Popper's **demarcationism** allows him now to say that a scientific hypothesis is one that can turn out to be false in this way. Put another way, science has a logic of justification based on hypotheses which can turn out to be false—they are *falsifiable*. (Of course, this is not to say that they are false, only that they take the risk). Non-scientific thinking, according to Popper, does not have this risk-taking quality. Such thinking may be perfectly all right in its own way, but it is to be excluded from the rubric of science.

Popper is also able to provide a logic of discovery. What the scientist must try to do is actively *refute* his or her hypothesis: he or she must try to test his own ideas to destruction. Again, non-scientists do not seriously try to do this, according to Popper. Popper is thus both a **falsificationist** and a **refutationist**.

These ideas have obvious appeal and power, and it will be no surprise to the reader to hear that Popper has been the most influential philosopher of science of the century. But since he wrote, there have been developments which have not only overthrown his or her system but also threatened the whole demarcationist enterprise.

Knowing the Facts

Many claims to superior knowledge depend, of course, on our knowing the facts when someone else does not. Behind these claims, there is often the assumption that there is a distinction to be made between *the facts* and *the interpretation*. The idea is that some truths are just given to us, to make of what we will: the parallel is that the artist or craftsman is given the materials, but uses his or her inspiration to make the materials into a work of art or craft. He or she might choose other materials, but the point is to make the work, not the materials.

This idea has some fancy versions, or rather has acquired some fancy names. *Datum* is Latin for something given, and *data* is its plural. So the idea is that we start off from the data available, and on that basis make our interpretation (inductive version), or think up our *hypothesis* and test it against the data (deductive version).

Not that there is inherently anything wrong with this idea. Obviously, reasoning has got to start somewhere, just as the artist has got to use *something* as his or her material. But there is a danger asleep within this idea. It is easy to make the further assumption that everyone should start at the same place, with the same materials, whereas often the more creative way to think is to start one step behind everyone else's assumptions, just as the creative artist may work on something which no one else considered even to be material for art, or perhaps something which has already been worked up into a work of art.

So the idea of a 'fact' is a relative one. The facts are the materials we start from, and interpretation is what we do with them. But others might start elsewhere, and so have different 'facts'. No statement proclaims that it is precisely where you have to start. And if it did, why ever should we believe it?

Theory-dependent Observation

We spoke above of recent developments which have threatened the demarcationist enterprise. The first of these criticisms turns on our ability to tell whether or not a prediction is true. Of course, we make the prediction, and then we compare it with the facts to see whether or not it is true. But we can see that there is a dangerous circularity here also, because we can only know the facts themselves by inference. Even observations made with the naked eye depend on the assumption that our eyes and brains are working properly. More complex observations, especially those made with instruments, depend for their accuracy on the theories behind their manufacture and calibration. And if those theories turn out to be wrong, then so do the supposed facts. So our ability to reason backwards from a false prediction as Popper recommends, depends on a lot of other theories. And how could they be tested? Not by deduction because that would lead to an infinite regress. And why should we start an infinite regress in the first place?

This is not to deny that it is important in science for our judgment to be **reliable** and **valid**. We say that our judgments, including our measurements, are reliable when they are consistent over time or over re-testing; or with the assessments of other trained observers. In this sense, our judgments must be objective, not subjective. Of course, it is possible for us all to be consistent, and all to be wrong (consistently) too. The extra element required goes towards our saying that our assessments are not only reliable but valid too.

Validity and Reliability

People often confuse these two terms. Let's unconfuse them. A measure of judgment or assessment is valid when it measures what it's supposed to measure, so that we can make inferences from it. For example, a thermometer is a valid measure of temperature: we can use it (correctly) to tell how hot someone or something is. But it is an invalid measure of, for instance, atmospheric pressure, or of voting intentions. Imagine putting a thermometer in someone's armpit to see if they are a Liberal or Labor voter!

This idea of validity has little to do with a judgment being *reliable*. A reliable measure should consistently give the same result under the same conditions. A reliable thermometer should consistently give the same result, both in measuring the same person twice (provided they haven't changed temperature in the meantime) and in comparing one person with another (providing they are comparable persons in the first place). Clearly, reliability is a good thing, but it is easy to see that an assessment could not only be consistent, but consistently wrong. That is what we mean when we say that an assessment can be reliable but not valid. Remember all those citizens of Salem who agreed very reliably on which ladies were witches.

Later on we are going to see that there are particular problems which arise in assessing the meaning of human behaviour. Often there we have to choose *between* validity and reliability. For example, a questionnaire about smoking may produce consistent results both in how a person will answer it, and how other people would answer it. It would thus be a reliable instrument. On the other hand, an in-depth interviewer might have good reason to believe that the questionnaire produced phoney or distorted responses, but be unable to agree with other interviewers on how to describe people's real attitudes. So his or her assessments of attitudes to smoking would lack reliability. This is one of many examples where reliability and validity are to be found together, on a see-saw.

What ways do we have of telling that judges are all correct, not just all consistently wrong? Well, their judgments have to be tested against the general beliefs of society or of the scientific community (how else would we do it?), and it's precisely the foundations of those beliefs that we are trying to assess in this chapter. Some scientists have argued that scientific theories are more likely to be valid if different methods of investigation produce the same or a converging conclusion. Comparing results produced by different methods is known as **triangulation**. Triangulation, then, is an attempt to produce theories which are both reliable and valid. Certainly, it improves our chances of escaping from merely subjective opinion forming; but you can tell at a glance that it could never solve our foundation problems, and was never intended to.

Holism

The second development is related to the first one. One problem with Popper's account of science is that it has never seemed to fit in with what real live scientists really do. Historians of science have shown that famous scientists like Copernicus, who was influential in bringing science to see that the earth revolved around the sun, not vice versa, did not abandon their hypotheses when they turned out to lead to false predictions. But far from being scientific frauds or dead ends in the history of science, such scientists are often its greatest figures.

A philosopher of science called Lakatos has shown that scientists hang on to their dearest held beliefs (the hard core of their science), but in exchange are happy to shed other beliefs which are less important to them (the protective belt of their beliefs). Another philosopher, the logician Quine, has shown that their doing so is well-founded in logic, and what's more, founded in the logic of deduction. When in real life we make a deduction, it is of the form,

All Xs are B, and Assumption One and Assumption Two and Assumption Three and . . .

This is an X

∴ This is B

For instance,

All trams are green and my eyes are working and this tram is not a fake and my friends are not deceiving me and . . .

This is a tram

∴ This is green

And if the deduction in fact makes a false prediction, it is easy for us to save our hypothesis; all we have to do is go back and reject one of the assumptions added to it. This according to Quine (1953) and Lakatos (1978a; 1978b) is both what scientists do and what they have to do. This is how they can hang on to their hard core of beliefs and let go of peripheral ones from the protective belt.

This is not to say that discarding beliefs is a matter of taste. It would be irrational or corrupt to add and subtract beliefs *ad hoc*. The rational person, including the rational scientist, will consistently order his or her beliefs from the most central to the most peripheral, and shed them under pressure of contrary evidence, in reverse order.

Notice that this account of science is still based on deduction, and that it still values consistency and rationality in the scientist. But notice also that what is now being evaluated is not an individual hypothesis, but a whole belief system. That is why this approach is known as **holism**. In each individual experiment or experience, what is being tested is not an individual belief, piecemeal, but the belief system as a whole. That is why the infinite regress of proof implied by Popper's approach does not occur here: there are local dependencies within the belief system, but there is no presumption made that the system can be grounded in something outside it. We just continue to believe it.

World views

We have been talking blandly about *belief systems* without saying too clearly just what we mean by these words. We say *system* because the scientist's beliefs interact with one another. One term (or *concept*) will occur in many sentences believed to be true. And if the scientist comes to believe that one of these sentences is wrong, or that the term should change its meaning, then these changes will bring about many others among his or her beliefs. No belief is an island.

Some thinkers have tried to express this by saying that everyone has his or her *world view*. (Actually they said it in German; everyone has his or her *Weltanschauung*. Except when we are quoting from the literature or trying to impress, we will leave this word to the Germans). The trouble with this idea is that it implies (in any language) that your opinions differ from mine because of *where you are*, really or metaphorically. All I need to do to agree with you on all matters is to swap places, really or metaphorically. Once we put it like that, we can see that the expression *world view* ignores the possibility that we might disagree because we have different theories, not just different access to experience—different views, perspectives, points-of-view or whatever. So, mostly, in this book, we prefer to speak of belief systems rather than world views.

Other people (Germans actually) have said that we *choose* in some sense to see the world in a particular way; and with a bit of effort we could choose to see it otherwise. They have wanted to draw attention to this possibility by calling the words we use *constructs*. For them, the word *concept* implies that you have to think about things in some particular way, as though words carried their own gospel. Mostly, in this book, we use either word indifferently, or we simply copy the word used by the thinkers we happen to be quoting at the time. Meanwhile, just try thinking about the world without using some tradition-given concept. If you like, start off with the idea of *up and down*. Or the idea of *home*. You may find dispensing with them harder than expected.

The Dominant View

This holistic account of science has become the dominant one in recent decades. It has seemed the most plausible and life-like explanation of why scientists do what they do. But if it is true, this explanation has an unexpected corollary: we can only settle disputes with other people who share most of our beliefs, and order their centrality in the same way. If they have different beliefs or value them differently, then their way of adapting their belief system may be just as consistent as ours, but it will produce different conclusions. There will thus be no coherent way of choosing between world views. So, along with holism must go a new tolerance for those who think differently.

Not only that, along with this new tolerance, we must give up much hope of excluding others who are not like-minded as not 'proper' scientists. Unless they are inconsistent, when we can simply reject them as irrational, there are no grounds for labelling them as unscientific, because there is no adhesive available for applying the label.

Lakatos (1978a; 1978b) has tried to find a way of comparing belief systems and showing how we might prefer one to another. He has done this by trying to evaluate competing research programmes. According to Lakatos' scheme, **progressive research programmes**, by making new discoveries, are to be preferred to **degenerating** ones, which are failing to make new discoveries. Few researchers have been very impressed by Lakatos' idea because it is all too plain from the historical record that the fortunes of schools of thought in science wax and wane in such a way that at any given time it is usually impossible to predict whether successes are in prospect or not. We may have a hunch that a particular programme is going to succeed; but a hunch is not a criterion.

Thus, there is no algorithm for either defining science nor for discovering it. There is no coherent or reasoned way of excluding a given body of knowledge from the corpus of acceptable thought, except by laying down a dogma and punishing non-adherents: in other words, we can only become exclusive by becoming a religion. If anything, the only difference left between science and religion would be that science might be more open to different points of view. And there is no philosophical reason to regard any one body of thought as more legitimate then any other. If that body of thought happens to receive state endorsement, then the grounds for that endorsement must be non-rational grounds. And if that endorsement has to do with grabbing and holding power, then that power must find what legitimacy it has elsewhere. Saying that something is science is only to say that it is one of a particular range of topics.

Prediction and Explanation

The emphasis so far has been on prediction, in the sense of confirming logical conclusions. Some people have thought that this emphasis is too narrow. They believe that the essential feature of science is explanation.

Theorists like Popper (1968) have emphasised the role of generalisations in making predictions, but this has perhaps obscured the fact that in most scientific explanations, to give the explanation is to give the cause of whatever phenomenon is to be explained. So, these other writers we have referred to have wanted to say that science is a matter of **causal explanation**. It is not that there are no generalisations involved; but the generalisations involved here are causal laws.

The Concept of Cause

What does it mean to say that one thing causes another? Various lists have been suggested to define the concept of cause, but there is no doubt that the list must be long and complex. At the least, we would have to have the following marks as necessary (though not sufficient) conditions of causal explanation.

1 The explanation must connect a pair of events, one explaining the other.
2 The pair of events must be close together in time and space—*contiguous*, as the jargon has it.
3 The event of the pair which is to be explained is the *effect.*
4 The event which explains the other is the *cause.*
5 The cause must *precede* the effect in time, or at least be simultaneous with it.
6 Causal connection allows for the possibility of *chaining*: if A causes B, then B can in turn cause C, which can in turn cause D, and so on.
7 It is not enough for the pairing of cause and effect to occur once. That may simply be a coincidence. For causation to occur, the two events must always occur together. That is, there must be a *covering law.*
8 Nor is it enough for there to be such a law. That implies only a correlation between events. It must also be possible to produce the event by *manipulating* the cause. A causal explanation is, among other things, a recipe for changing the world.
9 This condition is really a result of the previous two. It says that to be sure of a causal connection you must exclude *confounding variables* which *correlate*, i.e. pair up with the effect in question, giving a spurious appearance of causation but lacking the power to produce its occurrence through its occurrence. Research which is designed to exclude such spurious correlation is said to *control* for them.

These then are the conditions for **causal explanation**. Following them will produce a causal explanation but not one that will guarantee certain scientific knowledge. The argument from holism given above shows that nothing can do that. So moving the focus to causal explanation does not help us to evade the necessity for tolerance of variant belief systems which we argued for there. But it does help us to see that anyone claiming to give a causal explanation must meet certain standards in doing so; and can be criticised as *unscientific* if he or she fails to do so.

paired events
contiguity
cause precedes effect
cause explains effect
chaining
covering law
manipulation
control

Figure 2.1 The features of causal explanation.

The Medical Model

A great deal of fuss has been made in the last twenty years about the way doctors explain what is happening to their patients, and we ourselves make a bit of a fuss about it in chapter 8. For both these reasons, let us take a brief glance at medical explanation in particular.

It is easy to see that classical medical explanation is only a particular form of causal explanation. Medicine is concerned with the diagnosis and treatment of *illness*. Illness is defined as the presence of a *lesion* in the body. And a lesion is a *break* or *breakdown* in the normal causal chains occurring inside the body. *Symptoms* are the causal effects of the breakdown. *Treatment* consists in removing the lesion and thus the symptoms, thereby effecting a *cure*. In other words, all the classical medical terms can be redefined causally.

Recently, medical explanation and treatment have been criticised for concentrating their attention inside the body to the exclusion of the environment and lifestyle of the patient. But these criticisms do not undermine what we have been saying, for they only aim to put the patient in his or her causal setting: they aim at more elaborate causal explanations, not at non-causal ones.

Non-causal Explanation

We must not suppose that causal explanation is the only form of explanation possible. Magical explanations for instance have many of the features of causal explanation, but lack the ideas of contiguity and chaining. In that sense, they are sub-causal or quasi-causal explanations. For instance, during the recent Falklands War, it was reported that certain Haitian practitioners of voodoo were threatening to practise their arts on the British Prime Minister, Mrs Thatcher. Imagine the situation had they successfully done so. Just as Mrs Thatcher is haranguing the House of Commons, in far-away Haiti, Mother Obeah (our local voodoo 'practitioner') sticks a hat pin into Mrs Thatcher's image. Mrs Thatcher falls to the floor in mid-sentence, victim of a heart attack.

Notice that most but not all of the elements of causal explanation are present. The hat-pin stick and the heart attack occur together in time, and Mother Obeah certainly seems to have a recipe for producing the required result. Furthermore, unless it was a recipe which could be used repeatedly (on other Prime Ministers perhaps), we would not give her the credit for having done the trick even once. What the explanation of Mrs Thatcher's illness lacks is a postulated chain of events—radio waves across the Altantic or perhaps a volley of hat pins—connecting the action with the result.

Much more important are explanations which attribute the effect to be explained to the existence of a *mind*. Usually the thing to be explained is the action of the being to whom the mind is attributed. This kind of **mentalistic** or **Intentional** or **Interpretive** explanation—all these words are equivalent in our book—is usually restricted nowadays to human behaviour, or to the behaviour of *persons*, but this has not always been the case. Aristotle, for instance, thought that the stars followed circular courses in the heavens because circular motion was the most enjoyable for them. Many people have argued that causal explanation is the right sort of explanation for *natural* science, i.e. for the sciences of nature, but wrong for the *human* or *social* sciences. Causal explanation for things; Intentional explanation for people.

This distinction is often confused with the distinction between quantitative and qualitative research. The idea here seems to be that nature consists of measurable quantities but usually human behaviour or beliefs consist only or mainly of unmeasurable qualities. This shrinks the differences between people and things simply to the collection of different *items* of information about them. But it is easy to see on reflection that trying to distinguish the human sciences this way leads to confusion. For one thing, natural science often works with purely qualitative data, the colour of liquids or bird feathers for instance. For another, many aspects of human behaviour, including intentional behaviour, are entirely measurable—spending on theatre tickets, for example. So, concentrating on the kinds of data collected seems mainly to be a confused attempt to explain the difference of approach to the two broad areas of knowledge involved here. Referring to the holism of method has seemed a clearer way of making the distinction here.

We are going to discuss these matters in greater detail in the next chapter. For the moment we need only remind ourselves that causal explanation is certainly not the only kind of explanation available, let alone necessarily the best for understanding and explaining the behaviour of people, which is the primary concern of this book.

Conclusion—the Prestige of Science

Obviously, science as the concept has been commonly understood, has been one of the most prestigious ways of seeing the world in recent centuries. This prestige has increased with the vastly increased use of technology in our century. As a result, many groups, including professional groups, have wanted to claim that prestige, and the power that might be derived from it, by claiming that their professional practice was based on science in some way. This claim has often been part of a wider positivist desire to make science the dominant mode of thought in modern societies.

But the argument of this chapter has taken another direction. It has turned out that science is not one unique thing, and certainly not one thing that can be valued to the disadvantage of other ways of seeing the world. Indeed, science cannot be so clearly defined as to make any such odious comparison possible. More particularly, most science depends on causal explanation; and if we are doing causal explanation then we should try to do it as consistently and rationally as possible. But if, on the other hand, what we are doing is trying to explain human behaviour, then there is nothing in the philosophy of science or knowledge which obliges us to choose causal explanation, or if it comes to that, any of the currently fashionable approaches to human behaviour. In this book, we mainly adhere to the mentalistic approach, sometimes in combination with causal explanations.

Whichever approach or combination of approaches we choose, we can be sure that what we will be doing is constructing a whole belief system, not just testing particular hypotheses one by one. Therefore, the positivist programme of precise steps to precise knowledge can be regarded as a dead end, no matter what kind of science we seek.

Glossary

Algorithm A procedure which guarantees a result. By contrast, a *heuristic* only increases our chances of getting a result, without giving any guarantee of one.

Causal explanation Explaining events as due to some *cause*.

Deduction Reasoning from universal statements to singular ones.

Deductivism Belief that science can be founded on deduction.

Degenerating research programme One failing to make significant new discoveries.

Demarcationism Belief that a criterion (usually a logical criterion) can be found to distinguish science from non-science.

Epistemology The philosophy of knowledge.

Falsificationism Belief that a good scientific theory can in principle be shown to be false.

Holism Holds that our beliefs are tested as whole systems, not belief by belief. (Of course this is the philosophers' working definition we make use of in this book, but in other contexts, it means quite different things. Holistic medicine, for instance, has little to do with whole belief systems but a lot to do with the body and its environment as a whole *causal* system.)

Hypothesis An assumption we make for the sake of an argument, or to test a particular theory.

Induction Reasoning from singular statements to universal ones.

Inductivism Belief that science can be founded on induction.

Intentional explanation Explaining behaviour as due to mental contents, such as beliefs and wishes. Also known as *Interpretive explanation*.

Intuitionism We know, but we can't say how we know.

Logic of discovery Some method of reasoning leading to the discovery of scientific truth.
Logic of justification Some method of reasoning guaranteeing that a particular piece of knowledge is indeed scientific.
Methodology A rule-governed procedure aiding or guaranteeing scientific discovery. Methodological issues are concerned with the logic of enquiry—that is, how are we to discover and validate what we think?
Natural science The science of nature, usually using causal explanation.
Positivism Founding all knowledge on a methodical scientific procedure, and, as we said in chapter 1, on a basis of directly observable facts. As you know, we hold in this chapter that there are no such things.
Problem of induction The general conclusion never logically follows from the premises.
Progressive research programme One leading to significant discoveries.
Rationalism Belief that true knowledge is based on deduction from self-evident premises.
Refutationism Belief that good scientists actively try to refute their theories, not just confirm them.
Reliability A measure or a study is reliable if it consistently gives the same result. Of course there will be variant conceptions of reliability because there are variant conceptions of consistency. Contrast with *validity* below.
Scepticism about science Belief that there is no good justification for saying that one piece of knowledge or practice is scientific and another is not.
Theory dependency Reaching a conclusion, about for example what we see, depends on assuming some theory to be true.
Topic neutrality Logical reasoning is correct because of its *form*, not because of its *content*.
Triangulation The combination of different techniques of collecting data in the study of the same phenomena.
Validity A measure or a judgment or a piece of research is valid if it really shows what it is supposed to show, or seems to show. A thermometer is supposed to measure temperature and it really does so; so it is a valid measure of temperature (but not necessarily a valid measure of humidity, for example). Contrast with **reliability** above.

References

Chalmers, A.K. 1959. *What is This Thing Called Science*? St Lucia: University of Queensland Press.

Lakatos, I. 1978a. 'The Methodology of Scientific Research Programmes.' *Philosophical Papers* Vol. 1. Cambridge: Cambridge University Press.

—— 1978b. 'Mathematics, Science and Epistemology.' *Philosophical Papers* Vol. 2. Cambridge: Cambridge University Press.

Popper, K.R. 1968. *The Logic of Scientific Discovery*. London: Hutchinson.

Quine, W.V. 1953. 'Two dogmas of empiricism.', in W. Quine (ed.) From *a Logical Point of View*. Cambridge, Massachusetts: Harvard University Press.

Chapter 3 Understanding People–A Method?

In the previous chapter, we looked at the various ways in which people have tried to be scientific. Most of these attempts have been based on a notion of science as grounded on causal explanation. But social science seems often to be based on a different kind of explanation—explaining people's behaviour in terms not of causes but of their reasons.

Reasons and Causes

Reasons here seem quite different to causes. As we saw in the last chapter, a causal explanation looks for a contiguous antecedent event which might in principle be manipulated repeatedly to produce the same behaviour. But an **Intentional** explanation attributes the person's behaviour to the contents of his or her mind, and the contents are beliefs, wishes, intentions and other such *Intentions* (Searle 1983).

An **Intention** (with a capital 'I' to distinguish it from the ordinary meaning, which we mark by leaving in lower case) is any of those mental attributes showing aboutness. They are about the world outside our minds. So for instance when I believe that it is cold outside, the **proposition** that it is cold outside has added to it the mental attitude of belief. To specify the whole Intention, we must give both the attitude (here, the belief) and the proposition (here the sentence about its being cold outside).

Examples of Intentions are belief, fear, hope, desire, love, hate, aversion, liking, disliking, doubting, wondering whether, elation, depression, anxiety, pride, remorse, sorrow, acceptance, intention (without a capital 'I'), amusement and disappointment. Many but not all Intentions are described using the grammatical form of (verb + 'that' + sentence) of the so-called propositional attitudes. Intentions include propositional attitudes, as well as other mental states.

These Intentions are examples of the unobservable theoretical entities which we described in chapter 2. In that respect, they are like the viruses and atoms which occur in the sciences of nature. Like the existence of viruses, or atoms, the existence of a particular Intention has to be *inferred*. That is not to say, of course, that the *way* we infer their existence is the same. Most of this chapter goes to say that the way we make inferences about Intentions is very different.

Sometimes we can know about Intentions directly, in the sense that we can know directly that we are in pain (though we don't perhaps know directly whose pain it is). Sometimes we can have private access to some Intentions: the way in which I infer that I want an ice-cream is probably different to the way you would infer that I wanted one; but I'm still making an inference, and I could still be wrong. The general picture remains: Intentions and causes are both hidden away in different corners of the world, and we need to find them out by all sorts of different means.

Notice that the hope it would be cold outside is quite a different Intention, and so is the hope that it is hot outside. But all these Intentions are about a possible state of affairs outside the mind that has them. If I believe that it is cold outside, that is not to say that my mind is cold (nor in this case that the world outside my mind is cold either) but that my Intention refers outside my mind itself. In that way, it is like other aspects of language. Any meaningful sentence can refer outside itself; and this gives us a hint of the important role played in Intentional explanation by language generally.

If that is what it means to be a language user, then what does it mean to say that we have a language? What is a language? At the very least, a language is an ordered arrangement of signs. Signs themselves have been classified into various types, and what these types are will be helpful to our purpose here.

Signs

A sign which goes together in nature with what it signifies is said to be a **natural sign**; for instance, grey clouds are a sign of rain. The connection here between the two is of course a causal connection: one will be the cause or effect of the other. A sign which looks like or sounds like the object it signifies is said to be an **iconic sign** of it. There are strikingly few iconic signs in human languages, disregarding misplaced attempts to construe Chinese and Japanese and ancient Egyptian as languages all based on pictograms. Human languages are notable for the fact that their signs have no natural resemblance to the objects they signify: they are made up of **symbolic signs.** Symbols, in our definition, have a purely arbitrary association with their *referents,* the objects they refer to (Morris 1938).

This is not to say that any collection of symbols will constitute a language. Not only must the symbols have their conventional meanings, if any, in a language, but they also have to be ordered in a way that is acceptable and meaningful for that language. That is, they must conform to the grammar of that language. In this sense, so-called 'body language', whatever its value, is not really a language.

Next, we must be able to use the symbols, the 'words' of our language, in combination with the grammar for that language, to make an unlimited number of sentences which have never been used or heard before. So that when we give an Intentional explanation, we not only attribute a mind to the person whose behaviour we are explaining, but we are specifying the Intentions which are the contents of his or her mind; and those contents have partly to be specified in a language.

Of course any explanation has to be given in a language, causal explanation or mentalistic, magical or whatever. But when we give an Intentional explanation, we are implying also that the language is either the language of the person or a translation of his or her language. So we are implying that the person thinks, and that he or she thinks in some language. Intentional explanation is for language understanders and language users.

This partly explains why we are very reluctant to attribute very complex Intentions to animals who cannot give an account of themselves. I am quite happy to say that my cat is waiting at the back door wanting to go out because it believes that it is warm outside. But it is going too far to say that my cat is going outside to read *The Mayor of Casterbridge* in the sun, because that is attributing to my cat a whole range of beliefs and experiences for which there is little or no evidence. Similar borderline status is allotted to newborn babies, people who are chronically mad, and to the senile. And in all these cases, we have our doubts about many of the examples to be considered. The fact that there are these endemic doubts about these cases suggests that assessing them is indeed a matter of elaborate inference. More aspects of these borderline cases will be discussed below when we come to considering the concept of the **person**.

These Intentions together form an interlocking linguistic whole which constitutes each person's mind. Knowing the person's mind is the precondition to understanding and explaining his or her behaviour.

Language in this way is inherently creative. And for our purposes the signing system of bees, for instance, lacks creativity and so does not count as a language.

Finally, we must be able to use our symbols and grammar together to form new sentences which can have truth value; that is, they can be either true or false. A sentence is precisely the unit of language which carries truth value. An arbitrary collection of symbols need neither be meaningful nor truth valued.

These are the very same sentences which appear in our descriptions of Intentions. But they are embedded inside such descriptions. 'It is cold outside' is embedded within 'I believe that it is cold outside'. This embedding is part of the reason these two sentences do not imply the truth of one another. I can believe that it is cold outside, but I can be wrong. We can never infer with certainty from any mental state to the truth of any external state of the world beyond.

The reader will readily see that what we have here is an ascending hierarchy of concepts—onion rings of human thought—ascending from the symbolic sign, through the sentence to human discourse as a whole. There are probably numerous ways of dividing up these onion rings; but what we want to cling to here is

Natural sign
Iconic sign
Symbolic sign
Grammatical sentence
Proposition
Statement
Text
Interpersonal exchange

Figure 3.1 The hierarchy of communication concepts.

the idea of a hierarchy of concepts, less than we might fervently want to stick to particular ones particularly defined. It may be well to give a diagram straightaway of the various levels we are going to refer to.

When a sentence is used to state a truth about the world (rather then to ask a question or make a joke), then we say we have a **statement.** When these statements are formed into a tissue of interconnected sentences, then we have a text. The science of interpreting texts is called **hermeneutics.** Many thinkers have suggested that in explaining human behaviour, what we need is a hermeneutic approach, not a causal one. Human beings, according to them, are text-like, and should be read as texts: human behaviour has meaning in the way that a text has meaning, and to give a causal explanation of human behaviour is to erase its essential meaning. What then is this business of interpreting texts which is being proposed as the way for us to understand one another?

Interpretation of Texts

The essential feature of hermeneutics that we are concerned with will seem very familiar. We have already met with it in interpreting the belief systems of scientists. The only way we have to interpret a text is to give it an overall, global, holistic meaning.

This implies that the individual parts of a text cannot be given definitive meaning by themselves, although we can allow them provisional meaning while we go ahead with the interpretation of the whole from which they come. This alternation between the parts and the whole of a text is known as the **hermeneutic circle.** To understand the parts, we must understand the whole: to understand the whole we must understand the parts. But there is no doubt that the definitive interpretation rests on the coherence of the whole interpretation of the whole text.

This in turn implies that the more of a complete text we have available to us for interpretation, the better. Conversely, the more parts of the text that are missing, the more difficult it becomes to securely put the whole text together—to supply the missing pieces of the jigsaw, so to speak.

In practice however, we do not always know the limits of the text or how many parts of it are missing. If a book or a handout looks complete and there seem to be no numbered pages missing, for example, then we can be reasonably sure that we have the whole text. But when the text in question is the story being told to us by a client, there is no clear sign or indication that the story is complete or that it has come to an end. Often our clients tell us that the story has come to an end—'I guess that is about it,' they say, but that is precisely where we should be suspicious of premature closure. This problem of when to stop is one which is chronic in this kind of research, because there can rarely be found any reliable internal cue which signals 'The End' to a discourse. We are doing an archeology of fragments without knowing when we are to stop digging.

Other researchers have looked to the intentions (lower case here, please note) of the author of the text. A novel is written to amuse us, and the author will have in mind the sort of experiences and the sort of vocabulary which its readers could be expected to understand. In other words, one group of cues to understanding a text will be provided by a set of assumptions about what the author wanted to do with his or her communication.

While it is important to point to the existence of these, we should remind ourselves that looking for these intentions can present a minefield of disagreement among rival interpreters. For one thing, any piece of behaviour is open to rival interpretation, and writing a text is just one more piece of behaviour; for another thing, every text will have, in addition to its official intentions, a shadow set of unofficial intentions, a subtext. For instance, I might officially write to you to tell you what a good time I am having in Kashmir, but unofficially I might be giving a big hint that I am perfectly capable of living independently of you; and I might unconsciously be letting you know that this display of independence is something of a fraud, because reading between the lines it is quite obvious that I am missing you dreadfully.

Text-like Behaviour

These text-like properties are relevant to human behaviour for two basic reasons. First, human beings use and produce texts all the time. That is, they give an account of themselves all the time in their speech and writing. Second, even when they are not obviously producing text, their behaviour still has some of the characteristics of text.

The most important of these is something we have already mentioned in passing: no piece of human (or for that matter most animal) behaviour guarantees its own interpretation. Conversely, every piece of behaviour has a potentially infinite number of possible interpretations which could be placed upon it. That is not to say that all such interpretations would be equally good, valid or true; we usually have good reason to prefer one or two to the others; but nothing definitively rules the others out. Sometimes we want people to believe that our behaviour means just exactly what we say it means; and we get very annoyed when they seem to doubt our perfect sincerity. But no act can proclaim itself to mean what it says. Even a telegram from God saying that it was a telegram from God would still be open to doubt. Maybe the Devil sent it instead.

Others have wanted to bypass what people have said in order to look at the natural signs of people's bodies. What people say may be open to doubt, but what their bodies say cannot be doubted; so goes this line of reasoning. But this cannot be right. Our bodies can show a certain level of arousal, but they cannot tell us definitively what form of arousal is occurring and why. That is the problem of telling the difference between a blink and a wink; between a sigh and a simple exhalation. In context, we do make up our minds which is which, but this is an interpretation made on the balance of evidence. We never can read the meaning of the behaviour straight off, and we never could.

Global Interpretation

When we come to make this interpretation, it turns out that we do it in a way very similar to the way we interpret texts. We give the behaviour of the person an overall meaning, and the meaning of the particular parts of their behaviour falls into place within the context of the whole. The same problem of closure which we mentioned before occurs here too: we can never be absolutely sure that we have seen all the evidence necessary to assess someone's behaviour; but nevertheless we do make such judgments every day.

When we were interpreting a text, we tried to give the text as much overall consistency and intelligibility as we could. When it comes to assessing overall behaviour, including the 'texts' that people utter, we try to give a global interpretation of both their behaviour and their speech. This interpretation attributes to them, of course, Intentions. That is, we explain them and their behaviour by postulating theoretical entities; abstract things which cannot be directly seen—any more than an atom or a voltage can directly be seen. We know these theoretical entities only by their effects: they have a place in our theories of how the world works.

The theoretical entities involved in explaining people, then, are Intentions. And when we offer a global or holistic assessment of people's behavior we look at both their beliefs and their desires, among the whole range of their Intentions. We construe these to make the people we are explaining appear as rational as possible. Notice that rationality too is not a property of individual beliefs alone, but depends on the place of an individual belief in an overall belief system. Notice also that if there are two competing theories as to why someone does something, then we are bound to prefer the theory which makes the person out to be more rational then the other theory. In this way our understanding of people confers a status on them. Explaining people takes an effort, and it is an effort in which we can fail. But if we fail, then they are likely to be regarded as somewhat less human then if we had made the effort, at the least regarded by ourselves as less human, and very possibly by other people too. This is one of the many ways in which Intentional explanation has an inescapable moral and political quality that causal explanation does not.

Rationality

So we set out to understand our fellow creatures (and ourselves) by making them out to be as rational as possible. This certainly does not mean construing them as perfectly rational: no such idealism is required here; people are all too obviously not perfectly rational. All we are attempting is to see them as being as rational as possible.

Most of this rationality comes down to various types of consistency. We try to see the person's words today as meaning much the same as they did yesterday. And their aims today as being much the same as their aims yesterday too. These clearly are various kinds of self-consistency.

Then there is the kind of consistency which relates us to our culture. We prefer to make a person seem to sharc and cooperate in the beliefs and goals of his or her society. Again, this is not to assume that people are nothing but ciphers for their social setting; but it is to see conventionality as more intelligible than eccentricity. An attitude which described everyone as eccentric would seem very exciting at first, until one saw that in fact no one's behaviour had been explained at all.

This bias against eccentricity extends to a bias against conceptual schemes radically different to our own. If the person from Mars has a very different way of seeing the world, how would we know this? To understand him or her would be to see the points of similarity to ourselves, which is precisely to see him or her as not all that radically different. On the other hand, if he or she were radically different, we would not know that he or she was, just because he or she was radically different. To begin to be different, in a word, is to begin to be unintelligible. Disagreement must be seen against a background of fundamental agreement. Alas, this is not an idea that appeals to those who prefer exoticism to clear thinking. Some people think ethnicities make such nice pets.

These kinds of rationality have to do then with consistency of various kinds. They are said, in Jon Elster's (1968) phrase, to do with **thin rationality.** But there is another kind of rationality which goes further than consistency.

If we think about it, we can easily imagine someone who was perfectly consistent but at the same time perfectly mad, because their (consistent) beliefs or desires did not seem those which a human being, or a member of their society, should entertain. Someone, for example, who believed that the ultimate goal of human life was to weep as much as possible in our allotted lifespan would seem to lack this extra kind of **broad rationality.** Perhaps this broad kind of rationality comes down in the end to consistency too—consistency with the purposes of those around us. But in any case it goes beyond the simpler qualities of thin rationality. Notice that thin rationality is the rationality which the interpretation of *people* shares with the interpretation of *texts*: the meaning of the whole text we referred to before is largely a matter of overall consistency.

Functionalism

Some of this kind of explaining overlaps with other kinds of science. For example, in biology we sometimes explain physical features, such as the shape of a bird's beak, as having a *purpose* in furthering the survival of the species. This kind of explanation is called **functionalism**. But notice that the purpose in this kind of functional explanation is neither that of the beak nor the bird, but of the species as a whole or of its gene pool, which are not given minds in the explanation at all. Biological explanation is only superficially mentalistic.

Likewise when attributing a purpose to a tool like a washing machine. The purpose here is that of the maker or the owner, who have minds; not that of the washing machine, which does not have a mind. The washing machine's purpose is derivative; not original, not its own.

Animals themselves (rather than animal species) are a more complex case. We attribute original purposes to animals, and fully propositional attitudes; for example, we say that the cat wants to go outside to sit in the sun. And this implies that animals can have some sort of belief system expressible in a language; for example, that it is sunny outside, that this door is the way outside, that the cat wants to be in the sun, etc. But we are not prepared to attribute complex or reflexive Intentions to animals—their goals have been laid down by their biology, and do not include their attempting, for example, to make themselves more tolerant, or to explain the difference between Italian and English forms of the sonnet. Even if they were able to give us an account of themselves, it would not be a very complicated account.

Computers, or anyway computer programs, can give an account of themselves. They also have elaborate linguistic contents, and can to some extent define and refine their own goals. Perhaps it is just to the extent that they can be self-defining that we might some day be inclined to allow them full personhood.

The Concept of the Person

This discussion of functionalism and the previous discussion of reasons lead on naturally to discussing the concept of the person. So far we have only suggested indirectly what it is to be a person, by contrast with what it is not to be one. Persons act for reasons, not because of causes. In this sense their behaviour can be voluntary (though this is not to say that all the person's behaviour will be voluntary). Some of these reasons will be desires and wishes, not just beliefs; and in that sense a person is someone who has goals. Not only that, these goals will be original—they will be the purposes of the person himself or herself, not the purposes of some other being.

Something further distinguishes the full concept of the person. A person's goals may include plans to alter the person himself or herself, perhaps in quite novel ways. Say, for example, that you set out to be the first person in Melbourne to skateboard to Seymour while simultaneously reciting the Polish national anthem backwards: there would be no question of your simply doing that without reflection or practice. Your biological inheritance would not equip you to do so, because in itself such behaviour has no obvious survival value.

Moreover, it is certain that you would have to practice and rehearse such behaviour in order to turn yourself into the sort of person who could do such a thing. Part of your goal would therefore include changing certain aspects of yourself. More elaborately and more conventionally, you might set out at another time to be a saint or to tell the funniest jokes in your family. All such goals imply self-modification: in that sense they are **reflexive,** they turn back upon ourselves.

If then we say that persons are beings who have original goals, some of which are reflexive, then it becomes clear that persons are not exactly identical with human beings. Some human beings will lack these qualities if they are newborn or mad or senile; and some non-human beings will also have the attributes of persons: gods, ghosts, gremlins, angels, perhaps God Himself, will have complex, novel plans of their own, freely chosen.

In any case, there can be no doubt that persons have Intentions, and Intentional explanation is essentially used to explain the behaviour of persons. And we can see now that it is only marginally applicable to animals or babies or mad people because they precisely lack that ability to choose self-determining goals. Animals and babies are still carrying out Nature's plans, not (yet) their own.

Parts of the Mind

Being fully a person therefore implies that to some extent our minds have parts. At the very least, there is the part which wants to alter the other parts. Reflexivity entails some minimal specialisation of our minds, and to that extent our minds have compartments. Some thinkers—Freud for instance—have taken this compartmentalisation to far greater lengths. Maybe they are right, maybe not. We do not need to commit ourselves either way. But notice that if we say that there is an unconscious mind, then it must be an unconscious mind, and like any other mind or part of the mind, it must have Intentions for its contents: it must have unconscious wishes, beliefs, whims, doubts, intentions, and all the rest of the Intentional bag.

A separate question is whether there can be causal antecedents for parts of our minds. We argued before that Intentions cannot be connected up in any routine way with causes, because they are quite incompatible forms of explanation. But it is possible that certain groups of ideas we have might seem to have a rational framework, but in fact come and go depending on the causal state of our stomachs, or glands in our heads, or the presence of someone we are madly in love with. In these cases, we say that our reasons are not real reasons, but rationalisations, and that we are in the grip of an addiction or a drive which deprives us of our freedom.These addictions or drives then are causes of our beliefs and our behaviour; but they are not reasons for them. That is why we ignore their rationality when we use them to explain the addict's behaviour. If all our behaviour were determined by drives and addictions, then we could say that our behaviour was wholly caused, and that all our reasons were really rationalisations. But we have no good scientific grounds to believe that any such cynical possibility is true.

Reductionism

There is however a variant cynicism that we must consider. Some philosophers have argued that Intentional explanation is only causal explanation in disguise: Intentional explanation can be reduced to causal explanation. Intentional explanation may look different, but really we can treat it as the same, and use the same methods for investigating claims about mental phenomena as we do when investigating causal phenomena. The appearance of difference between them is an illusion.

According to them, the reduction is to be achieved by saying that events in our minds are only events in our brains, but under different labels. When I come to believe that it is cold outside, this is the same as particular neuronal firings or chemical changes taking place in my brain. What takes place is the same event, but in the first instance, the event is seen from within; in the second, the event is seen by an outside observer. However, it is nevertheless the same single event.

Other philosophers have replied that this equivalence may be right, in the sense that we do think with our brains, and there is no reason to believe that there is an independent mental realm which needs to be postulated to accommodate our mental attributes. But causation requires us to fit the events it describes into a pattern of laws; the pattern has to repeat itself, or anyway to be in principle repeatable for the causal explanation to hold true. But this is exactly what is not possible with mental events like beliefs, because there have never been any such laws discovered. And even if there were, it would be an extra thing to fit mental events and physical (brain) events into the same universal laws, because mental events have to be assessed under different holistic criteria to those affecting our assessment of physical events. The laws could never be confirmed because the grounds for assessing would always be shifting. So causal explanation cannot in practice be applied; **reductionism** does not work.

Other philosophers (Quine, for example) who oppose Intentional explanation have argued otherwise. Intentional explanation, according to them, is different to causal explanation, but also inferior to it—sloppy, uncertain, imprecise. The reply to them has been that Intentional explanation is all we have. The massive translation of mental into physical terms that they propose would be a translation which distorted the original mental *text*. For them to swap to causal explanation would only be to change the subject. Human problems as they actually exist are expressed in Intentional language, and must be answered in Intentional language.

Causal Narratives and Personal Narratives

We have spoken in chapter 2 as though the main task of natural science is the formulation of causal laws. This is not bad for a summary, but it conceals the extent to which some sciences, for instance cosmology and evolutionary biology, concern themselves not only with causal laws, but with how they combined with events to bring the world to its present state of affairs. They not only formulate explanatory laws, then, they tell a believable explanatory story.

These causal narratives are indifferent to human meaning except in the sense that we are interested in the results. On the other hand, we each have a personal narrative of how we and our tribe got to be where we are, and these personal narratives are laid out in the concepts with which we conceive human lives. Like causal narratives, they lay out a sequence of events over time; but personal narratives are largely made up of Intentional events. This distinction between causal and personal narratives will come in handy later when we discuss the differences between the medical case history and the clinical interview.

Doing and Saying

Of course, saying something is a particular sort of act, isn't it? It's doing something with words. Like any act, it has its associated intentions, for example, to inform or deceive; and possible unintended consequences. But there is another way in which doing and saying are opposed.

Saying you are going to do something is not the same as doing it, alas, and the fact that we are aware of many forms of rationalisation and of talk being cheap shows that we refer to this gap between word and deed all the time in explaining human behaviour: 'She said she wanted to come to our party but she was too scared of meeting her old boyfriend there.' We have discussed above the many forms of consistency we look for in attributing rationality to people; perhaps one of the most important forms is consistency of talk with action: we have to reconcile what people say with what they do in order to make sense of them.

This point connects with an important limitation on in-depth interviewing as a way of understanding people, which is what this book is all about. If you only do in-depth interviews of such a pure kind that you only get people's verbal account of what they think and do, then you are by definition excluding any check on how what they say squares with what they do. It becomes very hard to exclude the possibility that what you are hearing is one big self-deception, or interviewer deception perhaps. Luckily, very few in-depth interviews are really pure in this way, and life provides many means of cross-checking our interviewee's story against his or her behaviour. One day, for instance, he or she might turn up with a black eye and other bruises very hard to make consistent with the goody-goody image he or she has so far worked to project. These new signs imply behaviour inconsistent with his or her story thus far.

In a comparable way, pure observation of behaviour using a **participant observation** model has built-in limitations as an approach, usually because there are far too many possible stories consistent with what we manage to see of others' actions. But in practice, most researchers, like most people who are not researchers, ask people what they are doing, and so conduct informal in-depth interviews as they go along. Often we overhear what people have to say for themselves too, as if we were listening in on in-depth interviews conducted by other people on our behalf.

Understanding People—a Method?

These points about human action are not made to strike despair into your heart, or to make you cynical about this kind of explanation. After all, we all do it successfully every day. The American sociologist Garfinkel (1967) has made the point that our understanding of other people and our dealing with them depends on an enormous range of interpretive skills which we learn and exercise unconsciously and are unaware of but which are implicit in our social practice. We develop a natural mastery which is untaught, and only examined when there is a clash of interpretation—just as we mostly think about grammar only when we or someone else notices that we have made a mistake. As with grammar, the fact that social interpretation is not formalised and is not taught does not prevent us exercising a remarkable level of skill: most of us would find it hard actually to write a novel, but we all understand very well what the novelist is saying about the characters.

In any case, the fact that this kind of explanation is holistic, theoretical and indeterminate allows us to answer a question we set ourselves above: does social science allow us any greater certainty than natural science that our theories are right and our opponents are wrong? No. In social science we must be even more humble before the possibility that our understanding is provisional and local. Neither natural nor social science offers a logic of discovery, or a logic of justification. There are no algorithms here, only heuristics. We can adhere to certain basic principles, but there can be no guarantee that these principles will provide a correct answer.

This is perhaps the place to add that a whole school of criticism called **Deconstructionism** has arisen in recent decades, claiming that large parts of Western thought have been endowed with a spurious rationality and consistency, and that this has largely been done through a desire to control and impress others. We have no argument with such an approach, and to settle its claims would take us way beyond the scope of this book. But it is clear that Deconstruction mounts an attack on one or several kinds of rationality only to substitute a rationality of hidden motives. It therefore is no enemy to the position taken by this book.

The Validity and Reliability of the Interpretive Approach

Another feature of the way we explain people is implicit in what we have said already. *The fundamental unit of interpretive explanation is the individual person.* That is, people are explained, at least to begin with, on their own terms, rather than by being classified as a member of a larger group or class. Of course, once we have explained them, then we can classify them with the class of (literally) like-minded people. And even in explaining them, we take into account from the beginning their probable membership of social groups. Nevertheless, it is individuals, not families, classes or societies who are rational, consistent and meaningful; and in that sense explanation begins with individuals. The name of this assumption is **methodological individualism.** We have not sufficient space to explain here why we believe it to be not only the best approach but the only approach. These issues have been superbly discussed by Elster (1983).

You will remember the discussion in the last chapter about the validity and reliability of scientific explanations in general. These desirable attributes of explanations are sharply at issue in interpretive explanation, and now we are in a position to see why. The overall rationality attributed to an individual's mind is of course just what validity amounts to in this kind of explanation; in fact it is impossible consistently, in our opinion, to imagine what could possibly be *more* valid then that.

So far so good. The complications set in when we try to imagine what would be the equivalent in mentalistic explanation of scientific *reliability*. You could not independently value an interpretation for consistency over time or over different aspects of someone's behaviour, because that is exactly why we prefer the explanations we do in the first place: interpretations have a kind of built-in reliability, and they are constantly being updated to provide it. But they could never be found independently to be reliable; that would be cheating.

Remember too that there is good reason to believe that there may be no good way finally of choosing between certain competing explanations of someone's behaviour and talk. This itself places limits on what we can mean here by validity. It certainly does *not* mean that if one explanation is valid then all others must be invalid. Perhaps it would be better to speak about degrees of goodness for explanations, rather than their being absolutely in or out, which is what a term like *valid* implies.

The next complication is that interpretive explanations are hard to *generalise*. All along we assume that all minds are more or less subtly different from one another, and if this is so, then it follows directly that we can only make inexact or partial generalisations about more than one mind at a time. By contrast, the 'units' we explain in natural science are assumed to be pretty much the same; that, after all, is why we choose the units we do. For instance, sycamore trees get classified as a kind of maple because they are in most respects the same as maples; and one maple is the same as any other in even more respects. That is what makes talking about maples (the 'unit' of explanation here) worth doing. So the problem now looks like this: we can have one explanation for all maples, but for people we need as many explanations as there are people to be explained. This induces nightmare visions of endless explanation, driving people to take up botany (or to treat people as if they were trees).

Some theorists have said that natural science explanations are **nomothetic**—leading us to explain things by virtue of class membership, while social science explanations are **idiographic**— explaining each individual on his or her own terms. This distinction fits in more or less with what we have just said, but we dislike the distinction because we believe there is more to it than that. Remember that we said in an earlier section that part of attributing rationality to someone implies an assumption that they have more or less the same conceptual scheme as ourselves: eccentricity can be only partial to be intelligible. Remember also that societies go to a lot of trouble to make us intelligible to one another, at least when we are waiting at the traffic lights or submitting an essay to be marked. So there are good grounds, philosophical and sociological, for assuming that people's minds are largely the same. Their bodies also are pretty much the same;

and in a given society it is likely that their material setting—street lighting, shape of front garden, etc.—will also be comparable. Putting all this together means than we can with some confidence expect, in an Australian suburban house we have not previously visited, to be offered tea or coffee but not betel nut. So generalisation is possible; it is just a matter of finding what features of people's beliefs can be generalised and which ones cannot. Not in the end all that different from maple trees.

The Principles of Understanding People

This is a list of principles used in giving the best possible Intentional explanation of a given person's (P's) behaviour. These principles have been extracted from the philosophical literature in an attempt to find some kind of interpretive bedrock; without them, we would hardly have Intentional explanation at all. In this, they are more basic than such tricks of the trade as getting your P drunk to make him talk—tricks which have empirically been found to produce useful results.

Notice that we have no reason to assume that these principles listed below are a complete set, or that there is no overlap between them. Also, it may be that some of them should not be on the list: all are somewhat controversial. Nor can we assume that any two of these principles will always favour a particular interpretation of a given action. Indeed, when they conflict, we have not as yet any means of giving one principle precedence or dominance over another.

Therefore, we cannot assume that perfect application of these principles is possible, or that there will ever be one indubitably best explanation. Nor can we assume that there is any favoured place to start our investigations, or any right place to complete them: interpretation is in a constant state of revision, and the only reason we put up with such an unreliable mode of explanation is that, practically, it is all we have. Here then are the principles, together with references to some classic texts in which they have been defined.

1 *Rationality*. Construe P's behaviour so as to maximise the rationality of his or her beliefs, desires and actions (Davidson 1984). Maximise the mutual consistency—the thin rationality —of his or her beliefs, desires and actions; and their compat-

ibility—broad rationality—with what is known and valued in his or her culture (Elster 1968; 1983).

2 *Centrality*. Assume that some of P's beliefs are more central than others, that is, more firmly held and adhered to in the face of contrary evidence (Quine 1960).
3 *Cultural commonality*. Assume as much overlap as possible between P's beliefs and those of his or her culture.
4 *Methodological commonality*. Attribute as much commonality as possible between P's beliefs and your own (Davidson 1984).
5 *Cultural semantics*. Translate or interpret P's words so as to give maximum fit between his or her language and his or her culture (Quine 1960).
6 *Methodological semantics*. Translate or interpret P's words so as to give maximum fit between his or her language and your own (Davidson 1980; 1984).
7 *Intentionality*. Construe P's behaviour as far as possible as intentional, meaningful and voluntary (Elster 1968; 1983).
8 *Truth-telling*. Maximise P's truth-telling, both to you and to others.
9 *Social context*. Assume that P's behaviour, both verbal and non-verbal, is given meaning by his or her social context.
10 *Ideals*. Maximise the similarity between P's underlying aims or ideals and those of his or her culture.
11 *Self-directedness*. Maximise P's responsibility for being the sort of person he or she is—his or her self-directedness (Taylor 1985).
12 *Selfishness*. Maximise the selfishness of P's behaviour (Elster 1968; 1983).
13 *Creativity*. Minimise the originality of thought and action attributed to P; which is not to rule it out completely.

Holistic Methodology

Holistic methodology, then, starts off assuming others are as like us as possible, but assumes that any deviations in behaviour will probably best be explained as due to deviant beliefs. The researcher will try as hard and as persistently as possible to see P as rational, before assuming that P is in the grip of irrational forces, or non-rational causal mechanisms. He or she will assume methodological individualism, but place the values and goals attributed to P in the context of P's social and historical context. He or she will not assume that there is only one best way of interpreting P's behaviour (including his or her language), but that P himself or herself will be a significant source of confirmation and justification for his or her own behaviour as described in his or her own language, or anyway his or her own concepts. The art of *Interpretive explanation* consists of reconciling the variant interpretations which follow from the principles given above to give an overall sense of understanding of P's personality.

Glossary

Broad rationality Consistency with the goals and beliefs of the surrounding society.

Deconstructionism A school of philosophy which holds that most traditional rationalistic interpretations are spurious and motivated by hidden desires for power and social control.

Functionalism Explaining (usually biological) features by showing their *purpose* in helping group or species survival.

Hermeneutic circle If you start explaining a text by explaining the meaning of its parts, you have to explain the meaning of its parts in terms of the overall meaning of the text. But if you try to give the overall meaning of the text, you have to do this in terms of the meaning of its individual parts. So where do you start?

Hermeneutics The science of the interpretation of texts.

Iconic sign A sign which is visually similar (or sounds similar) to the object it signifies, as the road sign for a hump shows a schematic section of a hump.

Idiographic Describing the internal structure of an individual mind.

Intentionality Aboutness. Attributing to minds *properties* which refer outside the mind itself, as wanting an ice-cream is a property (wanting) referring to, about, the external ice-cream.

Methodological individualism Regarding the fundamental unit of explanation in the social sciences as the individual person.

Natural sign A sign which is causally associated with what it signifies, as clouds signify rain.

Nomothetic Studying individuals purely for the purposes of generalising to the classes of which they are a member.

Participant observation Studying people by participating in social interactions with them in order to observe and understand them.

Proposition A statement or assertion of the relationship between concepts. In philosophy, a proposition can be a true-or-false sentence which is expressed in a given statement.
Rationalisation A spurious explanation of one's beliefs, feelings or behaviour masking one's real reasons, possibly from oneself.
Reductionism For the purposes of this chapter, replacing mental explanations by would-be equivalent physiological explanations, usually in terms of brain neurones.
Reflexivity Having Intentional attitudes (see above) to oneself, for instance, trying to become a more modest person.
Statement A sentence which can be made true or false by the circumstances of its being uttered, as when 'It is raining' becomes true if it is raining nearby when I say it. What I say is the statement.
Symbolic sign A sign which has no formal or causal association with what it signifies. Rain is wet but the word *rain* is neither wet nor dry, nor does it make plants grow.
Thin rationality Internal mental consistency.

References

Davidson, D. 1980. *Actions and Events.* Oxford: Oxford University Press.

Davidson, D. 1984. 'On the very idea of a conceptual scheme.', in D. Davidson (ed.), *Inquiries Into Truth and Interpretation.* Oxford: Oxford University Press.

Elster, J. 1968 *Explaining Technical Change.* Cambridge: Cambridge University Press.

Elster, J. 1983. *Sour Grapes.* Cambridge: Cambridge University Press.

Garfinkel, H. 1967. *Studies in Ethnomethodology*. Englewood Cliffs, New Jersey: Prentice-Hall.

Morris, C. 1938. *Foundations of a Theory of Signs.* Chicago: University of Chicago Press.

Quine, W.V. 1960. *Word and Object.* Harvard: Harvard University Press.

Searle, J.R. 1983. *Intentionality.* Cambridge: Cambridge University Press.

Taylor, C. 1985. *Human Agency and Language. Collected Papers,* Vol. 1. Cambridge: Cambridge University Press.

Chapter 4
Preparation Work

The first step in conducting any research is to formulate a specific research problem and related research questions. The research problem posed at the beginning of any project is often very general. The research question needs to be focussed. For example, to simply state that you want to conduct a study of older people living in nursing homes is not very specific. What aspects of the institutionalisation process do you want to learn about? Do you want to study why older people are admitted into nursing homes, or what happens to them once they are admitted? Are you interested in examining issues which are associated with the pre- or post-admission stage, or both? Do you want to study the views of older men, older women, or both? The physically or mentally disabled? What conceptual framework will you be adopting? For example, will you apply a sociological or psychological perspective to study the admission process? These questions need to be answered prior to entering the field. Answers to these questions assist researchers to clarify and narrow their research focus. Researchers rarely enter the field on the day that they think of a research problem. Time is set aside to reflect on the question being asked. The question is posed in the context of previous work on the topic.

There are two types of preparation work that researchers engage in prior to entering the field. One type of preparation work, as discussed in chapter 9, relates to developing strategies for getting in, learning the ropes, maintaining relations, leaving the field and developing sampling and other method procedures. Preparation work discussed in this chapter relates to the conceptualisation of the research statement and research question. Although details of the researchers' preparation work are seldom reported in their final report, a considerable amount of time is spent on this activity. For example, Lopata (1980) reports spending a full year **reviewing the literature** on ageing, grief, divorce, ethnicity, and attending support group meetings for widows prior to undertaking her study on the support system of American widows. As a result of this work, Lopata developed a better understanding of issues associated with widowhood; such as changes in role involvements, social networks, types of loneliness and methods of coping with them, emotional support systems and forms of social interaction. Lopata's time spent 'researching' her research topic is not atypical of the experiences of other researchers or doctoral students (Shaffir et al. 1980).

Preparation work involves spending time in the library and locating and reading literature which will assist the researcher to further focus the question being asked. It may also involve documentary research and use of tools such as biographical dictionaries, membership directories of professional associations, newspapers, and *Who's Who in Australia* to learn more about specific individuals, places or situations.

Preparation work can also influence the researcher's success in gaining entry and establishing rapport with subjects once in the field. For example, Spector (1980) reports how he used documentary research to identify the central figures involved in the debate to demedicalise homosexuality. He developed a file on each of the public figures involved in the debate. This preparation work, before the interview, Spector argues, was crucial in influencing his entry into the field and getting public officials to take his work seriously. He notes,

> Well-known people tend to expect this work—in fact, [they expect] a mastery of what is in the public record. They may grow impatient with questions that could be easily answered by a look at public documents or their writings (Spector 1980: 100).

Sampling procedures can also be shaped by such preparation work. Spector identified his sample by examining who the media reported as being key figures in the debate. On the basis of this information, he contacted individuals for interviews. He also used public statements reported in the media to cross-check information he received while interviewing the informants.

This chapter will discuss why the review of the literature is an essential aspect of the research process, and describe how to use the library to locate pertinent information from different sources. A knowledge of how to access library information is essential for carrying out the preparation tasks underlying all research projects. While all researchers recognise the contribution a review of literature plays in the research process, there is some debate among qualitative researchers on the role it should play in assisting researchers to formulate their research questions.

Quantitative researchers identify the hypotheses that will be tested in their studies prior to entering the field. The purpose of conducting a review of the literature is to ensure that all relevant assumptions are incorporated into the study design. Hypotheses are spelled out, variables identified and questionnaires constructed on the basis of this knowledge. For example, there is little opportunity for the researcher to change or add new questions once the data-collection stage has begun.

Qualitative researchers, however, do not have to identify their propositions prior to entering the field. The methodological thrust of qualitative research is the possibility of the development of theory without any particular commitment to specific prior knowledge. They do not search out data to prove or disprove hypotheses they hold before entering the field. Rather, as Glaser and Strauss (1967) argue, propositions and theories are developed from the many pieces of evidence which are interconnected concurrently with the data-collection process. For this reason, the review of the literature plays a different role in qualitative studies. The literature acts as a stimulus for thinking.

Conducting a review of the literature throughout the project is an essential aspect of the qualitative research process. You should read the literature prior to entering the field to familiarise yourself with the crucial issues that others have identified, and to examine what has been neglected in the literature. Reading may stimulate you to think about issues and questions that you may want to pursue. In addition to reading the literature prior to entering the field, you should continue to read while in the field. The literature can provide useful clues that help you to interpret your data. However, it is important to remember when doing a search for a qualitative study that the literature should be viewed as a sounding board for ideas and that its suggestions and interpretations should not be taken for granted (Denzin 1989). In line with the theoretical principles underlying qualitative methodology (see chapter 3), the researcher measures his or her achievement by calling into question prior knowledge and discovering new ideas. For this reason, it is important that you do not enter the field with a fixed framework that will automatically interpret what you see or hear. As Bogdan and Biklen note,

> The danger in reading literature while you are conducting your study is that you may read and find concepts, ideas or models that are so compelling they blind you to other ways of looking at your data. Try to avoid jamming your data into pre-formed conceptual schemes . . . [It] is perfectly honorable to do research that illustrates others' analytical schemes, but try to distance yourself enough to formulate concepts of your own or to expand the work of others (1982: 153).

If the data fit the concepts from the literature, do not be afraid to borrow them. If they do not, it is an error to force the data to fit the concepts.

Why Conduct a Review of Literature?

There are many reasons for conducting a review of the literature. The most obvious one is to find out what is already known about the topic chosen for study. If you decide to investigate what younger people think about safe sex, then a good starting point is to find out if other researchers have asked this question and what they have reported. There is no point asking a question which has been the topic of extensive investigation unless your sole aim is to replicate the study on a different population (for example, Aboriginal youths/Australian youths). Research should never be conducted in ignorance of previous knowledge. The accumulation of knowledge depends on its being connected to current ideas. There are very few topics that do not have some published material.

For example, if you were to conduct a literature search on the topic of acoustic neuroma, a tumor found in the brain, you would discover that there are few publications on this subject. The nomenclature, acoustic neuroma, has only been used in the last ten years. However, this does not mean that there is no literature which is pertinent to a study that examines illness careers of people who have had an operation for acoustic neuroma. There is a rich sociological literature on the meaning of illness. Kaufman's (1988) study on the strategies stroke patients use to renegotiate their identity after the operation provides an interesting analysis of how people's actions can be influenced by their perceptions of illness. The issues which he describes as characterising the experience of recovering from a stroke, such as stigmatisation, the redefined self and attempt to return to normal, can provide a useful framework for understanding how individuals reconstruct their experiences in the pre-and post-operation acoustic neuroma stages.

An important aspect of the researcher's work is to place his or her study in the context of current knowledge and to broaden scientific knowledge. Researchers conduct a search of the literature not only to find what others have written on the topic but to justify the contribution their study will make to current knowledge. For example, the Minichiello et al. study (see Appendix A) addresses the issue of decision making for entry to nursing homes. They reviewed the literature on decision making and ageing and posed their question in the context of the psychosocial research on control and ageing. The contribution of the study to current knowledge of the topic is that it examines the different levels of engagement in the process of entry. Few studies have examined the actual processes by which older people are included or excluded in decision making to enter nursing homes. Research reports are often evaluated in terms of their contribution to knowledge. A study might be methodologically flawless but considered a failure by a critical reviewer if the study is not conceptually sound and advances knowledge.

The review of the literature also assists researchers to locate conceptual schemes which can act as a guide to raising questions and making sense of data. For example, Bowers (1987) develops a model of family caregiving centred on the purpose for the type of care that caregivers are providing (see chapter 1). Based on these findings, several other researchers have contributed to the development of theory about family caregiving by examining how staff and family members share the responsibility of providing care to nursing-home residents (for a review see Bowers, 1988). Researchers can also follow up an idea that has been mentioned in a report. Often research reports identify additional questions which can be investigated by other researchers. Below are some examples of issues raised in reports for further consideration.

> In order to better understand changes in people's experiences and feelings as they move from the community into nursing homes, longitudinal studies are required. Such an approach would give us a better understanding of the situations in which people find themselves and enables us to detect any discontinuities in personal perceptions of their situation once the change from pre-resident to resident has taken place. Future studies will need to examine the experiences of different segments of the aged population who enter and live in nursing homes. Are there class differences in the ways people make decisions to enter and select a nursing home? Do the ethnic aged encounter similar experiences in entering and living in a nursing home as do their Australian-born aged counterparts? Specific attention also needs to be focussed on examining how the current restructuring of nursing homes will affect the processes by which people enter them. Will the shift to recruiting a more dependent population affect the quality of life of those who live and work in nursing homes? Will such a shift create a custodial model of care? (Minichiello 1988: 220).
>
> At the intervention level, psychologists could conduct more studies aimed at improving the behaviour of the aged. For example, research can shed some light on the relationship between age and intellectual abilities. Decline in intellectual functioning with age is not necessarily inevitable or immutable. The extent to which older people's cognitive tasks are affected by age or societal attitudes is unclear. For instance, it is known that institutional living often encourages its inhabitants to take on a passive role. Staff members perform many of the activities of daily living for the residents, despite the fact that many are capable of performing these tasks for themselves (Avorn and Langer 1982). The extent to which clinical tasks and administrative routines can depress performance on cognitive tasks is a critical question that needs to be systematically investigated. There is an urgent need to distinguish between normal and abnormal changes in behaviour which occur with ageing, and to assess the extent to which learned helplessness is responsible for some of the physical and mental decline of the elderly. These are just a small sample of the many avenues for psychological research in the field (Minichiello, Alexander and Jones 1988: 8).

Finally, a review of the literature can provide useful suggestions on how to plan the method design of your study. Much can be learnt from the experience of other researchers regarding issues of locating and gaining access to subjects. In recent years, a rich literature has been published on researchers' personal accounts of their fieldwork experiences (Punch 1986; Shaffir et al. 1980; Sprinivas et al. 1979; Van Maanen 1988). The researcher can learn many lessons from both the successes and failures of other researchers (Dempsey and Dempsey 1986; Shaffir et al. 1980). For example, the ethical question of confidentiality which Laud Humphreys (1970) confronted after publishing the results of his study on impersonal sex in public places draws our attention to the difficulties researchers can face when conducting disguised research.

Becoming Familiar with the Library

A library can look intimidating to someone who does not know how to access the wealth of information it contains. The novice user entering the library is confronted with hundreds of journals, thousands of books, and computer terminals. Searching for the right book may be like looking for a needle in a haystack. The difference between a successful and unsuccessful library expedition will depend on your knowledge of the library. A lot of valuable time and energy can be saved by acquainting yourself with the library facilities and holdings. Anyone who has spent time doing library work can tell you how easy it is to be flooded with literature on a topic, and spend a great deal of time locating journals and books. These two factors probably account for why many people feel anxious about using the library. Librarians can, however, reduce such anxieties.

All libraries have a 'Reference and Enquiries' desk. Sitting behind this desk is a friendly librarian who is eager to acquaint you with the use of the **card catalogue**, the various **indices** (or *indexes* as they are referred to in some libraries), **abstracts** and **computer-assisted searches.** Librarians also offer guidance on the most appropriate reference works to be consulted for specific purposes. They can inform you about such things as conditions of borrowing, copyright, costs for interlibrary loans, photocopy services and loan materials available from cooperating libraries. The library offers a range of instructional programmes for users, including a tour of the library, instructions on catalogue use and sessions on information resources for particular subject areas. These orientation sessions are useful to both the novice and experienced users. Libraries vary in terms of the type of cataloguing system they use. It is advisable to consult the librarian to find out what classification system has been adopted in your particular library. Some libraries, for example, use the Dewey Decimal Classification System while others use the Library of Congress System. Depending on which system is used, the books will be given a different set of code numbers.

The range and volume of literature contained in the library is enormous and growing. Researchers continue to write, publishers continue to publish and libraries continue to purchase. This creates a problem for those of us who have to locate material within this growing collection. The problem we often face is not that the library does not hold information on our topic but how we locate the information. Fortunately, reference material is available to assist us to locate the pertinent literature. It is important to remember that a library's resources are not restricted to the collection contained in it. Interlibrary loan allows you to borrow books and journals which are not available in your library. Librarians can assist you to locate literature available in other libraries. It is advisable that you plan interlibrary loan requests well ahead as the item may take as long as three weeks before you receive it. The next section will provide a brief discussion on how these library resources can be used for this purpose.

Resource Material in the Library

There are a number of useful sources that can be consulted to locate books and articles. These include: the card catalogue, indices, abstracts and computer-assisted literature-search programmes. The card catalogue is mainly used to locate books in the library. The information contained in the card catalogue includes an alphabetical listing of books classified under the categories of the title of the book, the name of the author or the subject heading. Card catalogues in many libraries are now in microfiche format or stored on a computer. All books, audiovisual items and journals in the library are listed in the computer catalogue Online Public Access Catalogue (OPAC). These computer terminals are often located just inside the library entrance or close to the reference desk. OPAC is easy to use. You simply select the author, title or subject menu program and then type the required information. The computer will list the information on the screen and inform you whether the item is located in the library.

While the card catalogue is a useful place for researchers to begin their literature search it does not provide access to all published material on the topic. Excluded from the card catalogue are articles in journals. Unlike books, articles in journals are written and published much more rapidly and frequently than are books. These often represent the most recent literature on the topic. For this reason, journals are an excellent starting point to trace the literature. While articles can be found through a manual search of journals, a much more reliable way to locate the articles is by consulting indices or abstracts. Indices and abstracts are used to obtain information to periodicals and other literature which is not contained in the card catalogue. Most disciplines publish indices and abstracts which summarise the literature published in journals relevant to the field. Some indices and abstracts are interdisciplinary and cover published material from a number of disciplines.

Indices include reference materials on books and periodicals. Identification of relevant material is by means of subject terms in the form of keywords or thesaurus terms. An index does not reproduce the article but provides the information required to locate the article: name of author(s), title of article, name of journal, volume, year and page numbers. Abstracts provide similar information, but in addition include a short summary on the purpose, methods and major findings of the research studies, rarely exceeding 150 words. This information is useful when the content of the article cannot be determined simply by reading the title.

In addition to manual searches of the card catalogue, indices and abstracts, computer-assisted literature searches can also be used to identify relevant publications. Most libraries have access to computer-based bibliographic processing systems which contain a data base of hundreds of thousands of articles published in journals and other literature. The information held in the computer data base is similar to that found in the indices and abstracts. There are a number of computer-search programs available. Some of these are listed in Figure 4.1. The Directory of Onlinc Information Resources provides an exhaustive list of databases programs and a description of their contents.

Most of the computer-search programs provide access to journals only. The system is programmed by subjects and not authors. For this reason, it is important that users provide precise information on the topic to be searched. Most libraries will conduct a computer literature search at a charge. Cost is determined by the particular data base that is searched and the time it takes to complete the work requested. Time spent on selecting appropriate descriptors can save money in on-line searching time.

The term *institutionalisation* is too broad for describing a study which specifically focuses on the processes of admitting older people into nursing homes. The usage of this term will not allow the computer to distinguish literature written on older people admitted into nursing homes from the more general studies which include a wide range of people admitted into different types of institutions (for example, hospitals, hostels). If we want to locate information which is specific to our topic then we must construct a set of terms which will produce relevant information on older people living in nursing homes. We might therefore give the librarian the following set of words—*aged, nursing home admission.*

There are a number of indexing vocabulary manuals that assist the user to narrow topics which do not have headings specific enough for on-line searching. These reference sources provide a vocabulary of subject headings (For a detailed list see Haselbauer 1987).

Indices and abstracts

Indices and abstracts are published in many professional fields. Figure 4.1 provides a list of the major social and health sciences *indexing* and *abstracting* services and their equivalent computerised databases. Some of these will be briefly discussed below. (For a description of a comprehensive listing of indices and abstracts see Haselbauer 1987). It is important for researchers to become familiar with, and consult, the range of sources available to them. Too often, researchers restrict their literature search to sources within their discipline. For example, because health science is a broad subject area, there are many sources from other disciplines which include health science as subject matters. Given the title, *Sociological Abstracts*, a health-science researcher might not think to consult this source. However, a quick glance at *Sociological Abstracts* reveals that it contains references to numerous articles on the ethical and social aspects of health practice, and on policy-making issues related to public health.

Index Medicus is the major index to medical periodical literature and can be computer searched through MEDLINE (Medlars Online), the earliest on-line database. It is published monthly by the National Library of Medicine. The first volume was published in 1879, and an annual cumulation began in 1960. *Index Medicus* covers an international collection of over 3000 periodicals including life sciences, medicine and allied health topics. The index is arranged by subject headings. The subject headings are assigned by indexers using a controlled vocabulary, MeSH (Medical Subject Headings). It is important for users to consult MeSH for the appropriate subject heading before using the index itself. It may be frustrating to find nothing under the term *cancer*; however, looking it up in MeSH produces the information that *neoplasms* is the preferred term.

Indices/Abstracts	Computer searching databases
Arts and Humanities Citation Index	AHCI
Australian Public Affairs Information	AUSINET
Cumulative Index to Nursing & Allied Health Literature	CINAHL
Current Index to Journals in Education	ERIC
International Nursing Index	MEDLINE
Index Medicus	MEDLINE
Occupational Safety and Health	DIALOG
Science Citation Index	SCISEARCH
Social Science Citation Index	SOCIAL SCISEARCH
Physical Fitness and Sport Medicine	SPORT DATABASE
Public Affairs and Public Policy Index	PAIS
Biological Abstracts	BIOSIS
Clinical Abstracts	CLINICAL ABSTRACTS
Excerpta Medica	EMBASE
Mental Health Abstracts	NIMH
Nursing Abstracts	NURSING ABSTRACTS
Sociological Abstracts	SOCIOLOGICAL ABSTRACTS
Psychological Abstracts	PSYCHINFO

Figure 4.1 Indices, abstracts and computer searching databases in health sciences and related literature.

The *Cumulative Index to Nursing and Allied Health Literature* is a comprehensive index designed to meet the specific needs of nursing and allied health professionals. Some of the allied health fields included are occupational therapy, physiotherapy, medical records and health education. The index was first published in 1956. The index covers over 300 nursing and allied health journals and can be computer searched through the NURSING AND ALLIED HEALTH data base.

The *Science Citation Index* and *the Social Science Citation Index* are useful reference sources for science and social science researchers. The *Science Citation Index* is a multi-disciplinary science index and covers citations in over 3000 major journals of science. The *Index* has been published since 1961. It covers the pure and applied science such as biology, chemistry, physics and zoology. Approximately 54% of its coverage is literature in the life sciences and clinical practice. A library survey on the use of reference sources in biomedical libraries found the *Science Citation Index* to be the most heavily used reference tool (Haselbauer 1987). The Institute for Scientific Information offers portions of its database for direct on-line searching through SCISEARCH.

The *Social Science Citation Index* provides indexing for some 2000 periodicals in such fields as anthropology, economics, political science, psychology and sociology. The index has been published quarterly since 1962 and can be searched through SOCIAL SCISEARCH computer data base.

While the above describe indices, a number of useful abstracts are also published, for example, in the fields of biology, psychology, medicine and sociology. As was mentioned earlier, the additional information contained in abstracts is a statement on the research question, the specific method(s) of data collection, sample details, type of analysis used and results.

The most widely used medical abstracting service is *Excerpta Medica* which includes content coverage of over 3500 international journals in human medicine and biology. The annual abstract service was first published in 1947 and can be searched through the EMBASE computerised database. Abstracts are in English, regardless of language of the original article. Journal literature represents 95% of the citation; monographs, dissertations, conference papers and reports comprise the remaining 5%. The *Guide to Excerpta Medica Classification and Indexing System* provides detailed notes on how to use the abstract service.

Biological Abstracts provides a comprehensive coverage of the worldwide life-sciences literature and includes a wide range of topics from the medical, physiological and pharmaceutical literature. It was first published in 1926. *Biological Abstracts* scans 9000 journals, and abstracts only articles and other original papers published in periodicals. It consists of three sections: content summaries of research reports, with a subject-specific headings index at the beginning of the section; names of books, with complete bibliographic information and a brief synopsis; and scientific conferences, with bibliographic information on the conference plus names and addresses of speakers and the titles of their papers. The *Guide to the Use of Biological Abstracts* provides useful material for the beginning researcher to locate literature contained in the abstract. It can be searched through the BIOSIS on-line.

Psychological Abstracts has been published by the American Psychological Association since 1927. It covers the world's literature in psychology and related disciplines such as anthropology, education, linguistics, pharmacology, physiology, psychiatry and sociology. This source scans approximately 1000 periodicals and 1509 books, technical reports and monographs each year. This abstract can be searched through PSYCHINFO computer data base. Because *Psychological Abstracts*, like many other abstract services, uses a controlled vocabulary of subject headings, searchers are advised to begin their work by consulting the *Thesaurus of Psychological Index Terms*. For each entry, the *Thesaurus* supplies broader, narrower and related terms, and cross-references from terms not used.

Sociological Abstracts covers journals published by sociological associations and periodicals containing the word *sociology* in their title. It includes journals from the fields of anthropology, community development, economics, education, medicine, philosophy, political science and statistics. This source first began publication in 1953 and can be searched through SOCIOLOGICAL ABSTRACTS computer data base.

A useful Australian abstract source is the *Australian Public Affairs Information* (APAIS). APAIS is a comprehensive abstract service for Australian scholarly journals in the social sciences, humanities and public affairs fields. The *APAIS Thesaurus* lists the vocabulary of subject terms used to index articles. The first edition was published in 1981 and the most recent edition (third) in 1986. APAIS has been available as a computer-searchable database on AUSINET since 1978.

An Index-card System to Record Information

Once you have located pertinent literature material on a topic, the next task is to read and extract the relevant information from these sources. However, this poses a problem. The issue to be faced is, how do you retain this information given the fact that you may have read hundreds of articles? One strategy is to photocopy all these articles and to consult each original article when you are doing the analysis of the literature. However, this can be both time consuming and expensive. A more effective way of summarising and studying the information found in the literature is to store relevant information on an index card as you read the articles. A number of researchers have developed systematic card index storing procedures for recording a critical review of the literature (Seaman 1987). This section will discuss strategies for recording the content of literature reviewed.

What Information to Collect

The first step in reviewing the literature involves reading the report. Reports often follow a logical progression of ideas and arguments. The reader is provided with information about the (1) statement of the problem; (2) general question(s) asked; (3) theoretical position; (4) choice of research design and method; (5) choice of sample; (6) presentation of findings; and (7) a discussion of the implications of the results. When you read the report, it is helpful if you keep notes on each of these categories. These should be summarised in your own words rather than those of the authors. If direct quotes will be used make sure you copy the information and the reference details (for example, page number) accurately. If you do not record this information, you will find yourself making another trip to the library. Use quotation marks to indicate the quoted material.

An example of the type of information which can be included on an **index card** is presented in Figure 4.2. This example provides general format guidelines of how the information can be organised. Some researchers prefer to record their information in a spiral notebook because in this way the references are contained in one source rather than on separate cards (Nieswiadony 1987). The reader is encouraged to design a recording system that he or she finds most appealing and useful, as long as its content covers the information described below and the same format is used each time.

Each index card should begin with the full reference details of the report. The call number of the journal or book, and the library where it can be located should also be recorded. This information is valuable because it can save you considerable time if you have to consult the book or journal again. There are several systems prescribing the style of writing and referencing of literature, such as the Oxford and the Harvard. (For a detailed discussion on the presentation of reference material and guidelines on writing research papers, see *Publication Manual of the American Psychological Association* 1983; Walker 1987).

Most libraries hold the manuals describing these reference systems. We suggest that you adopt the commonly used Harvard system. The following information is included: the surname of the author or authors, followed by their first initials; the year of publication; the complete title of the book or article; the journal in which the article appears; the details of the volume and pages of the article, or if a book, the city of publication and the name of the publishing company.

Writers often describe the statement of the problem and the question(s) asked in the first page of the report. You should note the focus of the study and the theoretical perspective used by the author in a paragraph or two. Although most research reports provide a theoretical perspective that serves as a basis for the study, not every researcher makes it clear which perspective they have used in the study. Finding and analysing the theoretical perspective of a study can be tricky. Researchers often include a discussion of the theoretical perspective for a study among other information in the introductory materials. It is important that you try to decipher the theoretical basis of the study by examining and identifying underlying assumptions to the study and how these link to the broader universe of knowledge.

You should also note the substantive literature which is reviewed. Although references will appear throughout the text, particular attention should be paid to the literature that is used to substantiate the conceptual or content area of the study. This literature is easy to find because most reports begin with a substantive literature review. It is part of the background information of the report. Some substantive literature can also be found in the *Discussion* or *Implications* sections of the report. Your task is to note what material has been included, and assess how the literature presented has been used to provide a rationale for the problem statement.

Most reports include a separate section on methods. The index card should include a few sentences which summarise the methodological design of the study. This includes assessing the appropriateness of the research design to the question asked and evaluating sampling, data analysis and ethical issues. Did the study use a qualitative or quantitative design? A longitudinal or cross-sectional approach? Were structured or unstructured interviews conducted? Was the research design descriptive, exploratory or experimental? What sampling framework was used? What ethical issues were raised?

The final paragraphs of the index card can be used to briefly summarise the main findings, and the conclusions and/or implications of the study. You might also include reflections on how the report has influenced your thoughts on the topic. These comments can be included under the category of *Ideas*.

The *main purpose* of the literature review is to examine how your proposed study can fit into a broader knowledge base. In order to achieve this goal, you will need to identify the strengths and gaps in the current knowledge base. This requires an understanding of what was studied and how it was done. It was mentioned at the beginning of the chapter, that as a critic, you can learn much from the success and failure of other researchers' efforts. The main objectives are to identify *theoretical, methodological* and *substantive* contributions of a study so that these can be incorporated into your work, and to note the gaps in existing knowledge so that you legitimate your planned work. This analysis can assist you to identify productive avenues for further investigations, to place your study in context of existing knowledge, and to ask questions which have not been addressed in the literature.

Figure 4.2 An example of a review of the literature index card.

Minichiello, V. (1987) 'Someone's decision: that is how I got here', *Australian Journal of Social Issues 22: 345–356.* (Abbotsford Campus, La Trobe University NURS J: 62) (1 of 4)
Research Question: The study sheds light on the role *aged persons*, *family members* and *health professionals* play in the decision to seek nursing home care. The article also examines how the resident's living arrangement affects his/her perception of his/her situation, the options available to them, and who becomes involved in the decision-making process. The author notes that there have been few studies (he cites two studies—which I will follow up) which have paid systematic empirical attention to these questions. While there is no explicit reference to theory, the author is clearly working within a sociological framework and using a functionalist perspective. He argues that as family members turn to formal agencies to meet the daily needs of their aged relatives, they adopt an advocate role. For this reason, family members collaborate with gatekeepers of nursing homes and are influential actors in the decision-making process.

Minichiello article	(2 of 4)
Much of the literature cited to substantiate this position is written by authors using a functionalist perspective. **Method:** The author collected data by interviewing ninety aged residents and their next-of-kin. A semi-structured questionnaire was used. Qualitative data were collected on the residents' feelings about moving to a nursing home. All the interviews were tape recorded and conducted at the nursing home. The sample is not representative and includes only those residents assessed by the professional nursing home staff as capable of hearing and comprehending questions. This places limits on the generality of the results. **Main findings and conclusions:** The study found that people play different roles in the decision-making process. Most older people were minor participants in the decision to enter a nursing home. The qualitative data highlight the processes by which family members and health professionals exclude the older person from the decision-making process. Residents recognised that the person who first raised the topic of moving to a nursing home is not necessarily the most influential actor in the decision-making process.	

Minichiello article	(3 of 4)
While most residents identified the physician as the person who first raised the topic of moving into a nursing home, family members were seen as the most influential actors, although there were differences in which actors were identified as influential depending upon living arrangement. **Ideas:** There are a number of issues that the author does not address: is there an association between level of disability, marital status, gender and involvement in the decision-making process? The author does not tell us very much about the characteristics of people who make decisions for themselves. Who are they? What distinguishes this group from those people who find themselves in situations where others have acted on their behalf? Are there different levels of decision making? Of course there is the decision to move into a nursing home. But what about the decision of selecting a nursing home? Is it possible for some residents not to be involved in making the decision to move in a nursing home but to be involved in selecting the nursing home they will move to?	

Minichiello article	(4 of 4)
The concepts of power and conflict are all applicable to this study. The author has decided not to apply these concepts to understand the topic of decision making. The study has brought to my attention the difficulty of interviewing the more disabled residents. If I want to include this group in my sample, how do I collect data about them? Maybe through family members? The Minichiello article does not discuss whether there were similarities or differences between the stories of the aged person and the stories provided by their relatives about the decision-making process. If the two stories were similar, then family members can be used as a proxy interview in those cases where it is not possible to directly talk with the older person. I need to examine the literature specifically dealing with methodological issues in studying the institutionalised aged. This may give me ideas about data-collection strategies.	

Glossary

Abstracts Sources which contain reference material and brief summaries of periodical articles.
Card catalogue The main reference source for locating books in the library.
Computer-assisted searches Used to obtain periodicals and books which are stored in a central data base and are accessible by computer.
Indices card system Used to classify and store on index cards bibliographic and relevant information for each item in the literature review.
Indices Sources which contain reference material on books and periodicals.
Review of literature The analysis of existing literature pertinent to the area of study.

References

Bogdan, R. & Biklen, S. 1982. *Qualitative Research for Education. Boston*: Allyn and Bacon.

Bowers, B. 1987. 'Intergenerational caregiving: adult caregivers and their ageing parents.', *Advances in Nursing Science* 9: 20–31.

Bowers, B. 1988. 'Family perceptions of care in a nursing home.', *The Gerontologist* 28: 361–368.

Dempsey, P. & Dempsey, A. 1986. *The Research Process in Nursing*. Monterey, California: Wadsworth Health Sciences.

Denzin, N. 1989. *The Research Act: A Theoretical Introduction to Sociological Methods*. Third edition. Englewood Cliffs, New Jersey: Prentice-Hall.

Glaser, B. & Strauss, A. 1967. *The Discovery of Grounded Theory*. Chicago: Aldine.

Haselbauer, K. 1987. *A Research Guide to the Health Sciences*. New York: Greenwood.

Humphreys, L. 1970. *Tearoom Trade: Impersonal Sex in Public Places*. Chicago: Aldine.

Kaufman, S. 1988. 'Stroke rehabilitation and the negotiation of identity.', in S. Reinharz and G. Rowles (eds), *Qualitative Gerontology*. New York: Springer.

Lopata, H. 1980. 'Interviewing American widows.', in W. Shaffir, R. Stebbins & A. Turowetz (eds), *Fieldwork Experiences: Qualitative Approaches to Social Research*. New York: St Martin's Press.

Minichiello, V., Alexander, L. & Jones, D. 1988 'Australian literature in social gerontology: a content analysis of trends since 1980.', *Lincoln Papers in Gerontology* No 1. Melbourne: La Trobe University, Bundoora, Vic.

Minichiello, V. 1988. *Beyond the Medical Admission: Social Pathways*

Into Nursing Homes. Unpublished PhD thesis, Canberra: Australian National University.

Nieswiadony, R. 1987. *Foundations of Nursing Research.* Norwalk, Connecticut: Appleton and Lange.

Publication Manual of the American Psychological Association. (Third edition) Washington, DC: American Psychological Association.

Punch, M. 1986. *The Politics and Ethics of Field Work.* Beverly Hills, California: Sage.

Seaman, C. 1987. *Research Methods: Principles, Practice and Theory for Nursing.* Norwalk, Connecticut: Appleton and Lange.

Shaffir, W., Stebbins, R. & Turowetz, A. 1980. *Fieldwork Experiences: Qualitative Approaches to Social Research.* New York: St Martin's Press.

Spector, M. 1980. 'Learning to study public figures.', in W. Shaffir, R. Stebbins & A. Turowetz (eds), *Fieldwork Experiences: Qualitative Approaches to Social Research.* New York: St Martin's Press.

Sprinivas, M., Shah, A. and Ramaswamy, A. 1979. *The Fieldworker and the Field.* Delhi: Oxford.

Van Maanen, J. 1988. *Tales of the Field.* Chicago: University of Chicago Press.

Walker, M. 1987. *Writing Research Papers.* Second edition. New York: Norton.

Chapter 5 In-Depth Interviewing

> 'Prime Minister are you going to call an early election?'
> 'What sort of question is that? You know I have promised to run to full term.'
> 'Yes but . . .'
> 'There are no buts. When we make a promise to the electorate then we keep it!'
> 'You might wish to keep it Prime Minister, but your party might want a new leader at the helm. What is to stop them forcing you into an election situation where . . .'
>
> (Aroni, R. 1989: 1)

> 'Mr Woolley, are you worried about the rise in crime among teenagers?'
> 'Yes,' I said.
> 'Do you think there is a lack of discipline and vigorous training in our comprehensive schools?'
> 'Yes.'
> 'Do you think young people welcome some structure and leadership in their lives?'
> 'Yes.'
> 'Do they respond to a challenge?'
> 'Yes.'
> 'Might you be in favour of reintroducing National Service?'
> 'Yes.'
>
> (Lynn, J. and Jay, A. 1987: 106)

When we think of **interviews,** it is usually journalistic interviews as in the first quotation, or survey-style interviews as in the second, that come to mind. We rarely categorise interviews as conversations. Nevertheless, **in-depth interviewing** is conversation with a specific purpose—a conversation between researcher and informant focussing on the informant's perception of self, life and experience, and expressed in his or her own words. It is the means by which the researcher can gain access to, and subsequently understand, the private interpretations of social reality that individuals hold. This is made public in the interview process.

The preceding chapters discussed how we understand science and how we understand people. This chapter examines interviewing and the different methods of carrying out interviews. It then focusses on in-depth interviewing, what it is, how it differs from other forms of interviewing and why and when it can be used. Chapter 6 examines the skills used in doing interviewing as a research method.

What is an Interview?

There are a number of definitions of interviewing, each tied to the particular form or type of interview. The common elements of these definitions are

> a face-to-face verbal interchange in which one person, the interviewer, attempts to elicit information or expressions of opinion or belief from another person or persons (Maccoby and Maccoby 1954: 499; in Denzin 1989).

Essentially, interviewing is a means of gaining access to information of different kinds. It is done by asking questions in direct face-to-face interaction. For example, the researcher may ask you questions which range from the trivial (for example, what brand of toilet paper do you use?) to the serious and/or disturbing (for example, what is your attitude to compulsory A.I.D.S. testing?; do you believe certain ethnic groups should reside in Australia?; *or* what do you think of having exams?). One frequently used method for finding out about such things is the interview, where one can directly ask the person or group what they do, or what they think, about a particular subject. In-depth interviewing is one form of interviewing. But before we discuss in-depth interviewing, we examine other forms of interviewing that are available.

Interview Models

Interviewing can take a variety of forms. Most texts say that along a continuum you will find **structured interviews** at one end, and **in-depth interviewing** at the other (Babbie 1989; Bailey 1982; Kidder and Judd 1986; Taylor and Bogdan 1984). Other forms of interviewing lie somewhere between the two extremes.

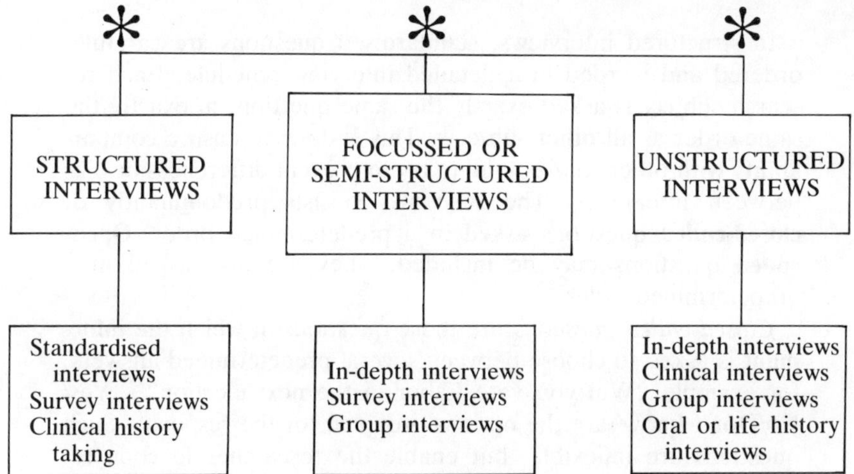

Figure 5.1 Interviewing methods: The continuum model.

Figure 5.1 gives us the traditional image of interviewing found in most methods text books. The following descriptions are given so that readers can differentiate between methods as they are practised, and not simply as they are written about in reports of research. The terms *structured, semi-structured* and *unstructured* refer to the process of the interview. There are debates about whether it is correct or necessary to make such distinctions. For our purpose, it is important to understand what these terms refer to. Armed with knowledge of the terminology, you can decide whether the debate is meaningful and whether you want to join in.

Structured Interviews

In social research, *structured* interviews (also known as **standardised** or **survey interviews**) are predominantly used in surveys or opinion polls. Writers of research methods texts which focus primarily on structured interviewing as the model that social scientists use, tend to neglect or devalue the in-depth interview. They assume that 'the asking of questions' is the main source of social scientific information about everyday behaviour and that the method of asking questions and receiving answers should not follow the usual patterns of informal conversation (Shipman 1972).

In structured interviews, standardised questions are carefully ordered and worded in a detailed interview schedule. Each research **subject** is asked exactly the same question, in exactly the same order as all other subjects. This is done to ensure comparability with other studies, and to try to prevent differences or bias between interviews. The schedule consists predominantly of **closed-ended** questions asked in a predetermined order. **Open-ended** questions may be included. They are also asked in a predetermined order.

Closed-ended questions are those questions in which the **informant** is asked to choose between several predetermined answers, for example, 'Will you vote Labor in the next election?'. 'Yes/No/Don't know' are the options provided for the response. Such questions are inflexible, but enable the researcher to code responses more easily and therefore cost less than open-ended questions. The underlying assumption made by the researcher using structured interviewing is that the questions he or she is asking are relevant to the area of inquiry. The primary criticism of closed-ended questions is that they do not allow the researcher to find out from the informant what is relevant to them or allow them to express different views. This shortcoming leads many researchers to consider alternative interviewing strategies such as in-depth interviewing.

Open-ended questions or free-answer questions are sometimes used in structured interviews. These are questions in which the researcher asks the informant how he or she feels or thinks about the topic under scrutiny; for example, 'How do you feel (or, what do you think) about the introduction of the *Dying with Dignity* legislation?'. The researcher then takes note of whatever the informant says in response to the question. These responses often lead to further questions which some authors argue increase data-coding difficulties and therefore research costs (Kidder 1981). However, we claim that when such questions are used in in-depth, focussed or unstructured interviewing, the richness of the data obtained is worth the cost.

Interviewer's Role in Structured Interviews

Another factor in structured or survey interviewing is the relationship between interviewer and informant and the respective roles they play. The assumption is that the researcher controls the flow of the conversation by asking questions and recording the responses of the 'subordinate' informant. In fact, the informant is usually referred to as the **subject** or **respondent,** because he or she is expected to *respond* to set questions rather than to *inform* through participation in a conversation. The interviewing situation is regarded as 'a one-way process in which the interviewer elicits and receives, but does not give information' (Roberts 1988: 30).

Face-to-face interaction may have its positive side in providing higher response rates than other survey methods, but in many texts, prospective researchers are warned of the dangers inherent in the interview process (Bailey 1982). The researcher may gain access by establishing trust and developing rapport with the informant, but is cautioned against over-involvement or getting 'too close' as this might influence objectivity and introduce bias into the research. As Roberts points out,

> . . . textbooks advise interviewers to adopt an attitude toward interviewees which allocates the latter a narrow and objectified function as data . . . interviews are seen as having no personal meaning in terms of social interaction, so that their meaning tends to be confined to their statistical comparability with other interviews and the data obtained from them . . . (1988: 30).

To summarise, researchers using structured interviewing assume that they know what sort of information they are after. Therefore, the role of the interviewer is to facilitate responses to the questions, that is, to be 'a neutral medium through which questions and answers are transmitted' (Babbie 1989: 245). The social interaction between the participants is formalised and highly structured to enhance reliability (that is, the extent to which the research can be replicated and tested for possible researcher influence or error). The underlying assumption is that objectivity is desirable and achievable.

Criticisms of the Structured Approach

There have been a number of criticisms of the structured approach to interviewing. Two of these criticisms are relevant to our discussion. Many researchers, (Bell and Roberts 1984; Finch 1984; Oakley 1988; Wakeford 1981), recognised that the idealised descriptions of structured interviewing in textbooks and research reports did not describe the social reality of interviewing. They illustrated how *real* research happens by publicly acknowledging this in accounts which accurately detailed the vagaries of structured interviewing.

In addition, in the 1970s, there was much discussion about the philosophical and political issues of research, particularly the question of the appropriateness or otherwise of the natural science model to the social sciences. It was argued (Taylor & Bogdan 1984) that experimental and survey methods did not adequately deal with the differences between objects and people, and that there were more valid ways in which to study *social* reality. In-depth interviewing was said to be one of these ways.

Focussed or Semi-structured Interviews

Focussed or semi-structured interviews are used either as part of the more quantitatively-oriented structured interview model, or of the qualitatively-oriented in-depth interviewing model. This is because researchers on either side of the two 'poles' of this arbitrary continuum use this strategy when it helps to answer their research questions. Essentially, this process entails researchers using the broad topic in which they are interested to guide the interview. An **interview guide** or schedule is developed around a list of topics without fixed *wording* or fixed *ordering* of questions. The content of the interview is *focussed* on the issues that are central to the research question, but the type of questioning and discussion allow for greater flexibility than does the survey-style interview. As with in-depth interviewing this may reduce the comparability of interviews within the study but provides a more valid explication of the *informant's* perception of reality.

Semi-structured or **focussed interviews** are modelled more closely on the unstructured than the structured model of interviewing. This means that the topic area guides the questions asked, but the mode of asking follows the unstructured interview process. Both unstructured and semi-structured (or focussed) interviews involve an in-depth examination of people and topics.

Unstructured Interviewing

Unstructured interviewing refers to interviewing which dispenses with formal interview schedules and ordering of questions and relies on the social interaction between interviewer and informant to elicit information. The **recursive model** of questioning (see discussion in this chapter) is often used in this method.

The unstructured interview takes on the appearance of a normal everyday conversation. However, *it is always a controlled conversation which is geared to the interviewer's research interests*. The element of control is regarded as minimal, but nevertheless present in order to keep the informant 'relating experiences and attitudes that are relevant to the problem' (Burgess 1982: 107).

In-depth Interviewing

Unstructured and *semi-structured* (or focussed interviewing) are two ways of doing in-depth interviewing. **In-depth interviews**, according to Taylor and Bogdan's useful definition, are '*repeated face-to-face encounters between the researcher and informants directed toward understanding informants' perspectives on their lives, experiences or situations as expressed in their own words*' (1984: 77).

There are several significant assumptions inherent in this conception. First, that these encounters are *repeated*, which implies that a greater length of time is spent with the informant. This is regarded as beneficial for rapport enhancement and for the greater understanding that may follow the increased social interaction. Secondly, that the encounter is *between researcher and informant*. This implies an egalitarian concept of roles within the interview which contrasts with the imbalance of power between the roles in survey methods. Thirdly, rather than focussing on the researcher's perspective as the valid view, it is the *informant's account* which is being sought and is highly valued. Finally, that we try to retrieve the informant's world by understanding their perspective *in language that is natural to them*. This reduces the possible distorting effect of symbols and language which are not part of their everyday usage. Hence, there is a significant move from the interrogative process used in a structured interview toward that of a more conversational process.

The fundamental legitimation for the use of in-depth interviewing is based on acknowledging that,

> The world of nature as explored by the natural scientist does not mean anything to molecules, atoms and electrons. But the observational field of the social scientist—social reality—has a specific meaning and relevance

> structure for the beings living, acting and thinking within it. By a series of commonsense constructs they have pre-selected and pre-interpreted this world which they experience as the reality of their daily lives. It is these thought objects of theirs which determine their behaviour by motivating it. The thought objects constructed by the social scientist in order to grasp . . . social reality, have to be founded upon the thought objects constructed by the commonsense thinking of men [*sic*] living their daily life within their social world (Schutz 1962: 49).

This quotation encapsulates the essential elements of the assumptions underlying **interpretive research**. In-depth interviewing is a method used in such research. The subject matter of the social scientist 'answers back', unlike the inanimate objects studied by the natural sciences. This is a fundamental difference between the natural and social sciences. Consequently, the use of natural science methodologies is regarded as inappropriate for the social sciences or at least some researchers think so. The underlying assumption of Schutz's statement is that we need to know what people think in order to understand why they behave in the ways that they do. This, in turn, is predicated on the belief that people act in the ways that they do because of the way in which they define the situation *as they see it or believe it to be.* That is, they interpret the facts as they see them.

Tied to this idea is the belief that when we are engaged in in-depth interviewing, what we are actually interested in is people's experience of social reality through their *routinely* constructed interpretations of it. If the researcher develops theories which are not grounded in the informant's experience of social reality, then he or she runs the risk of constructing and imposing on that informant a fictional view of their reality.

For example, let us say that a woman has just given birth to an infant. She feels depressed and lethargic, and this continues for months after the delivery. A doctor conducting a traditional clinical interview for the purpose of diagnosis and treatment may come to the conclusion that the woman is suffering from post-partum depression and needs treatment. Alternatively, if the doctor is aware of in-depth interviewing as a means of understanding the woman's interpretation of reality, then he or she might spend an hour engaged in such an interview and discover that there are alternative interpretations of the problem being discussed. The woman may tell the doctor how her body and self-image have altered in a negative manner due to physical changes during and after pregnancy; that she doesn't enjoy being overweight; that she is no longer independent because she has another human being totally dependent on her; and that her husband is not supportive. Her husband is reported to assume that all women 'get the blues' after giving birth and that she should 'pull herself together and not be neurotic'. She states that this lack of understanding and support is making her depressed. The woman's *definition of the situation* is that she is legitimately unhappy with the social situation in which she now finds herself. She argues that being depressed is a reasonable response under the circumstances. In this situation, the interviewer (doctor) can construct an interpretation based on the woman's own conception of her social reality. If the doctor accepts the meanings that the woman attaches to her actions he or she may be in a more advantageous position to 'diagnose' the problem than is the woman's husband. He has *imposed* his definition of the situation without taking his wife's understandings into account.

This example emphasises the interviewer's ability to reconstruct the reality of the informant through the process of listening to that informant. In other words, in-depth interviewing focusses on, and relies on, *verbal* accounts of social realities. This is somewhat different from participant observation which relies on participation *in*, and observation *of*, behaviour or action in the context in which it occurs. It is often argued (Taylor and Bogdan 1984) that the participant observer is in a better position than the interviewer to gain access to the everyday life of the informant or group of informants because the participant observer directly experiences the social world which the informant inhabits, rather than simply relating second-hand accounts. At one level, this is certainly true. However, each method has its advantages and disadvantages, depending on the research question that is being asked, and on the manner in which the researcher is seeking to answer it. Often the researcher is interested in the second-hand account. In that case, in-depth interviewing is regarded as one of the more effective means of gaining access to that account. This debate relates directly to the types of in-depth interviewing available to researchers and clinicians and the situations in which they choose to use them.

Types of In-depth Interviewing: When are they Used?

There are at least five distinct research situations in which one can use in-depth interviewing.

1 The in-depth interview is used to gain access to, and an understanding of, activities and events *which cannot be observed directly by the researcher.* Accounts of action and patterns of living are provided by those who have directly participated in or observed them, such as in Minichiello's (1987) study of decision-making processes related to the entry of the older people into nursing homes. He interviewed the older people living in nursing homes and members of their families in order to find out about events which he could not directly observe or participate in because they had occurred in the past. Eastop's (1985) study of the rural community's reaction to the Ash Wednesday fires is another example of this kind of interviewing.

2 In-depth interviewing is used in the life (or oral) history approach which is actually a more specialised form of the above-mentioned situation. Using this method, the interviewer attempts to *elicit and understand the significant experiences in the informant's entire life* by means of in-depth interviewing, sometimes combined with examination of letters, photographs and personal effects. This method has also been called a case study approach because it is the *individual* informant's subjective experience that is desired. The sociological autobiography differs from biography and traditional autobiography, in that the life history of the informant is produced as a result of interaction and collaboration with the researcher. A more detailed account of this type of in-depth interviewing can be found in chapter 7.

3 In-depth interviewing is also linked to the purpose of the research project. It is intended to enable the researcher to gain access to groups of people in order to provide a broad view of situations, people or settings. For instance, Aroni's (1985) longitudinal study of the impact of schooling on Jewish identity was based primarily on in-depth interviews with nearly 300 Jewish matriculation students attending Jewish and non-Jewish schools. This particular use of in-depth interviewing enables the researcher to study a larger number of people over a

shorter time than if they had chosen to use participant observation. If Aroni had decided on the latter method she would have had to have attended at least twenty schools and also participated in the home life and peer group interactions of 300 students. It would have taken a great deal longer to complete such a study.

4 The type of in-depth interviewing examined here is the **clinical interview.** It has been developed from three other kinds of interview: the sociological semi-focussed interview, the medical model of interviewing the patient to obtain a case history and the counselling interview. It has been adapted for use in the clinical setting. A more detailed examination of this type of qualitative interviewing can be found in chapter 8.

5 In-depth interviewing can be conducted with a group of informants. The **group interview** is where the interviewer gathers together a group of informants and provides them with the opportunity to engage in discussion. This can include analysis of any argument or debate that may arise if group members' subjective perceptions of the issues, context or subject do not concur. Alternatively, if there is an agreement then this is analysed. This type of in-depth interviewing enables the researcher to examine the dynamics of the group, and to interpret the views of the members of the group irrespective of whether their views are consensual or in conflict. One reservation about this method is that informants in a group interview will tend to provide views that can be publicly stated. If they had been interviewed separately perhaps there would be greater chance of hearing more private interpretations of their reality. Nevertheless, this method allows both meaningful use of the in-depth interview and different interpretations of the same experiences.

All forms of in-depth interviewing from semi-structured or focussed interviewing to unstructured applications rely on similar interviewing techniques.

Advantages and Disadvantages of In-depth Interviewing

There are advantages and disadvantages in trying to retrieve the world of the informant through in-depth interviewing. This is because, as many texts (Benney and Hughes 1970; Bogdan and Taylor 1975; Burgess 1982; Denzin 1989; Deutscher 1973; & Foddy 1988) point out, the researcher's *definition of the situation* is open to the vagaries of the informant's interpretation and presentation of reality. The researcher is not usually in the situation of being able to directly observe the informant in his or her everyday life. Thus they are deprived of the *ethnographic context* which would give a richer understanding of the informant's perspective.

If we return to our earlier example of the woman suffering from post-partum depression, we can illustrate the problems inherent in all forms of research relying on verbal accounts. One might ask how does the researcher (in this case the clinician) know that the informant (the patient) is telling the truth, and whether her definition of the situation is accurate? The interviewer cannot know for sure simply from engaging in the interview. The strategy of cross-checking through subsequent interviews can be used however to assess the accuracy of information. In the matter of 'truth telling' it is important to ask *who has the power to define what counts as truth* in the informant's social world. She, or her husband, or the medical practitioner? Secondly, whose definition of the situation can be regarded as accurate? How do we determine this and does it matter? The researcher who uses in-depth interviewing would argue that *the informant's definition is paramount,* because that is the focus of the research process. How we, the researchers, subsequently interpret and analyse that information depends on our aims in carrying out the research. This of course is directly related to the motive for doing the research. It may be to provide clinical understanding and advice, or to delve into the unresearched area of the post-natally depressed mother's perception of self and how it relates (or does not relate) to the social and political context in which all women and men live. These concerns are discussed in chapters 9 and 10.

This raises a serious question for the interpretive researcher. If you cannot determine such matters by using in-depth interviewing, why not use participant observation where the researcher is more directly involved in the informant's world? We argue that, even when researchers use participant observation, they are still seeking the 'definition of the situation' of the group or individual under study. This may be enhanced by their ability to interpret and reinterpret actions on the spot rather than relying on verbal accounts. However, if we are still trying not to impose our own assumptions of the informant's world, then the problem remains the same, irrespective of whether we are researching as participant observers or as in-depth interviewers. It is interpretation as such that is the issue and not the technique. This issue is discussed in more detail in chapter 12.

Some researchers (Klockars 1977; Oakley 1988) suggest that these problems can be overcome by the in-depth interviewer using intrusive yet ethically sound methods. That is, the researcher should adopt a highly interactive role in the interview process in order to allow a collaborative approach to be taken by the informant (see chapter 10).

Alternatively, Schwartz and Jacobs (1979) suggest that Cicourel's approach is useful in coming to terms with this issue. Their suggestion is that in an interview situation, the informant operates within an **ethnographic context,** that is, the informant has an everyday commonsense working knowledge of his or her own life history, the cultural milieu of which he or she is a part, and a sense of self identity. It is from within this ethnographic context that the informant makes decisions about what to say to the interviewer. The informant knows the exact meaning and significance of what he or she is saying (as it would be perceived by an insider of that ethnographic context, such as a family member or close friend). Schwartz and Jacobs (1979) point out that interviewers should try to make provision for the ethnographic context in which the informant is operating. Otherwise he or she risks the problems that we discussed above—that is, of trying to interpret what the informant means as opposed to what he or she says. The interviewer should confirm the interview using the *actual* version of the information sought.

In-depth Interviewing as the Method of Choice

Why and when does a researcher choose to use in-depth interviewing as a research method?

Why?

The decision to use in-depth interviewing as one's research strategy or data-collecting method is linked to theoretical and practical concerns. There are two major rationales given in the literature on choice of method. The first relates to the researcher's view of what social reality is and how it ought to be studied. As Bilton et al (1981) argue, different **ontological** and **epistemological** positions generate different **methodologies.** That is, different models of reality lead to different propositions about what reality is, and therefore demand different ways of establishing what can be accepted as real; different ways of validating or justifying the data relevant to reality; and different strategies for collecting such data. The way we go about getting at knowledge and the techniques we use to collect evidence are directly related to our image of social reality; the way in which we think we can know it and the way in which we think it ought to be studied. Therefore, if we believe (as most researchers using qualitative methods do) that social reality exists as meaningful interaction between individuals then it can only be known through understanding others' points of view, interpretations and meanings. If meaningful human interaction depends on language, then the words people use and the interpretations they make are of central interest to the researcher. In-depth interviewing is an appropriate method to gain access to the individual's words and interpretations.

The second rationale for deciding to use in-depth interviewing is based on the view that practical issues determine the choice of research method. Quantitative and qualitative research are simply names for different ways of conducting social investigations. They can be thought of as being appropriate for different types of research question. Bryman points out that when this view is taken, quantitative and qualitative research strategies are regarded as 'different approaches to data collection, so that preferences for one or the other or some hybrid approach are based on *technical issues*' (1988: 5).

When?

When you choose to use in-depth interviewing is also related to the *why* of your choice. If you opt for the first rationale (see the section above) and you hold a **symbolic interactionist perspective,** then you would use in-depth interviewing alone or in conjunction with participant observation.

If you opt for the second rationale then you would recognise that the types of in-depth interview described in this chapter are each appropriate for particular circumstances. For instance, when the researcher wishes to highlight subjective human experience, then the case-study or life-history approach is an appropriate form of in-depth interviewing. This methodological strategy enables the researcher to understand and interpret social reality through the meanings that the informant attaches to their life experiences. Thus, depth of understanding is achieved by focussing intensely on one person or one setting. Taylor and Bogdan point out that life histories enable the researcher to evaluate theories of social life by using them as 'a touchstone'; they refer to their own research with the mentally retarded whose life histories 'challenge myths and misconceptions of mental retardation' (1984: 81).

Another instance in which it is appropriate to choose in-depth interviewing is when the type of research depends on understanding a broad range of people or settings in a short time. That is, when there are research questions which lend themselves to in-depth interviewing rather than other qualitative methods because the researcher either has time constraints or has reasonably clear and well-defined research interests. Connell (1985) and Aroni (1985) both aimed at understanding a broad range of school students. Connell wanted a better understanding of children's constructions of politics. Aroni was interested in examining students' perceptions of their education in relation to ethnic identity. Both studies necessitated understanding the interpretations of *a broad range of people*. Participant observation would not have presented a useful alternative in these circumstances as it would have been too time consuming, and/or some of the activities (for example, playground discussion) were inaccessible to the researchers.

In-depth Interviewing and Theory Building

It is significant that all forms of in-depth interviewing are not predominantly used as hypothesis-testing modes of research but as theory-building ones. It is more usual to see this method being employed as part of an exploratory study where the researcher is attempting to gain understanding of the field of study, and to develop theories rather than test them. Leggatt's (1981) research on schizophrenia used in-depth interviewing to understand the relationship between schizophrenia sufferers and their families. She was not testing a hypothesis. Rather she went into the field with some hunches based on her reading of the sociological literature on mental illness.

She had a hunch that symbolic interactionist theory somehow was not dealing adequately with the nature of reality that these people experienced. She wanted to find a method which would enable her to understand and explain their 'definition of the situation'. During the research process she engaged in a process of theory building, based on the data she was gathering and her experiences of the actual interaction in the in-depth interviewing. Leggatt utilised the Glaser and Strauss (1967) model of **grounded theory,** that is, theory drawn or teased out of the data gathered. She developed a sophisticated interpretive approach and suggested that madness existed and in a fashion which was different from the symbolic interactionist portrayal. She concluded that government policies dealing with schizophrenia should be based on the informed view of the family members in whose everyday lives it plays a great part. The important point here is that Leggatt's conclusion rested on the views, attitudes and definitions of her informants. She had no formal hypothesis, and kept her hunches at the back of her mind while she listened and tried to comprehend the everyday reality of her informants. Further hunches were developed throughout the research, and when she had nearly completed the project these contributed to hypotheses or theories for further testing. More will be said on the topic of grounded theory in chapter 12.

Glossary

Aide memoire Another term for interview guide or schedule. See below.

Clinical interview An in-depth interview conducted by a clinician regardless of whether all or any of it takes place within a designated clinical building.

Closed-ended questions Those questions in which the informant is asked to respond by choosing between several predetermined answers.

Epistemology The philosophy of knowledge. Epistemological issues are concerned with *knowing* or deciding on what sort of statements we will accept to justify what we believe to exist.

Ethnographic context The everyday activities of the informant, his or her common sense working knowledge of that cultural milieu, and his or her sense of self-identity together form the ethnographic context in which the informant lives.

Focussed or semi-structured interviews Those interviews in which the researcher uses an interview guide which is simply a list of topics to be discussed with no fixed ordering or wording of questions. The content of the interview is focussed on the issues that are central to the research question.

Grounded theory The development of a theory by drawing or teasing it from the data gathered. The theory that is developed is then said to be *grounded* in the data.

Group interview Where the interviewer gathers a group of informants in order to engage them in conversation for the purpose of research. This is carried out using in-depth interviewing as the method for the conversation.

In-depth interviews Repeated face-to-face encounters between the researcher and informants directed toward understanding informants' perspectives on their lives, experiences or situations as expressed in their own words.

Informant The person whose thoughts, words and behaviour are studied in social research. When the person is informing the researcher of his or her views, attitudes and beliefs during in-depth interviews of any kind then the person is called an informant.

Interpretive research A form of research based on an approach which holds that social reality is consciously and actively created by individuals who mean to do things and who attribute meanings to the behaviour of others.

Interview A face-to-face verbal interchange in which one person, the interviewer, attempts to elicit information or expressions of opinion or belief from another person or persons, the informant(s).

Interview guide When used in qualitative research it consists of a list of general issues, topics, problems or ideas that the researcher wants to make sure are covered by each informant. It is used to jog the memory of the interviewer and is revised as different informants provide information which indicates the need to do this. It is also known as an **interview schedule** or an **aide memoire.** It does not act as a standardising instrument unless it is used in survey-style research.

Interview schedule Another term for interview guide. See above.

Life history interview A life history is the history of an individual's life given by the person living it and solicited by the researcher. It is a sociological autobiography drawn from in-depth interviewing and/or solicited narratives.

Methodology A rule-governed procedure aiding or guaranteeing scientific discovery. Methodological issues are concerned with the *logic* of inquiry—how are we to discover and validate what we think exists?
Methods Techniques for collecting data.
Ontology A branch of metaphysics concerned with the nature of existence, with what kinds of things may be said to exist and in what ways.
Open-ended questions Also known as free-answer questions. They are questions to which there are no sets of predetermined answers for the informant to choose from. Rather, the informant can choose to give any answer they wish to.
Recursive model of interviewing A form of in-depth interviewing in which the interviewer follows normal conversational interaction allowing the flow of conversation to direct the research process. It is regarded as the most unstructured form of in-depth interviewing.
Respondent The person whose thoughts, words and behaviours are studied in social research. When the person is responding to survey interviews and questionnaires, he or she is called a respondent.
Semi-structured or focussed interviewing Refers to interviews in which there are no fixed wordings of questions or ordering of questions. Rather the content of the interview is focussed on the issues that are central to the research question. Interview schedules are often employed to aid the interviewer in maintaining this focus.
Structured/standardised/survey/interview Refers to interviews in which the question and answer categories have been predetermined.
Subject The person whose thoughts, words and behaviour are studied in social research. When the person is subjected to experiments and observations he or she is called a *subject.*
Symbolic interactionist perspective A sociological perspective that emphasises the centrality of meaning in interaction. It is a view of the self–society relationship as a process of symbolic communication between people.
Unstructured interviews Refers to interviews in which neither the questions nor the answer categories are predetermined. They rely on social interaction between researcher and informant to elicit information.

References

Aroni, R. 1985. *The Effects of Jewish and non-Jewish Day Schools on Jewish Identity and Commitment.* Unpublished doctoral dissertation, Monash University, Clayton, Vic.

Aroni, R. 1989. Lectures examining research issues. Unpublished lecture notes. Lincoln School of Health Sciences.

Babbie, E. 1989. *The Practice of Social Research.* Fifth edition. Belmont, California: Wadsorth Publishing Co.

Bailey, K.D. 1982. *Methods of Social Research.* New York: The Free Press.

Bell, C. & Roberts, H. (ed) 1984. *Social Researching, Politics, Problems, Practice.* London: Routledge & Kegan Paul.

Benney, M. & Hughes, E.C. 1970. 'Of Sociology and the Interview.', in N.K. Denzin (ed.). *Sociological Methods: A Sourcebook.* London: Butterworth.

Bilton, T., Bonnett, K., Jones, P., Stanworth, M., Sheard, K. & Webster, A. 1981. *Introductory Sociology.* London: Macmillan.

Bogdan, R. and Taylor, S.J. 1975 *Introduction to Qualitative Research Methods: The Search for Meanings.* New York: John Wiley and Sons.

Bryman, A. 1988. *Quantity and Quality in Social Research.* London: Unwin Hyman.

Burgess, R.G., 1982. *Field Research: A Sourcebook and Field Manual.* London: Allen & Unwin.

Connell, R.W. 1985. *Teachers' Work.* Sydney: George Allen & Unwin.

Denzin, N.K. 1989. *The Research Act.* Third edition. Chicago: Aldine.

Deutscher, I. 1973. *What We Say/What We Do.* Glenview, Illinois: Scott, Foresman and Co.

Eastop, L.W. 1985. *A Study of the Attitudes of People Who Had Been 'Burned Out' in the Ash Wednesday Bushfire.* Unpublished paper, Monash University, Clayton, Vic.

Finch, J. 1984. 'It's great to have someone to talk to: the ethics and politics of interviewing women.', in Bell, C. and Roberts, H.(eds). *Social Researching: Politics, Problems, Practice.* London: Routledge & Kegan Paul.

Foddy, W.H. 1988. *Open Versus Closed Questions: Really a Problem of Communication.* Paper presented to the Australian Bicentennial Meeting of Social Psychologists. Leura, New South Wales, August.

Glaser, B.G. & Strauss, A. 1967. *The Discovery of Grounded Theory.* Chicago: Aldine.

Kidder, L.H. 1981. *Selltiz Wrightsman and Cook's Research Methods in Social Relations.* Fourth edition. New York: Holt Saunders International Editions.

Kidder, L.H. & Judd, C.M. 1986. *Research Methods in Social Relations.* Tokyo: CBS Publishing Japan Ltd.

Klockars, C.B. 1977. 'Field Ethics for the Life History.', in R.S. Weppner (ed.) *Street Ethnography.* London: Sage.

Leggatt, M. 1981. *Adaption to Psychiatric Disorder and Physical Disability.* Vols. 1 & 2. Unpublished doctoral dissertation: Monash University, Clayton, Vic.

Little, G. 1989. *Speaking For Myself.* Melbourne: McPhee Gribble Publishing.

Lynn, J & Jay, A. 1987. *Yes, Prime Minister : The Honourable James Hacker's Diaries.* London: BBC Publishing.

Mann, M. (ed.) 1987. *Macmillan Student Encyclopedia of Sociology.* Fourth edition. London: Macmillan Press.

Minichiello, V. 1987. 'Someone's decision: that is how I got here', *Australian Journal of Social Issues* 22: 345–356.

Oakley, A. 1988. 'Interviewing Women: A Contradiction in Terms.', in H. Roberts, H. (ed.). *Doing Feminist Research.* London: Routledge and Kegan Paul.

Roberts, H. 1988. *Doing Feminist Research.* Fifth edition. London: Routledge and Kegan Paul.

Schutz, A. 1962. *Collected Papers, Vol 1: The Problem of Social Reality.* M. Natanson (ed.). The Hague: Martinus Nijhoff.

Schwartz, H. & Jacobs, J. 1979. *Qualitative Sociology: A Method to the Madness.* London: Collier Macmillan.

Shipman, M.D. 1972. *The Limitations of Social Research.* London: Longman Group.

Stewart, C.J. & Cash, J.W.B. 1988. *Interviewing: Principles and Practices.* Dubuque, Iowa: Wm.C. Brown Publishers.

Taylor, S.J. & Bogdan, R. 1984. *Introduction to Qualitative Research Methods: The Search for Meanings.* Second edition. New York: John Wiley and Sons.

Wakeford, J. 1981. 'From methods to practice: a critical note on the teaching of research practice to undergraduates.', *Sociology* 15: 505–12.

Chapter 6 Interview Processes

Interviewing Techniques

There are no set rules for how to go about doing in-depth interviews nor for how to be a good informant. Yet we all have some idea of how we might behave in this situation. The following comments and suggestions are just that—comments and suggestions. It is not possible to provide rules because each in-depth interview will take place in a different socio-political and cultural context. These factors may influence the social interaction that occurs. For example, if I were interested in the views held by occupational therapy students of their own profession and its status in comparison with that of other health professions, I might decide to present my research problem in a very direct fashion. However, if I knew that there was conflict between these students and physiotherapy students then I might decide to present the research issue and myself as the researcher, in a less direct and obvious manner in order to create a non-threatening atmosphere. Alternatively, I might decide to heighten the focus of my research issue to the prospective informants in the hope that this would capture some of their current definitions of the situation more accurately. Thus, even the initial approach can differ depending on the social context as it is perceived both by the researcher and the informant.

The comments and suggestions that we provide are based on our experience and the experiences of other researchers who have used in-depth interviewing. Unlike some authors (Benney and Hughes 1970; Goode and Hatt 1952; Selltiz et al. 1959), we do not set rules, but we do talk about what was or was not helpful to us as researchers. Before you start your research, it might be a good idea to read chapters 4, 5, 6, 9 and 10 in conjunction with one another. This will help you to avoid some of the problems that others have encountered. In practice, the issues raised in chapters 9 and 10 are inextricably tied to the processes discussed here. For the ease of the reader, we have discussed these issues separately. However, when we reflect on the actual process of in-depth interviewing as most of us have experienced it, then integrating the material would have given a more accurate representation of those experiences.

Why Bother Discussing this at All? Specific issues of publication influence all who publish their research or write about the research process. Writing and publishing have an influence on, and are part of, the social context and structure of the interview and inevitably influence the process. It is important to recognise how such factors play a part in in-depth interviewing.

Strategies for Starting an Interview

Designing a piece of research, deciding on who should be interviewed, sampling strategies, and gaining access to your informant/s are all practical, ethical and political issues which are part of the research process. Let us assume that you have decided on a research strategy and informants have been selected on the basis of the sampling procedures you have employed.

How Many Interviews are you Going to Organise with your Informants? With in-depth interviewing, the researcher does not know, prior to speaking with the informant, how many interviews would be useful. They can range from one or two long sessions (anywhere between one hour to four hours) to more than twenty sessions in the case of life histories. This will depend on the relationship that builds up and on the informant's volubility.

How Do You Approach the Informant? The more complex answer to this question is another question, 'What impression do you want to give the informant about the research project and their involvement in it?'. We have found that most researchers wish themselves and others to see their research as bona fide and significant. Most people when approached to participate in a research project are willing if not flattered (Taylor and Bogdan 1984), and they will agree to be an informant if they 'can fit you into their schedules'. The opening gambit that Taylor and Bogdan use is very similar to those used by many researchers in the field:

> When approaching potential informants, we tell them that it seems like they have had something important to say and that we would like to sit down with them and talk about it some time, if they seem receptive to the idea, we schedule the first meeting (1984: 86).

Sometimes the researcher uses this approach. The notion of an unstructured interview with minimal direction from the interviewer even prior to the actual interview is appealing. It is one which provides the informant with little information about the research, aiming to avoid biasing the informant's understanding of the issue toward the researcher's interests. The intending interviewer is often counselled to behave as though he or she is unsure about which questions to ask and that they should be willing to learn from the informant (Taylor and Bogdan 1984).

Alternatively, the researcher may decide that this sort of approach is ethically and politically inadequate for what should be collaborative research, and will introduce him or herself, and the research issue in a more precise manner. This will be done by telling the informant a little about the general nature of the research issue, and how the researcher intends to conduct the entire project. This approach is usually taken when the researcher wishes to involve the informant in a collaborative undertaking (see chapter 9). The topics usually covered are confidentiality and anonymity, the motives and intentions of the interviewer, and who gets the final say on the manuscript. It may also be appropriate to discuss whether the informant should expect any remuneration, monetary or otherwise. Other pragmatic issues discussed are the interview schedule, place of interview, and what method is to be used to record the interview/s.

Many researchers talk about what will happen in the interview prior to its occurrence, thus structuring the mutual contact in so-called unstructured interviewing strategies. These discussions centre on **setting the tone**, producing a **productive interpersonal climate** or **establishing rapport**. Usually such issues are discussed in the framework of the practical details of doing in-depth interviewing. This issue is related to the social experience of the interview for both parties and to the structuring of the questioning process.

In-depth Interviewing: Control and Structure

In-depth interviewing, contrary to the image presented in Figure 5.1 (see chapter 5), should not be seen as unstructured interviewing in the psychoanalytic model of free association. The reality of the social experience is that the conversation process, while not formally structured, is controlled to a certain degree. This inevitably produces an inequality in the relationship between the participants. However in idealised accounts of in-depth interviewing, this is 'painted out' (Bell & Encel 1978; Oakley 1988). What is talked about is *establishing rapport* or establishing a *productive interpersonal climate*. These broad terms describe how interviewer and informant feel about their relationship. No researcher has suggested a specific method to create or guarantee rapport with the informant. However, it is regarded as important because it is assumed that if the informant and the researcher 'hit it off', then the informant will be more communicative. They will talk more freely because they 'get on' with the researcher.

How to Establish Rapport

Research methodology authors enthusiastically recommend that the interviewer establish rapport with the informant but none give the novice interviewer a specific technology for achieving this ideal. It is assumed to emerge somehow from a combination of the goal statement, and the individual's life experience. The question that remains in the mind of the novice is 'How do I actually do what is recommended?'. The *how to* of the interviewing process is addressed in another body of literature which we have not seen linked to research despite the obvious advantages of doing so.

Bandler and Grinder (1979), Bandler a mathematician and Grinder a linguist, have developed a technology of communication from an original interest in how some therapists (such as Virginia Satir, Milton Erickson and Jay Haley) achieved their successes. From comparative studies, they have distilled a description of how to understand another person's model of the world which in turn permits the establishment of rapport and the pacing of interaction for the desired outcome. This model (neurolinguistic programming) explains how some interactions are easy while others are very difficult for the interviewer and how the easy and the difficult interviews differ from interviewer to interviewer.

Bandler and Grinder (1979) show that people vary in the reliance and emphasis they place upon different aspects of the perceptual information which they receive from the world. The particular emphasis chosen will determine what they conclude about that world. Information about the world is received through vision, hearing, feeling or smelling. Our culture discourages using olfactory data so we will discuss the first three channels of information only. If you listen to what people say you will hear understanding indicated by: *I hear . . .*, *I see . . .*, or *I feel . . .*, then elaborated by using language which is systematically linked to the perceptual channel originally referred to. There are those who 'hear' their understanding, or talk in auditory terms of sounds and sound qualities, for example, volume, pitch, frequency; while the visual processors will 'see' brightness, colour, clarity; and the kinesthetic 'feelers' will express their meanings with emotional metaphors, and refer to such aspects as textures and temperature.

Different perceptual patterns link with different and characteristic eye movements, postures and breathing patterns. These can be used to guide the interviewer to understand the informant rapidly and accurately.

Rapport with another person is basically a matter of understanding their model of the world and communicating your understanding symmetrically. This can be done effectively by *matching* the perceptual language, the images of the world, the speech patterns, pitch, tone, speed, the overall posture and the breathing patterns of the informant.

Having matched and harmonised with the informant on these elements, the interviewer can lead the other person into areas of discussion which are significant in relation to the research problem, while maintaining understanding. (We strongly recommend that you follow up these brief comments by reading King et al. 1983).

Bandler and Grinder also propose a metamodel for effective gathering of information (Cameron-Bandler 1985). This will not be discussed here, because many of the recommendations concur with the sociological literature which is cited in this text. Suffice it to say, we find the model a valuable way of synthesising recommendations, and emphasising the claims that richer responses are elicited from informants by the use of open-ended, *how, when*, or *what* questions rather than by asking the unanswerable *why*.

Taylor and Bogdan (1984) talk of *setting the tone* of the relationship with the informant. This involves conversation with the informant prior to the interview. They caution the researcher not to ask directive questions when initiating the interview because this may predispose (bias) the informant's perception of what the researcher regards as important to talk about. Rather, the researcher should in the first few interviews, appear as someone who is not quite sure what questions to ask and is willing to learn from the informants.

Interview Structure: Asking Questions

A number of writers (Schwartz & Jacobs 1979; Stewart & Cash 1988) refer to the *patterned organisation* or structure of conversations and, specifically, interviews. They talk of three parts to the structure—openings or beginnings, topical sections or middles, and closings or endings. Each part of the structure is said to incorporate its own organisation. They also raise another model of interviewing structure and organisation called the **recursive model**.

The Recursive Model

The recursive model of interviewing refers to a form of questioning which is consistently associated with most forms of in-depth interviewing. It enables the researcher to do two things—to follow a more conversational model and by doing this, to treat people and situations as unique. *The interaction in each interview directs the research process.*

Recursive questioning relies on the process of conversational interaction itself, that is, the relationship between *a current remark and the next one*. The researcher chooses how to use this method to best effect. This choice, occurs at two levels. First, the interviewer needs to decide to what extent prior interaction in an interview session should be allowed to determine what is asked next. Secondly, the interviewer needs to decide on the extent to which the experiences and information of previous interview sessions with an informant or group of informants 'be allowed to determine the structure and content of current interviews' (Schwartz and Jacobs 1979: 45). This means, irrespective of the type of question you are using, whether open or closed ended, whether decided on in advance or asked spontaneously, that you choose how *recursive* you want the interview process to be.

The researcher who chooses the recursive model as the strategy for conducting in-depth interviewing, has chosen the most unstructured version of in-depth interviewing. This model relies on the natural flow of the conversation to direct it. The criticism levelled at the recursive model is that if the responses to the initial questions continue in the recursive manner, then it is possible for the interview to go off on a tangent. Interviewers have developed tactics to try to solve such problems. They use **transitions** to refocus the informant's attention on the topic or issue. *Transitions* are 'accomplished by connecting something the informant has said with the topic of interest, even if it is somewhat far fetched' (Abrahamson 1983: 339). The advantage of the recursive model of questioning is that it enables the interviewer to 'treat people and situations as unique and to alter the research technique in the light of information fed back during the research process itself' (Schwartz & Jacobs 1979: 45). This is close to the ideal form of research for those researchers who follow the **interpretive approach**.

As our discussion has indicated, there are a number of choices researchers need to make in relation to the degree of structure and control before and throughout the interview process. This includes the issue of how focussed on a particular topic, or problem the questions will be? It also raises the question of interview schedules or guides—to have or not to have?

The Interview Guide

When researchers are involved in large-scale survey research which utilises standardised (structured) interviewing techniques, they use a structured interview protocol or *schedule*. This usually includes the full list of questions in their appropriate order with instructions on how to ask certain questions, when to probe, how to cross-check and so on. This is obviously inappropriate in the context of in-depth interviewing, as it does not allow for recursively defined questioning, but rather a fully structured, controlled, survey-style interview. The quantitative model of interviewing ascribes various functions to the interview schedule which do not fit the **methodology** inherent in qualitative research. With the standardised or structured interview it is the interview schedule itself which acts as the standardising instrument by providing the question and response formats. Most research methods texts (Babbie 1988; Bailey 1982; Kidder 1984; Polgar and Thomas

1988) provide detailed discussions of the requirements for designing a *good* interview schedule for standardised interviews. They are usually less forthcoming about the different processes and needs of in-depth interviewing, and the nature and purpose of interview schedules in that context.

The in-depth interviewer needs to remind him or herself of certain areas which need to be discussed in the interview session/s. The researcher does not suddenly overnight become Superman or Wonderwoman by virtue of the fact of choosing to engage in in-depth interviewing. The researcher does not suddenly gain a flawless memory which can retain all the necessary information to be remembered in the interview setting. Rather, it is recognised that in such a predicament, the researcher utilises the means at hand to do a good interview.

So what does an interview schedule or guide, or as Burgess (1984) refers to it, an **aide memoire**, look like? Usually, it consists of a list of general issues that the researcher wants to cover. It is used to jog the memory of the interviewer about certain issues or concerns. Unlike the interview schedule used in survey interviewing, this interview guide is revised as informants provide information which has not previously been thought of by the researcher.

Knowing what to include in the initial interview guide involves researchers in some preparation work before they enter the field. For instance, Aroni (1985) knew something about the Jewish community in Melbourne because she was a member of it. However, until she did some preparation work, she was not aware of all the studies that had investigated Jewish identification and identity among adolescents or the methodology of such studies. After doing a literature search and review, she gathered copies of questionnaires and interview schedules that had been used in those previous studies and examined them in order to analyse the content of the material. She isolated several themes which kept recurring in all the different studies and topics which she felt had not been dealt with in these studies. At that point, she compiled a brief list of themes which she felt might be useful to her for in-depth interviews. These themes were revised substantially after the first five interviews because the informants had alerted her to a number of issues which neither she nor previous researchers had thought were significant. Those first five interviews followed the structure and approach of the *recursive model*. She gained a great deal of information from the informants in terms of *their* interpretations of the impact of schooling on their ethnic identity and identification.

The *aide memoire* or the interview schedule does not necessarily determine the order of the conversation in an in-depth interview. As Burgess (1984) points out, when he was interviewing primary school students, he had originally prepared to start each interview by explaining that he had an agenda. This included topics on themes that he wanted to cover in the discussion. His agenda or list of topics was structured around the chronology of the students' school lives. In keeping with this, he intended to start discussions with the obvious sequence of a chronology. However, even though he covered many of the topics and themes he had listed, he found that 'the order in which they occurred was different in each interview as these pupils had considerable freedom to develop strategies for answering my questions' (1984: 108). Rather than considering the issues chronologically, some informants started talking about the issues 'at the end, first'. In other words, they put the topic he had planned to ask about last 'at the top of the agenda'. He had to work his way back to the question he wanted to ask first about their early school experiences. This example highlights that one of the most significant aspects of the use of interview schedules in in-depth interviewing is that there is no set of preconceived, structured questions. Rather, the questions revolve around topics of conversations because the interview schedule merely suggests the kinds of themes, topics and questions that might be covered rather than any actual questions that might be used (Burgess 1984). The point here is that 'no individuals (other than perhaps other sociologists) think about themselves and their lives in the terms which sociologists use' (Burgess 1984: 1). A more detailed account of such background issues can be found in chapter 4.

Once a researcher has worked out some form of interview guide, made the introductions and set the scene or established rapport with the informant then he or she needs to start asking questions. But which questions? Do you start directly on the topic you are concerned with? Do you launch into asking about one of the themes on your interview guide and then quickly follow on with another theme question? Or do you opt for the *recursive model*? This reflexively defined structuring of the interview process, enables the researchers to start with some questions on a theme, and then he or she allows the conversation to meander according to the informants' responses and the subsequent verbal interaction between him or herself and the informant. Perhaps you opt for some form of descriptive questioning or follow the **funnelling** method or the **story-telling method?**

The choice of strategy is dependent on the perspective the researcher holds on theory and methodology, on the research question being asked, and on the social interaction between the participants of the in-depth interview. There is no best way to phrase, order or commence questioning. The following strategies have been useful to many researchers engaged in trying to answer different research questions.

Funnelling

Funnelling refers to a process of questioning in which the interviewer controls the flow and type of information being asked by starting the interview with questions of a general and broad nature. These initial questions are designed simply to start the informant thinking about the issue in general terms. Then, as the participants engage in conversation, the interviewer guides the informant's view towards more specific issues by using questions which narrow the area. Finally, the interviewer begins to ask specific questions directly about the issue being examined. By using this strategy, the interview process can be a more relaxed and non-threatening conversation. The informant can reflect at ease on general questions. It is only later in the conversation that he or she is required to be more specific in response.

For example, let us assume that you wanted to know something about adolescents' views of their body image and whether those views had any connection with eating disorders. Using this strategy, the researcher might start by asking some general questions about the media and body images of men and women. What are these images? How realistic are they? The researcher could ask the informant what he or she regards as healthy eating habits and unhealthy eating habits. Then, the researcher could continue by asking if the informant knows of any forms of eating disorders. From this point, the questions could narrow down by asking what the informant regarded as the ideal female and male body and what they personally regarded as an attractive body. Then, the researcher could ask the informant what actions, including eating habits could be taken to achieve their ideal body. The next step would be to ask questions dealing directly with the informant's own body and self-image, and eating habits.

The assumption made in using this strategy is that informants and interviewers would find it uncomfortable to start talking directly about an issue which may be personally threatening or uncomfortable to think about. It is often assumed that it is more difficult to commit oneself to personal, revealing commentary than to a general level of debate. Tied to this is the researcher's fear that the informant may decide not to continue the interview because it is too personal or invasive of privacy. General questions at the beginning of the interview allow the informant to consider issues at a non-personal level. Only as rapport develops are they asked to interpret their own personal circumstances. Abrahamson (1983) describes this process as being non-directive and yet, it is in many ways extremely directive though not to the same degree as standardised or structured interviews.

Story Telling

An alternative strategy is one suggested by Askham (1982). She proposes using the device of asking questions in such a fashion that the informant would respond with a story. The rationale for encouraging stories is that they can be used as part of the process of analysis specifically for purposes of clarification. Story telling is a feature of many non-interview, normal conversations. In-depth interviewing, it is used to parallel the social interaction of a normal conversation. She argues that there are basically two types of interview questions. The first one is similar to the notion of descriptive questioning *a la* Taylor and Bogdan (1984) where the interviewer asks for a record or description of an action, attribute or feeling, such as, 'When did you last see your ex-wife?'. 'How many brothers and sisters do you have?', 'Did you get bored waiting for the speech therapist?'. The second type of question she refers to is when the interviewer asks the informant to perform some more sophisticated analysis upon the raw data of their experiences before answering. These are questions which ask interviewees to generalise, classify, summarise, quantify or explain, such as, 'How often do you see your ex-wife?', 'What do you think the average family size is for people like yourselves?', 'Why did you get bored when you were waiting to see the speech therapist?' (Askham, 1982).

Interviewers rarely ask directly for a story. However, in the case of a life history, this is very often what is called for. The strategy that Askham used in her research on marriage was to imply that she wished the informant to talk in more detail about how an event occurred. She would phrase the question to refer to a specific time period, such as a month before the wedding or the time after the marriage, and then ask the informant to fill in the events occurring during the specified time, or as she puts it 'artificially forcing a story by setting its beginning and end, and requesting the recounting of more than one event within these limits' (1982: 561).

Another example of the first kind of question could be the one used by Aroni in her interviews with Jewish high-school students and their views on their schooling. All students were asked, 'Tell me something about how you came to be attending this school?'. The phrasing is significant because *something about* and *came to be attending this school* imply that attendance at that particular school was part of a process which needs to be answered in story form. The second type of story-telling question was one in which informants were asked if they could remember their last Jewish-studies class, or to inform the researcher about the schools they attended before the current one.

Not all these questions will result in stories. Often informants will just string a few sentences together. However, Askham (1982) and Aroni (1985) both found that one of the strategies which seemed to lead to story telling was to ask informants for examples of the generalisations which they made during the conversation. Stories also emerge from the informant's train of thought or speech when he or she is actually reflecting on something which is only indirectly connected to the preceding question or has nothing to do with it. The *kind* of question you ask does influence whether the informant responds with a story giving his or her interpretation and analysis but there are other influencing factors also. One of the ways in which the interviewer's behaviour can encourage this story-telling process is to *cue* the informants that one is receptive to listening to their stories. This can be achieved by 'showing a lack of any hurry, by engaging in preliminary chatter oneself, and by appearing to enjoy any detailed accounts from the start of the interview' (Askham 1982: 570).

Problems with Stories as Data

In-depth interviews are constantly referred to as providing rich and detailed descriptive information which is valued precisely for its *closeness* or *fit* with 'reality'. However, stories are usually structured and take on a form which may be excellent for listening impact. An informant may create a good story by distorting the discussion of his or her perceived reality, in order to enhance the interviewer's image of them. Conversely, stories can be used by informants to avoid providing analysis of a situation. The major advantage of the story-telling process for both interviewer and informant is that it allows the informant greater latitude in answering questions 'rather than having to mould his [*sic*] answers into a format which the question requires' (Askham 1982: 572).

Three other strategies need to be mentioned briefly. Taylor & Bogdan (1984) refer to these as solicited narratives, log interviews and personal document use. All three strategies are used predominantly by researchers attempting to engage informants in in-depth interviews of a particular kind—life histories. These strategies have also been used with in-depth interviewing of other kinds such as clinical interviewing.

Solicited Narratives

This strategy is best described by its name. **Solicited narratives** refer to the interviewer soliciting a written narrative from the informant. This is a story-like account written by the informant which is then used either as a discussion point for subsequent in-depth interview sessions or is added to the background knowledge that the researcher amasses in order to classify and analyse the received information. It combines the strategies of asking descriptive questions and eliciting stories from the informant. One can be more or less directive in asking the informant to provide a written narrative. Often researchers ask for the informant to produce a chronology of their lives prior to being interviewed or simply to write their own story. This latter approach is very similar to that mentioned by Askham. Others such as Taylor & Bogdan (1984) have used the solicited narrative approach to ask their informant to provide a detailed chronology prior to being interviewed. They then use the narrative as the basis for their in-depth interviewing of the same informant.

For instance, Shaw (1966) in his study of delinquents used a more directive approach in producing the life history of his informants. The sequence was a little different from those mentioned above. The youth 'Stanley' (a fictitious name) was first interviewed in order to ask him to prepare a detailed chronology of his delinquent acts and experiences. Shaw then gave the first solicited narrative back to 'Stanley' and asked him to use it to guide him in writing a second narrative—his life story. Stanley was directed to provide 'a detailed description of each event, the situation in which it occurred, and his personal reactions to the experience' (Shaw 1966: 23).

The advantages of such an approach are obvious. The informant is providing a written account of his or her life for the researcher who can then use it in a number of ways to inform the research process. It can provide the **ethnographic context** of the informant for the interviewer, or it can provide material for analysis and probing in the interview context. There are also disadvantages. Not all informants are able or willing to engage in research if it requires them to write about their views or experiences, or they may feel obliged to provide either an embellished account or a more socially acceptable one because it is in 'black and white'. It is a *captured* account.

Solicited narratives are also used by researchers in conducting **life-history interviews**. The advantage is that the account is written in the informant's words. Consequently, during in-depth interviewing, it is argued that the interviewer plays a less intrusive role in the informant's original account and interpretation of his or her own life. The life-grid approach is one form of solicited narrative. The informant is asked to complete a diagrammatic chronology of their life for the researcher. This approach is discussed in more detail in the next chapter.

This method is often combined with personal in-depth interviewing and/or with the **log-interview** method or **diary-interview** method. This method is a specific version of the solicited narrative. Rather than providing the researcher with a chronological account of his or her life and experiences up to date, the informant is asked to 'keep a running recording of their activities for a specified time period which is used to provide a basis for in-depth interview' (Taylor & Bogdan 1984: 91). **Personal documents**, such as informants' diaries, photos, letters, calendars, formal records and other memorabilia, are also used to jog the memory of informants regarding their life and experience.

These three strategies do not by their nature impose structure on the informants' interpretations of their own lives apart from asking for a chronologically ordered account. In most cases, they are used in conjunction with in-depth interviews to provide the researcher with some means of legitimately asking probing questions and addressing the informants' views in their own language as found in the written form. They provide a framework for the interviewing, that is, an interview schedule which is written by the informant.

Types of Questions

So far, we have discussed the asking of questions by examining the way in which they can be ordered to structure and control the interaction between the participants of the in-depth interview. Questions can also be related to the type of information which they are supposed to elicit. For instance, we could ask informants to provide descriptions of events, people, places and/or experiences. This is known as **descriptive questioning** (Spradley 1979; Taylor & Bogdan 1984), and is often used to start interviews. This is because it enables informants to discuss their experiences, placing their own interpretation on these in the process of describing them. In addition, it is regarded as a non-threatening strategy because the interviewer is not probing for specific answers to specific questions but is allowing the informant to take control of the flow of information.

Several researchers (Burgess 1984; Spradley 1979) mention two other types of questioning which are used in in-depth interviewing, often in tandem with descriptive questioning. First, **structural questioning**, by which we mean questions aimed at finding out *how* informants organise their knowledge. For instance, if the researcher asks a nursing student about how clinical training occurs at a particular hospital then he or she is asking a descriptive question. When the interviewer asks which areas of clinical studies the student has been involved with (other than the current one), then he or she is asking a structural question. The researcher is trying to determine the study categories which the informant perceives he or she has been engaged in, and the way in which the informant stratifies these studies.

Another form that questioning can take is **contrast questioning**. This enables the informants to make comparisons of situations or events within their world and to discuss the meanings of these situations. For example, the interviewer may then ask the nursing student during the same interview if he or she perceived any difference between the clinical training received by a tertiary-trained nurse and a hospital-trained nurse.

Patton (1980) mentions another question form apart from descriptive questioning. He mentions **opinion/value questions** which are aimed at gaining access to or understanding the cognitive and interpretive processes of people. That is, finding out what people *think* about a particular person, issue, event or experience. The interviewer might ask, 'What is your opinion of that?', or 'What do you think about it?'. In contrast to this, Patton discusses '**feeling questions** which are geared to understanding people's emotional responses. For example the interviewer might ask "How do you feel about that? Do you feel happy, sad, confident, intimidated, anxious . . .?"' (1980: 207).

A researcher might also want to ask the informant what Patton calls **knowledge questions** which are used to 'find out what factual information' the informant has. According to Patton (1980), the underlying assumption of questions is that the informant 'knows things'. The point is to find out what the informant considers to be factual, to elicit the informant's view on 'the empirical nature of the world that is being elicited' (1980: 208).

Sensory questions, as the name suggests, are those questions asking the informant about what has been seen, heard, touched, tasted and smelled. They are used in an attempt to induce informants to describe 'the stimuli to which they are subject'. For example, the researcher might ask the informant,'What did you see when you walked into the classroom?'. They are a form of descriptive questioning, as **background demographic questions** also are. These questions are used to provide the researcher with some characteristics which can be used to identify the person being interviewed in relation to other people in society. Therefore, it is usual to ask the informant to specify their age, sex, education, occupation, place of residence, and so on. As Patton so poignantly states, 'Background and demographic questions are basically boring; they epitomise what people don't like about interviews' (1980: 211). Some people argue that it is preferable to ask such questions at the end of the interview or tie them to the same phase as descriptive questioning at the beginning; nevertheless they provide valuable data for analysis.

Probing

Probing questions are used to elicit information more fully than the original questions which introduced a topic. In essence, it is the fact that probing is sanctioned as part of the research process that differentiates in-depth interviewing from normal everyday conversations. It is an indicator that the researcher is aware that he or she cannot take for granted the common sense understanding that people share because these may be differently interpreted by informant and interviewer. The example that Deutscher gives (1973) is appropriate. He points out that words which seem to be objective such as temperature descriptions *hot* and *cold* can actually have different meanings when used by different groups of people even though they are all speaking the same language. Translating his American example to the Australian context, we could say that an Australian truck driver may stop at the pub. The truck driver is complaining to the bartender that his drink is *warm* and the soup is *cold*. As Deutscher puts it,

> . . .the 'warm' liquid may have a temperature of fifty degrees fahrenheit while the 'cold' one is seventy five degrees fahrenheit. . . The standard for the same objects may well vary from culture to culture, from nation to nation, from region to region and, for that matter, within any given social unit—between classes, age groups, sexes; what is 'cold' soup for an adult may be too 'hot' to give a child (1973: 191).

The use of probing questions is a method of clarifying, and gaining more detail, especially when you are trying to understand the meanings that informants attach to **original** or **primary questions** (Stewart & Cash 1988). Original or primary questions are used to begin the interview or introduce new topics. They can stand alone out of context and still make sense. Probing or *secondary questions* are used as follow-up questions. They are introduced to elicit information of greater detail than that which was drawn from the primary question or previous probing. These probes are used when the informant's statements seem incomplete, and vague, or when the informant gives no answers.

Schatzman & Strauss (1973) suggest several question-asking strategies which act as probes. However, these suggestions are tied to that stage of interviewing where the interviewer feels that they have *established rapport* or, as Schatzman and Strauss phrase it, that they have developed *inter-personal familiarity and com-*

fort. These strategies are more directive and aggressive. Their first suggestion is eliciting new information from the informant by asking the **Devil's Advocate Question**. This form of leading question is often used for clarification. The question format 'deliberately confronts the informant with the arguments of opponents as abstractions within or outside the universe now being studied' (Schatzman and Strauss 1973: 81). The basic intent of this questioning tactic is to provoke the informant into elaborating on previous comments, either to provide the interviewer with more detailed information or to test the validity of the interviewer's interpretation of the informant's position on a particular issue or matter. It may provoke a specific retaliatory response or a more careful and detailed outline of a previous statement made by the informant.

Another means of *leading* the informant is to propose a **hypothetical question**. This is done by the interviewer suggesting a number of possible or plausible scenarios, options or occurrences and asking the informant to guess at his or her own attitude and/or behaviour response to such options.

A third means of leading the informant to further revelation is what Schatzman and Strauss (1973) call **posing the ideal**. This form of questioning can be used to ask the informant to describe and perhaps analyse the most ideal situation that they could conceive in relation to their current life situation. Another form of *posing the ideal* does not allow the informant to take the lead. Rather, it is the researcher who poses an ideal according to their perception of the situation. Whichever variation is used, the data elicited make the study available to the reader by allowing a comparison between the *perceived ideal* and 'reality'. These techniques enable the researcher to gain greater insight into the interpretations and views of the informant.

The most-often used form of probing is the **nudging probe** which is used when the informant has either given what the interviewer regards as incomplete information, or is hesitant to continue. Usually an interviewer will try to '*nudge*' the informant into speaking or continuing to speak by using body language. This can include silence on the part of the researcher perhaps combined with eye contact, quizzical facial expressions or nodding of the head. If this first strategy is not effective then the researcher might attempt to use *verbal nudging*. For instance,

Tell me more. . .
Oh, really.
Go on.
And then. . .
I see.
Is that so?
Please continue.
Yes?
Hmm. . .
What happened then?

Alternatively, if an informant has discussed an issue in a vague or superficial manner by using jargon or including generalisations, then you might use certain phrases to obtain clearer and deeper answers, such as,

Tell me a little more about. . .
Why did you?
What did you have in mind when you said. . .?
Just how small was . . .?
What happened after. . .?
I'm not sure I understand your point. . .

On the other hand, the conversation between you and the informant may have taken a different turn. You may feel that some statement the informant has given suggests a particular feeling or attitude on their part. If this is the case, the researcher might decide to ask,

How did you react?
What did you think and feel about that?
Is it the way you think and feel now?
Why do you think and feel that way?

Sometimes in the exchange of conversation a comment made by the informant may seem irrelevant. For example, if the interviewer asks the informant to answer a question about new regulations being administered in a public hospital, such as, 'What are your attitudes to the new regulations?', and the informant answered, 'A lot of my colleagues are grizzly and grumpy because of the implementation of the new regulations. . .', then the informant has avoided answering about his or her *own* attitudes. Rather, he or she has concentrated on analysing and reporting the definitions of others. The researcher might try redirecting the informant by repeating the question, 'What are *your* attitudes toward the new regulations?', stressing or emphasising *your* in order to elicit a more relevant response.

If the researcher is not sure that he or she has correctly understood what the informant has said or implied in answer to a question, he or she might try using the **reflective probe** strategy. This entails *reflecting* the answer back to the informant in order to clarify or verify the information. This double-checks the researcher's interpretation of an answer.

> You meant your daughter, didn't you?
> You mean the 1990s, don't you?
> She said that to you?
> Once every fortnight?
> Am I correct in assuming that you still hate his attitude?

The reflective probing strategy is similar to the **mirror** or **summary question**. When using this latter form of probing, the researcher is trying to ensure that they have gained an accurate understanding; the interpretation of the discussion summarises the conversation.

> Let me see if I have this straight? You actually. . . and then. . . and after that. . .
> So to summarise your situation, you began by telling me that. . .
> It is my understanding that in the past six years you have. . .

Researchers need to be very careful when using these two forms of reflective probe. In some cases, the use of such forms of probing can appear to be questioning the informant's integrity, knowledge or intelligence by communicating disbelief, undue pressure or even entrapment. This may result in the informant not answering or even discontinuing the interview. However, if either or both the reflective probe or the mirror probe are used effectively, they can help the interviewer avoid making the mistake of assuming that they have accurately understood the informant's statements or implied meanings. Foddy (1988) discusses this issue in relation to the utility of closed-ended and open-ended questions in eliciting information which is accurately communicated between the participants.

Non-answering

An informant may at some point in the interview decide not to answer a question. If the researcher assesses that the asking of such questions is not overstepping the bounds of privacy then he or she tries to change this by using a number of strategies. Of course, the informant may disagree with the researcher's assessment and decide not to provide any answer to questions that he or she regards as overly intrusive. This is the informant's right. The researcher may decide to restate the question, rephrase it, or if that fails, tactfully ask the informant why they did not answer. Sometimes an informant may decide that he or she is either unable or unwilling to answer a particular question or to allow the conversation to be directed to a particular area. He or she may or may not give a reason for this action. If you receive a reason *listen carefully* before deciding on which, if any, question you will ask next. Be prepared to either explain or expand on the answer or information required, why you have requested it and its potential use. If these forms of probing are unsuccessful be prepared to abandon questioning.

There are many reasons why informants may not adequately answer questions. Some are related to the social interaction of the interview process. First, the informant may be unsure of the type of comment or detail in which the researcher is interested. Does the researcher want a simple *yes* or *no*, or is he or she interested in a detailed explanation? Secondly, the informant may not understand the question. This may be because the researcher has relied on language use or phrasing which is unfamiliar to the informant.

Thirdly, the informant may not have adequately discussed a particular topic or issue because he or she does not have the knowledge or information required. Whether this is because he or she had not previously had access to the information or that it has been forgotten due to memory lapse is irrelevant. The point is that the informant in such an instance is unable to answer. Fourthly, the informant may be unable to express inner feelings and thus cannot adequately provide an answer for the researcher.

Several additional reasons may explain an inadequate answer or a non-response. The informant may feel that the researcher could not comprehend the answer because the topic or issue is outside the researcher's experience, or because it is too technical. Or, perhaps the informant thinks that a question is too personal and constitutes an infringement of privacy.

Cross-checks

It has been emphasised in this book that the in-depth interview is aimed at gaining access to the perspective of the informant. Thus, the researcher using the in-depth interview tries to elicit an honest account of how the informants see themselves and their experiences. How does an interviewer do this when people may be 'exaggerating their successes and denying or downplaying their failures' (Taylor & Bogdan 1984: 98); hiding important facts about themselves and their experiences (Douglas 1976); or that they 'lie a bit, cheat a bit' (Deutscher 1973) when giving their definition of the situation? It is obviously difficult for in-depth interviewers to know the difference between exaggeration and distortion purposefully employed, and authentic perspectives which are inevitably biassed and subjective. The answer is that the in-depth interviewer cannot be 100% sure about the difference. However, the qualitative researcher *is not primarily geared to finding out the truth per se but rather the truth as the informant sees it to be*. As Shaw puts it in his introduction to *The Jack-Roller*,

> . . . . the validity and value of the personal document are not dependent upon its objectivity or veracity. It is not expected that the delinquent will necessarily describe his life-situations objectively. On the contrary, it is desired that his story will reflect his own personal attitudes and interpretations. Thus, rationalizations, fabrications, prejudices, exaggerations are quite as valuable as objective descriptions, provided of course, that these reactions be properly identified and classified (1955: 2–3).

In essence, the interviewer is responsible for obtaining the informant's account and asking cross-check questions in order to make this genuine from the informant's perspective and to identify and classify distortions. This can be attempted in a number of ways. One can check the informant's stories and statements for consistency. This is done by seeing if the informant's description, interpretation or analysis of an event, experience or issue is consistent with his or her account of it in another interview or in some other part of the same interview. The interviewer can compare the versions given at the different times.

An alternative method of cross-checking that has been suggested as useful in dealing with seeming contradictions is to directly confront the informant with evidence of the problem, but in a gentle manner. For example, one could say, 'I'm a little confused. Perhaps you can clear this up for me. In one of our interview sessions you told me . . ., but this week you said . . .which doesn't seem to fit in with what you told me before. I don't understand this'. As Taylor and Bogdan point out,

> If you know a person well enough, you can usually tell when he or she is evading a subject or 'putting you on' and the interviewer can then gauge the degree to which he or she should press the point (1984: 99).

However, an important factor that needs to be kept in mind is that people can hold logically contradictory views simultaneously and that these form a valid part of the account. Cross-checking will not provide the researcher with a more genuine account if he or she discards these contradictions.

Closing the Interview

Let us assume that several in-depth interviews have taken place. You, the interviewer, have made your intentions clear as to the nature of your research and what you require from your informant. You gained access and began your interviews in a congenial atmosphere after establishing and maintaining rapport and the informant's interest in participating. You have related your questions to the overall intent of the research design and you have made them as clear to the informant as possible. In addition, you have listened attentively and sensitively to the comments, statements and queries made by the informant and progressively analysed this information in the process of the conversations. You have used probing questions to clarify and extend your understanding of the meanings they intended with their use of words. Now you wish to end the interview. How do you go about this?

Several factors must be taken into account. First, you may wish to re-interview the informant at some later date. Thus, you need to maintain rapport even though you are closing off the immediate relationship. Secondly, you should realise that the social process of in-depth interviewing creates a relationship between the participants and that such relationships create expectations. This may commit the researcher to fulfil prior promised actions such as contacting the informant when the research is published. The point is that taking a deep breath, heaving your shoulders and physically or verbally showing that you are glad it is all over may be gratifying to you as a tired researcher, but may be detrimental and hurtful to your informant and can be damaging to your research. It is important to show that you respect informants, their stories and their generosity in sharing them with you. There are both verbal and non-verbal cues that the interviewer can use to signal that the in-depth interview is coming to an end either for that session or for the total series of interviews with the informant.

Verbal Techniques

The most commonly used strategies are similar to those of normal everyday conversation. These can be listed as follows.

1 Explaining the reason for closing

This is a forthright method in which you, the researcher, tell the informant directly that you must close the interview and why it must finish at this point. This can take three distinct forms. First, you can announce that the task or purpose of the interviews has been completed to the best of your mutual abilities. For example, you might use any of the following or similar forms of phrasing.

> 'Well, all that we've discussed should give me plenty of food for thought.'
> 'Well, I have no more questions, just now.'
> 'Well, with this interview, the series is complete.'

Alternatively, if you have previously agreed on a time limit for the interview then *signalling that time is up* is another form of explaining the reason for closing. However, the researcher should be careful not to be in an unseemly hurry to quit the scene, nor should he or she be perceived as responding to the informant as one of many in a production line rather than as a unique individual. For instance one could say,

> 'Well, that's all the time we have for today.'
> 'Goodness, it's 10.30 p.m. already; our time just raced away today. Our time is up.'
> 'I'm sorry, we'll have to leave our discussion there today as I have an appointment waiting'.
> 'I must leave in five minutes because I have to teach a class at 4.00 p.m.'

2 Clearing-house Questions

Use *clearing-house questions* as an indication to the informant that you are closing the interview. Clearing-house questions enable the researcher to focus on areas which may not have been adequately covered up to that point. This can be done by asking the informant if you have answered all his or her questions or covered all the topics. For instance, one could ask,

> 'Is there anything else we should discuss before I leave? 'I think that we have covered everything that is necessary. Can you think of anything that I have missed?'

Alternatively, you can offer to answer questions such as the following.

> 'If you have any questions I would be happy to try to answer them'.
> 'Now it's time to ask if you have any questions.'

This signals your completion of the task and your desire to include them as a full participant.

3 Summarising the Interview

This is another conversational strategy which cues the informant that the interview is at the closing stage. It is a common form of closing which enables the researcher and the informant to formally recognise the areas of discussion that have been covered in the conversation:

> 'So do we agree that today we talked about a, b, c, d, and that we should continue next week by thinking about. . .?'

4 Making Personal Enquiries and Comments

Making personal enquiries and comments is another more involving manner of closing the interview. This strategy makes evident one's genuine interest in the informant. For example this can be done by asking about their family, job or situation.

> 'How is your son going with his final exams?'
> Do you think this is the right time of year to take a holiday in Hong Kong? It is the monsoon season.'

This type of question indicates two things to the informant. First, that the interview issues are no longer the centre of discussion, and secondly, that even though you are a stranger, you have taken an interest in his or her life and the things that he or she has mentioned to you. It indicates that you are really listening.

An alternative to this questioning is *exhibiting concern*. This does not mean that you should pretend to care. If you do not care or you have not developed a relationship of that type and level, then it is not only inappropriate but also unethical to claim otherwise by making such comments. However, if the relationship has developed to that extent then, comments such as these are appropriate.

> 'Please look after yourself and I will see you soon'
> 'I hope you pass all your exams with flying colours.'
> 'I know we didn't discuss this, but if you run into any problems like that just call me.'

5 Express Thanks and Satisfaction

Finally, one of the most obvious forms of closing a conversation is to *express thanks, appreciation and satisfaction* because you as the researcher have received information, from the informant, through the gift of his or her time and concentration. Thus, it is appropriate to close by saying something like this.

> 'Thank you for the time and effort you put in.'
> 'I have really enjoyed our discussions and I appreciate the fact that you agreed to participate in the study.'
> 'Well, now that we have covered the areas which are important, I want to let you know that we have done extremely well to get to this point in relation to. . . Thank you for your time.'

Non-verbal Closing Strategies

There are many non-verbal actions which can indicate to the informant that the interview is about to close. These range from looking at your watch or a clock in the room, to straightening up in your chair as if ready to move out of it, putting the cap on your pen and closing your notebook, unplugging the tape-recorder or offering to shake hands. Any one of these movements will cue the informant that you consider it is time to finish the conversation. There are obviously many more that could be mentioned. Most researchers find that the relationship with the informant will help determine what the best method is of closing the interview, and whether closing will be initiated by informant or interviewer. Researchers use verbal and non-verbal cues together.

One of the most significant factors in closing an interview is knowing when to stop. You do not need to drag it out until the allotted time if you have actually finished discussing the matters of interest. Nor do you have to probe everything in depth.

Your access to knowledge and information will be influenced by the relationship and the interaction you have developed with the informant. The previous sections dealing with structuring the interview process, and the forms that questions can take, are obviously not exhaustive. There are as many strategies and tactics as there are researchers. The aforementioned options have been discussed in order to give the reader some idea of these processes and situations as they have been experienced by others.

Recording the Interview

Interviewing as a method relies on the assumption that people are able (and willing) to give verbal accounts of their attitudes, beliefs and actions. This assumption is in turn dependent on the idea that human beings are reflective about their own actions, or can be put into a situation to become so. Keeping this in mind, most interviewers need to make a decision about how to record the interview.

Tape recording and note taking are two of the most commonly used methods and they are sometimes used in combination. There are advantages and disadvantages inherent in either technique. You can take notes during the interview, or if you think this is disruptive, rely on your memory to reconstruct the conversation soon after the interview. Or you can tape record the conversation and transcribe it after the interview. The questions that must be asked regarding note taking and tape recording as methods of recording interview material are as follows.

1 How effective is this technique in generating accurate data?
2 How fair is the use of this method to the interviewer and the informant?
3 How valid is the material gathered by this method?
4 How helpful is this method in analysing the material?

Note taking and tape recording should not be seen as simply alternative techniques or strategies for achieving similar ends but as different ways of doing research.

Tape Recording

Tape recording is one means of obtaining a full and accurate record of the interview. It can enhance greater rapport by allowing a more natural conversational style. The interviewer is free to be an attentive and thoughtful listener. The raw data remains on the record. Therefore, all the material is available for analysis when the researcher has the time to concentrate fully. Schwartz and Jacobs (1979) point out that there is greater analytic depth because the anecdotal information and the ambiguity of response is still available to the researcher. A more accurate picture remains because both questions and answers are recorded. Validity is enhanced by this preservation of authentic data.

If you are going to buy a tape recorder, we suggest that you purchase a small unobtrusive one which looks less intimidating than a large machine. Also, a researcher who constantly checks the tape recorder is distracting to the informant. Check that the equipment and batteries are in good working order prior to conducting the interview. It is frustrating to discover that the conversation was not recorded because the batteries were dead!

Tapes should be clearly labelled with the informant's identification, the topic and date of interview. Long-playing tapes should be used so that the conversation is not regularly interrupted because you have to change the tape. Low-quality tapes should not be purchased. They can be easily damaged by the machine due to frequent use.

However, there are problems with tape recording which are worth mentioning. Both interviewer and informant may find that the tape recorder inhibits interaction. Some people feel vulnerable, fearing that someone may recognise their voice if the interview becomes public. The informant may feel he or she has to be interesting or dramatic and this can bias the data. One of the most significant problems is that you cannot record the non-verbal data (unless you use a video camera).

In addition to this, there is the feeling that once something is on tape it is indelible. There may be concern that the recorded account may be misinterpreted at a later date when the informant is not present to interject, correct or change an interpretation. The ethics of using a tape recorder will be discussed in chapter 10. This gives the interviewer more control and power in relation to the informant and may upset the balance of interaction in the conversation. Tape recording can lead to a recessive style of research where the interpretive process occurs during the editing and selection of extracts from the transcripts rather than during the interaction process. Tape recorders can also lull the interviewer into a loss of concentration.

One of the most tedious and time-consuming aspects associated with tape recording is transcribing the data. Taylor and Bogdan (1984) estimate that a one-hour interview will result in up to forty typewritten pages of data. The work associated with transcribing can be reduced if you use a transcriber. A transcriber is especially designed to play back the tape at slow speeds. A clear tape can also save many hours of trying to transcribe inaudible words and sentences. The tape recorder should be strategically placed so that it can pick up the conversation effectively without being obtrusive.

If you plan to have someone else transcribe the tapes then it is important that you work closely with that person. The transcript must accurately reflect what was said. It should not only include sounds but also the non-verbal messages (for example, pauses) expressed by the researcher and informant. This contextual information can influence how you listen to and interpret the text. It should be pointed out that the major advantage of typing your own transcript is that you become more familiar with the data. As you are taking down the text, you become engaged in data analysis.

Note-taking

Note-taking pulls the researcher into analysis and interpretation earlier in the research than tape recording. As you make notes, you tend to use your own version of shorthand which also incorporates interpretation. In researchers' interview notes, it is quite common to find commentaries about the discussion offered by the informant. This is a useful practice to adopt. Note taking also enables the researcher to record body language in relation to speech patterns, although a tape recorder is a better way of recording the modalities of speech.

Note-taking allows partial analysis to occur. However, this can also lead to a prematurely fixed conception of data where little or no reselection of raw data occurs. This is because the notes are in a form that makes deletion and addition unattractive. Nonverbal contact may be restricted and discourse constrained because the researcher will be taking notes rather than interacting naturally. Rapport with the informant is obviously at risk. Nevertheless, note-taking tends to make the researcher listen more carefully to what the informant is saying.

If you decide to rely on your memory to reconstruct the interview, then we recommend that you follow some simple rules about note-taking. First, you should concentrate your attention on key words and ideas, and follow these as they develop in a conversation. The emphasis is *not* to recall and reproduce all that was said in exactly the same words, but to recall the *meanings* of remarks. Recalling conversation is a skill. It involves learning how to be attentive and reflective. Researchers who have mastered these skills can conduct up to two hours of interview without the use of a tape recorder (Bogdan and Biklen 1982). Second, we repeat, it is important that you write your fieldnotes soon after you have finished the interview. We suggest that you should not spend more than one hour in the field and that the fieldnotes should be written on the same day. The day after may be one day too late. Diagrams of the setting or *sitting charts* can help you to trace the conversation and recall its details.

Many researchers use tape recorders in conjunction with taking notes. This is usually done in the hope that one can gain the advantages of both and cancel out their disadvantages.

Listening Analytically

The role of the interviewer is not simply to record and process responses but to *participate in a conversation* with the informant. Participation means more than listening, nodding and note-taking. It means answering, commenting and attending to conversation sensitively. It also means thinking about each verbal interaction, and its theoretical direction: when to probe for clarification or elaboration, and when to sit quietly and acknowledge the silence of the informant. Thus, the researcher needs to fully participate in the initiation, maintenance and closing of the in-depth interview but at the same time to sustain a *critical inner dialogue*. As Adelman points out,

> One problem with using talk lies in its familiarity. To penetrate beyond the 'ordinariness' of talk, to attribute social categories, value judgements and other cultural features requires the researcher to separate out his [*sic*] own knowledge as a member of the culture from the talk being used by a fellow member of the culture. This separating out allows the researcher to sustain a critical inner dialogue. . .Such reflexibility comes through attention to what people say. . . (1981: 24).

The process of listening is a crucial part of the interview process. It acknowledges the value of the informant's participation in the interview. For the researcher, it is the means of engaging in the conversation as part of normal social interaction while at the same time being distanced enough to sustain that critical inner dialogue which enables analysis of the data. This analytical ability enables the researcher to analyse what is happening at the same time as participating in the interaction and the discussion.

Some researchers regard listening as 'art' (Douglas, Roberts and Thompson 1988) whereas others regard it as a strategy (Schatzman and Strauss 1973) for maintaining the flow of communication. Both interpretations are applicable. The most significant point to remember is that the in-depth interview is social interaction, and listening can act as a stimulation for further interaction or as a response to such interaction. The fundamental principle of in-depth interviewing is to provide a framework within which informants can express their understandings in their terms. That framework is negotiated through talking, listening and reflecting.

Listening as Support and Recognition

In-depth interviews should operate as two-way communication and not feel like interrogation to the informant. This involves letting the informant know that you support his or her continuing comments and discussion of issues by listening carefully and indicating this attention both verbally and non-verbally. This can include 'smiling' with your eyes, nodding and making 'listening noises'. Empathic listening allows the researcher to reduce emotional tension by providing a supportive response and endorses the informant's feeling of value.

Careful listening cues the informant to refine his or her ideas and interpretations while articulating them because he or she has a sympathetic and patient listener. This assumes that the researcher is non-judgmental. Frowns on the interviewer's face should indicate lack of understanding, not disapproval! The tendency to evaluate, judge, approve or disapprove of a statement made by another person occurs in everyday conversation. However, in-depth interviewing requires the researcher to give a non-judgmental or tolerant appearance to the informant because the continuation of the social interaction may rely on such perceived tolerance. When we use the term *non-judgmental*, we are not advocating the same sort of distancing as is used in survey-style research. Rather, we are suggesting that the researcher should not come across as being overly critical. Nevertheless, listening involves response. A glassy-eyed passive interviewer, hanging on every word leaves the informant feeling unrecognised, uncared for and often intimidated and unsure of how to interact with that interviewer. Useful and effective listening involves giving feedback to the informant in a normal conversational form.

Modes of Listening

It is obvious that listening occurs at more than one level. Listening is not just hearing words spoken. We have all sat in a lecture theatre and forgotten what was said. This is hearing—listening at a superficial level. Yet, when the lecturer introduces material that is directly examinable we 'tune in' to understand, and record. During an in-depth interview, you can focus on information on at least two levels. One level is the explicit content or verbalised information given by the informant. The second is the implied or unstated information, or what is not said. Listening at both levels helps you to decide what you want to listen to, that is, when you want to probe. This gives you, the researcher, a certain degree of power and control over the structure of the conversation.

Listening Skills

Researchers often need to develop their listening skills. One way in which we can improve our listening skills is to work out what some of the 'subskills' of listening are. Some of the ones we have noted during our own interviewing are as follows:

- adjust to the informant;
- identify the informant's attitudes;
- perceive and recognise differences between similarly worded statements;
- resist being overly influenced by emotion-laden words and/or arguments;
- distil the meaning intended by the informant by making valid inferences;
- use 'contextual clues' to determine the meanings of words and phrases used by the informant;
- take note of the sequence of ideas, comments and details;
- try to avoid the effects of projecting one's own perceptions on informants' statements;
- try to reflect on and analyse one's own listening;
- capture the main ideas being put forward by the informant;
- recognise supporting ideas put forward by the informant;
- learn to listen in undesirable or bad conditions;
- learn to check the accuracy of new information;
- learn to retain all relevant information;
- maintain sensitivity to persuasive techniques used by the informant;
- be alert to contradictory statements made by the informant.

Obviously, there are many other subskills involved in listening. The question is not how many subskills there are, but how can one develop these skills. Some people have developed such skills as part of their natural repertoire in their everyday interaction and they simply need to practice and refine them. (It is for this reason that interviewing is often referred to as an *art*, rather than a science.) However, most people have not adequately developed these skills. One means of developing such skill is to adopt Adelman's notion of *critical inner dialogue*.

What the researcher might think would be as follows: 'What is this informant saying that I can use? Is this interesting in relation to my research problem? What are the central ideas this person is putting forward in this account? OK. Have I fully understood what this person is saying? Maybe, maybe not. I had better use a probe. Oh, yes I did understand. Now I can go on with a follow-up question.'.

We think a great deal faster than we speak and this enables us to develop and use to advantage critical inner dialogues during the interview process.

Another means of improving our listening skills is to concentrate on the *preparation* aspect of listening. If you are as fully prepared and informed as you can make yourself on a topic, issue or person then you may be more capable of hearing and appreciating the implications of the comments and statements made by the informants. This preparation can be carried out by reading, immersing yourself in the social setting or taking studies examining the area. You must also involve yourself in the social interaction of the interview situation. This is essential as involvement prevents a lack of interest which might encourage concentration lapses. Concentration is a matter of both involvement and self-discipline. If you focus on what the informant is saying, how he or she is saying it, the body language that accompanies the verbal message, and the relevance the comments have to what has gone on before in this or previous interviews, then you won't have time to allow for mental wanderings!

A strategy for doing this is to link information by making mental links between the original questions, the answers and the logically following questions. This is called *recursive structuring of the interview* or following the *recursive model of questioning*. Recursive questioning is an excellent means of maintaining concentration. When researchers use this strategy, they tend to integrate the informant's statements and comments into organised patterns or trends which help arrange the pieces into a total picture. They then reinterpret and analyse the information as it is given. The use of the *critical inner dialogue* is part of this overall process. Obviously, we have not given a total account of the strategies and processes involved in doing in-depth interviewing; as such a task is impossible by its very nature. What we have provided in this chapter are some features which we have noted in our own research practices.

Glossary

Aide memoire Another term for interview guide or schedule, see below.

Background demographic questions Used to provide the researcher with some characteristics which can be used to identify the person being interviewed in relation to other people in society. Such questions ask the informant to specify their age, sex, education, occupation, place of residence, etc. These questions are a form of descriptive questioning.

Contrast questioning Questions asking the informant to make comparisons of situations or events in their world and to discuss the meanings of these situations.

Descriptive questioning Asks informants to provide descriptions of events, people, places or experiences. It is often used to start interviews.

Devil's advocate question A form of probing. It is a question which deliberately confronts the informant with the arguments of opponents as abstractions within or outside the 'universe' which is being studied.

Diary interview method See **log-interview method** below.

Ethnographic context The everyday activities of the informant, his or her common sense working knowledge of that cultural milieu or his or her sense of self-identity, together form the ethnographic context in which the informant lives.

Establishing rapport Refers to the establishment of a positive easy-going relationship with the informant. No researcher has a specific method to create or guarantee this.

Feeling questions Questions which are aimed at understanding people's emotional responses.

Funnelling Refers to a process of questioning in which the interviewer controls the flow and type of information being asked by the informant. This is done by starting the interview with broad general questions and continuing it by narrowing the discussion using more specific questions which ask directly about the issues that are of interest to the researcher.

Hypothetical question A form of probing. It is a question in which the interviewer suggests a possible or plausible number of scenarios, options or occurrences and asks the informant to guess at their own response to such options in attitude or behaviour terms.

Interpretive approach An approach that holds that social reality is consciously and actively created by individuals who mean to do things and who attribute meanings to the behaviour of others.

Interview guide or schedule When used in qualitative research it consists of a list of general issues, topics, problems or ideas that the researcher wants to make sure are covered by each informant. It is used to jog the memory of the interviewer and is revised as different informants provide information which indicates the need to do this. It is also known as an **interview schedule** or an **aide memoire**. It does not act as a standardising instrument unless it is used in quantitative research.

Interview schedule Another term for *interview guide*. See above.

Knowledge questions Aimed at finding out what factual information the informant has, that is, to find out what the informant considers factual.

Life-history interview A life history is the history of an individual's life given by the person living it and solicited by the researcher. It is a sociological autobiography drawn from in-depth interviewing and/or solicited narratives.

Log-interview method A specific version of the solicited narrative. The informant is asked to keep a log or diary of daily events either *in toto* or using a set of themes provided by the interviewer. They are asked to keep the log for a specific time period. It is used as a basis for further interviews. It is also another version of the diary-interview method.

Methodology A rule-governed procedure aiding scientific discovery. Methodological issues are concerned with the *logic* of inquiry, that is, how we discover and validate what we think exists.

Mirror or summary question A form of probing. It is a variation of the reflective probe. One uses the same strategies but the interviewer also clarifies the informant's comments by summarising them and then reflecting them in the question form.

Nudging probe A form of probing in which the interviewer uses verbal cues or body language cues to elicit further information from the informant.

Opinion/value questions Aimed at gaining access to or understanding what people think about a particular person, event, issue or experience.

Original or primary questions First questions used to ask an informant about an issue, event, person, place or attitude.

Personal documents Informant's diaries, photos, letters, formal records, calendars, scrapbooks and all memorabilia which can be used to jog the memory of the informant regarding their life and experiences.

Posing the ideal A situation in which either the informant or the interviewer describes and perhaps analyses the most ideal situations they could conceive of in the life of the informant.

Probing questions Questions used to clarify, gain more detail and understand the meanings that informants attach to original or primary questions and answers to them. This is why they are also known as *secondary questions*.

Productive interpersonal climate Another term used for *establishing rapport*. See above.

Recursive model of interviewing A form of in-depth interviewing in which the interview follows normal conversational interaction allowing the flow of conversation to direct the research process. It is regarded as the most unstructured form of in-depth interviewing.

Reflective probe A probing strategy which entails the researcher reflecting the answer given by the informant in order to clarify or verify the information. It is also known as a *mirror or summary question*.

Sensory questions Those questions asking the informant about what has been seen, heard, touched, tasted and smelled. They are used to induce the informant to describe the stimuli which they have experienced. They are a form of descriptive question.

Setting the tone Another term for *establishing rapport*. See above.

Solicited narrative Refers to the interviewer soliciting (asking for) a written narrative (story-like account) from the informant. Researchers often ask for a chronology of the informant's life prior to being interviewed, or the informant is asked to write their own story.

Story telling A means of directing interview interaction. The researcher asks the informant questions which requires the telling of a story as part or all of the response.

Structural questioning Questions aimed at finding out *how* informants organise their knowledge.

Transitions A means of shifting the conversation to another issue or topic by connecting something the informant has said with the topic of interest to the interviewer, (even if this connection is a little far-fetched).

References

Abrahamson, M. 1983. *Social Research Methods*. Englewood, New Jersey: Prentice Hall.

Adelman, C. (ed.) 1981. *Uttering, Muttering: Collecting, Using and Reporting Talk for Social and Educational Research*. London: Grant McIntrye.

Askham, J. 1982. 'Telling Stories.' *Sociological Review* 30: 55–573.

Aroni, R. 1985. *The Effects of Jewish and non-Jewish Day Schools on Jewish Identity and Commitment*. Unpublished doctoral dissertation, Monash University, Clayton, Vico.

Babbie, E. 1989. *The Practice of Social Research*. Fifth edition. Belmont, California: Wadsorth Publishing Co.

Bailey, K.D. 1982. *Methods of Social Research*. New York: The Free Press.

Bandler, R. & Grinder, J. 1979. *Frogs with Princes, Neuro- linguistic Programming*. Utah: Real People Press.

Bell, C. & Encel, S. 1978. *Inside the Whale: Ten Personal Accounts of Social Research*. Oxford: Pergamon.

Benney, M & Hughes, E.C. 1970. 'Of Sociology and the Interview.' in N.K. Denzin (ed.). *Sociological Methods: A Source- book*. London: Butterworth.

Bogdan, R. & Biklen, S. 1982. *Qualitative Research for Edu- cation*. Boston: Allyn and Bacon.

Burgess, R.G. 1984. *In the Field, An Introduction to Field Research*. London: Allen & Unwin.

Cameron-Bandler, L. 1985. *Solutions: Practical and Effective Antidotes for Sexual and Relationships Problems*. Ann Arbor, Michigan: Future Pace, Inc.

Deutscher, I. 1973. *What We Say/What We Do*. Glenview, Illinois: Scott, Foresman and Co.

Douglas, L., Roberts, A. & Thompson, R. 1988. *Oral History: A Handbook*. Sydney: Allen & Unwin.

Foddy, W.H. 1988. *Open Versus Closed Questions: Really a Problem of Communication*. Paper presented to the Australian Bicentennial Meeting of Social Psychologists. Leura, New South Wales, August.

Glaser, B.G. & Strauss, A. 1967. *The Discovery of Grounded Theory*. Chicago: Aldine

Goode, W.J. & Hatt, P.K. 1952. *Methods in Social Research*. New York: McGraw Hill.

Kidder, L.H. 1981. *Selltiz Wrightsman and Cook's Research Methods in Social Relations*. Fourth edition. New York: Holt Saunders International Editions.

King, M., Novik, L. & Citrenbaum, C. 1983. *Irresistible Communication: Creative Skills for the Health Professional*. USA: W.B. Saunders Co.

Oakley, A. 1988. 'Interviewing women: a contradiction in terms.', in H. Roberts, (ed.) *Doing Feminist Research*. London: Routledge and Kegan Paul

Patton, R. 1980. *Qualitative Evaluation Methods*. Beverly Hills: Sage.

Polgar, S., & Thomas, S.A. 1988. *Introduction to Research in the Health Sciences*. Melbourne: Churchill Livingstone.

Schatzman, L. & Strauss, A.L. 1973. *Field Research: Strategies for a Natural Sociology*. Englewood Cliffs, New Jersey: Prentice-Hall.
Schwartz, H. & Jacobs, J. 1979. *Qualitative Sociology: A Method to the Madness*. London: Collier Macmillan.
Selltiz, C., Jahoda, M., Deutsch, M. & Cook, S.W. 1959. *Research Methods in Social Relations*. Revised edition. New York: Holt.
Shaw, C.R. 1966. *The Jack Roller: A Delinquent Boy's Own Story*. Chicago: University of Chicago Press.
Shipman, M.D. 1972. *The Limitations of Social Research*. London:Longman Group.
Spradley, J.P. 1979. *The Ethnographic Interview*. London: Holt, Rinehart and Winston.
Stewart, C.J. & Cash, J.W.B. 1988. *Interviewing: Principles and Practices*. Dubuque, Iowa: Wm.C. Brown Publishers.
Taylor, S.J. & Bogdan, R. 1984. *Introduction to Qualitative Research Methods: The Search for Meanings*. Second edition. New York: John Wiley and Sons.

Chapter 7
Life History

A **life history** is precisely what it says it is—the history of an individual's life given by the person living it and solicited by the researcher. It is a sociological **autobiography** drawn from in-depth interviewing and/or solicited narratives (see chapter 5). It is an attempt to gain an account of a person's life told in their own words. This chapter discusses oral or life history as a means of extending and developing our understanding of in-depth interviewing. The concept of an oral or life history is defined and a rationale for its use is provided.

The usual form in which life histories can be found is in full-length accounts of the person's life, stated in their own words. Sometimes, these accounts appear with the introduction and conclusion written by the researcher in order to frame the informant's account in a sociological context; or an informant's story may be interspersed with a great deal of the researcher's interpretive material. The life history can be regarded as distinct from traditional autobiographies because it is recognised that in the more conventional autobiography what we read is what the author wishes us to know. In the sociological version, what we read is mediated by the researcher's interaction with the person during the telling of the story, the coding, analysis and interpretation of it.

The life history has also been called *oral history*, *life story*, *document of life*, *case history* or *personal history*. These terms, which are often used interchangeably, all refer to specific forms of research. For instance, the **case history** is drawn from clinical models in which the informant is asked questions so that the clinician can determine a more fitting diagnosis of the informant's 'state of health' in the light of past experiences. The aim in **oral history** is to gain information about the past whereas the central concern of the **biographical life history** is to elicit information detailing the individual's development. The sociological life history aims to understand the ways in which a particular individual creates, makes sense of and interprets his or her life.

Life histories are not simply the domain of sociologists. They will inevitably be different in form and content, even when the substantive research area is the same, because different people will have done the history for different purposes. These can range from sociological research to psychoanalytic investigation; from work histories to clinical profiles.

According to Denzin (1989), if we clarify the various terms used to describe this method, it is easier to understand the forms it can take. So, for our purposes a *life* is the unfinished process of the lived experiences of a person and is given meaning by that person and his/her significant others. *History* is an account of an event or events including an attempt to explain why it occurred. A *story* is a recounting of events which is subjective and may be fictional. A *life history* is the experience of a person, group or organisation and is somewhat different to a *case history* which is a 'full story of some temporal span or interlude in social life' and focusses on a process not a person (Denzin 1989: 185). Oral history should not be confused with personal history which reconstructs a life based on interviews and conversations. *However, it is quite obvious that in practice most researchers merge the two.*

If we examine Figure 7.1, we can see that elements of these *terms or methods* can be utilised depending on the purpose and aim of the research project.

The wavering between the terms *life-history* and *oral history* in fact reflects the disciplinary antecedents, history and sociology.

Term/Method	Key Features	Forms/Variations
1 History	What happened? How?	Oral, life, personal.
2 Fiction	An account, something made up, fashioned.	Story (life, self).
3 Biography	History of a life.	Autobiography.
4 Story	A fiction, a narrative.	Life, personal experience.
5 Discourse	Telling a story.	First, third person.
6 Narrative	A story, having a plot and existence independent of the teller.	Fiction, epic, folklore.
7 Narrator	Teller of the story.	First, third person.
8 Life history	Account of life based on interviews and conversations.	Personal history, edited, complete, topical.
9 Case	An instance of a phenomenon.	Event, process.
10 Case history	History of an event or social process, not of a person.	Single, multiple, medical, legal.
11 Case study	Analysis and record of a single case.	Single, multiple.
12 Life story	A person's story of his or her life, or a part thereof.	Edited, complete, topical, fictional.
13 Self-story	Story of self in relation to an event.	Personal experience, story, fictional, true.
14 Personal experience	Stories about personal experience.	Single, multiple episode. Private or communal, folklore.
15 Oral history	Recollections of events, their causes and effects.	Work, musical, family.
16 Personal history	Reconstruction of life based on interviews and conversations.	Life history, life story.

Figure 7.1 Forms and varieties of the biographical method.[1]

[1]Drawn from Denzin (1989: 188)

Whenever you read the terms (used interchangeably), it is because the author is utilising aspects of both traditions. (The less charitable view of course is that he or she is simply unsure of the exact meaning and is having a bet 'each way'). Many social scientists prefer the term *life story* to designate the retrospective information itself without the corroborative document evidence often implied by *life* or *oral* history. Researchers using this method assume that informants can make sense of their past and that public records are not always meaningful or the most valid source of information. For example, if gerontologists wanted to understand the impact of ageing on Australian lives, they could examine and analyse statistical evidence derived from the Australian Bureau of Statistics or tabulate responses from surveys dealing with independence of the elderly. However, it is only from such life history interviews as provided by Blythe (1979) in *The View in Winter: Reflections on Old Age* that we vicariously experience the meanings of ageing in our society. We gain access by reading from the personal and subjective accounts given by the elderly about their lives and their perception of the progression from youth to old age.

A History of Life Histories

Life histories, as they are currently used in sociological research, follow the examples given in other disciplines particularly history, anthropology and clinical work (case histories). Each discipline focusses on the *individual case* for different reasons, in order to achieve different aims.

Oral History

The telling of one's life story is not unique to the social sciences. Most societies have some oral tradition of passing on information from one generation to the next. Autobiographies can be attested to even in ancient tomb inscriptions (Misch 1951). The use of oral evidence in historical research is not new. Much knowledge and information (evidence and data) in literate societies has been passed on by word of mouth. Throughout western history, from the Middle Ages until the beginning of the Enlightenment, there were very few examples of introspection about the nature and concept of one's inner self. Most personal accounts were documents either of 'memorable events (*memoirs*) of great deeds done (*resgestae*) or philosophers' lives' (Plummer 1983: 9). From the Renaissance and Enlightenment periods came the diaries of Samuel Pepys, and the autobiographies of Rousseau and Goethe. These latter documents were seemingly motivated by a search for an understanding of one's inner self. Later in the Victorian era, biographies became popular.

In Australia, the oral tradition was significant in Aboriginal life whereas written documentation was not. According to Douglas et al. (1988) Australia's first white settlers wrote a group of foundation narratives predominantly based on oral evidence. In the eighteenth and nineteenth centuries, historians also relied a great deal on oral evidence to write their accounts of history. Yet by the nineteenth century, when the writing of history became a professional occupation, the critical analysis of written documents became the preferred mode of 'doing history'. Oral sources of knowledge were spurned as limited, inadequate and biassed compared with the reliability of documents.

In the last forty years, this method has regained popularity for both theoretical and political reasons. In the 1960s, oral history in Australia developed as part of the increased interest in social history. There was a movement away from simply examining chronologies and biographies of great men and great events to a 'people's history'—an understanding of history through the eyes of ordinary folk by talking and listening to them. Their views were regarded as politically worthy. The examination of written documents coming from kings, queens and various social institutions was replaced by the methodology of oral history. (For a more detailed account of the development of oral history in Australia see Douglas et al. [1988] particularly chapter 1, from which this discussion has been drawn.)

Here it is sufficient to point out that oral history is currently flourishing. At least three significant oral-history projects were publicly funded in Australia in the 1980s. The *Migrant Oral Histories* project invited members of various ethnic groups to do their own recording under the direction of an experienced oral historian. This project was initially funded in 1984 by the New South Wales Ethnic Affairs Commission. At the same time the La Trobe Library funded an oral history project eliciting responses from the Chinese in Victoria (Douglas et al. 1988). One of the largest and most recent oral-history projects was established in 1985 at the federal level by the Community Employment program in conjunction with the National Library of Australia—*The Cultural Context of Unemployment: An Oral Record.* Over sixty people were employed to capture and document the personal experiences, traditions and contemporary culture of groups of the unemployed. These projects indicated, both in the political arena and the academic domain, a shift in what was and is regarded as legitimate historical evidence.

These developments in the discipline of history intersected with developments in the theory and practice of Australian sociology. The life histories which were produced by sociologists had a profound influence on the acceptance and encouragement of oral history within academic and non-academic history circles.

There has also been a modest spillover in the last fifteen to twenty years in the clinical research fields (for example, from nursing, occupational therapy and physiotherapy journals) as is shown by the increase in discussion of qualitative methods in general. As will be seen in the next chapter, clinical interviews have drawn on a combination of this model and the medical traditions.

Life History

The history model has been discussed above. The anthropological antecedent was **ethnography** in which researchers were also trying to illustrate a true-to-life picture of what people say and do in their own words. Psychology's use of the case history was also known to sociologists, particularly the works of Freud such as his accounts of 'Dora' and 'Little Hans' (Freud 1925).

Life History and Symbolic Interactionism

Over the last thirty years in Australian academic sociology, the symbolic interactionist perspective and the qualitative methods which came with it became very popular (Davies 1966; Bryson & Thompson 1972; Wild 1974; and Connell 1985). In sociology, the use of personal document and life history has been related to **symbolic interactionist** theory and to the perception that case histories, oral histories and life histories were useful in providing 'the salient experiences of a person's life and that person's definitions of those experiences' (Taylor & Bogdan 1984: 78). In fact, it has been argued (Schwartz and Jacobs 1979; Plummer 1983) that there is a fundamental affinity between the central tenets of symbolic interactionism and life-history research, especially in the legacy of the Chicago school of sociological thought and practice of the 1920s and 1930s. There are three theoretical assumptions which are common to life-history research and symbolic interactionism: (1) life is viewed as concrete experience; (2) life is regarded as an ever-emerging relativistic perspective; and (3) life is viewed as inherently marginal and ambiguous. The following discussion is drawn from Plummer (1983: 52).

Life as a Concrete Experience

This was central to the view of 'doing sociology' held by the Chicago sociologists. Their view held that there was no point in studying abstractions of individuals or of social life. Rather it was more pertinent to recognise that 'a separate individual is an abstraction unknown to experience, and so likewise is society when regarded as something apart from individuals. The real thing is human life' (Cooley 1956: 67). The central consequence of being concerned with life as concrete experience is that 'in every case of study, we must acknowledge that experiencing individuals can never be isolated from their functioning bodies and their constraining social worlds' (Plummer 1983: 54). The Chicago sociologists focussed on the necessity of considering the combination of a social and an individual phenomenon. Life-history research is in accord with this view because it is aimed at examining life as concrete experience.

Life as an Emergent Perspective

This is central to symbolic interactionist thought. The social world is seen as constantly changing and in a state of flux. W.I. Thomas' dictum 'If men [sic] define situations as real, they are real in their consequences' is applicable here. Human beings experience reality through their definitions of it. These definitions of the situation in turn alter in relation to their experience of it. 'The reality shifts with a person's life and people act towards things on the basis of their understandings, irrespective of the "objective" nature of those things' (Plummer 1983: 56). If we accept this view then it must be acknowledged that we can gain access to the objective world only through our precariously negotiated subjective views of it. These subjective views and conceptions of reality are inherent to the people who experience them. Thus, if one accepts these theoretical assumptions then the most central and fundamental source of knowledge is the personal document, the life history which elicits 'the sense of reality' that human beings hold about their own worlds.

Life as Ambiguous and Marginal

This is tied to the previously mentioned views. If we have taken one person's subjective reality seriously in a life history, and then consider it in relation to another persons', then there is always the possibility that ambiguity and incongruity will become evident in their definitions of the same situations. This is also related to the informants who have traditionally been chosen for such research particularly by members of the Chicago School. The informants are often from marginal groups—those with less credibility than other groups in social hierarchies; members of so-called deviant groups—thieves, trans-sexuals, the mentally retarded, the immigrant, and so on. As Plummer (1983) points out, the researcher using the life-history approach operates with these three assumptions, the first two leading them to study marginal groups 'whose voices may not be so readily heard'. This issue is discussed in more detail in chapter 10.

The message to the researcher was to move away from studying abstractions and get at the particular, the detailed and the experiential, that is, 'concrete human experience'. It was said that this allowed the researcher to grasp the ambiguities and inevitability of different perspectives, particularly those of marginal individuals and groups.

An Example of a Life History

The most well-known and discussed life history in sociology which is also claimed to be the first major one in the twentieth century was Thomas and Znaniecki's (1918–1920) *The Polish Peasant in Europe and America.*

The significance of this piece of research lay not in its size (originally five volumes) but in the use of the life-history method as a means of examining a social issue and its concern with developing social theory. Approximately one quarter of all immigrants to the United States between 1899 and 1910 were Polish. The impact of immigration, settlement, marginality, and community were questions of public concern. The method used by Thomas and Znaniecki was regarded as distinctive. The study included an abridged but major life-history statement made by a Polish peasant named Wladek, and then several other life histories; over 700 letters which were arranged into fifty series; third-person reports drawn from court records and social work agencies; documents collected through social agencies dealing with people who wished to emigrate from Poland and those arriving to settle in the USA; and a set of newspaper documentation taken from the archives of a Polish peasant newspaper. (See Plummer 1983 for a more detailed account.)

The use of the life-history method and the letters made this study famous. The same period gave rise to a number of life-history studies being done by American sociologists, (Anderson 1961, Burgess 1925, Cavan 1929, Park 1930, Shaw 1966, Sutherland 1937). There has been a revival of interest in the life-history method in sociology since the 1960s and 1970s at approximately the same time that symbolic interactionism was also coming into vogue. This is evidenced in the appearance of research methods texts such as Taylor and Bogdan's *Introduction to Qualitative Research Methods* (1984); N.K. Denzin's *The Research Act* (1970) and H. Schwartz and J. Jacobs *Qualitative Sociology* (1979). All these volumes dealt with qualitative methods which included life-history methods. Later, we have the appearance of Thompson's (1978) *The Voice of the Past* which examines the resurgence of interest in *oral history* and D. Bertaux's (1981) focus on the renewed interest in the *life story*.

The use of the labels *life history, oral history* and *ethnography* in Australia also indicates that the tradition of doing such research crosses disciplinary boundaries. The labels depend on whether the researcher is employed as historian, anthropologist, or sociologist. The use of this particular form of in-depth interviewing is evident in works such as A.F. Davies' *Private Politics* (1966) which was an examination of five Australians and their political socialisation; B. Wilson & J. Wynn's *Shaping Futures: Youth Action for Livelihood* (1987) which used four case studies to highlight attendant research on youth, education, work and inequality; Claire Williams' *Open Cut and The Working Class in an Australian Mining Town* (1981) and R.W. Connell's *Teacher's Work* (1985) which provides five personal accounts of teachers' perceptions of their lives in relation to their work.

Types of Life History

There are two basic approaches which underpin the type of life history the researcher might choose to carry out—the nomothetic approach or the idiographic approach.

The **nomothetic approach,** as discussed in chapter 2, is based on the idea that theoretical generalisations are drawn from systematic experimentation which usually employs statistical validation and on the idea that such generalisations should be applicable to *many* individuals. Researchers adopting a nomothetic approach believe that the life history or case study is only useful as a means of learning theoretical constructs in the social sciences or perhaps generating new discoveries. However, that is where their utility ends because they argue that one cannot generalise from single cases (Schwartz & Jacobs 1979).

On the other hand, the **idiographic approach**, as we defined it in chapter 3, advocates that it is *scientifically valid and methodologically correct* to examine the behaviour and/or perceptions of one individual as an independent totality. Generalisations may be developed from the individual's story. This approach stresses that the goal of the social sciences is *understanding* human behaviour and social realities not *quantifying* them. Schwartz and Jacobs point out that these two approaches can be seen as complementary so that 'in the course of acquiring and analysing the contents of a series of life histories, and searching for patterns *within* each one, the researcher may purposefully or serendipitously uncover patterns *between* them' (1979: 69). Whichever approach is adopted, it will inform the type of life history the researcher will engage in.

Several researchers (Allport 1942; Denzin 1989; Tagg 1988) assume that the variations can be encompassed in three essential forms of actual practice.

1 *The complete or comprehensive life history* which aims to incorporate the full range of the individual's life experiences. It is usually a long and complex account and is a rarity in research practice, for example R.W. White's *Lives in Progress: A Study of Natural Growth of Personality* (1975) in which he focusses on the overall flow of life of three people.
2 *The topical life history* which focusses on only one phase, aspect, or issue of the individual's life. This can take either the comprehensive or limited mode. *The comprehensive topical life history* mode does not try to focus on the full life history but

rather examines a particular issue. Good examples of this form of practice are Shaw's (1966) study of 'Stanley', examining his delinquency; Sutherland's depiction of *The Professional Thief* using Chic Conwell's information; Hughes' (1961) study of Janet Clark and her drug use; and Bogdan's (1974) research of Jane Fry's trans-sexuality. *The limited topical life history* is actually the same as the above form except that less material is covered. Usually these life histories will include more than one person per volume. For example, the Davies study (1966) of five people.

3 *The edited life history* may use either the topical or the complete life history. Comments and analysis by the researcher are then either interspersed with the narrative or in a combination which includes introductory passages and analytical commentary after the narrative, or incorporated in a combined form Examples of this include Wilson and Wyn's *Shaping Futures* (1987) and Connell's *Teacher's Work* (1985).

These three types of life history are differentiated in terms of the *aims of the research process* and what the researcher is looking for or trying to illustrate; and *the degree of intrusion* made by the researcher in the production of the final document.

Aims of Doing Life-history Research

The aims of the research process will inevitably influence the choice of research area and the type of research you choose to do. Glaser and Strauss (1977) have examined this issue in relation to doing life-history research. They point out that researchers need to decide whether they are producing a **case history** or a **case study.**

The *case history* has as its central goal the eliciting of the fullest possible story for *its own sake*, such as that of the mining community (Williams 1981) or the bushfire disaster (Eastop 1985). The case history is inductively evolved. The *case study* on the other hand tries to utilise personal documents, oral or written, for a theoretical purpose. You start with a theory or *analytic abstraction* and use the life history to illustrate or to verify some theoretical abstraction. An example of this is Douglas' (1967) use of suicide stories to lend validity to his version of suicide definitions.

Researcher Intrusion in the Life-history Document

The degree of researcher intrusion in the final document is the other distinguishing feature between types of life-history research. Such intrusion usually occurs in the process of interpreting the story and/or editing it.

Interpretation of a life-history document can occur at several stages and is predominantly done by the informant and the researcher. It can occur during the in-depth interview stage when the researcher listens to the informant and decides on what to ask next. Interpretation can also occur when the researcher decides on whether to use alternative sources of personal accounts such as letters, diaries, photos, etc. to accentuate or verify the story as told in the in-depth interview. Which of these elements he or she regards as significant is also a matter of interpretation. Obviously the informant is engaged in interpretation throughout the process by deciding what to mention or what to highlight. Finally, interpretation occurs in the written presentation of the life history.

Editing is the form that interpretation takes in the written presentation of life histories. It can range from minimal interpretation by the researcher where the raw data is presented *in toto* without any interpretive commentary, through to 'verification by anecdote' (Plummer 1983: 115) in which the researcher's theoretical understandings of a particular sociological problem are predominant. The informant's interviews or quotations drawn from them are used as examples to illustrate and highlight the theoretical position being argued.

The most crucial methodological issue confronting the researcher using the life-history method is the problem of *interpretation* and selection of data at all stages of the research process but particularly in the final publication. As has been pointed out by Allport, it is 'This process of interaction between theory and inductive material . . . [which] is the essence of the methodological problem with personal documents' (1942: 21).

Editing occurs in the presentation of all forms of life history. We have not yet found a publication of life history which did not use some form of editing. This can range from simply cutting out the verbal repetitions and the *ums* and *ahs*, to extensive cutting of the account and arrangement in chronological sequence, to the use of selected quotes to accentuate theoretical arguments. Plummer notes in his discussion of this issue that,

> The Polish Peasant story was twice as long in its original form, the Letters from Jenny were abridged to approximately one third of their original length . . . Don, the Sun Chief's 8,000 page diary was reduced (for publication purposes) to one fifth of its original length (1983: 108).

In many cases, editing is carried out with the purpose of easing the work of the reader. The researcher attempts to make the life-history interview a more communicable experience on the page by reformatting the text which is then used as the major empirical component of the research (Bertaux and Bertaux-Wiame 1981; Chalasinki 1981). In other cases, the researcher does a great deal more in editing the material. Connell, in his examination of school teachers, makes comments about the necessity to maintain confidentiality, and says that to do this, he and his colleagues felt constrained not to 'print actual biographies, even names, dates and places are changed' (1985: 3). We feel it is worthwhile reading his rationale as an example.

> Given the rule of confidentiality under which this research was done, we did not feel entitled to print actual biographies, even with names, dates and places changed. Yet as we worked through the evidence it seemed more and more important, for readers' understanding of the social processes we were studying, to convey in the published report the sense of biography, the way things hang together and take shape (and sometimes fall out of shape) in teachers' lives. As a slightly uneasy compromise, I have settled for constructing composite biographies, which are presented in Part One. Every detail in them comes from the interviews, but they come in each chapter from more than one. 'Terry Petersen', 'Rosa Marshall' and the others are therefore not real people. But I think reading chapters 1–5 as if they were, will give more insight into the lives of the actual teachers from whom the evidence comes than would a topic-by-topic, cross-sectional presentation of the same evidence (Connell 1985: 3).

Doing Life-history Research

The actual research processes used in life-history research involve the same issues as outlined in chapter 5 as well as issues relating to the researcher's choice of informant and the inclusion of alternative sources of data (other than the in-depth interview).

As can be seen in Figure 7.2, there are innumerable variations to choose from when one engages in doing life history research.

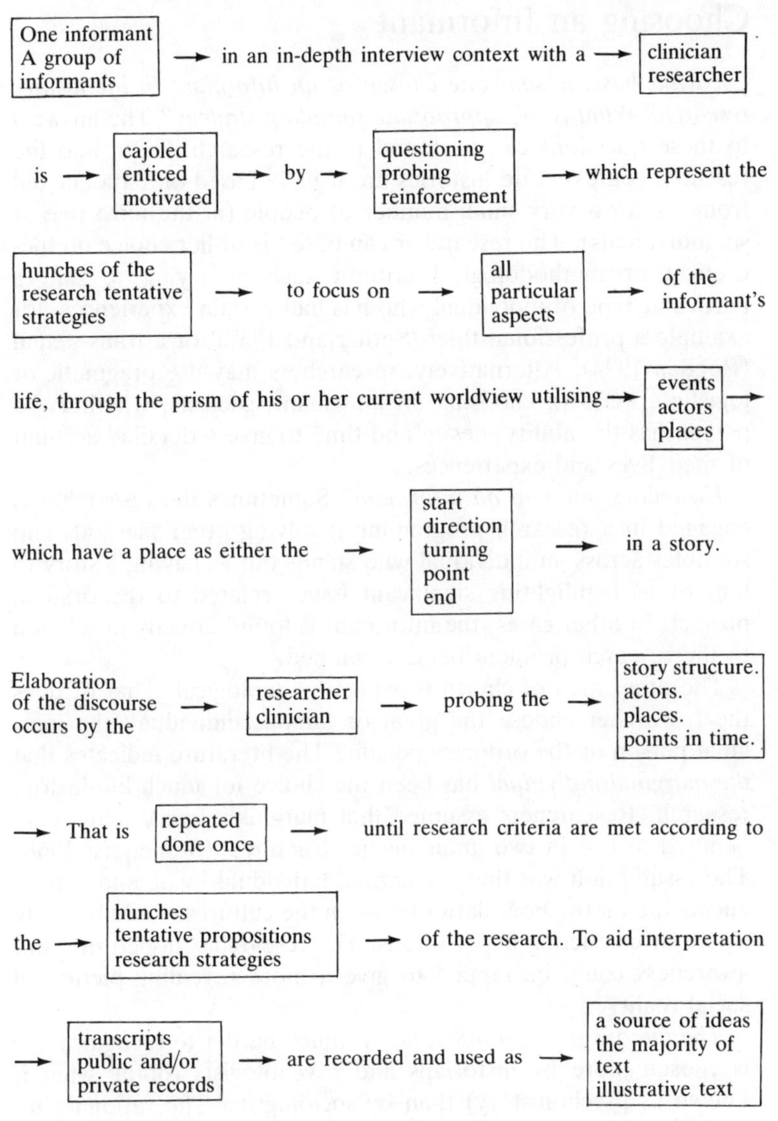

One informant
A group of
informants
in an in-depth interview context with a
clinician
researcher
is
cajoled
enticed
motivated
by
questioning
probing
reinforcement
which represent the
hunches of the
research tentative
strategies
to focus on
all
particular
aspects
of the
informant's
life, through the prism of his or her current worldview utilising
events
actors
places
which have a place as either the
start
direction
turning
point
end
in a story.
Elaboration
of the discourse
occurs by the
researcher
clinician
probing the
story structure.
actors.
places.
points in time.
That is
repeated
done once
until research criteria are met according to
the
hunches
tentative propositions
research strategies
of the research. To aid interpretation
transcripts
public and/or
private records
are recorded and used as
a source of ideas
the majority of
text
illustrative text
in the analysis and publication of the research.

Figure 7.2 Variations of doing life history research.[1]

[1]Drawn from Tagg (1985)

Choosing an Informant

On what basis is someone chosen as an informant in life-history research? What is the appropriate sampling strategy? The answers to these questions can be found in the research design and the research context. Life histories are usually based on data elicited from one or a very small number of people (at the most five or six individuals). The researcher can base his or her choice on theoretical or methodological criteria such as trying to find a particular type of individual who has had certain experiences, for example a professional thief (Sutherland 1937), or a trans-sexual (Bogdan 1974). Alternatively, researchers may use pragmatic or logistic criteria in choosing an informant, such as, whether the person has the ability, desire and time to give a detailed account of their lives and experiences.

How does one find an informant? Sometimes the researcher is engaged in a research programme involving other methods and stumbles across an individual who stands out as having a story to tell, or as highlighting significant issues related to the original project. In other cases, the informant is found directly in relation to the research problem being examined.

The other area of choice is explicitly ideological. That is, does the researcher choose the great or famous individual, the marginal person or the ordinary person? The literature indicates that *the marginal individual* has been the choice for much life-history research. Researchers assumed that marginality was being 'condemned to live in two antagonistic structures' (Stonequist 1961). The assumption was that a marginal individual living and experiencing life on the boundaries between the cultures would be more aware of conflicting expectations. The researcher hoped that this awareness could be tapped to give a more revealing picture of social reality.

The famous or great individual is much harder to recognise and is chosen more by historians and psychologists (doing what is known as psychohistory) than by sociologists. The rationale for choosing such an informant is that they can illuminate the issues, values and crises of a particular time due to their significance in that era. Erikson's case histories of Luther, Gandhi and Hitler (Erikson 1959) are well-known examples of this approach. A more recent example is psychologist Graham Little's (1989) publication of his television interviews with currently famous individuals in Australian society.

Choosing an ordinary person as an informant is not as simple a task as one might think. After all, how do you define someone as *ordinary*? The actual basis for choosing someone as a life-history informant, using the idiographic approach, is that there is something unique about them (Plummer 1983; Schwartz & Jacobs 1979). However, sociologists have sought out those informants who are not particularly famous or marginal (as Connell chose teachers, and Wilson and Wyn chose teenagers). The oral historian often tries to choose an ordinary person for ideological reasons. Part of the popularity and resurgence of oral history as a research method at present is tied to the political and ethical concern with expanding knowledge of the interpretations of ordinary people in contrast to an earlier emphasis on the wealthy or famous.

The most significant factor about choosing an informant, maintaining a relationship with that informant and publishing his or her life history is that the person be someone who is *aware of, informed about and involved in* his or her own cultural world and able to articulate his or her own views. This is what the researcher can define as *a good informant*.

Data Gathering

There are three major modes of data gathering when doing life histories.

1 Soliciting narratives.
2 In-depth interviewing of many sessions.
3 Use of multiple research strategies which may or may not include 1 and 2.

Soliciting narratives

In chapter 4, we said that soliciting a narrative account from an informant is often used to gain access to the person's story either through the **log-interview method** or the **life-grid approach.** Diaries of a more extended nature than log interviews have also been used to good effect but they have been used more often by psychologists and anthropologists than sociologists. Anthropologists and sociologists found it difficult to legitimate such usage as scientific, whereas psychologists argued that such methods directly revealed the subject matter in which they dealt. The assumption by researchers incorporating this data is that it provides a daily record of events which are regarded as significant by the informant. These are two of the three ways in which diaries are used. The third is an analysis of a single day in the life of the informant.

In-Depth Interviewing as Life History

The nature of in-depth interviewing when it is used to elicit life-history information is not different from anything described in chapter 5. However, the researcher usually needs many more interview sessions. Establishing and maintaining good relations with the informant is vital to success. The life-history in-depth interview is also more dependent on tape-recording so that a full account is available and the relationship between researcher and informant is not overly hampered by detailed note-taking. The conversation between researcher and informant in the life-history interview is often dominated by the voice of the informant. This is sometimes difficult for the informant to get used to because his or her perception of an interview is one in which the researcher asks lots of questions and the informant simply answers them. The researcher needs to facilitate story telling as in Askham's model delineated in chapter 5. To do this, he or she must create a situation in which the informant not only feels at ease but wants to discuss details in full.

One strategy for extracting further detail is the **informal post interview.** The researcher ties up loose ends by thanking the informant, going over some or all of their discussions in an informal manner, and checking on the informant's feelings about the sessions and the extent to which they made clear what they were trying to say. In effect, the informal post-interview chat is an attempt to make some checks on the validity of the account according to the informant's perception.

A number of ethical considerations are raised by life-history research such as, 'Who owns the account or holds copyright?', 'What does the informant get out of participating in the research process?'. In addition, there are the other usual issues of confidentiality, anonymity and control. These issues are discussed in detail in chapter 10.

Use of Multiple Research Strategies

There are a number of sources the researcher can use to elicit personal accounts which do not rely on in-depth interviewing. Denzin (1989) points out that life histories can use any record or document, including the case histories of social agencies, if they throw light on the subjective behaviour of individuals or groups. This same point is made somewhat more expansively by Plummer (1983) who lists nine sources of personal accounts which include life histories and oral histories. He aptly calls them 'documents of life'. We agree with his assertion that life history 'at its best' incorporates in-depth interviewing with intensive observation of the informant's life, interviews with the informant's friends and/or family, and access to and analysis of pertinent 'documents of life' such as diaries, personal letters and photographs.

Life-history researchers may employ more than one form of personal document. We have already mentioned in-depth interviewing, solicited narratives, diaries and letters. These accounts may be used individually or together to provide a cohesive or more informative description of the life experiences of the informant. Alternative sources of data are also available to the researcher. The researcher may decide to use questionnaire data in the same way as the diary- or log-interview method, that is, to help initiate the interviews. Photographs, films, self-observations and possessions can also be used to provide data for cross-checking against interview material. Systematic self-observation can also be used, although it is often regarded as not being adequately scientific (see chapter 2). According to Plummer 'We can never *really* know another's world, we might *just* know our own' (1983: 34). The example he cites is Anderson's publication of *The Hobo*. Anderson used his own life experience as a member of a hobo family to inform his research even though he did not admit or discuss this until much after the publication.

The informant's possessions may be used as talking points to trigger discussion with the informant. They can be examined as a means of identifying the significance that individual informants attach to them and to the events or people which they symbolise. Films and photos can be utilised in the same manner. Another factor which should be taken into account is that informants may emphasise or de-emphasise their own role in difficult periods of their lives depending on how they wish to present themselves and so on. As stated earlier, the researcher will recognise this possibility and in some instances may wish to cross-check information to define a *true account* according to the informant's subjective reconstruction.

Utility of Life Histories

The significance and utility of the life history in sociology is based on the central tenet that it provides 'an account of individual experience which reveals the individual's actions as a human agent and as a participant in social life' (Blumer 1939: 29).

Yet, there is more to it than that. In many ways, the life history is a means of focussing on the relationship between biography, structure and history. It is unique as a form of social research because it can actually encompass those features of social life by dealing with concrete human experiences such as *talk, feelings and action* as they occur within the constraints of the social structure. The social structure is unique to the historical period in which the informant lives. The constant criticism of life histories has been that they are too individualistic, neglect history and are therefore not theoretically useful. This criticism has been made without taking into account that the life history enables us to view the *totality* of the biographical experience.

> This totality enables us to see an individual in relation to the history of their time, and how he or she is influenced by the religious, social, psychological, political and economic ideas available to them in their world. It enables us to perceive the intersection of the life history of human beings with the history of their society, thus enabling us to comprehend and develop theories about the choices, contingencies and options open to the individual as they move through history and structure (Plummer 1983: 69).

In addition, it must be pointed out that life histories constitute a significant strategy in incorporating history within the theoretical framework of symbolic interactionism. Plummer argues that this is achieved by the dual focus that occupies life-history research—'The changing biographical history of the person and the social history of his or her lifespan' (1983: 70). This is evident in the three modes of life histories: *the oral history* in which the historical problem rather than the biography becomes the key issue; *the 'career' approach* which is derived from symbolic interactionism and focusses on the changing meaning of an individual's life course as he or she moves through personal crises side by side with a given age cohort in an evolving historical culture; and the *psychohistory* approach which consists of two streams. The first stream, following Erikson and Lifton's work, examines the 'great men' [sic] of the period in order to illustrate that the concerns of the historical period are mirrored in the concerns of these 'great men' [sic] (see Plummer 1983). The second stream focusses on shared psychohistorical themes such as those things which are regarded as collective symbols of an historical period. Lifton's examination of the collective trauma of the survivors of Hiroshima (*Death in Life*) is a good example.

Social Processes and Social Change

Life histories enable the researcher to examine the ambiguities and inconsistencies which are a part of everyday experience. Most social scientists speak of social change, social process and the constant state of flux in which human beings interact. Many researchers using attitude scales or questionnaires end up providing accounts of social reality which are far more ordered, rational and unambiguous than the way in which we experience it. It is with life history that the researcher can capture some of the ambiguity that is evident in our lives. As Becker so succinctly points out '. . . sociologists like to speak of on-going processes and the like but their methods usually prevent them from seeing the processes they talk about so glibly' (1966: xiii).

Glossary

Autobiography Life story written by oneself.
Biographical life history A life history in which information is elicited from the informant detailing his or her individual development.
Case history The history of an individual in which the informant or client is asked questions so that the clinician can determine a more fitting analysis of the informant's state of health in the light of past experiences.
Case study The collection of data, both formal and anecdotal, on a single individual or single social unit (for example, family), with all available evidence from records, observations, and interviews used for a theoretical purpose.
Editing A form of interpretation and rewriting of given texts.

Ethnography The direct observation of the activity of members of a particular social group, and the description and evaluation of such activity, constitute ethnography. This research technique is used predominantly by anthropologists, sociologists and psychologists.
Idiographic approach Refers to the individual case or event. In single system strategies, idiographic refers to any system for the assessment of behaviour or performance derived from a particular individual rather than from the average of many individuals' performance.
Informal post interview A conversation between researcher and informant in which the researcher ties up loose ends by thanking the informant and going over some or all of their discussions in an informal manner in an attempt to make some checks on the validity of the account according to the informant's perception.
Life-grid approach One which the researcher provides a means of aiding the informant to write down their life story. This is usually in the form of a diagrammatic representation such as a grid. For example, the grid might have sixty rows representing the informant's years of life, and columns could represent areas of change. It is a diagram version of a diary.
Life history The history of an individual's life given by the person living it and solicited by the researcher. It can be drawn from in-depth interviewing and/or solicited narratives and personal documents.
Log-interview method One in which informants keep a running record of their activities for a specified period of time. This is then used to provide a basis for in-depth interviews.
Nomothetic approach In behavioural science research, nomothetic refers to any system for the assessment of behaviour or performance which is based on the average of many individuals' performance.
Oral history The aim in oral history is to gain information about the past. It includes retrospective information and corroborative evidence. It is the recollection of events, their causes and effects.
Symbolic interactionism A sociological perspective that emphasises the centrality of meaning in interaction. It is the study of the self-society relationship as a process of symbolic communication between people.

References

Abercrombie, N., Hill, S. & Turner, B. 1988. *The Penguin Dictionary of Sociology*. Harmondsworth: Penguin Books.

Allport, G.W. (ed.) 1965. *Letters from Jenny*. London: Harcourt Brace Jovanovich.
Anderson, N. 1961. *The Hobo*. Chicago: University of Chicago Press.
—— 1975. *The American Hobo: An Autobiography*. Leiden: E.J. Brill.
Becker, H.S. 1963. *Outsiders: Studies in the Sociology of Deviance*. New York: Free Press of Glencoe.
—— 1971. 'Introduction.' to 'The Jack Roller.' by Clifford Shaw, in H.S. Becker (ed.). *Sociological Work*. London: Allen Lane.
Bertaux, D. (ed.) 1981. *Biography and Society: The Life History Approach in the Social Sciences*. Beverly Hills: Sage.
Bertaux, D. & Bertaux-Wiame, I. 1981 'Life Stories in the Bakers' trade.', in D. Bertaux (ed.). *Biography and Society: The Life History Approach in the Social Sciences*. Beverly Hills: Sage.
Blummer, H. 1939. *An Appraisal of Thomas and Znaniecki's 'The Polish Peasant in Europe and America'*. New York: Social Science Research Council.
Blythe, R. 1979. *The View in Winter: Reflections on Old Age*. London: Allen Lane.
Bogdan, R. 1974. *Being Different: The Autobiography of Jane Fry* London: Wiley.
Bremmer, M., Brow, J. & Canter, D. 1985. *The Research Interview: Uses and Approaches*. London: Academic Press.
Bryson, L. & Thompson, F. 1972. *An Australian Newtown: Life and Leadership in a Working Class Suburb*. Melbourne: Kibble Books.
Burgess, E.W. 1925. 'What social case records should contain to be useful for sociological interpretation.', *Social Force* No. 6: 524–32.
Cavan, R.S. 1929. 'Topical summaries of current literature: interviewing for life history material.', *American Journal of Sociology* 15: 100–15.
Chalasinski, J . 1981. 'The life records of the young generation of Polish peasants as a manifestation of contemporary culture.', in D. Bertaux (ed.). *Biography and Society*. London: Sage.
Chambliss, B. 1972. *Box Man: A Professional Thiefs' Journal* (by Harry King as told to and edited by Bill Chambliss). New York: Harper and Row.
Connell, R.W. 1985. *Teachers' Work*. Sydney: George Allen & Unwin.
Cooley, C.H. 1956. *Human Nature and the Social Order*. Glencoe, Ill: The Free Press.
Davies, A.F. 1966. *Private Politics: A Study of Five Political Outlooks*. Carlton: Melbourne University Press.
Denzin, N.K. 1970. *Sociological Methods: A Sourcebook*. London: Butterworth.
Denzin, N.K. 1970. *The Research Act*. Chicago: Aldine.
—— 1989. *The Research Act*. Third edition. Chicago: Aldine.
Dollard J. 1935. *Criteria for the Life History: with Analysis of Six Notable Documents*. New Haven, Connecticut: Yale University Press.
Douglas, J.D. 1967. *The Social Meaning of Suicide*. Princeton: Princeton University Press.
Douglas, L., Roberts, A. & Thompson, R. 1988. *Oral History: A Handbook*. Sydney: Allen & Unwin.
Eastop, L.W. 1985. *A study of the attitudes of people who had been 'burned out' in the Ash Wednesday Bushfire*. Unpublished paper, Monash University, Clayton, Vic.

Freud, S 1925. *Case Histories: 'Dora' and 'Little Hans,'* Vol. 8. The Penguin Freud Library, Harmondsworth: Penguin.
Glaser, B.G. & Strauss, A.L. 1967. *The Discovery of Grounded Theory: Strategies for Qualitative Research.* Chicago: Aldine.
Heilman, S. 1980. 'Jewish Sociologist: Native-As-Stranger.', *The American Sociologist* Vol. 15: 100–108.
Hughes, H.M. 1961. *The Fantastic Lodge: The Autobiography of a Girl Drug Addict.* Boston: Houghton-Mifflin.
Lifton, R.J. 1968. *Death in Life.* New York: Random House.
——1973. *Home from the War.* New York: Simon and Schuster.
Little, G. 1989. *Speaking For Myself.* Melbourne: McPhee Gribble Publishing.
Mann, M. (ed.) 1987. *Macmillan Student Encyclopedia of Sociology.* Fourth edition. London: Macmillan Press.
Misch, G. 1951. *A History of Autobiography in Antiquity,* tr., E.W. Dickes, 2 vols. Cambridge, Massachusetts: Harvard University Press.
Park, R.E. 1930. 'Murder and the Case Study Method.', *American Journal of Sociology* Vol. 36. November: 447–454.
Plummer, K. 1983. *Documents of Life: An Introduction to the Problems and Literature of a Humanistic Method.* Sydney: Allen & Unwin.
Schwartz, H. & Jacobs, J. 1979. *Qualitative Sociology: A Method to the Madness.* London: Collier Macmillan.
Shaw, C.R. 1966. *The Jack Roller: A Delinquent Boy's Own Story.* Chicago: University of Chicago Press.
Spradley, J.P. 1979. *The Ethnographic Interview.* London: Holt, Rinehart and Winston.
Stonequist, E.V. 1961. *The Marginal Man: A Study in Personality and Culture Conflict.* New York: Russell and Russell.
Sutherland, E.H. 1937. *The Professional Thief by a Professional Thief.* University of Chicago: Phoenix Books.
Tagg, S.K. 1985. 'Life Story Interviews and Their Interpretation.', in M. Brenner et al. (eds). *The Research Interview: Uses and Approaches.* London: Academic Press.
Taylor, S.J. & Bogdan, R. 1984. *Introduction to Qualitative Research Methods: The Search for Meanings.* Second edition. New York: John Wiley and Sons.
Terkel, S. 1970. *Hard Times: An Oral History of the Great Depression.* London: Allen Lane.
—— 1977. *Working.* Harmondsworth: Penguin.
Thomas, W.I. & Znaniecki, F. 1958. *The Polish Peasant in Europe and America.* New York: Dover Publications (Orginal editions published 1918–20).
Thompson, P. 1978. *The Voice of the Past: Oral History.* Oxford: Opus Books, Oxford University Press.
White, R.W. 1975. *Lives in Progress: A Study of Natural Growth of Personality.* Third edition. New York: Holt, Rinehart and Winston.
Wild, R.A. 1974. *Bradstow: A Study of Class Status and Power in a Small Australian Town.* Sydney: Angus & Robertson.
Williams, C. 1981. *Open Cut and the Working Class in an Australian Mining Town.* Sydney: Allen & Unwin.
Wilson, B. & Wynn, J. 1987. *Shaping Futures: Youth Action for Livelihood.* Sydney: Allen & Unwin.

Chapter 8 The Clinical Interview

IT'S NOT
THE FRACTURES
......
IT'S THE FAMILY

Defining the Clinical Interview

By *clinical interview*, we mean interviews which take place in the clinic. And by *clinic* we mean some professional setting in an institution, agency, or surgery; or some encounter in which both parties understand that one of them is there as a representative of some such institution. The clinical interview is understood by all parties concerned as a mode of discovering information, part of the professional practice of one of the participants. In that sense, the clinical interview is an interview conducted by a recognised *clinician,* regardless of whether all, or any of it, takes place within some designated clinical building.

Having defined the clinic, we can now say that the clinical interview is a part of *applied social science.* In particular, it is an applied in-depth interview, hence its inclusion in this book. This book is devoted to the in-depth interview, and argues throughout that the in-depth interview is the best way (or one of the best) to investigate people's minds. But in the practice of applying the general principles of the in-depth interview to clinical work, various adjustments have to be made: especially theory which gets bent in the practice of being applied. This separate chapter exists mainly to show how the bending takes place, and how to do it well.

We have already described in previous chapters how to go about doing an in-depth interview. In this chapter, we are going to confine ourselves to how one might adapt the techniques previously described to the applied clinical setting. But before we do that, we must look at the ways in which the clinical interview differs from the research interview, as well as the ways in which it is the same. In passing, we discuss a number of other ways, derived from other sources, of conceptualising the clinical interview—in our view, these other approaches are somewhat misleading. However, we must discuss them in order to get them out of the way.

The Clinical Interview is the Same as the Research Interview

The clinical interview, we have said, is an applied piece of social research using the in-depth interview as its research technique. That implies, given what we have said in earlier chapters of this book, that it will take an open loose-textured form to facilitate the holistic interpretation which is such an interview's aim. It may have a **protocol**, but any such protocol will be determined largely by the course of the interview itself, rather than by the prior expectations or interpretations made either by interviewer or client.

The questions asked will be *open-ended* and *recursive* as we defined those terms in the previous chapter. That is, they will not close off the possible range of responses, and their form will often be determined by previous responses.

The aims of the interview will be subject to change at any time during its course. So will the meaning ascribed to the statements of the client (and of the clinician for that matter) as the interview proceeds. The interview will acknowledge throughout that its process is one of inter-subjective interaction and interpretation, just like any other well-conducted in-depth interview.

The Clinical Interview is Different from the Research Interview

This process of inter-subjective interaction which we mentioned above is likely to be more complex in the clinical interview than in the in-depth interview directed at research. The aims of the participants in the research interview are likely to be relatively simple, **symmetrical** and mutually congruent: the researcher wants to understand what is going on, and—more or less—the informant wants to tell the researcher. For instance, the researcher wants to know what it feels like to have a diagnosis of breast cancer, and the woman with the diagnosis tries to tell her. Of course, both of them may have other, extra or hidden agendas for the interview, and these may make it hard enough for the two of them to find and hold onto one another's wavelengths, but usually both understand fairly well what they (both) are about.

In the clinical interview, however, there are apt to be *systematic* differences of perception between the two in terms of both the aims and meaning of the interview. For instance, the client or patient may be sure that she has heart trouble (her mother had it too at the same age) and that the solution to her problem is to be put on Workcare before death has a chance to deprive her of a chance to further her career in retailing. The clinician, on the other hand, sees her as having terminal breast cancer, and as a success for diagnosis, a problem for medical research, and a failure for chemotherapy. In the clinician's eyes, she has the personal and social problem of coming to terms with her imminent death as quickly as possible. They are both therefore likely to misunderstand what the other is saying, and why they are saying it. (The dialogues quoted from Taylor in chapter 1, are painful instances of such mutual struggles towards comprehension.) In this way, they resemble domestic disagreements over sex or annual holidays. Instances like the above one in which the patient has made her own diagnosis and determination of treatment are only extreme forms of the chronic problems of translation and **negotiation** which occur in all social interactions.

Expertise

In the research interview, there is a general presumption that the informant has the required information which the researcher lacks. The researcher may add a few details, but essentially his or her aim is to interpret the experiences of the informant by placing that informant in a social and theoretical context which may be of little or no interest to them. In the traditional textbook version, the informant provides the data and the researcher provides the explanation, so allowing a neat division of expertise between them. The client at least is the expert on himself or herself.

In the clinical interview, as in other types of in-depth interviewing, this neat division between data-expert and interpretation-expert breaks down. The clinician may see something straight away about the client—'Have you noticed that your eyes are bright yellow?'—which supplements the facts supplied by the client, alters their interpretation, and sharpens the aims of the client from a general desire to feel less awful, to having his or her illness treated. All this depends on clinician and client negotiating a shared perception of the facts as they go along. The client for instance agrees that he or she has been feeling very weak and feverish since dining at the restaurant last Saturday, acknowledges that he or she has a temperature, volunteers that he or she has not had hepatitis before, and accepts the volunteered knowledge of the clinician that he or she has both signs and symptoms of hepatitis.

Using the Expert's Authority

It is clear too from this example that the expertise of the clinician has a different import to the expertise of the research interviewer. The clinician's opinion makes a big difference to how the client sees his or her world, and to how he or she achieves goals within it. Their interaction is not simply a meeting of minds; it depends on a shared understanding that the beliefs and aims of both will *change and develop*. Indeed the expectation of learning has always to be counted as part of the aims of both parties in a way which is not always true of the research interview.

Finally, this growth towards change and development in the participants' belief structures is directed towards *action*. The clinician's expertise is legitimated by the State, and carries with it a license to *treat*, that is, to act on the client's body or property or social circumstances. We have already discussed, in chapter 2, the general role played by science in legitimating professional membership and practice. Now we see the in-depth interview itself providing part of the legitimation of clinical work. The clinician is licensed to collect the information, and certified by his or her education as being capable of doing it well.

The client may resent the fact of the clinician's licence to act, may try to ignore it, or try to coerce the clinician into trying to do things the client's way; but none of this can alter the asymmetry of social legitimacy: the clinician is the expert in a way that the client is not.

Signs and Symptoms

Medical writers often distinguish between **signs** and **symptoms** in discussing the information gathered in a clinical interview. Signs are the pieces of information collected by the clinician, regardless of whether they have been noticed by the patient. Symptoms are the pieces of information noticed by the patient; in that sense, they define the problem, at least at first. They have their meaning within the personal world of the client: the signs have a meaning within the worldview of the clinician.

We think this distinction between signs and symptoms is a useful one for dividing the *origins* of the pieces of information used in the interview. It is not useful as a way of indicating how they might be used. Both signs and symptoms have to be evaluated and used within the belief-systems of both client and clinician. Ultimately, those belief-systems must come to coincide for effective diagnosis and treatment to occur, and in that process signs and symptoms will become assimilated to one another.

Dialectical Processes in the Interview

It is clear from the above examples that the clinical interview proceeds by mutual exchange, each step depending on the previous ones. In this sense, it has an intrinsically **dialectical process.**

Of course, the argument of this book is that all meaningful conversations proceed in this way; but the clinical interview has a stepwise dialectic of a very forceful kind. The clinician may from the start have a general aim to exercise his or her expertise, and the client a general aim to experience it. But for such expertise and experience to occur, the client needs to disclose the facts as he or she experiences them (the *symptoms*), the clinician needs to collect information possibly unsuspected by the client (*signs* like having yellow eyes), make a preliminary interpretation, elicit further signs and symptoms, share further possible interpretation with the client, and discuss possible courses of action with him or her. In this dialectical process, the meaning of each step depends on the preceding ones. The only fixed assumptions are that full information is needed to act correctly, and the clinician is State-licensed to act correctly. A prior assumption which of course is open to question is that the clinician will interpret correctly. This issue is raised in more detail in chapter 9.

Process Models Versus Goal Models

A distinction has often been made between the *goals* of the interview, on the one hand, and the *process* of the interview on the other. According to us, the goal of the in-depth interview is the understanding of the world of the informant by the researcher. The goal of the clinical version of the in-depth interview is the development of a shared understanding of the world of the client, leading to concerted action by both clinician and client to alter that world for the better.

The process of the in-depth interview is one of testing and negotiating theories about the meaning of the informant's world. We have already said that the process of the clinical interview is a dialectic in which the interviewer contributes facts as well as interprets them. This process will be one of accumulating facts and increasingly sharpening and redefining therapeutic aims.

Positivist Models of the Clinical Interview

We have discussed in previous chapters, especially in chapter 2, the positivist desire for algorithms and set procedures as guarantees of scientific legitimacy. It is not surprising that in the clinical literature, this desire often appears as a taste for checklists and step-by-step procedures. Our attitude to such desires has two parts. Firstly, these are a very good way of checking out causal hypotheses about clients, where there is no question about making any fundamental reassessment of scientific truth, but only of applying conventional truths in a conventional way to the client's particular case.

Secondly, checklists and fixed routines provide a poor way to reach interpretive understanding of anyone, and are likely to lead the interviewer into a false sense of security, believing that understanding has been achieved because the standard procedures have been followed. The best they could safely provide would be a heuristic reminder that we should not jump to conclusions too soon about what the client is on about; we should move from areas of neutral and unalarming detail towards more important matters only after we have established rapport with our client; we should observe a general movement from sharing facts to sharing decisions; and we should be conscious at every stage of the need to negotiate the client's understanding of, and consent to, our clinical decisions.

These recommendations may seems harmless enough, and possibly bland and useless too. On the other hand, we are very conscious that most nostrums for conduct of the clinical interview which occur in the published literature have about them a spurious air of professionalism, and in fact work to close off our receptivity to *what the client is actually saying and doing.*

Most such models of the clinical interview are taken either from medical practice or from the practice of counselling. We should get these out of the way as paths we should not take.

The Medical Interview

Here the goal is to elicit facts about the patient that the physician needs to know as a basis for treatment. To a large, though not complete extent, the patient is a biased and ignorant witness to his or her own body processes; he or she is a collaborator whom the doctor cannot do without. No doubt the body of the patient works as a system, but it is a causal system having very little relation to the logical system of the patient's mind. The correct analogy here is with the driver who takes his or her car to the mechanic for advice and repairs. True, the *'car'* here is the *'driver's' own body*, but we have very little more privileged expertise about our bodies than we do about our cars.

Nor can there be any question of the patient's illness being such-and-such because he or she *thinks* it is such-and-such. For the clinician in a medical setting, there is only the reality as seen by him or her and his or her colleagues. There is no question of an inter-subjective reality negotiated between clinician and client. In this sense, the clinical practice of medicine is a simply applied natural science. If the patient takes a different view of the value of his or her own opinions and self-diagnosis, then the doctor may humour him or her with the best possible grace, but humour the patient he or she does nevertheless.

Checklists

Seen in this way, it becomes clear why medical clinicians place so much emphasis on *checklists of symptoms* and on what we might call **bleaching the interpretation** of the patient: for instance, when the patient says he or she had pneumonia last year, the clinician should not simply accept this account, but conservatively conclude that the patient was sick, probably with a high temperature, at some time in the recent past, perhaps last year, perhaps not; and may have received treatment then. Bleaching the interpretation of the client, then, is as matter of redescribing symptoms in a manner as neutral as possible.

Symptom checklists make sense from the point of view of causal explanation. There are only so many probable illnesses, and each is defined in terms of a handful of discrete (separable) symptoms; so by collecting lists of symptoms, it should be possible to decide within limits what the illness of the patient is. Bleaching the interpretations of the client is of course a necessary preliminary step to making this clinical decision. The background to this procedure is the one we have seen before in previous chapters: causal explanation allows us to a large extent to fragment the evidence and to deal with experience in separate parcels.

None of this will apply of course to the attitude of the patient to his or her illness, nor to large parts of psychiatry. This is precisely because we are dealing there with the holistic aspects of people's minds. This is not to say that this has always been understood in medical training or practice. Neither is this to say that there should be no place in non-medical clinical practice for checklists or for taking a detached view of the client's memory or the validity of his or her interpretations. Because the client knows that he or she has a problem and you have a role to play, it is likely that the stories you hear in the clinic will have recurrent *themes;* and checklists will often give you a quick way of eliciting them. But, for holistic work, checklists can never have more than a loose, heuristic value. It is often alarming to see clinicians who confidently believe that going through their checklist with the client constitutes most of their diagnostic work.

Clinical Objectivity

Medical training also stresses the value of detached, objective observation, leading to publicly inspectible records. To do this, is of course, simply to reach for the goals of valid and reliable measures which we summarised in chapter 2. This is a perfectly legitimate aim of causal explanation, which as we have seen is precisely what medical explanation is. But we must remember that this kind of public objectivity is just what we cannot hope for in holistic explanation. To aim for it there would be to apply the right standard to the wrong material. Medical explanation is a good form of explanation in itself, but a bad model for other clinical work.

Often though, the clinician will be imitating the information-collecting path of the medical interview. That is, he or she will partly be interested in how the world or the client's body *is,* not in *how the client sees it.* So far as that can be discovered without aid of the client, a search for neutral bleached information will be appropriate. What he or she does will be similar to taking a case history, rather than a personal life history or oral history of the client of the kind we describe in chapter 7. For the purposes of taking a case history—so far as the client is the source of information about physical or social facts—the clinician will master the client's interpretation only to dispense with it. The clinical interview will be concerned then with a hybrid of causal and interpretive explanations.

The Counselling Interview

In some ways, the counselling model is at the opposite pole to the medical interview. Especially (but not only) with Freudian approaches to psychotherapy, enormous emphasis is placed on allowing the client time to unfold his or her own story in his or her own way. Obviously, this fits in very nicely with the holistic approach we are taking here. We have two reservations about it, however. These are, first, that counselling usually allows a very small place to providing or feeding back information or attitudes to the client; second, that most counselling theory plays down the goal of understanding in favour of talking about such personal attributes of the therapist as warmth and liveliness.

In most counselling, at least as conventionally described, most of the information provided in the interview flows one way, from client to therapist. Rightly or wrongly, many therapists refuse to provide information about themselves or about sociable circumstances, on the grounds that these are outside their professional role, or would constitute an irrelevant change of topic within the interview. According to them, the client is likely to find out of his or her own accord most of the relevant information about himself or herself and his or her attitudes if the therapist acts as no more than a 'mirror' to him or her. These clinicians may indeed see the interview as 'intersubjective', but most of the 'perception' allowed to occur is of the client only. Clinicians coming from this background will accordingly often be shocked by the directness of client demands for information in other clinical settings. For instance,

> *AIDS patient:* 'How long have I got to live?' *or*
> *AIDS patient's mother:* 'How did he or she get it?'

These are everyday demands in some clinical settings, which it would be grossly inappropriate to meet by replying, 'That's a matter of how *you* see it, don't you think?'. Most clinical interviews are more fully inter-subjective in the sense that both parties to the exchange are likely to alter their views and attitudes, and are in some sense committed to doing so.

Much of the literature on counselling, and by extension on the clinical interview generally, places great emphasis on the personal attributes of the therapist. The therapist in particular should be 'psychologically-minded', a skilled helper, a good listener with an empathic attitude who knows how to prevent his own feelings and attitudes from interfering with the therapeutic process. Given the relatively passive role taken by the therapist in much counselling, this is not surprising.

The approach taken in this book does not take exception to this approach in counselling. What it does say is that dwelling on the attributes of the therapist is no excuse for not defining the *goals* of therapy, and essential to any goal of therapy must be reaching a shared understanding with the client of how he or she experiences the world. Once we can see that, it also becomes easy to see too that often the wider goals of treatment will differ from those of counselling, and will often be reached by different routes.

Most strikingly, in a clinical setting, client and therapist will disclose information to one another about how the world works, including how bodies work, and how institutions such as hospitals work. In this way, clinical work becomes an aspect of *teaching,* and educational methods will become appropriate. For instance, we often check whether our client correctly understands medical or legal terms; whereas in a counselling setting the question of correctness does not arise.

Even more strikingly, one of the goals of the clinical interview, as we have said, is likely to be an action taken by the professional on behalf of the patient, either because the patient has not got the skill, or the knowledge or the status to carry the action out. This action might be anything from cutting out an ingrown toenail to issuing a writ against his mother for making nuisance phone calls to his wife; from putting a patient on the right kind of anti-depressants to writing a certificate for his or her employer. This overlaps the classic meaning of the word *patient,* which implies that he or she is the passive recipient of someone else's (the *agent's*) action. We are including here also the cases where the action bears on some third party (for example, his mother who is making the nuisance calls).

So, to summarise the argument so far, clinical interviews are something between medical case-history taking on the one hand, and counselling on the other. Clinical interviews must take a holistic view of the client's belief system (not just a case history), but they must also include a mutual inter-subjective exchange of information, including specialist education of the client (unlike most counselling), and can lead to the therapist using this information to become an effective agent on behalf of the client (like a doctor but unlike a psychotherapist). Perhaps the following table will make these points clearer.

	Doctor	Clinician	Counsellor	Social researcher
Holistic	*no*	*yes*	*yes*	*yes*
Education	*yes*	*yes*	*no*	*no*
Agent	*yes*	*yes*	*no*	*no*

Figure 8.1 Attitudes to and views of clients' belief systems.

(Notice that, in many ways, the role of the psychotherapist emerges as parallel to that of the sociologist doing in-depth interviews for research. The reader might want to think about why that should be so.)

Stages of the Clinical Interview

Ivey (1988), among others, (for example, Bernstein & Bernstein 1985; Egan 1982) has attempted to outline stages which should be followed in a successful interview, including the clinical interview. According to him, they are as follows.

Rapport/Structuring

This stage concerns the explicit or implicit definition of the relationship between interviewer and interviewee, including an understanding of what is beyond its limits.

Gathering Information, Defining the Problem, and Identifying the Client's Assets

This is obviously an important task, and obviously Ivey has put it in the right place: it would be very odd if, as clinicians, we provided the treatment before finding out what we were treating. Describing it as a *stage*, however, conceals the way in which we often go back and redefine the meaning of the *information* we have received, and so recast the problem—narrow it down, sharpen its definition, or reframe it in some way. On the whole, we prefer to emphasise an overall process of *funnelling*, as we call it in chapter 5, where the definition of both purposes and roles moves from the broad to the narrow and from the vague to the precise as the interview proceeds. What we find valuable in Ivey's formulation is not the supposed existence of stages but his implied setting of *goals* for the interview; and these goals we completely agree with.

Defining Goals

At this stage, client and counsellor determine what goals the client wants to reach, at least if he or she dared. This stage, of course, would be modified by learning from the therapist that certain goals were unattainable and others not—for example, that an overseas trip next year is impossible because you have terminal lung cancer. It could also be modified in a different way by the therapist's inability to facilitate those goals—we don't give handouts for overseas trips at this agency, but you *are* eligible for sickness benefits. In any case, it is of cardinal importance for the client to have it made clear what counts for him or her as a solution to his or her problem, and this must be established somehow and somewhere in the interview. A useful comparison could be made with hairdressers who cut your hair the way they believe you want it (or the way they believe suits you), and express surprise or hostility if you complain about the result.

Exploring Alternatives and Confronting Client Ambiguity

Ivey means here that the clinician should work over with the client how consistent his or her goals are with one another, and how consistent they are with his or her means to achieve them. In psychotherapy, these inconsistencies of the client's will often be inexplicit and unconscious, and the clinician's task will mainly be to bring them to awareness and confront them. In the clinical interview, on the other hand, this will mean, as we have said above, providing factual information and saying what the clinician is prepared to do.

Generalisation and Transfer of Learning

Here, Ivey (1988) makes the important point that 'change that is not carried beyond the laboratory of the interview to the real world is not change'. A clinical interview must make provision for checking that both clinician and client do what they say they will do. Explicit recording of goals and 'contracts' is a good start towards this. In other settings, the clinician and client will conduct role-plays as part of their rehearsal for the real world outside.

Modifying the Social Science Approach

So far, we have seen that the clinical interview is somewhat different from the most famous models of clinical work. It applies the social-science model to institutional practice. The constraints on doing this, which we have listed, occur because the professional becomes in the clinic both an educator and an agent of the client. He or she has in a very active way to *work* for the client. These constraints serve mainly to modify the medical and counselling models of clinical work. Other constraints however modify the social-science approach we have outlined in the previous chapter. These modifications we must turn to next.

Information Capacity—Communicating with the Client

Many studies have shown that there are severe limits on the capacity of human beings to retain and process information. Even under ideal conditions, few people can juggle more than eight or so items of information in their heads and retain the items in memory. It follows that clinicians should not expect their clients to remember to tell them all the details which the client thinks to be relevant if the details are numerous and varied. Often these details will only be offered with prompting in the course of the interview. Nor should the clinician expect himself or herself to be any better without taking careful notes. The moral should be clear.

Moreover, clients in the clinic are very likely to be tired, confused, in pain, disoriented, depressed or anxious. All these factors have been shown severely to limit whatever capacity for processing information the client may possess, and the clinician should take it for granted that severe limits are being placed by the clinical set-up on getting and giving information. There seem also to be only a few realistic ways around this: whenever possible, we should place our clients at ease and give them time to get used to us and the clinical room. Taking notes for them as well as for ourselves is often useful. And having a friend or relation of the client present is often a good way of checking, extending and corroborating stories—theirs and ours.

Social Aspects of the Clinical Population

One of the most striking facts about most clinical populations is the oppressed and downtrodden nature of many of the people coming (or being brought) for institutional help. Working-class people are far more prone to illness of most kinds, and far more prone to seek assistance from hospitals and other helping agencies. So are people who are habitually heavy users of drugs, including alcohol and tobacco; and people who are intellectually retarded or educationally disadvantaged. To these we can add those people who are criminally or sexually or psychically or interpersonally **deviant** (for instance, those of us who are inarticulately angry about the state of the world much of the time; or those of us who were sexually exploited as children. Working-class clients are not necessarily deviant by virtue of their being working class, but they are just as likely as any social deviant to feel defensive and lacking in legitimacy; so if the following discussion lumps them in with deviant groups, this is not without reason.)

Worse, if someone is a member of one of these groups, then he or she is very likely to be a member of one or more of the other groups too: deviant and disadvantaged groups have a high tendency to overlap. So, for instance, the level of alcohol and drug abuse is statistically very high among gay men: the level of heart disease is unexpectedly high among people with criminal records.

Worst, those members of society who are found among these overlapping deviant groups are the heaviest users of our helping institutions. No reader will be surprised now to read that 70% of males in Australian prisons are there for drug-related offences; but not everyone knows how much time and money in welfare agencies, schools and hospitals is consumed by these multiply deviant groups. To the clinician, it often seems that these people are taking away all the clinic's time from its proper clients. To the outsider, it often seems that in fact these multiply-deviant clients *are* the clinic's proper clients.

Therefore, the clinician can expect similar themes to recur in the stories and worldview of these clients. These recurrences allow him or her many shortcuts in dealing with them. They also can lead to many traps of **stereotyping** clients as supposedly typical drug-users or prostitutes. None so deaf as the clinician who has turned off his or her hearing-aid the better to listen to his or her prejudices.

These deviant clients, being human beings, know all too well that they come from deviant groups. They know all too well that they are not highly regarded by the custodians of society's values, and rightly or wrongly they usually see clinicians as such custodians. This is to say that these clients are **stigmatised** and will behave so as to manage the 'spoilt social identity' that being stigmatised entails. Because stigma leads clients actively to alter or suppress information, it can decisively affect the success of a clinical interview; and we will spend a little time thinking about it.

Client Information Control—the Presentation of the Therapeutic Self

Goffman (1959) has given a useful account of the general manoeuvres we use to clean up the presentation of information about ourselves to give an acceptable social impression. In presenting ourselves to others, we are not usually concerned in letting others see us as we really are, but as we want them to perceive us. We are involved, in all our transactions with other people, with controlling the flow of information about ourselves, including deleting and sometimes inventing information, so as to *manage the impression* others form of us.

We have already said that the clinical interview is concerned with the two-way flow of information between therapist and client. Now we can see that if either or both of these people engage in large-scale 'impression management', then the ideal we have set ourselves of achieving a shared holistic understanding in the clinical setting is likely to be threatened, or achieved only in a fake or spurious form.

According to Goffman's (1959), *The Presentation of Self in Everyday Life,* clients (and therapists) are apt to show a *front* to the therapist rather than passively or unreflectively letting the facts about one's self unfold. Few of us trust the conclusions others might draw about us so completely to chance and charity. Front is the actively presented body of information we show to others. Often, this performance requires us to make visible—give *dramatic realisation* to—information which might otherwise be sceptically regarded. It is is always useful to have the temperature or the coughing fit right in front of the doctor, rather than limply telling him that you had one at home just before coming to the surgery.

We notice others' limited capacity for accommodating complex information, and so present an *idealised* simplification of the facts: our leg has been hurting non-stop since Thursday, we have never missed a day at work, and we love our spouse without qualification and without ceasing. And we only maintain such unbelievable things . . . in order to be believed.

We preserve the pretence that most, if not all, the things that happen to us and to our bodies are intended by us. We *meant* our children to become motor mechanics, and we *meant* to burp just at that point in the interview. We *meant* to get angry when you pointed out that we had burped, and then *meant* to start coughing just when we did start. Throughout, we kept to the *maintenance of expressive control*, as Goffman calls it. Obviously, the problem of the maintenance of expressive control is going to be particularly pressing when we are working with physically damaged clients, especially in hospitals.

Finally, when necessary to preserve the desired impression, we are prepared to lie, concoct false identities and false histories—to misrepresent ourselves, or to leave large and deceptive areas of mystification about potentially embarrassing areas of our lives. The doctor didn't need to know that I drink two bottles of wine a day, or that my wife earns twice as much as I do. If the doctor wants to know those things, let the doctor find out for himself or herself.

Stigma-management

Goffman (1963) has paid special attention to the impression management of those people who have a social stigma: something to be ashamed of. (Note that *shame* has to do with what others think is wrong with us, regardless of our own opinion of ourselves. What we find wrong with ourselves is a matter of guilt.) Regardless of whether we are personally responsible for, our failure to measure up to society's norms—whether we wear a coleostomy bag, beat up old men in parks or were born a dwarf—we are charged by normal people with the responsibility for endorsing those norms by *appearing* as normal as possible. Obviously, the different ways—the ruses—which stigmatised people use to preserve social appearances will vitally affect their behaviour in the clinical interview.

By far, the most common way of managing stigma is suppressing the information or putting out counter propaganda designed to lead people to believe that you are not stigmatised. Because the point of this exercise is to pass yourself of as 'straight,' this form of stigma management is known as *passing*. Alternatively, you might try *migration* away from sources of social exposure, for example, the country town you grew to feel ashamed in, or *withdrawal* into having as little contact with others as possible (a major source of depression among people from stigmatised groups). *Brazening it out* is another possible solution. You dare the 'straights' to put you down; to refuse to accept your shame. Or you might attempt to form an improvised 'ghetto' of the excluded.

The word *splitting* usually refers to divisions within the individual mind. Here we use the word to describe a process of coping with stigma. The ruse here is to divide your stigmatised group into two: the socially acceptable and the socially unacceptable—good Jews and bad Jews, for example. Clients choosing this ruse will launch fierce verbal attacks on 'poofs' or 'dole bludgers' who to all external appearances are little different from themselves. The clinician should be alert to the personal defensiveness implied by these attacks, and fail to join in. Both good Jews and bad Jews are still Jews; 'poofters', however defined, are just one sub-group of gay men and women; and encouraging our clients to split their group is only to feed their sense of social insecurity.

By now, the reader will be getting a sense of how, underlying all these ruses, and many other such ruses we haven't space to deal with, is one fundamental stratagem: angling for acceptance in the way likely to be most acceptable to the belief system of your interlocutor.

An experienced therapist will forestall all such ruses by showing from the very beginning that he or she is **wise**—though he or she may not be a member of the stigmatised group, he or she nevertheless understands *what it feels like* to be a member of the group. (Often one finds inexperienced therapists pretending to phoney group membership in a futile attempt to curry respect: but as Groucho Marx said, 'Who wants to be a member of any club that would let [him] in?' *Acceptance* is what is required, not fellowship.) And showing that you understand what it feels like to be a member of the stigmatised group is none other than our old friend holistic understanding.

Institutional Limitations on the Clinical Interview

We have seen so far how the flow of information from client to therapist might be distorted or constricted by stigma; in managing his and her image so as to minimise has social shame, the client may mislead the therapist about what his or her real problems are and what might be their real causes and solutions. Now we turn to the ways in which the institution itself can constrain the clinician.

So far we have outlined the limits on clinical understanding imposed by the client's 'front'. But there are many other limits which are likely to be imposed from outside the clinical room.

Foremost among these is the limitation of time. The in-depth interview is necessarily time consuming, and the extent of the interview is to some extent unpredictable because of the holistic nature of the material. Yet almost all institutions and clinics in our society are overcrowded with clients waiting to see too few therapists. Even in private clinics or in private practice, the pressure to earn enough money to cover costs means that time is scarce. Therefore, the in-depth interview is apt to remain rather shallow, and its validity and reliability rather doubtful.

The Clinician as an Agent of the State

Second among these limitations must rank the justified suspicion that the institution, of whom like it or not the clinician is a representative, is seen by the client as potentially hostile to his or her interests. Only the naive among clinical workers believe that their hospital is purely interested in the welfare of its patients: hospitals are primarily clients of State governments, and must constantly refer to State government priorities on health, employment and welfare spending. These priorities insinuate themselves into the clinical interview whenever the clinician finds himself or herself saying that you can go on the methodone programme; you can't get free access to a hospital bed no matter how distressed you might feel; or you should have an abortion in the next two weeks (enquire at Reception) otherwise it will certainly damage your health, if not your work prospects. Moreover, when the client realises that you are indeed an agent of the State (like it or not), then he or she is likely to tell you the versions of the truth best calculated (by him or her) to produce the action from you which he or she desires. In other words, he or she is likely to become manipulative rather than frank. And when you think about it, your own attitude as agent of the State is likely to be a manipulative one too, though you will try to conceal this fact from yourself. Obviously, when both parties to the social interaction are trying to manipulate the other, largely through the control of information, then hope for the kind of shared holistic understanding, which we set as the *goal* of the clinical interview, is likely to be dashed.

The Client as an Agent of Others

If the clinician is apt to be a stand-in for wider institutions of the State, so too is the client likely to be present on behalf of other groups—pursuing the agendas of his or her family or his or her workmates or his or her church. He or she may only have come to the clinic at their behest in the first place. Even when he or she has his or her own intentions for treatment, they are likely to be modified or censored by his or her awareness of what, for instance, would be acceptable to his or her children when it comes to admission to a retirement home. So, both clinician and client are sitting there in the room secretly wired for messages back to an unseen headquarters.

Then, there is likely to be definite ideas in the head of both client and clinician of how a clinician is expected to behave, in other words, what it is to be professional. We have discussed in great detail in a previous chapter what it means to society as a whole for someone to be professional, but for clients it usually means that the clinician will be punctual, well-heeled in appearance, confidential, not impertinent, not advance his or her sexual or status interests through the interaction, and generally preserve an air of middle-class decorum. But having expected, and sometimes insisted, that the clinician will gaze at him or her from an alabaster pedestal, the client is likely also to be intimidated by his or her perceived social distance from the therapist; just as the therapist is likely to feel cut off from his or her client, while at the same time hiding his or her own anxiety behind a cool professional front.

Subverting Preordained Clinical Roles

But there are good ways around these problems, so long as we are aware that they are indeed problems. The clinician should make it clear at the appropriate time that he or she is unwilling to be manipulated without a corresponding exchange of true confessions by the client; and he or she will usually find in any case that the client sets him or her a test of his or her integrity—not as State agent, but as fellow human being who knows what it is like to struggle with and through bureaucratic systems.

Most useful here is a habit on the part of the therapist of self-disclosure. Telling the client relevant facts about yourself can throw light on the client's problem. But even better it can show the client that you are quite capable of hopping off your pedestal when required (you might even make a game of hopping on and off several times in each interview; but beware of stigmatised clients who are determined to knock you off it for good), and perhaps share his or her attitude—and might even be prepared, if the situation forces it on you, actually to subvert the system in order to see that justice is done to him. In other words, you show yourself prepared to play with the professional role that has been allotted to you, in order to show the sincere human being who might otherwise have remained hidden beneath the mask.

But the clinician has to be prepared really to commit himself or herself to this line of action, and possibly suffer the institutional consequences: fake radicalism doesn't fool the humblest and slowest client when his or her welfare is at stake. On the other hand, the inter-personally committed therapist is likely to win the most intense loyalty from his or her clients, and spend a lifetime receiving invitations to dinner, christenings and bar mitzvahs, which of course he or she will refuse with warmly gratified thanks.

Intimacy

Social science theory often disputes whether there is any such thing as a real self beneath or beyond the social roles we have internalised. We needn't buy into such discussions here. What is not in dispute is that there will be aspects of the client which might be excluded by his or her playing the narrow range of roles seemingly allotted to him in the hospital or clinic. When we allow the client to step outside these, he or she has the *sense* of unconstrained personal expression. It feels to him or her (and to us) as though he or she has been permitted to be his or her real self. And when that free-floating expressive self is acknowledged, most clients find the experience deeply satisfying. We are satisfying what seems to be a deep need for intimacy, a need to be acknowledged as a person beyond the nuts and bolts of playing a mere social part. And to share that intimacy can be for the clinician a motive more powerful than any other for continuing and enriching his or her work.

How to do a Clinical Interview—a Summary

There are various models of clinical interviewing, mostly adapted either from the standard medical interview, or from counselling. It is argued here that both these models are inadequate and misleading for most interviews in clinical settings. This is particularly because they have not thought through the holistic approach to the client and his or her world which is advocated in this book.

On the other hand, the approach suggested here is to see the clinical interview as primarily applied social research. In other words, we take the approaches on in-depth interviewing advocated in chapter 3 and adapt them to the clinical setting. The interview will of course concern mainly a 'two-group' and its ability to negotiate a shared view of reality; but outside social forces will always be listening at the clinic door trying to regulate and police whatever transactions might take place there.

So this chapter concentrates on how we must adapt the social research approach to the clinical interview. This adaptation comes about through two main constraints: first, the demography of the clinic; second, the inescapable fact of the clinic being part of an institution.

The demography of the clinic means that a very high proportion of clients will be poor, old, sick, passive, addicted welfare recipients from multiply-stigmatised groups. Therefore, the social-research approach will adapt itself to the special needs and perceptions likely to be induced in clients by having some or all of those attributes. The theory of stigma is especially applied to see how client responses can be coloured or hidden by a perceived need to manage 'spoiled social identity'.

The constraints imposed by the institution place different limits on the two group's transactions. Virtually all clinicians will be expected to see too many clients in too short a time for genuine holistic understanding to occur. What's worse, virtually all institutions, rhetoric notwithstanding, will set *measurable positivistic goals* for themselves and their clinicians (employees in their eyes), and put pressure on both clinician and client to come up to an external standard which they impose. Families and employers might in this way be said to behave in a way similar to the institution.

Ways have been suggested in which the agents of social control can be side-tracked or placated while interpersonal reality can be given a space and time to breathe. Within that space and time, the client can be given a chance to define and make explicit his or her real beliefs and wishes, make them as consistent with one another and the 'facts' as necessary, and form an alliance with the therapist, based on mutual understanding and respect, to make some of those wishes come true.

Glossary

Bleaching the interpretation Finding some objectively observable meaning for the client's expressions.
Deviant Not fitting socially acceptable norms.
Dialectical process Resulting from a dialogue or some back-and-forth exchange.
Legitimation Made officially acceptable to social values.
Negotiation Reaching agreement by stages of proposal, rejection and acceptance.
Protocol A standard format for an interview (a piece of research generally).
(clinical) Signs Indications noticeable to the professional observer, though not necessarily to the client.
Stereotyping Assuming that someone with some standard attribute (for example, black skin) will have other standard attributes to match (for example, be an unemployed alcoholic). A stereotype is usually an exaggerated and prejudiced view of a group of people.
Stigmatisation Making some personal attribute a source of shame.
Symmetrical relationship When *A* loves *B* and *B* loves *A*, symmetry; but when it is unrequited, asymmetry.
Symptoms The features of an illness as experienced by the patient.
Wise Understanding what it is like to be a member of a stigmatised group.

References

Bernstein, Lewis & Bernstein, Rosalyn S. 1985. *Interviewing: A Guide for Health Professionals.* Fourth edition. East Norwalk, Connecticut: Appleton Century Crofts.

Egan, Gerald. 1982. *The Skilled Helper: Models, Skills and Methods for Effective Helping.* Second edition. Belmont, California: Wadsworth.

Goffman, Erving. 1959. *The Presentation of Self in Everyday Life.* New York: Anchor Books.

—— 1963. *Stigma: Notes on the Management of Spoiled Social Identity.* Englewood New Jersey: Prentice Hall.

Ivey, Allen E. 1988. *Intentional Interviewing and Counselling: Facilitating Client Development.* Brooks/Cole Publishing Company.

Chapter 9 The Pragmatics Of In-Depth Interviewing

The pragmatics of conducting research using in-depth interviewing as the primary method are inextricably interwoven with the methodological stance we take; the moral and ethical issues that are raised throughout the research process and the political context in which the research takes place. More will be said on this subject in chapter 10. Here we examine the pragmatic issues raised in the doing of research.

By *pragmatic issues* we mean the practical concerns of the researcher in accomplishing his or her task. These practical concerns include how one designs and does research, decides on sampling procedures, gains access to informants, establishes rapport, and leaves the field. They also involve assessing bias and objectivity throughout the research process, gauging the validity and reliability of the research process and the data, and deciding whether to employ multiple methods.

Research methods texts usually present the reader with a linear model of research; a sanitised, idealised account of how research ought to be done, progressing tidily from research design to data collection and then from data analysis to publication of results. Or, they tell us how complex and untidy research is, and that one must recognize that 'social research is not just a question of neat procedures but a social process whereby interaction between researcher and researched will directly influence the course which a research programme takes' (Burgess 1984: 31).

We argue that the research process *is* complex and untidy. Rarely does it follow the path laid down in the traditional texts. However, using a linear profile of the process of in-depth interviewing is helpful for heuristic reasons. It is the simplest way of incorporating into the discussion some of the issues, problems and untidiness that may arise in the research process. It is obvious, however, that each piece of research will raise its own dilemmas for the researcher and the researched. This chapter discusses the pragmatics of doing in-depth interviewing, that is, how one goes about designing and doing research, gaining access to informants, explaining the aims of research, avoiding bias and so on.

Research Design

Linear models of research describe specific stages of a project. These usually include generating or testing hypotheses, gathering data, analysing data, and then writing a research report. However several researchers (Bell & Encel 1978; Bell & Newby 1977; Burgess 1984; Roberts 1988; Shipman 1976) have acknowledged that the reality is far more complex than it is usually portrayed. The social interaction between informant and interviewer can influence not only the direction of the discussion but the research project itself. Throughout in-depth interviewing research, the methodology and the research design are negotiated and renegotiated by both researcher and informant. However, prior to entering the field the researcher needs to make an initial choice of a research problem or question.

Selecting a Problem

You might decide to examine a particular question or issue because it is an important social issue of the day, an assignment problem set by your lecturer, or an issue related to your experience and understanding of the world which you wish to further explore. Whatever the motivation, research begins with *asking a question* and is carried out in an attempt to answer it. It is a means of understanding and explaining the world. Research begins *before* you put together a research design.

An Example

Initial motivations are numerous. Often researchers are interested in a particular issue and decide to read more about it. They discuss it with friends and/or colleagues. Personal experiences may induce an interest in an area. A research problem may be developed or generated by the interplay between the researcher's theoretical and methodological training and personal experiences within a social setting (Burgess 1984). For instance, Aroni (1985) selected her research topic after many dinner-table conversations. These discussions included speculation about the relationship between Jewish schooling, and the production and maintenance of Jewish identity. Her sociological training enabled her to perceive it as a topic for research. It was only after some preparation work (see chapter 4), which included reading research literature in the field and talking to other researchers, that she designed a research project. Even then, the sociological problem was revised several times after preliminary discussions with some informants, members of the Jewish community and her doctoral supervisor. She then formulated a research problem and turned it into a working title. After this, she wrote a research proposal outlining a design for the research project.

James (1984) provides detailed discussion of the practical issues facing a researcher prior to defining the research problem and subsequent reclarification of the research topic. Her account of doing research as a nurse in a cancer ward outlines how the entire process began, how she narrowed the question and then how she began with a research proposal or design which altered in response to suggestions made by prospective informants. Her account provides commentary on her position as a postgraduate student, the manner in which this influenced the framing of the topic, the people she discussed the project with and the help and encouragement she received in actually selecting a suitable topic.

The Process

You begin the process of defining the research problem by working out why you are asking the questions. This is an important issue because it will influence (a) the sort of research you would like to do; (b) what you in fact are able to do; (c) who it is for; and (d) how you go about doing it. The questions you might ask at this point are,

- What prompted me into thinking about this problem?
- What is the real problem that underlies this?
- What are my values and interests in relation to asking this as a research question?

Most researchers begin with general topics and then clarify or narrow these to a few questions. A good way of doing this is to write down everything you can think of in relation to your topic. Then choose those ideas on which you want to focus and write a clearer statement of your research question. Once you have selected the issue of particular interest, reformulate it and and revise it *in the field*. We have found that it is useful to broaden the research problem or topic again at the end of the research process as it helps to balance your overall understandings of the theoretical issues.

Substantive and Theoretical Questions

There are two categories of questions that researchers operate with—*substantive* and *theoretical*. *Substantive questions* focus on particular problems or issues in a specific setting such as nursing homes, schools, hospitals, and so on. *Theoretical questions* are those which relate specifically to conceptual categories such as deviance, social control, identity formation, group identification. A good research design is one which asks both questions. Also, as mentioned in chapter 1, the research problem or question in qualitative studies is usually flexible and open to change throughout the research process.

A Manageable Research Question

A manageable research question is one that is clear, concise and answerable within the practical constraints imposed on the study. These include limited time and money and the ability of the researcher to maintain sanity throughout! But how do you make a research project manageable? There are no hard-and-fast rules. One useful way is to 'unpack' it and examine the assumptions underlying the asking of the question in the first place. For example, take the question, 'Does body image have an influence on eating habits?'. You might ask yourself, why would we be interested in examining the relationship between body image and eating habits?. The following statements are hypothetical answers.

- *I have experienced bulimia* and want to understand myself better.
- *I am a psychologist* working with anorexia nervosa sufferers and I want to know whether there is any real relationship between body image and eating habits.
- *I am a feminist* with theories about societal influences on women's health; and since it is predominantly women who suffer from eating disorders, I want to find out if body image influences behaviour. If this is the case, I want to find out where people get their ideas about bodies from.
- *I am a nurse* who wants to explore this commonly held assumption because I have worked with people who have a negative body image but do not suffer from eating disorders.

The implication one can draw from the given statements is that *who you are* will influence what assumptions you bring to the asking of the question and how you go about narrowing it down to a specific research project.

The research design should outline the initial aims and objectives of the project and give an indication of the methodology to be employed. The researcher should provide a preliminary indication of the theoretical concepts to be used. This includes their relationship to the research problem, and the methods employed to collect and analyse data. The research design should not be rigid but should be used as 'a base against which modifications can be made as the research continued' (Burgess 1984). After all, you may find, even with preparation work behind you (reviewing the literature, talking to informants socially), that your original research question is inappropriate and does not fit with the data 'on the ground'.

Sampling

The purpose of sampling, be it in qualitative or quantitative research, is to produce either a sample which is representative of a chosen population or which may 'illuminate a situation, get insight, or collect information about a particular event' (Wadsworth 1984). Below are a set of terms used to define different forms of sampling.

Population Sampling

The **population** refers to the entire set of people you intend to study. A **sample** is a subset of that population which is considered to be representative of it in some fashion. Population sampling strategies can be divided into two basic types, **probability sampling** and **non-probability sampling**. The difference between these two types of sampling can be explained as follows.

> In probability sampling every unit in the universe under study has the same calculable and non-zero possibility of being selected. Meanwhile with Non-Probability Sampling there is no means of estimating the probability of units being included in the sample. Indeed there is no guarantee that every element has a chance of being studied (Burgess 1984: 54).

Probability Sampling

There are several forms that probability sampling can take. Some examples which are well known are *random sampling* and *stratified random sampling*. (For a detailed discussion see Bailey 1982; Polgar & Thomas 1988.)

Random Sampling is regarded as providing the most representative form of sampling, because the sample is chosen so that every member of the population being examined has the same probability of being included. You list all members of the population. Then, using some method such as dice or random number tables, you select your sample from the list of the population. The advantage of random sampling is that it provides a group that is representative of the population. The major disadvantage is that you need to be able to list every member of the population. As Allen (1989) points out, in many clinical settings this is just not possible. Also, in many instances, the cost is prohibitive, being much more expensive than using readily available groups.

Stratified Random Sampling is a variation of random sampling in which quotas are filled rather than a random sample being taken right across the population. The advantages of stratified random sampling are that all the significant groups are proportionately represented and the exact representativeness of the sample is known. The disadvantages are again a prohibitive cost for a very small gain in accuracy and the need for a remarkably detailed amount of information about your population.

Non-probability Sampling

There are a number of forms which non-probability sampling can take. These include: *incidental sampling*, *quota sampling*, *snowball sampling* and *theoretical sampling*. These are briefly discussed below.

Incidental sampling (also referred to as *Judgment, Convenience or Opportunistic Sampling*) involves the selection of people, actions or events at random. When a TV interviewer stops passers-by in the street and interviews them, that is incidental sampling. Replication is impossible.

Consecutive or quota sampling is an improvement to incidental sampling in that, if you were the TV interviewer standing on a street corner, you might keep on interviewing until you had interviewed forty-nine men and fifty-one women because those are the proportions of each sex in the population. The problem is that the fifty-one women you met would not necessarily be representative of all women in the community.

Snowball sampling relies on the researcher's knowledge of a social situation. This approach involves using a group of informants with whom the researcher has made initial contact and asking them to put the researcher in touch with their friends, then asking those people to be informants and in turn asking them to put the researcher in touch with their friends and *so on* as long as they fit the criteria for the research project.

Theoretical sampling is a process of data collection which is generated by, and is used to generate, theory. The researcher concurrently collects, codes and analyses his or her data. He or she then makes decisions about what further data should be collected in order to develop the emerging theory. This is explained in more detail below.

Sampling in Qualitative Research

Qualitative research tends to rely mostly on the use of non-probability sampling, particularly snowball sampling and theoretical sampling. Burgess (1984) argues that in theoretical sampling, case data collection is essentially controlled by the developing and emerging theory. The researcher has to decide for what theoretical purpose the groups and sub-groups are used, and which groups or sub-groups are used in data collection. As he puts it, 'Theoretical sampling . . . involves researchers in observing groups with a view to extending, modifying, developing and verifying theory' (1984: 56). The term **saturation** when used in conjunction with theoretical sampling refers to a process where no additional data can be found that would add to the categories being developed and examined. That is, you have reached saturation level. It is this process that makes qualitative research systematic.

Let us provide an example. Aroni (1985) drew informants from both Jewish and non-Jewish day schools in the Melbourne metropolitan area in order to provide a comparison of the patterns of identification in their responses. The choice of metropolitan schools was made not simply for pragmatic reasons but in direct relation to demographic data. This showed that the majority of Victoria's Jewish population are urban dwellers congregating in enclaves within various suburbs of Melbourne. Only students from schools located within or close to these enclaves were approached. A major problem in the sampling procedure arose in deciding who was to be included as an informant (in the absence of agreement regarding objective criteria for determining who is a Jew in the modern context). Aroni decided that for the purposes of her research the only objective criterion designated was that of having a Jewish parent (not necessarily the mother as designated by Orthodox Jewish Law as this would exclude a number of individuals who subjectively perceive themselves to be Jewish).

In addition, identification of Jewish students in non-Jewish schools was a legal problem in two ways. First, schools are prohibited from differentiating their students on grounds of religious criteria. Secondly, they are bound not to release certain information about students such as their home address and phone number. To do so is regarded as infringement of privacy. The snowball technique of sampling was used to overcome this problem. Students at Jewish day schools were asked to introduce the researcher to their Jewish friends attending non-Jewish schools, where she did not already have initial contacts. It was also an attempt at gaining access to informants who did not publicly identify with being Jewish.

Issues in Sampling

Sample size is an issue which is often raised by researchers and students. In most qualitative research, the sample size tends to be small for a number of reasons. First, in-depth interviewing is time-intensive research. Unless there is a research team engaged in the project, it is very difficult for a single researcher to be involved in more than 100 long and complex social interactions. Secondly, there is a tendency for qualitative researchers to utilise theoretical sampling. This does not encourage large samples by its very nature (especially when linked with the concept of saturation).

Time and Space Sampling

The *time/space dimension* is one of the least discussed aspects of doing qualitative research. Where it has been discussed, it has been in relation to how much time the interviewer has available to complete a research project, how long it actually takes to complete it, and how that relates to a budget (Wadsworth 1984). The would-be in-depth interviewer is charged with several pragmatic concerns including arranging times with informants, not overtaxing their own or their informants' concentration span, and making a choice between doing longitudinal or cross-sectional (static comparison) studies.

It seems to be stating the obvious when one points out that social activity occurs in time and space but that 'neither have been incorporated into the centre of social theory; rather they are ordinarily treated more as environments' (Giddens 1979: 202). Nevertheless, the geopolitical context may have some bearing on your choice of topic, access to informants, and the willingness of informants to trust you. For instance, in the case of Aroni's research, had she decided to do her research a year earlier perhaps she might have gained access to one of the schools using 'front-door methods'. Perhaps if she had conducted the interviews during the 1973 Middle East War the informants' perceptions of their Jewishness might have been different. Perhaps if she had decided to interview Year 11 Students instead of Year 12, the students would not have been as willing to talk because they didn't need to create displacement activity to the same extent as those studying for final year high-school exams.

It is important to remember that informants are not 'cultural dopes' or 'clean slates' but rather individuals involved in everyday living. This includes a consciousness of relations to family and peer groups, exposure to media discussions and active participation in the historical context. In addition, it is important to remember that informants will have different activities occurring in relation to their own social rhythms. Thus, if you are interviewing people who are health professionals working in hospitals, they will be involved in the routines that are associated with such institutions and may be influenced by such, in their ability and desire to converse with you. For instance, if a person has just finished a long night shift, he or she may not be interested in, or capable of, engaging in an in-depth interview. In addition, if a hospital staff or nurses' strike has just been announced, the political climate may not be conducive for conducting interviews or for gaining access to informants.

The time and space dimensions of social reality lead one to consider the twin issues of selection of research location and selection of time. The space dimension is closely tied to the time dimension in that it forms part of the structures that individuals create and yet are restrained by. Growing up in Melbourne, or any other city for that matter, may play some part in the formation and reproduction of both informants' and researchers' world views.

The selection of research location is not always a matter of choice but is tied to the exigencies of the research project. It may be tied to access. Gatekeepers may have specified certain locations as available or unavailable to the researcher. The researcher may also be concerned about the physical comfort which can be attained in certain locations in order to put the informant at ease. For example, Aroni found that students did not wish to be interviewed at the school they attended as they regarded the school precincts as 'enemy' territory.

Longitudinal Research

The selection of time varies according to the nature of the research project itself. There are some projects where the passage of time is significant to understanding the phenomena being researched. It provides 'the possibility of comparing changes in identifiable individuals over time and the possibility of meeting the criticism . . . that . . . (other studies) cannot identify *who* actually changes in some respect' (Bulmer 1977: 11).

Bulmer's description of **longitudinal** research design is a traditional explanation of its advantages over other forms of research labelled as **static group comparison, single case study** or the comparison of different populations at two points in time. However, if we examine Aroni's research, the advantage of using a longitudinal design was not only tied to the identification of who actually changes, but also to the understanding that 'the study of social activity involves the elapse of time just as that activity itself does' (Giddens 1979: 199). In addition, it must be pointed out that conducting a longitudinal study does not necessarily involve an expectation of social *change* (as implied by Bulmer's statement). Rather, it may be examining the *continuity* over time of the meanings and values informants attach to events, behaviours and attitudes. Thus, a longitudinal design *allows the recognition and examination of patterns*.

In this context, the longitudinal design also enables the investigation of time-space relations by following informants through cycles of social activity which are demarcated through 'time-geography (which) deals with the time-space choreography of individuals' existence over given time periods: the day, week, year or whole lifetime' (Giddens 1979: 205). Thus, in Aroni's research, the subjective meaning structures of the students typifying their Jewishness were examined in their relationship to the locale of the school. The term **locale** here refers to regionalisation on a time-space basis by which the 'aspects of . . . settings . . . are normatively implicated in systems of interaction, such that in some way they are "set apart", for certain individuals, or types of individuals' (Giddens 1982: 40). The informants are then followed through from the end of that episode in their lives through to alternate locales, regions and episodes (university, work, college or unemployment). Thus, the researcher is able to analyse the continuity or otherwise of the informants' meaning structures from one episode in their everyday living to another, by means of a longitudinal research design.

Gaining Access ('Getting In')

Once a sample has been decided upon, how does the researcher get people to agree to being interviewed? How do you gain permission and from whom? Which strategies are useful in seeking cooperation? How do you present yourself? How much detail or information about the research project do you disclose to the informant? Is your study an overt or covert one? Do you need to 'strike a research bargain'? Do you need to promise your informants anything in the research process or after it? To what extent does the manner in which you present yourself influence your ability to gain access to the informant and/or the setting? There are a number of discussions about the difficulties of gaining access to informants (Cohen & Taylor 1972; Pettigrew 1988; Spender 1988) but they do not provide adequate information regarding negotiation techniques for overcoming the problems nor who one negotiates with.

Gatekeepers

Gaining access is fundamentally an issue of getting permission to do in-depth interviewing. The question is, from whom do you need permission? If you are engaged in research with a small sample, such as in a life-story project, then it would be the informants who need to give permission. However, you may wish to interview patients in a hospital, school children, factory workers, or prisoners. These people as we have identified them in the previous sentence are members of a bureaucratic hierarchy. In order to gain access to them you may confront what are known in the jargon as *gatekeepers*. **Gatekeepers** are 'those individuals in an organisation that have the power to withhold access to people or situations for the purposes of research' (Burgess 1984: 39).

The problems raised by asking permission from gatekeepers are related to how the researcher comes to be seen in the eyes of the informant. Burgess (1984) raises this issue in the context of researcher/informant relationships. Let us assume that you are interested in exploring factory hands' perceptions of their working lives. What credentials do you, the researcher, come with if you have to contact both the head of the firm and the shop floor steward in order to gain access to your informants? What sort of rapport and trust can you build if the initial contact with the factory worker is predicated on contact with those who have control over him or her? The inevitable question will be *whose side are you on*? Will the worker suffer or feel pressure to participate because they are fearful of the job consequences if they do not participate? In these circumstances, the researcher needs to clarify his or her position in order to establish a good relationship with the informant. Is the owner or manager of the factory acting as a sponsor of the research project? How much access will he or she have to any cassettes or notes of conversations? Answers to such questions have to be given before they are asked. Assurances need to be made.

Examples

One example where access was denied by gatekeepers was found in Aroni's (1985) research. In order to actually speak to informants, she used what are known as *back-door* or illegitimate measures to find her sample. She was denied access at the 'front door' by the gatekeepers, so the strategies she used involved going to other individuals in the organisational hierarchies and changing her sampling strategy to the snowball technique whenever she was confronted with poor or no access. Some prospective informants did not agree to participate because she did not have the appropriate credentials. That is, she did not have the school's 'blessing' and people wondered why she had been denied it. Others who did agree to participate did so on the understanding that if she did not have the school's blessing 'she must be okay' because she must have done something to 'buck the system'.

In Aroni's case, access was denied to the class lists of the school that was sponsoring another research project. The board members refused access. This presented a serious threat to the viability of her research as the school was, in enrolment terms, the largest Jewish school in the State. Most of the other schools (both Jewish and non-Jewish) agreed to allow access to student lists although some sent letters home to parents to request permission for names and addresses to be released. In other cases, the principals of the schools allowed senior staff to make the decision to grant access. Other principals refused to provide any class lists with Jewish students' names listed on the basis that this might be prejudicial or at least seen that way by parents, peer group or teaching fraternity. Other schools, particularly the Jewish ones, allowed Aroni access as she had 'insider status'. As a member of the Jewish community, she was regarded as 'friendly' toward the community and as not harbouring any sinister or ulterior motives. More will be said on this later in the chapter.

Another example is given by Burgess (1984) who interviewed school students while also being their part-time teacher. He comments on how his access to students increased because they negotiated interviewing times to coincide with unpopular classes in order to avoid those classes. He highlights that gaining access is not just access to informants, but also to print documents which might provide a broader understanding of the research environment and the informants.

Access needs to be clearly negotiated with all parties involved. Obviously, the research activities that occur during this part of the research process 'will influence the ways in which those who are to be researched define the research and the activities of the researcher' (Burgess, 1984:85). Once permission has been given by an informant, an agreement or a research bargain should be established between the researcher and the informant regarding the type of interviewing to be engaged in or the use of other research strategies, and how and when they will be employed (see chapter 10 for greater detail).

Leaving the Field

Most qualitative methods texts refer, at least briefly, to 'leaving the field' when discussing various forms of ethnographic research, particularly participant observation. The problems of leaving the field for the researchers engaged in in-depth interviewing are much the same. It has been recognised that disengaging from the research context is a process rather than a single event. This process can have a significant impact on the informant/s, the researcher and possibly future researchers depending on how the process was orchestrated and carried out. The political and ethical aspects are obviously tied to the practical concerns of successfully leaving the field.

The researcher should realise that leave taking is inherently influenced by the manner in which he or she entered the field, the bargains they made throughout, and the nature of the social relationships that they had formed during the interviewing. In recognising these influences, the in-depth interviewer—whether engaged in eliciting a life history, a clinical interview or in any other form of in-depth interviewing—would have to face the knowledge that there is more to this process than their physical removal from the research setting. Emotional disengagement for both researcher and informant occurs. Much of the literature focusses on the hurt that might be experienced by the informant and provides details of how to extract oneself causing the least amount of distress to the informant or the research community.

If we accept that in-depth interviewing necessitates establishing and maintaining a good rapport with informants then it should also be recognised that such a process is never devoid of some form of emotional commitment from both sides of the fence. If emotional commitment is a two-way process then emotional disengagement must also be such a process. Yet, very few researchers prepare themselves for exit, and even fewer report on the process when providing details of their project. It is usually in the reporting of life-history research (Liebow 1967; Whyte 1955) that there is discussion of the intimate relationships that exist between the researcher's academic and personal involvement with the informant/s (Altheide 1980). In these discussions, it is acknowledged that the pragmatic concern of finishing one's involvement with informants is a psychological and social problem as well as a tactical one.

There are at least three ways of leaving the field that have been suggested to researchers: withdraw gradually, withdraw by cutting relations quickly and completely, or do not ever withdraw entirely. For instance, for Aroni (1985) being a member of the community she studied meant that in many respects she could never leave the field. The three options are tied to one's view of the research process. *There are no natural or routine means by which one can end the researcher/informant relationship*. The strategies employed vary with the setting or research context.

This aspect of research is not always as easy as it sounds. In the process of disengaging from the informants and the context, there are certain moral obligations which must be fulfilled, the most obvious being that the researcher should thank all participants in the process appropriately. Questions that the researcher should ask himself or herself are, Have all agreements been adhered to? Who benefits from the process and the publication of the research?. The research process can be regarded as successful when the researcher can answer these questions with a sense of having sustained a position of personal and professional integrity in relation to the informants.

Pragmatic Concerns

The pragmatic concern is with what is the most advantageous way of leaving the field. That is, to decide which process is going to enable the researcher to complete the research project successfully. Our interpretation of *successfully* includes maintaining access to informants during the analysis and writing-up stages so that the interviewer is not prohibited from obtaining any other critical data. After completing the task according to one's research design, totally distancing yourself from informants may disadvantage you if during a later stage you need to clarify some points. *Successfully* also means not disappointing, offending or distressing informants throughout the research. This includes the process of leave-taking so that if you, or some other researcher, wishes to engage in further research, you have not 'queered the pitch'.

To achieve these goals, the researcher can at the beginning of the process set a time frame so that both parties are prepared for a leave-taking to occur. If one has made promises, one should keep them. Another strategy is to gradually break the routine that has been established. For instance, if you have completed the supposedly last interview, tell the informant that this is the formal end of the research but that you will maintain contact. Then gradually ease down the number and type of contacts so that hopefully the emotional and intellectual impact of the breaking down of the routine of the research process is not so great. Contact can then be maintained, or not, at a level which is negotiated between researcher and informant.

Alternatively, you may feel that setting up social distance and cutting relations totally and quickly is the most appropriate form of leave taking. You regard it as a clean break and as the mode of leaving the field which would provide the least possible future complications. Researchers using this approach have negotiated set time frames with informants at the beginning of the research process and have renegotiated them throughout so that when the last interview has taken place both parties expect a leave taking to occur. Obviously, if you wish to do follow-up research, or you are involved in a longitudinal study, then this would not be an appropriate approach to take. *There are no rules.* The pragmatics of leaving the field are directly tied to the foregoing research process, and the political and ethical stance the researcher has adopted in that process.

Objectivity

> Be a good craftsman [sic]. Avoid any rigid set of procedures. Above all seek to develop and use the sociological imagination. Avoid the fetishism of method and technique. Urge the rehabilitation of the unpretentious intellectual craftsman yourself. Let every man [sic] be his own theorist; let theory and method again become part of the practice of a craft (C.W. Mills 1959: 224).

Nearly every student entering introductory sociology courses would have heard the above quotation in Australian lecture theatres for at least the last twenty years. The underlying premise is a sound one. Mills is arguing for flexibility and creativity of thought. Nevertheless, the validity and reliability of qualitative research is often examined closely *precisely because* researchers try to carry out Mills' exhortation.

Objectivity: Validity and Reliability

It has been argued that **objectivity** can be divided into two components: reliability and validity. **Reliability** is the extent to which a measurement procedure yields the same answer. **Validity** is the extent to which it gives the correct answer, or a finding is interpreted in correct ways (Kirk & Miller 1986). How are these concepts applied in qualitative research? As we pointed out in chapter 2, people often confuse the terms and cannot perceive how they are distinct and yet related notions.

Objectivity is a difficult concept to define because the term is used to refer to different ideas and is often used ambiguously. Usually it is used to describe the goal or aim of scientific investigation, that is, objective knowledge. The assumption underlying this usage is that objective knowledge is free of bias or prejudice. Abercrombie et al. (1988) suggest that there are divisions of opinion as to whether objectivity or objective knowledge can be achieved. They also debate whether it is possible to be objective in social science research, and in particular qualitative research, using such strategies as in-depth interviewing. They present five arguments which have been advanced to say that social science research is not and cannot be objective.

1 Social science judgments are subjective, being coloured by the actors' own experiences.
2 All propositions are limited in their meaning to particular language contexts.
3 All social science theories are produced by, and limited to, particular social groups. Such a doctrine is often taken to be an outcome of the sociology of knowledge which treats all knowledge as a function of social location.
4 All observations are necessarily theory-laden.
5 In that all members of society have different values, social scientists will unconsciously, but necessarily, have their arguments influenced by their values (Abercrombie et al. 1988: 170).

The significance of this approach to objectivity is that the arguments used to state that social science research is not objective can be applied to all forms of science (Kuhn 1970). Objectivity is an aim or goal which is not really an achievable one. In fact, many theorists (Fay 1980; Wadsworth 1984) argue that it is not necessarily desirable. The researcher should be critical and espouse particular values in an explicit fashion.

The second usage of the term (which is related to the first) is one which is generally acknowledged (Douglas 1971; Kirk & Miller 1986). The aim of objectivity in research is making knowledge shareable. As Douglas (1971) points out, *shareability* is defined by members of the academic community who are interested in such knowledge. Truth (or what provisionally passes for truth at a particular time) is bounded by the tolerance of empirical reality and by the consensus of the scholarly community (Kirk & Miller 1986). If one takes this consensus into account then the objectivity of a piece of qualitative research can be examined and evaluated in terms of its validity and reliability.

Validity

In in-depth interviewing, the researcher tries to stay close to the empirical world in order to ensure a close fit between the data and what people actually say and do. According to Taylor and Bogdan (1984), this is attempted and achieved by calling things by the right names or being concerned with the validity or correctness of one's understanding of the informant's perceptions, view, attitudes and behaviours (see chapter 2).

> . . . our ability to identify a perverse use of terms as perverse depends on the assumption that there is such a thing as calling things by their right names, and this in turn depends on the assumption that there is a common world and that language's relation to it is not wholly arbitrary (Graff 1979: 90).

The in-depth interviewer is constantly engaged in checking perception and understanding against a host of possible sources of error to draw tentative conclusions from his or her current understanding of the situation (Kirk & Miller 1986). Probing, cross-checking and recursive interviewing are forms of validity checking. When using these techniques, the interviewer will sooner or later discover the discrepancies in the informant's story.

Why are such discrepancies a matter of interest for the researcher? Interview statements should not be treated as accurate or distorted versions of reality. We would argue, along with Silverman (1985: 176), that interview data 'display cultural realities which are neither biased nor accurate but real'. The researcher's focus should be aimed at analysing the moral and cultural forms that are displayed as they can provide a rich source of data of how people 'account for both their troubles and good fortune'. Therefore, bias and accuracy are still relevant issues. However, they should rather be seen as problems arising 'only in the analysis of data, not in the form or content of data (except in so far as participants are troubled by bias or accuracy)' (Silverman 1985: 176).

In-Depth Interviewing as a Validity Check

There are three types of error which are said to make research invalid. A *type one error* is believing a principle to be true when it is not. A *type two error* is rejecting a principle when in fact it is true. A *type three error* is asking the wrong question. The *latter* is the source of most validity errors in qualitative research (Kirk & Miller 1986). A wrong question is one which is not understood by the informant or is regarded by the informant as evidence of misunderstanding on the part of the researcher. Employing strategies to avoid asking the wrong question are vital to the in-depth interviewer. The use of multiple research methods is a commonly used strategy. If understanding derived from the asking of a question or series of questions in a conversation can survive 'the confrontation of a series of complementary methods of testing, it contains a degree of validity unattainable by one tested within the more constricted framework of a single method' (1986: 30).

Research has **external validity** when it shows something that is 'true' beyond the narrow limits of the study. If the findings are appropriate and 'true' not just for the particular time, place and people in the study but are generally so, the research is regarded as externally valid. The only way that one can 'objectively' assess external validity is to see if the results can be repeated in another time and place with different people and procedures. The more variations in places, people and procedures a piece of research can withstand and still yield the same findings, the more externally valid the conclusions. External validity is similar to reliability.

The researcher can never be ultimately sure that he or she has understood all the meanings and cultural implications elicited in the in-depth interviews. However, as Kirk & Miller suggest, 'the sensitive, intelligent fieldworker armed with a good theoretical orientation and good rapport over a long period of time is the best check we can make' (1986: 32). Enhanced validity is one of the legitimations for the enhancing of rapport and building a good relationship with your informants in the face to face interaction of the in-depth interview.

Reliability

For a technique of data collection to be reliable, we must show that the research can be repeated or replicated. However, it is not often that researchers are rewarded for simply repeating research, either their own or someone else's. Replications are often regarded as less creative and interesting than new discoveries, and are more difficult to publish.

Research that repeats the ideas or concepts rather than the procedural details of previous studies serves two purposes. First, it may provide some new discoveries about another set of events; and secondly, it can provide a conceptual replication of previous ideas. Exact replications of procedures and results demonstrate that the results are reliable. Conceptual replications of ideas and conclusions demonstrate that the research is externally valid.

Reliability in in-depth interviewing involves checking the strength of the data. The concern is whether or not, and under what conditions, the interviewer would expect to obtain the same finding if he or she tried to do the research again in the same way. The question to be asked then is how one assesses the reliability of research projects using in-depth interviewing as their primary method.

It is often pointed out that 'the claim to fame' of qualitative research is its ability to provide valid understandings of the meanings informants attach to behaviour, events, attitudes. It is also claimed that its major flaw is in providing and assessing reliability because of the difficulty of replicating such research. In order to reasonably assess reliability when using any research method, including in-depth interviewing, it is necessary for the researcher to document his or her procedure. This should be done in such a manner that any reader or prospective researcher can find details of how and why the researcher made certain decisions in the research process; their perceived impact on researcher and informant/s; how the data were collected (interviews only or personal documents in addition to in-depth interviews or multimethod use); and how they were analysed. Thus, the researcher provides a fully documented account of ethnographic decision making (Kirk and Miller 1986).

One way of improving the researcher's ability to provide an account which enables replicability is to adopt a language for coding the scientific behaviour of the researcher. Kirk and Miller (1986) propose that in writing an account of the research process, interviewers (or rather, qualitative researchers or ethnographers as they refer to them) might wish to use their four-phase model of science to outline their procedures and processes. They argue that qualitative research is the same as all other forms of science. There is an *invention phase* in which the research question is decided and a research design developed; a *discovery phase* in which data are collected; an *interpretation phase* during which analysis and theory building occurs; and an *explanation phase* in which the entire research process is packaged for communication.

This approach is useful in aiding the interviewer to write a detailed and literate account of the research process to allow for an assessment of reliability. However, there is a limitation in using this model when a research project is based on in-depth interviewing. This is because attendant analytical processes occur *throughout* the project. It is not so easy to determine when a researcher is engaged in which phase. They might, when engaged in probing, be involved in both the discovery phase and the interpretation phase. It is essential that, as researchers, we acknowledge the non-linear nature of research. Analysis in research using in-depth interviewing does not occur in a neat ordered fashion immediately after the data gathering but in fact simultaneously with it.

Objectivity in Selection of Research Problem

Let us assume that I have a certain piece of research in mind. How did I come to choose this topic? What were the motivations? Is it chosen because I am studying research methods and I have been given a limited choice? Perhaps I have chosen to examine physiotherapists' attitudes to body image—their own and that of patients—because I have been treated by a physiotherapist, noticed some disparaging responses from her during treatment and wondered if it affected her ability to treat me. Or perhaps I've decided to interview nurses about their vision of the role of nursing because I have been politically active on behalf of my own union for twenty years. I want to know what might motivate nurses to be more or less involved in industrial action. On the other hand, I may be a sociologist, psychologist, or clinician who has been working in a particular field, and I wish to expand my knowledge of that field by conducting research. Even at this stage of the research process, that is, the choice of research area or topic, the decision is very rarely a detached, neutral, objective, value-free choice. As was discussed in chapter 6, the rationale, and/or motivation will inevitably be predicated on my worldview, my life experiences, my age, ethnic background, gender, class and occupation. These factors are usually discussed as possible influences on researchers regarding their ability to ask questions appropriately. They are only fleetingly glossed over as factors focussing choice of research area.

> 'You can divorce your wife or abandon your child, but what can you do with yourself?'
> 'You can't banish the world if it's in you. Is that it, Joseph?'
> 'How can you? You have gone to its schools and seen its movies, listened to its radios, read its magazines. What if you declare you are alienated. You say you reject the Hollywood dream, the soap operas, the cheap thriller? The very denial implicates you' (Bellow 1973: 113).

The above quotation makes it abundantly clear that human beings cannot escape the social world which they have not only socially constructed, but also internalised. The question that should be asked is should they feel that they need to, in order to be *scientific?* This is a methodological issue for the researcher. As previously stated in chapters 2 and 3, the concept of an objective, neutral, value-free stance has been arbitrarily agreed upon by some members of the community as a useful criterion by which to judge research as being within the domain of science.

'Different ontological and epistemological positions generate different methodologies and methods for research' (Bilton et al. 1981: 630). Methodologies and methods are not constructed or chosen in isolation from ontological and epistemological positions. Rather, the manner in which we gain access to knowledge and our choice of the techniques for collecting evidence are directly related to our image of reality and the way we think we can know it. Obviously, our choice of research topic or question will be influenced by our worldviews or meaning systems.

The issue of objectivity within interpretive approaches to social science is a contentious one. There are those theorists who argue that when one has attempted to understand and interpret the actor's view of reality then one is in a position to give an objectively valid explanation of the nature of this socially constructed reality. On the other hand, there are theorists who argue that objectivity is not really possible. The researcher is simply another social actor interpreting and attributing meaning to the world through his or her interaction with others.

The researcher's account, even though it allows for a critical and professional understanding, does not necessarily provide a more objectively true account of society than the competing versions of others, whether they are social scientists or not. Therefore, the researcher's explanations and understandings, even of the topic, are subjective. The view put by some theorists such as Giddens (1976, 1982) is that the construction of social science explanations (in choice of topic, area, analysis and so on) is predicated on analysing a preinterpreted world in which knowledgeable social actors create and reproduce frames of meaning in conditions not of their choosing. To be able to analyse social life, the researcher has to penetrate these frames of meaning using skills similar to those whose conduct or action he or she is attempting to understand. According to Giddens, the purpose of mediating these frames of meaning is 'to generate descriptions of them that are potentially available to those who have not directly participated in them' (1976: 145). The researcher is then able to reinterpret or transform these frames of meaning into 'the technical terminologies invented by social scientists' (Giddens 1982: 13).

Subjectivity is almost a requirement for interpretive research such as in-depth interviewing. The notion of *bias* however is still there. After all, if I am a pro-nuclear activist, an anti-nuclear activist or a journalist, and I wish to interview members of a local community about their attitudes and understandings of nuclear energy, then whichever stance I take, I could still be accused of bias, irrespective of my personal and professional integrity. The assumption is that all our understandings of the world are theory laden, and that this is something which must be accounted for in the research process. There are a number of ways of doing this. One can either take an explicitly political stance and state one's own position throughout the various stages of the research project, or one can state prior assumptions and understandings of the research area at only the writing-up stage and let the reader be the judge. The bias is inherent, it does not go away. It is simply *counted in* to the research process. Taylor & Bogdan (1984) suggest the option of critical self reflection, that is, examining one's own 'perspectives, logic and assumptions'.

This methodological issue is raised before the researcher has made contact with the informant/s and is also tied to a number of other factors. These are: for *what purpose* is the research being undertaken, or as Wadsworth (1984) puts it, *for whom* is the research? This is a question that is not dealt with in most introductory research methods text. There is usually a sharp division drawn between 'knowledge and the uses of knowledge, between questions in the philosophy of social science and those in political philosophy, between scientific activity and political activity, and between theory and practice' (Fay 1975: 12). What Fay is ultimately drawing our attention to is the 'role which values have as part of the conceptual framework which defines what it is to have real, i.e., scientific knowledge about some phenomenon' (1975: 15).

If we accept a critical and interpretive framework and assume that there is an inter-relationship between *the actor's and the researcher's typifications and frames of meaning*; and that social agents (human beings—both researchers and researched) are both *knowledgeable* and *capable,* then we are not simply engaged in an analysis of action, but are also implicitly taking a political stance. This is because we recognise that the findings of the social sciences can be understood and taken up by those to whose behaviour they refer and that this is integral to their very nature.

As Giddens notes,

> It is the hinge connecting two possible modes in which the social sciences connect to their involvement in society itself: as contributing to forms of exploitative domination, or as promoting emancipation (1982: 14).

Researcher Bias?

This last point raises two methodological issues: first, the insider/outsider status of the researcher; and secondly, the time and space continuum in which research takes place (examined earlier in this chapter).

Although there is now a growing literature on the effects of gender in qualitative research (Oakley 1981; Roberts 1981)—and it is recognised that a fieldworker's gender, age, prestige, expertise or ethnic identity may limit or determine what he or she can accomplish—very little has been written on the effects of ethnic identity in the field, especially in terms of research strategies employed. We wish to elaborate on this particular aspect of the interviewer's identity and image because it provides a good example of the possible impact that the researcher's attributes may have on the informant and his or her relationship with that researcher.

Even though much attention has been focussed on the ethical problems of minority or ethnic research, very little has been directed at the methodological problems raised, and the techniques used have not been modified to any degree (Montero 1977). Also there is little written regarding the conditions faced by ethnic scholars conducting research in ethnic communities.

An Example: the Insider-outsider Controversy

The most commonly discussed methodological issue in research examining ethnic groups has focussed on the 'insider-outsider' controversy (that is, who should carry out such research?). It is argued on one side of the debate that insiders have a special knowledge of their own group, that they are 'endowed with special insight into matters necessarily obscure to others, thus possessed of a penetrating discernment' (Merton 1972: 11). On the other side, it is argued that 'unprejudiced knowledge about groups is accessible only to non-members of those groups' (Baca Zinn 1979: 210). This controversy is also applicable to other social groups, such as professions. Thus one could ask whether only nurses should research nurses, or occupational therapists research occupational therapists, and so on.

Merton's (1972) position paper on the sociology of knowledge was written as a response to the view held by many black American scholars that white researchers ought to be excluded from research in black communities (a view which he considered elitist and exclusionary). In this paper, he concludes that the debate can be overcome if researchers take heed of his plea for 'insiders and outsiders in the domain of knowledge [to] unite. You have nothing to lose but your claims. You have a world of understanding to win' (Merton 1972: 44).

Obviously, Merton did not consider several important methodological and empirical issues which are directly related to the politics of the setting. One of these is the perception that members of the ethnic group (with minority status) might have of the research enterprise itself. Past studies, particularly in the USA (Blauner and Wellman 1973; Moore 1967), have revealed a hostility toward and distrust of researchers by the communities being investigated. In the case of Jews in Melbourne, a community suspicion of non-Jewish researchers exists (Aroni 1985). Merton's call for unity ignores the larger context of ethnic relations in which the research process is carried out. For instance, in the case of Aroni's study, the advantage of being an insider was that her 'credentials' were evaluated as acceptable because of past associations with members of various groups in the Jewish community. She was identified as politically non-threatening in the context of Jewish and non-Jewish relations in the public arena. It was assumed that she 'understood' the community and would not 'misinterpret' various practices and the meanings attached to them. However, within the Jewish community any investigations of Jewish day schools not sponsored by communal organisations was regarded as potentially threatening to their image. Even though she was an 'insider' in terms of the Jewish community, she was not an 'insider' as far as the administrators of one of the schools was concerned.

In considering the insider/outsider controversy in terms of entrance to the field, insider status can have advantages in gaining access to the field. Of course, by the same token, that status also has its limitations if one is not readily identified as being politically sympathetic toward the institutions under examination. Ethnic researchers conducting studies within their own communities may experience problems common to all researchers, as well as the dilemmas posed by their own ethnic identity.

The methodological issue inherent in the insider/outsider controversy focusses on who can provide more satisfying or better sociological knowledge. In discussing this issue, Zinn (1979) contends that it is the lens through which minority scholars see that enables them to ask questions and gather information others could not. A number of researchers (Blauner and Wellman 1973; Ellis and Orleans 1971; Valentine and Valentine 1970; Zinn 1979) believe that insider researchers pose different questions due to their insight into various nuances of behaviour which an outsider may interpret as merely typical of the entire sample under investigation. Ellis and Orleans in their discussion of 'race research' in America argue:

> Undoubtedly, white social scientists are as capable of engaging in race research as their non-white colleagues even though their everyday experiences differ. However, because they come to the task with different backgrounds they are likely to see different problems and pose different questions. The intellectual and practical concerns may overlap, yet their analyses and recommendations will almost necessarily differ insofar as these are tempered by differences in the individual sense of urgency and conception of the possible (1971: 18).

The view attached to this position is that traditional theoretical frameworks do not fit minority experiences. Insider researchers are more likely to challenge such frameworks due to their supposedly more attuned interpretation.

The most obvious objection voiced against this view is that the subjectivity of insider researchers 'will lead to bias in data gathering and interpretation' (Zinn 1979: 213). However, those who voice this objection assume that somehow the observations and interpretations of outsiders are value-free. This in turn implies that social science and/or natural science is based on a perspective which sees the logic of knowledge construction as being neutral. As has already been stated, if one accepts the view that *all* observation is theory-laden (following Feyerabend), it seems logically, and politically, impossible to accept such a view.

Making knowledge *shareable* is the goal and aim of objectivity. This shareability is defined by members of the academic community who are interested in the collection and use of such knowledge (Douglas 1971). The researcher needs to provide systematic evidence of the actual research methods used to collect and analyse data so that there is some possibility of replication. This is one means of acknowledging one's stance as a researcher who retains political and personal integrity by maintaining *scientific* reliability and credibility.

However, even though the ethnic researcher (insider) may be more attuned to the informant's meanings, this in itself could present a problem. The ethnic researcher (insider) must guard against assuming a taken-for-granted stance toward the informants' meanings, languages and conceptualisations. The danger is that the researcher might not probe for details which may or may not indicate different interpretative schemes being used and/or relied upon by the informants. The assumption that an insider researcher is privileged in terms of 'in-group understanding' presupposes that the ethnic community is monolithic in nature and that there is little differentiation between various individuals' views on certain subjects. To retain the integrity of the phenomena, the ethnic researcher must attempt to straddle his or her insider's perspective with his or her outsider's stance.

An additional methodological problem is raised by doing research in one's *own* community. Once the existence of a research project becomes public knowledge in that community, it may or may not be considered that the degree of perceived political significance may impinge on the researcher's consciousness in a number of ways. Actual research strategies and methods need to be evaluated in terms of being appropriate within the political environment (which is also part of the process of the research project). For clarification and elaboration of this point, one can consider the impact of the political context of the Jewish community for Aroni as a researcher.

Apart from the work of Bullivant (1974–5), who was not regarded as an insider, most research conducted in Melbourne by Jewish social scientists examining issues of identification and/or education had relied on data elicited by the administration of a questionnaire. Bullivant's ethnography of the Yeshivah Boys' College was informed by a phenomenological and social anthropological methodology. It provided subsequent researchers (Aroni included) with sociologically useful and relevant material. However, the study raised much controversy within the Jewish community when it was published. The discussions centred on the claim that Bullivant's interpretations were derived not from proper scientific techniques but from his personal, subjective participation in school life as a teacher who was not an insider (and therefore whose ability to understand was curtailed by his status as *ethnic outsider*). The ethnographic mode of research was tarnished in the eyes of various members of the Jewish community because the results were evaluated as being *ethnically based* misinterpretations. Tied to this are the understandings, meanings and values various influential members of the Melbourne Jewish community have and hold regarding what constitutes valid knowledge upon which to base policy decisions. Their interpretations of validity (which will be discussed later) were influenced by their knowledge and experience of prior researchers in the area, most of whom opted for methods usually associated with positivistic methodologies. Apart from being professionally socialised in the positivist paradigm (most of them being 'trained' at the time when that paradigm in sociology was predominant), they were aware that facts and figures were what was required of them by communal policy-makers in order for their data and conclusions to be acceptable and used. In the case of Aroni's research project, the political implications due to the history of sociological enquiry in the Melbourne Jewish community influenced her choice of research strategy to include the administration of a questionnaire, even though in-depth interviewing remained the central strategy.

Obviously other factors were also involved in this choice, such as enabling comparability with previous research—thus partially satisfying the requirements of the academic sociological community as a critical reference group. If one accepts Merton's (1972) references to the 'corrupting influence of group loyalties upon the human understanding', the 'native' or 'insider' must somehow acquire distance in order to gain some objective perspective. Heilman (1980) argues that the researcher's status becomes that of 'stranger', as Simmel defines it, and not that of outsider.

The conceptualisation of objectivity inherent in the stranger's role 'does not signify mere detachment and remoteness, but is a distinct structure composed of remoteness and nearness, indifference and involvement' (Levine 1971). Obviously, the issue is related to the negotiation of position of the researcher in constructing sociological explanations as both participant and researcher. What has to be taken into account is that such categories as *insider*, *outsider*, *native* and *stranger*, should not be conceived of as absolute, but rather as terms of type and of degree. By conducting in-depth interviewing, the researcher (particularly the 'native-as-stranger') is in a good position to access social cues and intended meanings which would not be accessible to more structured methods.

Bias: Interviewer and Informant Relationships

To this point, we have discussed one example of how the interviewer's non-professional identities (that is, other than that of researcher) might infringe on the informant's perception of the researcher and the interview process altogether. There are a number of other perceptions that may influence or bias the informant's communication during the interview.

The background of the informant is something that he or she will inevitably bring in to the interview. When we are interviewed by someone, we do not suddenly discard the fact that we belong to a family, an ethnic and/or religious group and are members of a class or gender. We also see ourselves as being members of a particular age group, working in a particular occupation, and having a particular physiological status. We have all grown up in a particular time and place, in a particular group with a particular set of circumstances which we have experienced. This background comes with us into the in-depth interview. Obviously, not every role or group membership has 'potency or relevance' (Kadushin 1988) for developing or determining the informant's interaction/s in the interview situation. Rather those roles, attitudes and beliefs which the informant has decided are most relevant and relate to the perceived purpose of the interview will be drawn upon. The perceived purpose of the interview can be what the interviewee interprets as being the reason that the researcher has engaged in the research process but it can also refer to the reason for the informant's participation in that process. This can range from simple curiosity through to a desire to portray oneself in a favorable light even if only in the eyes of a social researcher. Even though it is understood that interviewers can influence an informant's discussion, the reverse is also the case.

Informants can manipulate the researcher's interpretation and definition of the situation—just as the researcher can—by half answering questions, not answering them, or making misleading statements. This may be done for a variety of reasons ranging from trying to impress the researcher, to simply trying to control any social interaction in which he or she might engage. For instance, the informant may have perceived the researcher to be someone who holds a very strong feminist stance, and may then gear his or her communication with the researcher to take this into account. They may wish to portray themselves as sympathetic to such a stance and frame their language to fit in with it; or they may wish to antagonise the researcher by using overtly sexist language to illustrate their own non-adherence to or defiance of such a perspective.

How does the researcher deal with these intended and unintended consequences of the in-depth interview situation and their relationship with the informant? There have been a number of suggestions made in chapter 6 as to how to carry out the interviewing process in a manner which enables the researcher to gain as accurate an understanding of the informant's interpretations as possible. However, as we discuss in chapters 3 and 12, the process of analysis involves a great many decisions about the unit which you are examining and *how* you can examine it—are you analysing the words, the phrases, the stories or the beliefs and meanings the informant attaches to these when you are interpreting their communications with you? This issue is discussed in greater detail in chapter 12.

One way of dealing with these issues is to try and use different methods to cross-check information so that even though you are focussing on the subjective view of the informant, you take into account and examine what you regard as possible sources of bias in his or her account and your own analysis and interpretation.

Use of Multiple Research Methods

In-depth interviewers are often confronted with problems of validity when they are asked what effect the interviewer's presence has on the informant's generation of data (that is, internal validity) and whether the data that are obtained in studying one situation can be generalised to another situation (external validity) (Burgess, 1974). Many researchers advocate the use of **triangulation** which is also known as **multiple strategies** of field research or **mixed strategies** as a means of overcoming problems of validity and bias (Burgess 1984; Campbell & Fiske 1959; Phillips 1985; Webb et al. 1966). **Triangulation** refers to the combination of different techniques of collecting data in the study of the same phenomenon, and its most well known proponent is Denzin.

There are two reasons for the use of triangulation. First, that the 'deficiencies of any one method can be overcome by combining methods and thus capitalising on their individual strengths'

(Blaikie 1988:1). Secondly, that it can be used to overcome the problems that stem from studies relying on 'a single theory, single method, single set of data and single investigation' (Burgess 1984: 144). All the advocates of this strategy only provide us with more variations on the same theme. It is regarded as a means of enhancing validity and decreasing possible bias.

Blaikie (1988) argues that triangulation is a metaphor that was originally drawn from surveying and that it is an inappropriate one for social science researchers. This is because in attempting to overcome problems of bias and validity 'the ontological and epistemological incompatibility of some methods is ignored' (Blaikie 1988: 7). In fact, Blaikie points to the fallacy of Denzin's arguments by asserting that 'he has abdicated the interpretivist concern for the primacy of meaning in favour of a positivist concern about validity and bias' (Blaikie 1988: 11). Blaikie is not the only critic of Denzin's lapse. Silverman also provides a very telling critique of the misuse of triangulation,

> . . . to overcome partial views and present something like a complete picture. Underlying this suggestion is, ironically, . . . elements of a positivist frame of reference which assumes a single (undefined) reality and treats accounts as multiple mappings of this reality. Interestingly, Denzin talks about 'measuring the same unit' and quotes from a text which supports multiple methods within a logic of hypothesis testing. Conversely, from an interactionist position, one would not expect a defence of hypothesis-testing nor, more importantly, of social 'units' which exist in a single form despite their multiple definitions.
>
> For an interactionist, ... without bias there would be no phenomenon. Consequently, . . . actions and accounts are 'situated'. The sociologist's role is not to adjudicate between participants competing versions but to understand the situated work that they do.
>
> Of course, this does not imply that the sociologist should avoid generating data in multiple ways . . . The 'mistake' only arises in using data to adjudicate between accounts. (Silverman 1985: 105–106).

The relevant point for qualitative researchers is the final one made by Silverman. There is nothing wrong with generating data in multiple ways. However, if one wishes to remain ontologically and epistemologically consistent then one might conceivably use 'different methods in a time sequence stage in the research process' (Blaikie 1988: 15). Aroni does this by using a questionnaire to initiate data collection in her research on Jewish identity and schooling. The material drawn from the questionnaire was used as a 'bouncing off' point for her in-depth interviews. The questionnaire was the method used in the brief initiating phase of the research and the process of administering it personally was used as a means of establishing rapport prior to the interview. Informants were also offered access to their questionnaires and to the research results.

Glossary

Cross-section A broad sampling of persons of different ages, income levels and ethnic background.
Cross-sectional study One that studies a cross-section of the population at a single point in time.
Epistemology A philosophical concept or term which is used as a technical definition of a theory of knowledge or how human beings come to have knowledge of the external world. In sociology, the term is often used to refer to the methods of scientific procedure which lead to the acquisition of sociological knowledge.
Gatekeepers Those individuals in an organisation that have the power to withhold access to people or situations for the purposes of research.
Ideal types Heuristic aids used in the construction of hypotheses. It is an exaggeration or idealisation of certain features of phenomena which are present in reality.
Incidental sampling (judgment and opportunistic sampling) Involves the selection of people, actions or events. Replication is impossible.
Locale Regionalisation on a time-space basis. The aspects of settings are normatively implicated in systems of interaction so that in some way they are set apart for certain individuals.
Mixed strategies See *triangulation*.
Multiple strategies See *triangulation*.
Participant observation A method of research widely used in sociology and anthropology in which the researcher takes part in the activities of a group or community being studied while also acting as observer.
Population Refers to the entire set of people you intend to study.
Random sampling Representative form of sampling where you list all members of the population and using some method such as dice or random number tables, you select your sample from the list of the population.
Reliability The extent to which a method of data collection gives a consistent and reproducible result when used in similar circumstances by different researchers and/or at different times.

Sample A subset of the population which is considered representative in some fashion.
Sampling The taking of a proportion of individuals or cases from a larger population, studied as representative of that population as a whole.
Saturation Refers to a process where no additional data can be found that would add to the categories being developed and examined, that is, you have reached saturation level.
Snowball sampling Involves using a group of informants with whom the researcher has made initial contact and asking them to put the researcher in touch with their friends; then asking them about their friends and so on, as long as they fit the criteria for the research project.
Stratified random sampling A variation of random sampling in which quotas are filled rather than just taking a random sample right across the population.
Theoretical sampling The process of data collection for generating theory whereby the analyst jointly collects, codes and analyses his or her data and decides what data to collect next and where to find them, in order to develop his or her theory as it emerges.
Triangulation The combination of different techniques of collecting data in the study of the same phenomenon. It is also referred to as the use of *multiple strategies*, *mixed strategies* or *multi method*.
Validity The extent to which a method of data collection represents or measures the phenomenon which it purports to represent or measure.

References

Abercrombie, N., Hill, S. & Turner, B. 1988. *The Penguin Dictionary of Sociology*. Harmondsworth: Penguin Books.

Allen, F.A. 1989. *BH101 Research Methods*. Unpublished lecture notes. La Trobe University, Bundoora, Vic.

Altheide, D. 1980. 'Leaving the field.', in W. Shaffir, R. Steffins & A. Turowetz (eds). *Fieldwork Experiences: Qualitative Approaches to Social Research*. New York: St Martin's Press.

Aroni, R. 1985. *The Effects of Jewish and non-Jewish Day Schools on Jewish Identity and Commitment*. Unpublished doctoral dissertation, Monash University, Clayton, Vic.

Bailey, K. 1989. *Methods of Social Research*. Fifth edition. New York: Free Press.

Bellow, S. 1973. *The Dangling Man*. Ringwood, Victoria: Penguin Books.

Bell, C & Newby, H. 1977. *Doing Sociological Research*. London: Allen & Unwin.

Bell, C. & Encel, S. (eds) 1978. *Inside the Whale: Ten Personal Accounts of Social Research.* Sydney: Pergamon Press.

Bilton, T., Bonnett, K., Jones, P., Stanworth, M., Sheard, K. & Webster, A. 1981. *Introductory Sociology.* London: Macmillan.

Blaikie, N. 1988. *Triangulation in Social Research: Origins, Use and Problems.* Paper presented at the Conference of the Sociological Association of Australia and New Zealand, Canberra.

Blauner, R. & Wellman, D. 1973. 'Toward the decolonisation of social research.', in J. Ladner (ed.). *The Death of White Sociology.* New York: Vintage Books.

Bullivant, B. 1975. *The Way of Tradition: Life in an Orthodox Day School.* Canberra Australian Council for Educational Research.

Bulmer, M. 1979. 'Concepts of the analysis of qualitative data: A symposium.' *Sociological Review* 27: 651–677.

Burgess, R.G 1982. *Field Research: A Sourcebook and Field Manual.* London: Allen Unwin.

Burgess, R.G. 1984. *In the Field: An Introduction to Field Research.* London: Allen Unwin.

Campbell, D.T. & Fiske, D.W. 1959. Convergent and Discriminant validation by the multitrait—multimethods matrix., *Psychological Bulletin* 56: 81–105.

Cohen, S. & Taylor, L. 1972. *Psychological Survival: The Experience of Long Term Imprisonment.* Harmondsworth: Penguin.

—— 1977. 'Talking about Prison Blues.', in C. Bell and H. Newby (ed.). *Doing Sociological Research.* London: Allen & Unwin.

Denzin, N.K. 1970. *The Research Act: A Theoretical Introduction to Sociological Methods.* London: Butterworth.

Deutscher, I. 1973. *What We Say/What We Do.* Glenview, Illinois: Scott, Foresman and Co.

Douglas, J.D. 1971. *Understanding Everyday Life.* London: Routledge and Kegan Paul.

—— 1976. *Investigative Social Research.* Beverly Hills, California: Sage.

Ellis, W. & Orleans, P. 1971. 'Race Research: Up against the Wall in More Ways Than One.', in Orleans, P. & Ellis, W. (eds). *Race, Chains and Urban Affairs Annual Review*: 5. Beverly Hills: Sage.

Fay, B. 1980. *Social Theory and Political Practice.* London: George Allen & Unwin.

Giddens, A 1979. *Central Problems in Social Theory: Action, Structure and Contradiction in Social Analysis.* London: Macmillan.

—— 1982. *Profiles and Critiques in Social Theory.* London: Macmillan.

Glaser, B.G. & Strauss, A. 1967. *The Discovery of Grounded Theory.* Chicago: Aldine.

Graff, G. 1979. *Literature Against Itself.* Chicago: University of Chicago Press.

Heilman, S. 1980. 'Jewish Sociologist: Native-As-Stranger.', *The American Sociologist* Vol. 15: 100–108.

Huberman, A.M. & Miles, M.B. 1983. 'Drawing valid meaning from qualitative data: some techniques of data reduction and display.', *Quality and Quantity* 17: 281–339.

James, N. 1984. 'A Postscript to Nursing.', in C. Bell & H. Roberts (eds). *Social Researching: Politics, Problems, Practice*. London: Routledge and Kegan Paul.

Jick, T.D. 1979. 'Mixing qualitative and quantitative methods: triangulation in action.', *Administration Science Quarterly*. 24: 602–611.

Kadushin, A. 1988. *The Social Work Interview*. Second edition, New York: Columbia University Press.

Kidder, L.H. 1981. *Selltiz Wrightsman and Cook's Research Methods in Social Relations*. Fourth edition. New York: Holt Saunders International Editions.

Kidder, L.H., & Judd, C.M. 1986. *Research Methods in Social Relations*. Tokyo: CBS Publishing Japan Ltd.

Kirk, J. & Miller, M. 1986. *Reliability and Validity in Qualitative Research*. Beverly Hills, California: Sage.

Kuhn, T.S. 1970. *The Structure of Scientific Revolutions. Second edition. Chicago: University of Chicago Press.*

Liebow, E. 1967. *Tally's Corner*. Boston: Little Brown.

Mann, M. (ed.) 1987. *Macmillan Student Encyclopedia of Sociology*. Fourth edition. London: Macmillan Press.

Merton, 1972. 'Insiders and Outsiders: A Chapter in the Sociology of Knowledge'. *American Journal of Sociology*

Mills, C.W. 1959. *The Sociological Imagination*. London: Oxford University Press.

Moore, J.W. 1973. 'Social constraints on sociological knowledge: academics and research concerning minorities.', *Social Problems* 21: 65–77

Oakley, A. 1984. 'Interviewing Women: A Contradiction in Terms.', in Helen Roberts (ed.). *Doing Feminist Research*. London: Routledge and Kegan Paul.

Patton, R. 1980. *Qualitative Evaluation Methods*. Beverly Hills, California: Sage.

Pettigrew, J. 1988. 'Reminiscences of fieldwork among the Sikhs.', in Helen Roberts (ed.). *Doing Feminist Research*. London: Routledge and Kegan Paul.

Phillips, B. 1985. *Sociological Research Methods: An Introduction*. Homewood, Illinois: Dorsey.

Polgar, S. & Thomas, S. 1988. *Introduction to Research in the Health Sciences*. Melbourne: Churchill Livingstone.

Roberts, H. 1988. *Doing Feminist Research*. London: Routledge and Kegan Paul.

Shaffir, W.B., Stebbins, R.A., & Turowetz, A. 1980. *Fieldwork Experience: Qualitative Approaches to Social Research*. New York: St Martin's Press.

Shipman, M.D. 1972. *The Limitations of Social Research*. London: Longman Group.

Silverman, D. 1985. *Qualitative Methodology and Sociology*. Aldershot, Hants: Gower Publishing Co. Ltd.

Spender, D. 1988. 'The gatekeepers: a feminist critique of academic publishing.', in H. Roberts (ed.). *Doing Feminist Research*. London: Routledge and Kegan Paul.

Valentine, C. & Valentine, V. 1970. *Making the Scene, Digging the Action and Telling It Like It Is: Anthropologists and Work In a Dark Ghetto: Contemporary Perspectives.* New York: Free Press.

Van Maanen, J. 1970. 'Qualitative methodology.', *Administrative Science* Quaterly 24: 4 + (Special Issue).

Wadsworth, Y. 1984. *Do it Yourself Social Research.* Collingwood, Victoria: Victorian Council of Social Service.

Webb, E.J., Campbell, D.T., Schwartz, R.D. & Sechvest, L. 1966. *Unobstrusive Measures: Non-Reactive Research in the Social Sciences.* Chicago: Rand McNally.

Whyte, W.F. 1955. *Street Corner Society.* Chicago: University Chicago Press.

Zinn, M. 1979. 'Field Research in Minority Communities: Ethnic, Methodological and Political Observations by an Insider.', *Journal of Social Problems* Vol. 27, No. 2, December, 208–214.

Chapter 10
Ethics

There are a number of factors which must be clarified and reiterated at the outset of a chapter on ethics. The politics and ethics of social research are not divorced from any part of the research process. Each decision that we, as researchers, make, involves not only a practical or **methodological** component but also an ethical and political one, even if this is not immediately apparent. The interrelationship between these various elements of research is inevitable in the practice of research. The reasons we have separated these factors into distinct chapters are twofold. First, if we tried to capture the complex interrelationships on paper, then we would have no chapters or headings, because in the process of writing a book on in-depth interviewing, we would simply try to follow the intertwined complex relationships between theory, method, pragmatic issues and political and ethical concerns as they have occurred in the research process. This would be good as an appendix or an accompanying volume providing a **phenomenological** account of in-depth interviewing, but in and of itself may not clarify the issues that are raised if one is planning to engage in in-depth interviewing for the first time. Secondly, we think it is important to highlight these issues as central to any research enterprise. As previously stated, the political and ethical factors inevitably influence the theoretical, methodological and practical choices that are made.

We are not providing a list of *do's* and *don'ts* because each researcher will have to decide those for himself or herself in relation to the context of the research. The rest of the chapter will delineate the dimensions of politics and ethics as part of the researcher's explicit recognition of the impact of power on social relations—including the special social relations encountered in doing in-depth interviewing.

Ethical and Political Issues

Each research process will engender its own ethical and political dilemmas. Research projects which are essentially based on in-depth interviewing may strike all the same possible ethical quandaries as other forms of research. The political context of the research can influence the nature of the ethical considerations brought to bear during the process. When we use the term **political** here, we include the politics of interpersonal relations, the politics of intergroup relations, the cultures and resources of research organisations—including universities and government research units and the power of the state. The politics of these contexts influence not only the outcomes of research projects, their design and implementation, but also what the researcher will perceive as presenting moral dilemmas.

Ethics is the study of standards of conduct and moral judgment. In this context, the term is used to denote the system or code of morals we apply to the research process, be it as individuals and/or as members of a profession. Social research ethics involves the consideration of the moral implications of social science inquiry. There are three elements which are usually considered when examining research in terms of ethics and politics.

1 The morality of the practices used, and the personal and professional morality of the researcher who used them.
2 The integrity, both personal and professional, of the researcher.
3 Social justice in relation to the informant/s, the community, the profession and/or the society at large.

The central ethical and political questions that must be asked of any research programme are, 'Who is it for?' and 'What is it for?' (Wadsworth 1984), and 'How can the research be done so that the abovementioned three elements are sustained?'.

There is a question which underscores all these elements and highlights their contentious nature. Who decides what counts as personal and professional morality, integrity and social justice in any circumstance, including the research one? The answer we give is that those individuals, groups or institutions who hold power are the ones who usually decide what counts. Power and control in social research is also specifically raised in the social interaction between the interviewer and the informant. Figure 10.1 gives a brief suggestion of some of the ethical and political issues raised in research using in-depth interviewing. This is not an exhaustive list (see Punch 1986).

As mentioned in the previous chapter, one's choice of research topic and research design is influenced by who you are, the socialisation processes that you have been involved in (both personally and professionally) and the social and political climate of the era. Thus, if you grew up in Australia in the 1960s and 70s, and studied social sciences in the 1980s during your nursing studies, then your choice of research topic and method would be influenced not only by your personal background but also by the theoretical perspective you learned; your views as an individual and as a member of the nursing profession; and the exigencies of trying to complete a piece of research within a limited time period for a specific reading audience. This sentiment was stated much earlier by Max Weber (1958) in his essay 'Science as a Vocation', where he discusses the relationship between facts and values and their implications for policy. Weber argued that all research is tainted to some degree by the values of the researcher. In most Australian tertiary institutions, the research project would also have to be approved by their **ethics committee**.

Research Processes	Ethical & Political Issues
Design of Research Project	• Is the researcher competent and capable of conducting research? That is, were they credited with professional integrity?
Sponsorship	• Does the researcher pay for the research, or is it some other group or institution? • Who benefits from the study? • Who has access to data and results? • How do you maintain confidentiality of informants if you are not the only 'owner' of the raw data (tapes/notes/ transcripts, personal documents)?
Access	• Who controls the research process? • How ethical are the methods that the researcher is prepared to use to gain access to informants?
In-depth Interviewing	• Who has control of the interactions? • Whose interpretation of the situation is accorded validity? • How is confidentiality maintained and trust developed? • What effects does the research have on the informant? • To what degree can the participants strike and keep a bargain? • If the researcher controls the recording process, is the informant's view of what should be recorded given equal weighting?
Analysis	• Who has control of storing of data and the maintaining of confidentiality? • Is the researcher's analysis 'keeping faith' with the informant's account?
Presentation of Data	• What effect does the informant as audience have? • Who owns the research report—sponsor/s researcher/s, or informant/s? • What is the purpose of publication? • Who has control of publication and/or censorship of the report?

Figure 10.1 Idealised account of some ethical and political issues raised during research.

Costs and Benefits: a Difference in Values

The ethical and political questions raised in the choice of topic and the design of research revolve around weighing the potential benefits of asking the research question against the anticipated costs. This is of necessity a subjective assessment of two sets of values. One value or right is that of the social scientist to inquire, to gain knowledge and to advance scientific theory. The social scientist hopes to advance knowledge which will be of practical value to society and the research participants (Kidder 1981). The other value, or right, is that of the informant to maintain privacy, dignity, and self-determination (Kidder 1981). As Kidder points out,

> A discussion not to conduct a planned research project limits the first of these rights. A decision to conduct the research despite its questionable practices with research participants limits the second (1981: 368).

Ethical Absolutist or Situational Relativist?

The researcher can be an **ethical absolutist** or a **situational relativist** in dealing with ethical and moral dilemmas in the research process. The ethical absolutist position is one in which researchers want to establish specific principles to guide all social research. Such principles are often developed and devised into a professional code of ethics which is to be adhered to by all members of the profession.

The situational relativist holds that there can be no absolute principles of ethical research behaviour or absolute guidelines. They argue that the social science researcher is faced with the same ethical and moral issues that he or she confronts in everyday life and has to handle them both in the same way. That is, they have to come to an ethical decision according to their individual interpretation of the situation at hand. Ethics are up to the individual's conscience.

There are advantages and disadvantages in taking either stance. If social science researchers hold to the absolutist position then there is some form of collective responsibility which helps to prevent individual researchers besmirching the integrity of all researchers. On the other hand, the use of a formalised code of ethics may end up producing social research which is unadventurous and sterile. Researchers may be too confined to ask useful and creative questions which overstep guidelines.

The option that seems to take into account the informant, the researcher, and future potential researchers is the one where the professional body representing the discipline devises a set of guidelines or a code of ethics which still allow the researcher to make some personal ethical choices in the context of the research process itself.

Who and What is it for?

A significant part of one's choice of topic is working out what it is you actually want to find out. This is to begin with, a practical problem but it is tied to two questions, 'What are my values and interests in choosing this topic?;' Who and what is the choice of this research project for? The identification of *who* and *what* the research is for is crucial for any research undertaking.

These questions, 'What is the research for?' and 'Who is it for?', are interdependent and have an impact on the research design. Who is the **critical reference group?** What are its interest according to its members? Is the research area, topic or group being chosen to provide the researcher with increased status in the academic community by being able to complete a Ph.D.? Does the researcher wish to provide the group being researched with some information which may empower them in the political arena? Is the researcher trying to achieve both aims? Or is the researcher employed by other interested parties or groups such as universities, foundations, charitable institutions, government bodies, unions, etc. where the critical reference group is the employing body?

Wadsworth (1984) clarifies this issue in her discussion of critical reference groups. She points out that, in answering these questions, the researcher needs to understand that the *who and what* research is for will be tied to the research design, practice, ethical stance and what the researcher does with the results once the research is completed. She designates *who* as 'the critical reference group or groups' and then lists some, 'the researcher or researchers, those the research is for (to help meet their interests, solve their problems); the researched . . .' (1984: 8).

If you are a member of the group that you are researching, then determining the values and interests of the group beforehand may be easier. However, it is important to remember when interviewing members of the group that the group is not monolithic, that all members do not necessarily all have the same views or values, that you, as the researcher, may need to 'sort out what the shared interests, views, ideas, etc. are that the research is intended to serve'. The assumption made by Wadsworth is that research should be done to aid those being researched and that this is essential to a form of research known as '**action research**'. Action research is research 'in which the knowledge and techniques of social science are combined with practical policy initiatives to plan and achieve social change' (Mann 1987: 2). This brings us back to the audience for the research and the issue of access and sponsorship. The critical reference group might include your Ph.D. examiners and other sociologists, psychologists and/or clinicians, the people who were the informants, the people who you wish to influence by doing the research and/or the general public.

An Example: History of a Process

Let us examine the initial stages of Aroni's (1985) doctoral dissertation as an example of our discussion to date. She had decided on a research question after hearing an issue discussed at many dinner-table conversations among her peer group. In the Jewish community of Melbourne (of which she was a member), there were many assumptions made regarding the impact of schooling—just as in the general community there is a belief that schooling makes a difference. However, the precise nature of the effects of schooling was a debated issue. Jewish communal leaders, teachers and parents commented on the rise in the assimilation and intermarriage rates of Jews into the surrounding non-Jewish society. They assumed that if their children attended Jewish day schools then this might prevent or at least slow down the rate—because Jewish children would be inculcated with Jewish values and the schools would instil Jewish identity. They felt that this was the task of the school, just as they felt it was the task of the school to provide the students with an education that would enable them to succeed in the majority culture while retaining their own ethnicity.

She noted that the majority of the comments were made by concerned Jewish adults—either parents, teachers, communal leaders and/or Jewish social researchers—and not by those who were directly affected by the results of decisions regarding Jewish schooling in Melbourne, namely, the students. The purpose of Aroni's research was to examine if *in the view of the Jewish students*, attending or not attending a Jewish day school had any impact on their sense of Jewishness in terms of identification and/or personal identity. If so, in what manner and to what degree; and if not, what other factors did they evaluate as significant.

From the perspective of the researcher, the study had four critical reference groups—members of the Jewish community who participated as informants; those Melbourne Jews who are involved in forming the Jewish schools' educational policy; the academic community of sociologists; and the researcher herself. All these groups influenced the researcher, not only from the point of view of ethical commitments, but also in terms of methodological stance and choice of research techniques and strategy. She herself shared the values and interests of some members of the Jewish community. These values and interests included the perpetuation of a strong, viable and committed Jewish community in Melbourne. However, she also shared the values and interests of the academic community of sociologists. This meant that she had to display personal and professional integrity not only to the group which was being researched but to the group which would critically examine the research from an alternative perspective. The questions of bias and objectivity are again raised here as issues of personal and professional morality and integrity, not simply as concerns of methodology.

Punch (1986) points out that when reading field research, the reader is heavily reliant on the integrity of the researcher in terms of detailing the nature and number of interviews, the data analysis process and the criteria for the selections included in the research report. Usually the personal logs and diaries of the researcher are not available, the interviews are not always quoted at length and the reasons for selecting and specifying particular quotes and incidents are not articulated (Van Maanen 1984). The reader is then reliant on the academic integrity of the researcher,

> in coming clean not only on the nature of his [sic] data, how and where it was collected, how reliable and valid he [sic] thinks it is, and what successive interpretations he [sic] had placed on it—but also on the nature of his [sic] relationship with the field setting and with the 'subjects' of the inquiry (Punch 1986: 15).

The researcher needs to maintain his or her personal and professional integrity by establishing competence in choice of research topic, research design and conduct of the research project. This involves establishing credibility in the eyes of the critical reference groups. In the case of the academic community and the Jewish community, Aroni's research design needed to indicate that her personal commitments were clearly stated so that they could be taken into account by anyone assessing the research project.

Sponsorship

Who intiated the research project? Was it the researcher? The group being interviewed? Or another interested party such as a government research body or private industry? How can this affect the research project?

Discussions of this issue usually refer to the impact of **sponsorship** on researchers' conduct, loyalties and understandings of why they do research. As Roberts so succinctly put it, 'To whom does our primary duty as researchers lie and how can we maximise the effectiveness of the work we do?' (1984: 201). Does our loyalty go to those being interviewed or those who commissioned and funded the research project (assuming that they are not the same)?

If we return to our earlier example of Aroni's research, we can see some of the problems raised by sponsorship of research. One of the members of the governing body of one of the Jewish day schools had sponsored another researcher to investigate almost exactly the same research question. Aroni discovered this and discussed two issues with her supervisor. First, did it matter if there was more than one research project examining similar issues and dealing with the same informants, and, secondly, would it be appropriate to join the research team that was being employed by a member of the school board?

These questions were discussed in terms of whether another researcher would 'spoil the field', that is, make it difficult for future researchers such as Aroni to interact with informants (who were already jaded by participating in a research project, particularly one dealing with similar issues). By joining a research team paid for by a member of the school board, what sort of control would each team member have in deciding the research strategies to be employed and the mode of analysis to be used?

To what use would the research be put, and how would the time and manner of the publication of results be influenced? Would there be problems with the sponsor if some or all the analysis was unfavourable to his or her school and if so, would there by any attempts to suppress data? Aroni, in conjuction with her supervisor, decided that the independence of her research might be threatened—independence was a critical factor in the assessment of doctoral dissertations—and that the costs both ethically and methodologically were too great. She decided to make contact with the informants without the backing of the other parties in the field. After informing them of her decisions to go it alone she discovered what the term **gatekeepers** meant! This brings us to the political and ethical concerns of gaining access to the population which you wish to study.

Gaining Access and Informed Consent

What sort of methods are you prepared to use to gain access to your informants? Will you be overt or covert in your approach? How ethical are these methods particularly when your research is jeopardised by intransigent gatekeepers? Are you prepared to use back-door methods? How do you decide if the end justifies the means?

Access and acceptance are critical to in-depth interviewing (as they are to any form of research). For instance, the reputation of one's institutional affiliation can influence access in either a positive or negative fashion. If you are a researcher who has presented documentation and credentials establishing your project as being carried out under the auspices of a prestigious university, you are more likely to gain access to informants than someone who simply knocks on the front door and introduces himself or herself as a student who wants to ask about attitudes to euthanasia. However, in some settings, certain credentials may be irrelevant or harmful. You may be investigating attitudes to euthanasia with predominantly devout Catholic informants. They may know that the head of department who has authorised your research and signed your letter of introduction is well known for his or her humanist views. They might not be happy to participate in a study that was associated with this individual. In this case, the research would suffer from being seen as an extension of the academic sponsor. The politics of the social context will have determined the prospective informant's perspective of the researcher's integrity and ethical stance.

The term **informed consent** is drawn from the medical sciences where there is a possibility that actual physical harm can be done to participants and patient's rights can be violated. It is important to acknowledge this background because the attempts that have been made to control biomedical research and protect patients is the model upon which social science has based its codes of ethics in relation to informant participation and protection. It has been pointed out (Punch 1986) that we attempt to protect the rights of vulnerable groups (children, the aged, prisoners, the institutionally confined mentally ill, etc.) because their rights have been violated in past research, particularly in biomedical research. Professional and ethical codes have been drawn up to include principles which cover the 'dignity and privacy of individuals, the avoidance of harm and the confidentiality of research data' (Punch 1986: 35).

The question that has been raised is, how applicable is this model to social science research? The concept of informed consent presumes that the informants participating in research have the right to be informed that they are being researched and what the nature of the research is. How appropriate is this concept to in-depth interviewing? Informing someone that they are being interviewed is not usually problematic. However, how much do you wish to tell the informant about the nature of the research project, particularly if you feel that it will influence their discussion of the area which you are examining? In many cases, to provide full information would destroy the research project. In other cases, it may be the only way to secure access. Do we take the ethically absolutist position, or opt for the situational relativist one?

Researcher/Informant Relationships

This brings us back to the political and ethical problems in research relations. The questions that each researcher must ask are, 'What are the risks and benefits for those individuals who participate in research? What should participating individuals be told about the nature of the research project? How essential is informed consent? What form of protection might individuals who participate in social research need? How far does the researcher intrude before there is an invasion of privacy which is intolerable to the informant? What *is* the relationship between the researcher and informant?

The Debate: Overt or Covert—Do the Ends Justify the Means?

When establishing the researcher/informant relationship, it is also important to establish the moral ground. This is done by providing the informant with accurate information such as your aims and goals in doing the research, how the interview data will be stored, what you the researcher will do with the information and whether your plans for the final product will be of any benefit to the informant.

This is the ideal version. Yet as has been debated by many researchers (Bulmer 1980, 1982; Denzin 1978; Erikson 1968), whether one should be involved in overt or covert research is a moot point. Erikson has argued that the researcher is being unethical if he or she deliberately misrepresents his or her identity for the purpose of securing access to the 'private domain' of the informant/s. Also, the researcher is being unethical to misrepresent the character and nature of the research in which he or she is involved. Denzin has responded to Erikson's comments by arguing that there can be no invasion of privacy if one does not accept the disfunction between the public and private domain. All methods can pose a potential threat to colleagues. The essential debate boils down to whether one accepts that 'what is good for social science is inherently ethical', which is what Erikson accused Denzin of doing. The related question is whether certain pieces of research should be carried out at all, if they are so dangerous to individuals.

> Anyone who has been interviewed, even on trivial topics (such as which television programmes they watched last week) will know that the interview is a rare enough event for it to leave a mark on the interviewee. You find yourself rethinking what you said, aware of the gaps between what you wanted to say and what you were able to say. When interviewed on deeper topics, such as how you see your work or relationships within the family, or your feelings about death, the effect is more marked. The interview both opens up areas of dialogue in taken-for-granted areas of your life, and at the same time, perhaps because of the conversational asymmetry in the relationship between the interviewer and the interviewee, fails to offer a sense of closure. As a result the interviewee typically emerges from the interview with a feeling of being left stranded. It is the researcher who goes away with the data to rework it in his or her own fashion, to gain satisfaction from making it make sense, and who indeed has the context to do so (Walker 1989: 37).

This vision of the relationship between researcher and informant is unfortunate but seems reasonably accurate if one examines published accounts of the research process. The researcher very rarely addresses the **social justice** issue of who the research is for, because it seems that it is for him or her. Establishing rapport for a period of time is regarded as a reasonable cost if it means publication of research! The nature of such a relationship is hardly ethical when one is being entirely exploitative. This issue has been raised by Oakley (1984) in her discussion of 'feminist interviewing' where she examines the nature of the relationship between women who are informants and those who are researchers, using herself as the example. She points out that inherent in the nature of *normal* human relationships is reciprocity of conversation. While she is doing the interviewing, the least she can do for her informants is answer their queries and share their problems in the context of their social interaction. However, she points out that most textbooks would suggest that this is inappropriate behaviour for an interviewer. Wadsworth (1984) has also raised this issue in the context of talking about action research and who it is done for—the answer for Wadsworth being *those who are studied*. She also comments that the least one can do is to prevent the research being used to hurt or offend those who have helped. She also refers to the avoidance of causing *social hurt* by keeping promises of confidentiality.

Confidentiality and Anonymity

People often given consent to be interviewed when they know that they will not be individually identifiable because their **anonymity** has been guaranteed by the researcher. Hence, the researcher who promises to use pseudonyms is more likely to gain access to a sample. **Confidentiality** does not refer simply to protecting names and keeping confidences but sometimes to protecting other information about the informant. This is often done by altering details in description of people, places and/or events. The entire process takes the form of a bargain. It is based on the notion that the individual will agree to taking part in the research process and become the informant *if* the researcher keeps his or her side of the bargain by promising to create and maintain anonymity and confidentiality. The pragmatics of this process are not always as simple and easy as the texts make them sound. Where does the researcher store his or her own personal research diary (which probably includes the names, addresses and phone numbers of the informants particularly when constant use is made of this to arrange interview times)? If one promises to keep it under lock and key then is it to be kept locked in the home of the researcher or in the workplace or elsewhere? The ideal situation would be strict adherence to whatever is promised but this is rarely the case. The problem is that it is necessary to make bargains and promises which can be kept! Making initial contact with informants is not simply a matter of gaining access and being courteous. The informant must be able to trust the researcher and be confident in what you say. This is essential to successful social interaction in most conversations.

As we have stated, much of the material written on the ethics and morality of the research process utilise concepts from medical research (such as informed consent). Many comments have been critical in relation to the applicability of these concepts in non-medical research. On the other hand, the basic underlying concepts are the same—the integrity of the researcher in carrying out research, the morality and ethics of the relationship between researcher and researched, and the consideration of social justice issues in determining who benefits from the research process and the publication of results.

Data Collection and Dissemination: Control and Privacy

Let us again assume that you, as the researcher, have gained access to informants; you have given them a brief introduction and explanation of the research project as you see it and now you proceed to the asking of questions and discussion of topics which might bear on your research problem. How invasive should you allow your questions to be? At what point is the informant's privacy infringed? Do you use trick questions to elicit sensitive and private material from your informant? In some cases, the informant will let you know in no uncertain terms that you have infringed his or her privacy when you ask questions which overstep their subjectively determined boundary. In other cases, you may decide that unless you elicit information on certain areas and issues that an informant regards as private and confidential, then you will not have a valid understanding of those issues and your research project will not be worth doing. The decision is based on your subjective consideration of the ethical choice and whether your choice is morally allowable within your own ethical framework and boundaries, or, morally reprehensible and not allowable within that same framework. The political pressures in such a situation are twofold. At one level, the pressure to produce many good research reports quickly may be very strong, particularly if future promotion and status are dependent on such publications. At the other level, there may be political pressure to present oneself as being a researcher of great integrity who maintains an ideologically and ethically sound stance in relation to participants (that is, in research projects which you initiate and carry out). Both pressures may be applied to the researcher and the choice is both a political and ethical one.

As stated in chapter 5, the interviewer usually has control of the interactions during the interview even though this may not be apparent to the informant. In many cases, it is an intended control. In others, even where the researcher has negotiated a more egalitarian relationship with the informant, it becomes an unintended consequence of the research process itself and of the social and political structures and settings in which it takes place. In this context, even though in-depth interviewing is oriented around placing the informant's interpretations and meanings at centre stage, it is often the interviewer's interpretation of the situation which is accorded greater validity. This can include decisions about which subject matter is to be regarded as private and confidential and which should not. This becomes most obvious in negotiations about record keeping and note taking. In some instances, an informant will ask the researcher to turn off the tape recorder while he or she refers to something which he or she has defined as private or confidential. The researcher is often reluctant to do this because he or she anticipates that the forthcoming information might be significant to the research project. For the informant, the privacy issue is translated from the immediate context of the research process to the promises of confidentiality and anonymity which he or she had been given in terms of the storage of the data and its subsequent publication and future dissemination.

Again, there are no set rules apart from the subjective deliberations one makes in determining whether an action is ethically sound. Perhaps the most significant factor to remember is that researchers, like other professionals, are held accountable for their actions—be it by an ethics committee, a research methods lecturer, the group or individual being researched and the researcher's own conscience.

Analysis and Publication

The presentation and dissemination of data is also a stage of research which is fraught with political and ethical dilemmas. In relation to anonymity and confidentiality, the researcher should again try and keep faith with informants by disguising their identity and information so that the individual is not identifiable. This is usually achieved by the use of pseudonyms and slight changes of descriptive information. Is it desirable if you want to provide your readers with accurate information? The researcher is usually placed in the position of trying to balance the needs of the informant for privacy with the needs of the audience for accurate and detailed data. In many instances, this is not possible, especially when the group researched is part of a small community or the research was focussed on well known or famous individuals. Then the initial promises should not have been made or at least stated in a qualified and realistic form.

It is often the case that when a researcher is engaged in coding and analysing data that he or she will discuss queries and problems with relevant associates and colleagues. When promising confidentiality and anonymity to informants, did the researcher explicitly extend his or her own access to and reading of the data to these colleagues? Were informants aware that someone else might read or listen to their statements in unreconstructed and undisguised form? We think that the most useful way to overcome such possible violations of promises is to try and identify ethical issues before they become problems (although foreseeing all such problems is not possible). For instance, the researcher should gain informed consent from the informant for the use of a tape recorder during interview sessions. This should be done with full explanations of the problems of maintaining confidentiality and anonymity in all research.

Who is the Research for?

Another issue raised at this stage of the research echoes our initial question of who the research is for. Was the research sponsored? Were there any expectations on the part of the sponsor and/or the researcher which were not specified at the beginning of the project? Did any stated expectations change? The power relationship between sponsors and researchers exists whatever the topic of research and is often most felt when the researcher wishes to publish the results of his or her research and make the material public. It is when the research takes an unexpected turn, or the researcher comes up with embarrassing findings, or the analysis and explanation made by the researcher is not in keeping with the interests of the sponsors, as they see it, that the exercise of power is most likely to pose difficulties for researchers and expose their vulnerability in sponsored research. The ownership of the report is often at issue in such circumstances.

If the research was initiated by the researcher alone, there are still ethical and political concerns which must be faced. Data dissemination includes not only publication but also communication of the report orally and visually. Researchers, in the age of electronic media, are often invited to comment about their research on television and radio programmes particularly if their findings are regarded as controversial. Once data has been widely disseminated in the public arena, it means that anyone can utilise it for their own purposes. Researchers need to make political and ethical decisions in relation to how widely their reports should be disseminated and if they should have any legal brakes applied to them. In some cases, the researchers' interpretations of the meanings and events in informants' lives may differ from the informants' interpretation to such an extent that the informants might wish to prevent further publication or dissemination of the report. This can occur even though the researcher and informants agree that the report is truthful and accurate. It may nevertheless, or in fact because of this, be seen as harmful.

Some researchers, particularly those who have made the political decision to engage in action research, provide their informants with an opportunity to validate their studies. In some instances (Whyte 1955), this involves the informant reading the entire manuscript prior to publication or the researcher discussing drafts of the report with informants. In many ways, these approaches act not only as a means of maintaining an ethical stance in relation to informants but also as a final verification of the validity of the research. However, as Burgess (1984) points out, there are no solutions which are foolproof. It has been said that the 'only safe way to avoid violating principles of professional ethics is to refrain from doing social research altogether' (Bronfenbrenner, 1952: 453).

The best one can do is to consider the ethical and political issues in asking a particular research question, determine the areas of concern prior to the research, take into account professional standards that have been established and then consider the ethics of the entire research process as an individual case with its own social and political ramifications.

Glossary

Action research Research in which the role and political stance of the research is aligned and interventionist. This is because research is joined with action in order to plan, implement and monitor change. Researchers choose to become participants in planned policy initiatives and use their knowledge and research expertise to aid their informants.
Anonymity In this context refers to the informant being anonymous or not individually identifiable. This is usually achieved through the use of pseudonyms.
Confidentiality Refers to protecting names of informants, keeping confidences and protecting information about the informant.
Critical reference group A group, person or collectivity which is taken into account by an individual as being significant in determining his or her attitudes and behaviour. In this case, the researcher takes into account the individuals or groups which he or she regards as significant in determining his or her approach, and behaviour in the research.
Ethical absolutist Researcher who wants to establish specific principles to guide all social research and who wants to have these principles produced as a code of ethics to be adhered to by all members of the relevant profession. In general terms, an ethical absolutist would argue that there can be no deviation from the principles which he or she regards as ethical. These principles are to be adhered to absolutely.
Ethics The study of standards of conduct and moral judgments. In this context, it refers to the system or code of morals we apply to the research process, be it as individuals and/or as members of a profession.
Ethics Committee A committee set up by an institution or organisation to act as a moral watchdog upon its own members.
Gatekeepers Those individuals in an organisation that have the power to withhold access to people or situations for the purposes of research.

Informed consent Consent being given by an informant or client for research to be carried out, when those requesting this consent have provided the informant with full knowledge of what it is that they are consenting to.
Methodological Pertaining to a rule-governed procedure aiding or guaranteeing scientific discovery. Methodological issues are concerned with the *logic* of inquiry, that is, how are we to discover and validate what we think exists?
Phenomenological Pertains to phenomenology. Phenomenology is the study of the forms and varieties of consciousness and the ways in which people can apprehend the world in which they live. It is the study, in depth, of how things appear in human experience. The practice of phenomenology as developed by Brentano and Husserl, involves the 'bracketing' or laying aside of preconceptions (including ones derived from science) in order to be able to inspect (one's own) conscious intellectual processes more purely.
Political Usually refers to a situation when people cannot agree voluntarily about allocations of all kinds in societies. If and when such agreements are not automatic then some binding arbitration or settlement is required or will appear.
Situational relativist A researcher who holds that there can be no absolute principles of ethical research behaviour or absolute guidelines because ethical decisions are dependent on the individual's interpretation of the particular research situation and the context in which it occurs.
Social justice Refers to a particular form of justice. Justice is defined as *giving each person his or her due* and is *treating equals equally*. These injunctions to impartiality can be given either a purely procedural interpretation (that is, in adjudicating between conflicting claims) or a substantive one (that is determining what entitlements each person has). Interpreted substantively, justice is a distributive principle prescribing a certain dispersion of liberties or benefits over a population. Theories differ over the appropriate criterion for this allocation. One debate raised is the tension between individual and social justice. While the former is consistent with an emphasis on procedural justice, the latter focusses on the structured location of groups (for example, ethnic minorities, women, the poor) and highlights the impact of the content of law and regulation upon the category.
Sponsors In this context refers to those individuals or groups who initiate and/or pay for research to be conducted.

References

Abercrombie, N., Hill, S. & Turner, B. 1988. *The Penguin Dictionary of Sociology*. Harmondsworth: Penguin Books.

Aroni, R. 1985. *The Effects of Jewish and Non-Jewish Day Schools on Jewish Identity and Commitment*. Unpublished doctoral dissertation, Monash University, Clayton, Vic.

Bronfenbrenner, U. 1952. 'Principles of Professional Ethics: Cornell Studies in Social Growth.', *American Psychologist* Vol. 7, No. 8: 452–455

Bulmer, M. 1980. 'Comment on the Ethics of Covert Methods.', *British Journal of Sociology* Vol. 31, No. 1: 59–65.

Bulmer, M. 1982 (ed.). *Sociological Research Methods: An Introduction*. London: Macmillan Press.

Burgess, R.G. 1984. *In the Field: An Introduction to Field Research*. London: Allen and Unwin.

Denzin, N.K. 1968. 'On the Ethics of Disguised Observation.', *Social Problems* Vol. 15, No. 4: 502–504.

Denzin, N.K. 1978. *The Research Act*. Second edition. Chicago: Aldine.

Erikson, K.T. 1968. 'On the Ethics of Disguised Observation: A Reply to Denzin.', *Social Problems* Vol. 15, No. 4: 505–506.

Kidder, L.H. 1981. *Selltiz, Wrightsman and Cook's Research Methods in Social Relations*. Fourth edition. New York: Holt Saunders International Editions.

Mann, M. (ed.) 1987 *Macmillan Student Encyclopedia of Sociology*. Fourth edition. London: Macmillan Press.

Oakley, A. 1984. 'Interviewing Women: A Contradiction in terms.', in Helen Roberts (ed.). *Doing Feminist Research*. London: Routledge and Kegan Paul.

Punch, M. 1986. *The Politics and Ethics of Fieldwork*. Beverly Hills: Sage Publications Inc.

Roberts, H. 1984. *Doing Feminist Research.*. Third edition. London: Routledge and Kegan Paul.

Van Maanen, J. 1984. 'Tales of the Field.', in D.H. Berg & K.K. Smith (eds). *The Clinical Demands of Research Methods*. Beverly Hills, California: Sage.

Wadsworth, Y. 1984. *Do it Yourself Social Research*. Collingwood, Victoria: Victorian Council of Social Service.

Walker, R. 1989. *Doing Research: A Handbook for Teachers*. Cambridge: Routledge.

Whyte, W.F. 1955. *Street Corner Society*. Chicago: University of Chicago Press.

Chapter 11 Assembling and Organising the Data

The next two chapters provide a review of methods used for coding and analysing data. Few other publications examine the procedures for organising qualitative data. Learning how to store and manage the data is a crucial step in the research process because the quality of data analysis partly depends on the systematic recording of fieldnotes. (For a detailed discussion of the general issues presented here, see Bogdan and Biklen 1982; Lofland and Lofland 1984; Miles and Huberman 1984; and Strauss 1987.)

Although qualitative data are not usually susceptible to computerisation, they do need to be transcribed, coded and filed. This chapter discusses how to store the data into files. These files assist the researcher to sort, focus and organise information in such a way that patterns and themes within the data become clearer. Specific attention will be paid to the following questions, What data do you record? How do you record it? What fieldnote system can be used for storing the data collected? Chapter 12 will discuss methods for discovering and testing concepts contained in the fieldnotes.

Data analysis includes both a mechanical and an interpretative phase. The work which surrounds the mechanical phase involves designing operations which retrieve, modify and transform data. Physically sorting out the data into files provides easier access to sections of it. Researchers often end up with over 3000 pages of fieldnotes. Trying to make sense of those pages without ordering and storing may turn the interpretative work of data analysis into a nightmare. It is important for the reader to recognise that while the mechanical and interpretative aspects of data analysis are discussed in separate chapters, these two tasks are interrelated and occur simultaneously. The interpretative work presupposes that the data are organised according to a set of mechanical operations. Yet, at the same time, the interpretative work will dictate how the data will be sorted.

Fieldnotes—What do they Contain?

Fieldnotes contain a record of conversations the researcher has had with people, observations about their actions in everyday life and procedures for collecting such information. While the data may be collected through a combination of asking, listening and looking, which of these activities is dominant in a study will vary with whether the researcher is using in-depth interviewing or participant observation. It should be stated, however, that whether we are conscious of it or not, all these skills are put into practice in our everyday lives. When we sit in a classroom, we listen to what is presented, ask questions to clarify issues, and observe the non-verbal gestures of the lecturer to assess the importance of what is being said. Unlike the ordinary person, however, researchers are more conscious of using these skills to study human life. As it was noted in chapter 6 when using in-depth interviewing, listening and asking are important skills to master. The interviewer, of course, is also observing as he or she talks to the informant. Much of what is written in the fieldnotes can be derived from observations made about the informant, the setting and the interview.

Fieldnotes contain more than a transcription of what the tape recorder has registered. Experienced researchers include information in their notes that was invisible to the tape recorder but perceived by the trained interviewer. The formal interview is only one component of the fieldwork experience. It may constitute about 60% of the total time spent collecting data in the field. The rest of the time is spent contacting people on the telephone and talking to them before and after the formal interview. The researcher is also an observer. Information is collected about the facial and physical expressions of the informant, the details of the setting and perceptual impressions. This information places the interview in its larger context and provides additional information on the informant, the setting and the topic.

Fieldnotes include the researcher's reflection on what was said (or not said) and observed. The reflective account can include speculation about themes and connections between pieces of data; issues which arise while entering and leaving the field; reflections on methodological, sampling and ethical issues; and ideas on report writing. Researchers often prefer to keep the descriptive and reflective parts of the notes separate (Burgess 1982). It is important to recognise that the reflective content of fieldnotes is a personal activity. The researcher is encouraged to adopt a writing style that will not inhibit notetaking.

The reflective comments should include information the researcher thinks is relevant at the time. An inexperienced fieldworker would complain that he or she did not write any notes because there was nothing important to report. Rosalie Wax (1971) warns fieldworkers to think twice about following the example of those would-be ethnographers who assert or boast that they take few or no fieldnotes. The fact is that most of the people who say that they are able to get along without taking notes do not write anything worth reading. While notetaking may appear to be tedious, and indeed even simply boring, it is crucial for the analysis.

Guidelines for Writing Fieldnotes

There are a number of basic principles for data recording that can facilitate the task of writing fieldnotes. (Burgess [1982] and Webb [1982] provide excellent illustrations and we highly recommend that the reader consult these sources.) The first basic rule is to write down any idea that enters your mind. These ideas can be lost if you do not write them down immediately. Many researchers carry with them a little notebook during the course of their study and enter comments at all hours of the day or night. Many good ideas are composed while you ride the tram, have a long hot bath, or pretend to be listening to a boring conversation.

A second rule is to set aside time for writing the fieldnotes. Your memory can play tricks. You must adopt the attitude that unless you write down everything you are thinking about, there is a danger that it will be lost. It is a serious error not to record or reflect on the data as soon as it has been collected. It is so easy to allow one's fieldnotes to pile up. As a general rule the researcher should write the fieldnotes no later than the day after the interview. The objective is to minimise the period between data collection and data storing, and to reflect on the data before commencing the next interview. Most experienced fieldworkers note that the quality of their notes diminishes with the passage of time. Details are lost and episodes are forgotten or muddled (Hammersley and Atkinson 1983).

Note-taking should be viewed as compulsory. Like maintaining a personal diary, it involves discipline and hard work. Many of us at one time began writing a diary but gave it up because we did not invest enough time in the project. Fieldnotes, like diaries, must have periodic entries and include information that you might find of interest at some later stage.

Another important rule to follow is to make duplicate copies of your fieldnotes and to store these in separate places in the event of a fire or theft. There is nothing more frustrating than losing your data and realising that you do not have another copy. Hours of hard work can be lost. As chapter 12 will illustrate, the duplicate copy can be used for cutting and pasting accounts of a single event or situation onto index cards.

Finally, the task of data coding and data analysis should not be separated. Both these tasks need to occur at the same time. As well as spending time to write and code the data into files, the researcher should be searching for emergent ideas in the data and sketching research strategies. Researchers can ask themselves how much knowledge they have gained, what they know and do not know, the degree of certainty of such knowledge and further lines of inquiry. Of course what the researcher writes will depend on a continual reassessment of purposes and priorities. As Hammersley and Atkinson (1983) note, the standard practice of writing down everything you see and hear fails to take into account that with the accumulation of data, the researcher focusses his or her attention on what to write down, how to write it down and when to write it down. During the first days of a research project, the focus of the researcher will be general. As a result, fieldnotes will be much broader in scope. As the research progresses, and themes and concepts are identified, the notes will become more focussed and selective.

Different Types of Fieldnote Files

Although there are no general rules on what sort of information should be included in your fieldnotes, a number of researchers have suggested that the notes should address the who/what/when/where/how questions that surround the study (Bogdan and Biklen 1982; Burgess 1982). *Who* involves reporting the identity of the participants and their relationships to others. *What* involves describing the activity or conversation seen or heard. *When* involves noting the reference to time, with special attention to recording the actual sequence of events. *Where* involves describing the location of the activity. *How* involves a description of whatever logistics were used to collect the data and an analysis of how ideas and patterns in the data have emerged.

The answers to the above questions, as illustrated in Figure 11.1, are stored in the following separate files: a transcript file which contains the raw data of the interview; a personal file on the fieldwork experiences; and an analytical file which discusses ideas and conceptual issues. The rest of the chapter will discuss the form and content of these three files and present examples of each.

The Transcript File

As we discussed in chapter 6, there are a number of ways one can record the interview. We have stated that the use of a tape

Transcript File	Personal Log	Analytical Log
Includes the transcription of the interview, observer's comments and a cover page. The text is centred in the middle of the page with margins containing observer's comments on both side.	Includes a descriptive account of the actors and their settings, reflective notes on the fieldwork experience and methodological issues.	Includes a detailed examination of the research questions asked, and ideas emerging as the study progresses.

Figure 11.1 File system for storing data.

recorder in conjunction with notetaking is the most useful means of capturing the full dimensions of the conversation. Regardless of whether or not you used a tape recorder, the transcript file is a reproduction of the formal interview which took place between researcher and informant. The depth of information contained in the **transcript file** may be slightly different, depending on which of these two methods is used (Ives 1980). A conversation that was reproduced from a tape recorder will contain an exact reproduction of the verbal conversation, while a memory recollection of a conversation will contain a combination of what was said and approximate remarks. Strauss (1987) suggests that researchers use quotation marks for exact recall, apostrophes to indicate less precision in wording and no marks to indicate proxy recall.

Typed notes are preferable to handwritten notes. For one thing, they are much more legible. It also makes it easier to code and cut up your notes to create index cards at a later stage (More will be said about this topic in chapter 12). Another way the transcript file can be prepared for analysis is to break up sentences into paragraphs which are organised around ideas or topics.

An example of a transcript file is reproduced in Figure 11.2. This conversation was transcribed from a recorded conversation between one of the authors and a clergyman. The focus of the study was to identify how ministers construct eulogies. This was the first of several interviews and only the first four pages are reproduced here. We include this transcript to illustrate guidelines for formatting the transcript file and provide an example of the rich data that can be collected through in-depth interviewing.

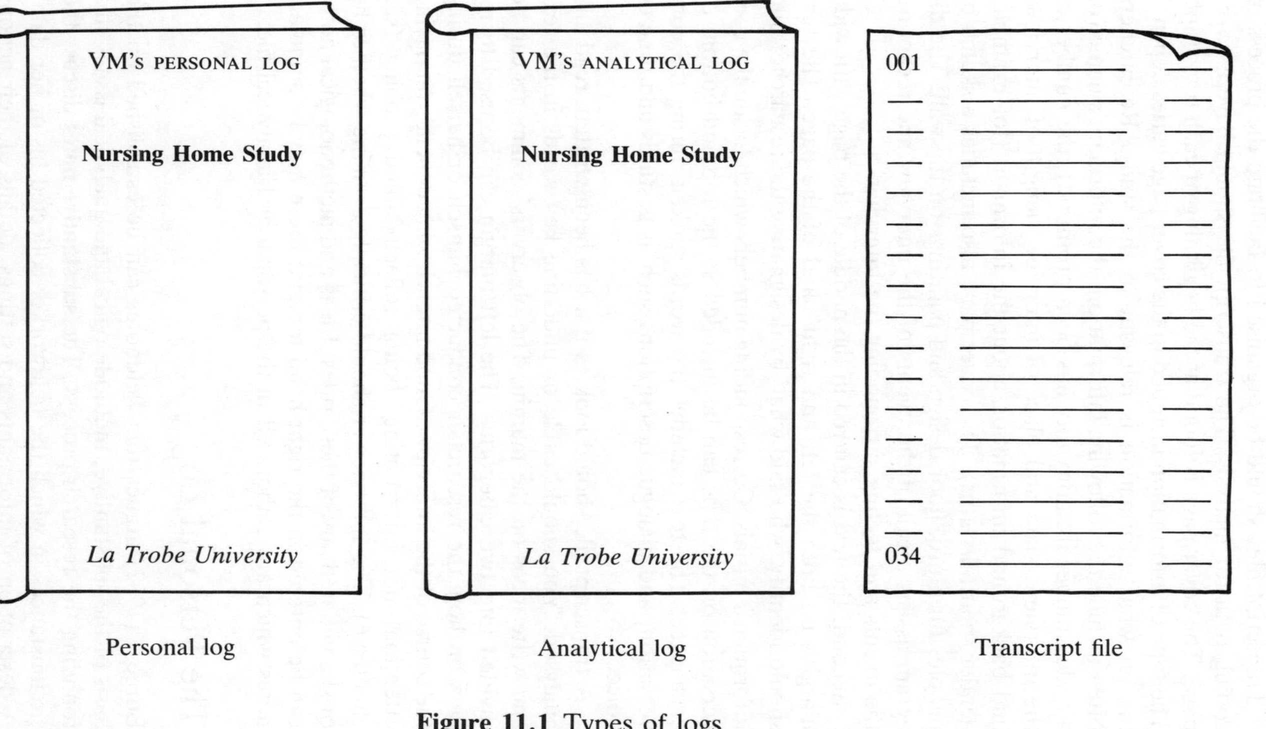

Figure 11.1 Types of logs

Transcript files should be organised to facilitate the process of coding data for analysis. The transcript file should have a cover page. The cover page is found at the beginning of each transcript. The type of information included in the cover page varies depending on what information is relevant to the study. Researchers often include the following information: the informant's name (or a code number if anonymity has been promised), the number of the interview, data and place of interview, length of interview, and background information about the informant (for example, gender, marital status). The cover page also includes a sketch of people, furniture, floor design and paintings on the wall. The diagram assists recall of the events of the interview and recapture the events and feeling surrounding the interview.

Second, the text is centred in the middle of the page with wide margins on both the left and right hand of the page. The text should identify 'who said what' by designating the researcher and informant's initials. Corresponding numbers which locate the conversation on the tape can be included at the top and bottom of each page. The text includes the words spoken during the conversation, and dialogue descriptions such as gestures and tone of voice.

A transcript file should look as if it has been written, read and analysed. You should circle or underline key words in the text and write ideas on the margin. The observers' comments can be divided into two categories. The left margin can be used to reflect on how the researcher conducted himself or herself during the course of the interview. Good interviewing depends on paying attention, not interrupting, being reflective and probing (see chapter 6). The interviewer should critically examine whether he or she violated any of these rules. Ideas and methodological notes can be entered in the right-hand margin; these may be summary notes which are elaborated in the personal and analytical file.

The Personal Log

Burgess (1982) argues that fieldnotes can be established on the basis of the substantive, methodological and analytical issues surrounding the research process. The **substantive notes** discuss the circumstances in which the fieldworker collected his or her data. A description of informants and settings, details of their actions and personal impressions of situations are included. The **methodological notes** contain a first-hand account of the processes involved in doing the research. The **analytical notes** record the researcher's initial questions and the ways in which these questions have been revised.

The **personal log**, described here, is an annotated chronological record or diary of the researcher's reflections of the substantive and methodological issues which arise in the course of the study. The log is produced over a period of time. It is an impossible task to write the personal log at the end of the study. It becomes an instrument for discovering and organising ideas only if it is written while you are collecting data. There are a number of questions that need to be addressed concerning the format of the personal log. How do you record this information? Should you write down everything you are thinking about? Should you write in simple language? These are important questions. Before we proceed to discuss the specific contents of the personal log, a few words need to be said about the practice of writing it.

Figure 11.2 Example of a transcript file.

Informant:	Rev. David Hodges, Interview No 1.
Topic:	How do ministers construct eulogies?
Date:	8 January 1987.
Place:	Rev. Hodges' home—lounge room, Melbourne.
Time:	Arrived at DH's home 1.10 pm; chatted for 20 minutes; formal interview began at 1.30 pm and finished at 3.00 pm; left DH's home at 3.45 pm.
Relevant Information:	United Church Minister for 30 years, recently retired, delivered many eulogies, trained in Scotland.
Special Circumstances:	Hot day (35°C), permission to use tape recorder was granted.

Transcript data

	0000	**VM** David, I would like to begin by asking you what is a eulogy?	
		DH Well an eulogy is an address (*cough*) to honour a person either living or dead I presume. But in my case (*smile*) it would be given for the dead.	*Did not realise that a eulogy can be delivered for a person who is not dead. Need to understand if the construction of such eulogies are different from the funeral address.*
A case interrupting.		**VM** So it is . . .	
		DH So it's a funeral address.	

I think this is a good question to ask David as it opens the conversation

VM What is the purpose of the address?

DH I think the purpose of it as far as a Christian service is concerned is to . . . it is part of a *ritual*. I think we need rituals at birth and birthdays and so we need a ritual for death because I think that just helps us to get through what can be a difficult time—so that is part of it. It's a part of a ritual which is a Christian ritual if you're a Christian. It's one of those *rite-of-passage* things in a way and that is common to everybody, not just Christians; when it is for a particular person in a particular situation then it becomes a recognition of their life. And I think usually a thanksgiving for their life. I think that is the main point.

Need to examine how the concepts of rituals, rite of passage can be applied to study eulogies.

Eulogy is a way of giving recognition to life. Would all ministers agree with this statement?

Picked up point of inconsistency

VM You said 'I think'. Is there a difference between what you think and what the Uniting Church would think is the purpose of the eulogy?

Very informative response. David is doing most of the talking.

DH No, I think different Ministers would have different emphases. So there would be some ministers who would think that the important thing at a funeral service is the reading of the Bible, the preaching of the word on this particular occasion with an emphasis on the Church's belief in eternal life, resurrection or whatever.

0024

Question—does the minister's views on the purpose of a eulogy influence how he constructs it?

One type of eulogy has a 'doctrinal emphasis'.

0024	So some ministers would have that sort of, if you like, doctrinal emphasis in a service. They would emphasise that largely and they would minimise any recognition of the particular person. They would say that a service is about celebrating the gospel and the resurrection rather than celebrating the life of a particular person.	
	I would not deny that (*DH means he would not deny the importance of celebrating the gospel—the Christian aspect of the funeral address*) but there are other ministers, and I would be one of them, who would see a major focus of a funeral service and a eulogy in a service to be a thanksgiving for the particular person for whom the service is being conducted. So I would make that a very important part of what I am doing and of course, it would be related to the Christian gospel.	*Another type—'Thanksgiving' Are there other types?*.
	But then I think that if you spoke to a minister who took a different approach, the opposite stance to the one I gave you, he would say that the important thing is 'here is a congregation, a lot of these people have got a very hazy idea of what the Christian faith is about and this is a real opportunity to	*Negative case—Uniting Church Minister who uses the 'doctrinal emphasis'. What about ministers from other churches?* *An aim of doctrinal emphasis is to preach the gospel to those in attendance.*
0048	preach the Gospel you	

0048 see'. You say bam, bam, bam, which I think is . . . frankly.

I think that the occasion, the people have come because they knew, respected, loved this particular person. I think that they ought to be able to move through this critical point in their lives by being able to have expressed by me, what they want to say about him, what they want to think about him, what they want to feel about him. So my objective is to try to make the person who has died a sort of continuous living presence in that group. It's all about the person who has died for me.

DH sees himself as a voice which represents the audience. But who is the audience?

I should have asked a clearer question. What do I mean by 'that'?

I am following the conversation and picking up on David's ideas for follow-up discussion.

VM How do you do that? It must be a difficult thing because sometimes you come across people you knew, sometimes you come across people that you did not know very well and then you come across the in-between people.

DH Well it probably sounds, it would be a strange thing to say I think that I find it easier if I do not know the person terribly well (*laughs*). Because the way I do it is to listen to the family and to friends and I would see them before the service.

VM You would arrange to see them?

DH Oh yes always.
0072 And I would spend

I should have followed through and asked why DH thinks it is easier to do a eulogy for someone he does not know well. Instead I introduced a different topic.

0072 sufficient time with them. I would just simply talk to them about him and some of the things would be quite formal things, such as he was born in the country, or he was an accountant, or he had a partner who was so and so. The factual things about families. Those factual things do not worry me much. I do not believe the eulogy should be full of these sort of facts—Bill Smith was born in Mansfield in 1892 and lived here and moved there and qualified here and did this at this university, had so many children etc . . . I think that is all adequate but everybody who is there knows most of those things anyhow.

By talking to people, they will tell me the factual things of the person. But they will tell me about it in a particular sort of way, you know. They might say he always loved the country, and although his job brought him to the city he always had a great love for the country. And so I would just put that at the back of my head and you build up a sort of picture in your mind of the sort of person. You talk to his family, you talk to some of his friends. Even if you have not known him at all, why that is sometimes easier is because they distill the essence
0116 of him.

What are the factual things about families?

An example of retrieving the 'essential thing' about a person and building a portrait of the person

(This interview continues for another 27 pages).

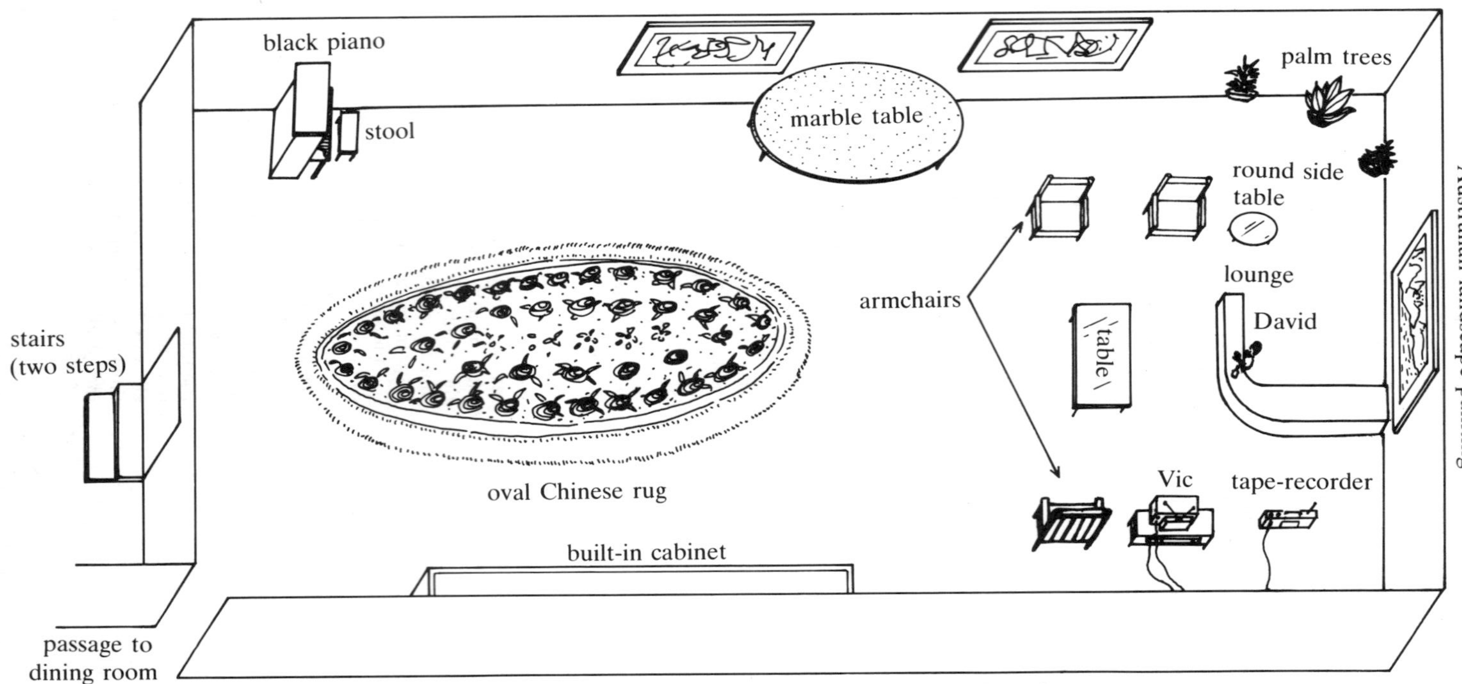

Figure 11.3 Transcript file: diagram of setting.

Writing a Personal Log

While each researcher is encouraged to devise a set of instructions which are congruent with his or her writing style and research interests, the following guidelines provide a framework for constructing notes. We suggest that you enter your thoughts in a journal. Put down on paper all of your thoughts and impressions. Do not omit events because they seem mundane. As discussed in chapter 1, you only partially know what particular events or situations will be relevant for the discovery of ideas when you are collecting data. What may seem irrelevant at the time can turn out to be a significant piece of information.

Your notes should be frank and unrestricted in length. Try to be detailed in your description. The notes must provide a full account of people, situations, decisions rather than summaries of these. For example, instead of, *Mr Rhodes looked distinguished*, you could write something like, *Mr Rhodes wore a three piece black suit with a matching vest and red tie. The suit was bespoke tailored and immaculate. He spoke with a soft gentle English accent. He was very articulate. I was not surprised when he later told me that, prior to his retirement, he was the vice-president of an insurance company. He projected the image of a business man. My first impression of him, based on visual cues, was of an independent elderly man who made up his own mind about things. The interview confirmed this assessment. He had made his own decision to move to a nursing home.*

Information can be entered under a principal heading to which the notes relate. The heading can be the name of the person or the title of the particular institution, depending on your unit of analysis. For example, if the investigation is centered around examining how the organisational structure of nursing homes influences staff behaviour, the essential item to record is the type of nursing home (for example, private nursing home, state nursing home, voluntary nursing home). On the other hand, if you are interested in studying how residents explain their admission to nursing homes, the major heading is the name of individuals. Sub-headings are used to further organise the material contained within the major heading. This carefully planned organisation of the material brings the facts under review in an arrangement that facilitates the discovery of ideas (Webb 1982).

People, Settings and Activities

Words taken out of context are difficult to interpret. Your fieldnotes should read like a play script. A descriptive account of the actors involved and the setting must be conveyed. This information places the interview encounter in its larger context and is extremely valuable during the analysis phase of the research. For example, one of the authors studied elderly people living in geriatric wards. The paintings on the walls made a strong impression on the initial visit. A number of the paintings were about clowns and animals. These are the sort of paintings one would expect to find in a child's room or kindergarten class. This observation proved to be very important when the researcher analysed the interview material. Patients spoke about staff members treating them like 'babies'. The decor of the geriatric ward certainly gave credence to the residents' views that staff perceived them in childlike terms.

In line with the theoretical underpinning of interpretative research (see chapter 3), the fieldnotes must reproduce the perceptual states experienced in the interview. The intent is to reconstruct the conversation within the context in which it occurred. To simply rely only on the verbal text ignores that the interaction evolved from assumptions people were making about themselves, others and the setting. These assumptions influence what people say.

People should be carefully described in the notes. First, a short biographical history that is relevant to the study should be given. This biographical history could include information on a person's age, gender, marital status, type of living arrangement, occupation and other information that would appear to be relevant to subsequent analysis. For example, if you were studying older people living in a nursing home you might include their medical history prior to entering the nursing home. A study on prostitution may contain information about age of profession entry, educational level and social class.

Second, a description of how people dress and present themselves is included. You can learn important things about a person on the basis of his or her general appearance and manner. People use 'impression management' to influence how others think about them through their looks and actions (Goffman 1967). The person's style of talking and acting, as well as the mood of the interaction, can also be observed. Researchers, like Goffman (see chapter 8), rely on their eyes to reach interesting conclusions about human behaviour. For example, by observing waiters working in a restaurant hotel, Goffman (1967) noted that waiters presented themselves differently when they were in the dining room than when in the kitchen. He developed the concept of 'front and backstage behaviour' to distinguish between people's presentation of self in formal and informal situations.

You, of course, are also an actor. The notes should include an account of your own behaviour in the field. People's words and actions can only be understood if they are examined in the context in which they are staged (Bogdan & Taylor 1975; Schwartz & Jacobs 1979). As an actor in the script, you are influencing how others act. An examination of your role in the field helps to access the influence your actions have had on the subject's remarks and behaviour. It also allows you to revise your field tactics or develop new ones.

Like people, settings need to be carefully examined and described. These can be sketched out in sufficient detail to enable imaginary recreation. An assessment of your impressions of the setting can provide useful insights and substantiate conclusions reached from other data sources (as illustrated in the above example of the geriatric ward study). An example of a personal log is presented in Figure 11.4. You will notice that the personal log includes a detailed chronological description of the social experience of doing research and methodological issues which arise in the field. The personal log reproduced here was written by a student doing a fieldwork assignment. It is presented as it appeared in the student's diary. This has been done purposely because we did not want to mislead the reader into thinking that a personal log is written like a paper. A personal log should read as you speak, capturing your thoughts without being inhibited by the formalities of writing well as presented in a final manuscript. The student was studying how people define *love*. We include these notes to provide an example of the type of information that can be included in a personal log and to illustrate the discussion that follows. We suggest that you read through Figure 11.4 before you go on, and then refer to it as you read.

Figure 11.4 An example of a personal log. A student's personal log on *Perceptions of Love Project,* April 1989. Peter—Informant Number 1.

Getting In

I briefly considered who I could approach to be my first informant. I had decided that my sample had to include a cross-section of people from various social and cultural backgrounds, of varying age and a mixture of male and female participants. Age and gender would allow me to capture people who may be in different stages in the life cycle and experiencing different types of love. The person's social situation (e.g. in a relationship) and cultural background may shape how they talk about and experience love.

Inspiration visited me one evening while I was watching television. The news mentioned the terrible battle that had taken place between two rival bike gangs a few years ago. I cannot remember the details of the news item. But the story immediately reminded me of one of my clients' husband that I had met last November. Peter and his wife had interested me a lot when I met them. I had never met a bikie before and was curious to know where all of Peter's scars came from. I had summoned up the courage to ask him about a particularly large scar at the top of his thigh (a large chunk of muscle tissue was missing, the scar was clearly visible as he was only wearing a pair of shorts). Peter's reply was 'someone's [*sic*] didn't like me and took a shot at me'.

Peter fitted the type of informant I wanted to interview. For my first interview I had a strong preference for someone of approximately my age, male and relatively unknown to me. I had met him before when I was present at their home birth, as their own midwife, Bettye, was unavailable that night, attending another client. I had spoken to Sue on the telephone just once before she went into labour when I agreed to be 'backup midwife' and only once more after their son was born. Bettye had continued on with the post-natal care, and I had visited them briefly once just before Christmas. I certainly did not consider them friends—simply very friendly people with whom I had shared a significant and moving experience; the birth of their son, Jesse. I suppose a certain degree of trust and rapport had already been built prior to the interview, and this made it easier for me to inquire into the private world of Peter's feelings about love.

On Sunday (23/4/89) I telephoned Sue and Peter's home and spoke to Sue. I asked Sue whether she thought Peter would mind being interviewed and explained to her the topic. I was anxious to ask Peter directly and wanted to hear Sue's opinion about the topic and whether she thought Peter would mind being interviewed on the topic. (Looking back I guess I was uncomfortable approaching a married man.) I figured that if Sue thought that Peter would not mind being interviewed then I could proceed and interview him without being too concerned about revealing the topic prior to the interview. I did not want Peter to know the topic beforehand as I wanted his responses to be spontaneous. Sue promised me that she would not reveal to Peter the topic.

When Peter came to the telephone he willingly agreed to be interviewed. There was no hesitation. After I put the telephone down I felt somewhat guilty at the conspiracy that I had engineered and wondered whether I should ring back and 'come clean'. I decided, however, that it was important to keep things as I had arranged. I felt good to talk to them again. They both expressed their delight at having the opportunity to see me again. Naturally when I spoke to them I inquired about their son's progress and was pleased to hear that he was healthy and had quite a fan club amongst their friends and family. I looked forward to seeing him again and seeing how much he had grown.

I telephoned Pete and Sue again on Friday (28/4/89) to confirm my visit the following day. Peter answered the call and in reply to my question, 'How are you Peter', he said in a flat tone, 'Could be better', and handed the receiver over to Sue. Sue told me that Jesse had died suddenly on Wednesday. He had died of 'cot death'.

Sue gave me a vivid account of the events that took place on the evening that Jesse died and talked for a long time without stopping. I listened and at the same time wondered what, if anything, I could say. When Sue stopped talking I found myself saying how sad I was at the terrible news and was there anything I could do. (I also remembered our lecturer saying that when doing fieldwork one of the risks of establishing rapport with informants is that we can become involved with their world. In such moments we can share feelings such as embarrassment, sadness, excitement and so. I now knew what he was talking about.) Sue said that she was coping reasonably well. She asked me to attend the funeral to be held after the autopsy the following week. Sue did not cry on the telephone and said that she would let me know if there was anything I could do to help in the meantime.

When I put the telephone down and found myself alone in the house I poured myself a drink and sat in a daze for about an hour. I had never had the experience of losing one of 'my' babies before and did not know how to respond to Sue and Peter. I did not know how to handle my feeling of inadequacy. I did not know how to cope with my feeling of rage at this injustice. I still feel a physical pain in my throat and chest at the thought of Jesse's death. Indeed, in writing this account I find myself in the midst of these feelings again. I cannot see the keyboard because of my tears. I eventually rang a colleague of mine who is also a good friend. She had [had] a similar experience with one of her clients. She was lovely to talk to and after speaking to her I cried, off and on, for the next few hours.

On Saturday morning 1/5/89 I visited Sue and Peter. I ended up staying at their house for most of the weekend. The house was in semi-darkness because the curtains had not be [*sic*] drawn. Sue's mother was there. Sue and Peter talked constantly about many different topics, including Jesse. There were Jesse's toys and baby paraphernalia all over the house. Jesse's cot had been folded up and rested against the wall; his soiled nappies and clothes sat on top of an overfull laundry basket.

I stayed with Sue and Peter all day on Saturday and went home mid-evening. Both of them seemed to want me to stay and talk about Jesse. We looked at the photograph album which contained all of their son's pictures. Sue and Peter took great delight in talking about their son's birth. Sue's mother was very cheery and chatty for most of the time; but every now and then someone was crying.

The next day I rang Sue and Peter to see how they were. I was invited up to spend the day again. Sue's mother had gone home and we spent the day in much the same way as the day before. Sue and Peter talked about the funeral arrangements. I let them lead the conversation and I followed. As the hours went by I relaxed and so did Sue and Peter. Sue at one point commented that she had entirely forgotten about her loss more than once during the day.

I had naturally come to the conclusion that Peter would be in no mood to go ahead with the interview. I was wrong. Peter told me that he still wanted to do the interview. We arranged to do the interview on the following Tuesday; the day following the autopsy and the day before the funeral. I wondered whether I would end up with an interview on love or a discussion on grief. When I explained to Peter the topic and said that I would understand if he did not want to go ahead with the interview, he insisted on being interviewed.

Ethical Considerations

Even though there had been a change in my relationship with Peter over the past few days, and the grief Peter was experiencing, it seemed to me wrong not to proceed with the interview because Peter wanted to do so. I wondered why he still wanted to go ahead. I often thought about the many times they had indicated how pleased they were that I was their consistent [*sic*] companion over that weekend. Was I taking advantage of their gratitude? Or was this their way of carrying on as though nothing has happened? I made it clear to them, and in particular Peter, that I would totally understand if the interview did not take place. They both made it clear to me that this was what they wanted to do.

I was deeply concerned that the actual interview situation may prove to be stressful for Peter. The topic of love—love for one's child—could surface in our conversation. I wondered about the use of the tape recorder and wondered whether Peter would 'clam up'. Peter has expressed his feelings quite openly to me up until this point. I had valued his confidence in me. I wondered how much of an influence the tape recorder would have on the conversation. I decided to go ahead and use the tape recorder and explain to Peter why I wanted to use it.

The Interview

On the day of the interview I thought about some of the important techniques about in-depth interviewing. I must remember how important it is to ask for permission to use the tape recorder and to point out to Peter that the recorder can be turned off at any point. I wanted Peter to have control of the tape recorder.

I wrote down some topic areas I wanted to cover during the interview as a guide I could refer to if I needed to do so. I decided that because I could remember the topics quite easily I would keep the notes in my bag unless I was at a loss for direction or words. I reminded myself to be reflective, not to interrupt or fill silent spaces with talk. I could remember quite clearly the words of our lecturer saying that we were after the interviewee's point of view, not ours. For reassurance I reminded myself that the interview was a form of conversation. In fact what I was about to do was no different to what I had been doing over the last few days: listen to Peter talk, that is, let Peter talk and I will follow 'his' conversation.

I arrived at Pete and Sue's home late morning. As usual their dog, Sheila, came trotting to the car in her usual friendly way; wagging her tail and waiting for a friendly pat. She escorted me to the front door and Sue was waiting to let me in. Their house is in the 'bushland' area of the north-eastern suburbs of Melbourne. Not an easy house to find without directions. Two houses share the same land. The tenants next door are friends.

Peter, Sue and I shared the usual hug that we had grown accustomed to over the last few days. Sue made a 'cuppa'. We sat and chatted in our usual relaxed fashion. Sue showed me some newspaper clippings about her son's funeral notice. I was reluctant to instigate any move toward starting the interview. After half an hour Peter suggested 'we get started'.

I explained to Peter that I was doing this interview as part of a learning exercise for my qualitative methods course. I explained to him, for the first time, why the class had chosen the topic of love. I explained why it was important for nurses to understand what love means to people and its implications for nursing and midwifery. I said how important it was for nurses to understand what lies behind people's emotional experiences; that this understanding assists us to provide care and support to individuals in times of stress. As I was explaining this to Peter I was aware that what I was saying was very pertinent to his recent experience (loss of child). I was aware of my own discomfort but Peter showed no sign of being upset. I made a mental note that if I was too concerned about trying not to talk about sensitive topics that [*sic*] I was not going to get very far in my interview. At this stage I came to terms that I was talking about a very sensitive topic and that it was foolish for me to be too sensitive. I wanted to know what Peter thought about love—and this was going to mean talking about happy and sad times.

I reached into my bag and produced the tape recorder. Peter did not object to the use of the tape recorder. The tape recorder, however, reminded Sue of the researcher who came to interview her the day after Jesse's birth. She told me how shocked she was at the time when the reporter produced a tape recorder and she had been given no prior warning that one would be used. She had felt intimidated. The presence of the tape recorder had greatly affected what Sue said during the interview as she imagined that the tape would be played to others without her consent. Her trust in the interviewer disappeared with the presence of the tape recorder. Sue's comments gave me the opportunity once again to reassure both of them that the only person to hear the tape was I. I did, however, mention to Peter that the class would be reading the first few pages of the transcript. Peter was unconcerned. I could not help but think that the difference between myself and the researcher was that I had established rapport with Peter and Sue prior to the actual interview. Now I understand why establishing rapport is so very important. A trust is built and people are more likely to agree to participate in your study, and confide in you, than if you were simply a stranger who will have a brief encounter with them.

Peter and I were seated at right angles to each other. I was seated on the settee. Peter was sitting in an armchair. The large, heavily littered coffee table was directly in front of me. I placed the tape recorder on it; on top of a pile of magazines and newspapers. I explained to Peter how the tape recorder could be switched on and off, emphasising that he was welcome to stop the tape at any time he wished.

Sue asked if we minded her presence in the room. We both said we did not mind. It was difficult to ask her to leave the room as there was only the bedroom and bathroom available for her to retreat to; the kitchen was part of the living room. Sue was busy reading newspapers; searching for death notices addressed to Jesse. She was kneeling on the floor, on the other side of the coffee table with a pair of scissors in her hand.

As I was interviewing Peter I was aware, every now and again, of Sue cutting another notice out of the paper. Whenever she did this Peter would turn his gaze in her direction. I do not think I would interview another person in the presence of others. It was obvious that on more than one occasion Peter's train of thought was influenced by Sue's activity, and maybe even her presence in the room.

Peter looked very tired and was not as chatty as he had been recently. He told me later that he had been having trouble sleeping since Jesse's death. There were several references to Jesse's death during the course of the interview. Each time Peter referred to Jesse there was a long pause in the conversation. One such pause was particularly long and I just had to say something, anything to fill the silence.

He told me about his boyhood days. He had a succession of dogs as companions as a boy. But he lived close to a busy highway and the dogs kept getting killed on the road. He was talking about how he saw love as partially being a learned emotion. He quickly learned not to become so emotionally attached to his dogs as he knew that sooner or later they would be killed and he would feel sadness. It was almost like a self fulfilling prophesy as each dog in succession (as though) obligingly ran onto the road.

I asked him if loosing Jesse was seen by him to possibly have an influence on the love he will feel in the future for another child. He emphatically replied, 'No, no way. That is completely different!'. His reply was so forceful that I was immediately worried that I had hurt his feelings. Was I too presumptions to think I had the right to ask him such a personal question? Peter must have noticed my dismay and concern as he quickly followed his reply with a wide beaming and reassuring smile.

I was thrown off balance once again when during the course of our conversation Peter took a tray off the bookcase and proceeded to construct an immaculate, large cone shaped 'joint' cigarette. He casually lit the end, took a few large puffs and handed it to me. I declined the offer but the smell of the joint brought me back to my younger days. I was hoping he would roll another joint before I left.

The joint in no way seemed to affect his behaviour. The conversation continued on as before. I asked him about his experience when he was falling in love with Sue. He said that he felt silly and related a delightful story of how each of them made it clear to the other that they were 'interested'.

The interview did not seem to come to a logical conclusion as I had expected. We both simply became tired and stopped. I suppose this is what Glaser and Strauss mean by 'saturation' or stopping when nothing else needs to be said. I think Peter was clearly restrained whilst the tape recorder was on. He never really warmed to the subject as I had hoped would have happened. It may have been that the topic was something that he had never really given thought to or I was looking at it from the perspective of a women. [*sic*] (I suspect there may be some validity to the later explanation because Sue said that she was surprised at some of Peter's comments. Sue told me that she would have given me a completely different story and believed that she would have offered more freely her thoughts). His vocabulary seemed to let him down. He was floundering on many occasions for the right word, and several times simply resorted to saying variations of roughly synonymous words in quick succession. This made it difficult for me to follow what he really was trying to say. The interview ended when Peter looked at me with an expression which indicated he had enough. I switched off the tape recorder and Peter said, 'Will that do you?'

When the recorder was switched off we both let out an audible sigh and we laughed. Peter mentioned that he felt that it was a very hard task to describe the topic of love into words. Sue felt that she would have had no trouble at all and argued that women thought about such things much more than men.

Peter rolled another joint and we all shared a smoke together (my wish has come true). Peter noted that if his mates had not brought him over a bag of 'home grown stuff', he would be on 'the Valium'. I must admit that

I felt that this type of social self-medication (joint) appeared to be therapeutic. I was feeling very relaxed and content with the world at that moment! Peter took me for a walk down the garden to inspect the crop of plants that they were in the process of saving from the voracious local snails. On the way back up to the house he told me how happy he and Sue were that I had reappeared in their lives. We shared a big hug together and we both cried. At this stage I felt I had been immersed into their lives.

Maintaining Relations

I telephoned Peter and Sue today (9/5/89) to see how they were. Peter was drunk. Sue told me that their dog, Sheila, had been destroyed by the rangers today because she was worrying the sheep. Peter is pretty cut up about it. It must be a terrible slap in the face for him.

I feel that I have developed a good and trusting relationship with Peter and Sue. I do not think I would have any difficulties in asking Peter to be re-interviewed. Given that this is my first interview, and my ideas will continue to develop as I listen to other people's stories about what love is, I may want to ask Peter further questions or get him to clarify some of his statements.

I visited Sue and Peter yesterday (28/5/89) in the evening and brought with me a copy of the transcript. Their friends, John and Ros, also dropped in to see them. John belongs to the bike club. Peter and John went out together for the night, leaving Sue, Ros and myself to chat. The conversation was a real education for me and provided further insights on the topic. (I suppose this is another advantage of qualitative methods; data collection does not have to be restricted to a point in time. It is continuous and in fact when it happens naturally, as with my conversation with Sue and Ros it provides real insights on the topic). Ros and Sue were talking about their partners and the way the men's violent outlook on life affects their lives. Ros spoke to me about her concern over John's obsession with weapons, and particular guns and knives. She showed me her birthday present given to her by John. It was a ladies flick knife. It was a very heavy but it sat in Ros' hand very comfortably. The blade was razor sharp, 'good for cutting up steak' Ros informed me.

Getting Out

I have no doubt that I will remain in contact with Peter and Sue. Sue and Peter were not at all interested in the transcript or what the group analysis revealed on love. I did not keep my original bargain of providing Peter with feedback on the research findings.

Reflections on the Social Experience of Doing Research

The social dimension of the fieldwork process involves four steps—getting in, learning the ropes, maintaining relations and leaving the field (see chapter 8; Shaffir et al. 1980). An account of how the researcher has designed and executed each of these is important for two reasons. First, the researcher can learn new ways of behaving while in the field and possibly develop further fieldwork skills. Learning new skills is crucial for being successful in the field. Second, the final written product is the result of many decisions. These decisions influence the quality of data that is collected. A study cannot be properly evaluated unless it is placed within the larger context of how the data were collected.

Getting people to agree to be interviewed is a difficult task. Many anxious moments are spent thinking about ways to get people to say *yes*. Yet the way you go about getting others to accept you and your study can either open or close doors. The personal log contains a detailed account of how you gained permission and the strategies used to seek cooperation. How did you present yourself? How much information about the study did you disclose? Were you doing covert or overt research? Did you strike a research bargain? What did you promise your informants? Did you present yourself differently to informants?

There are no simple formulae that guarantee successful entry. The tactics you use, and the issues you encounter, will depend on the research question and informants. For example, on first reflection, it would appear easy to interview people who are sitting in a park. After all, you do not need to negotiate with a gatekeeper (see chapter 9) to gain permission to go up to a stranger and talk to them. However, Karp (1980) notes that studying people in public places is not so easy.

> Strangers in public settings largely avoid each other. We try to maximise public privacy as we travel on buses, sit in waiting rooms, stand in lines, or simply walk along the street. The researcher is no different. Those who study conduct in public places will, like everyone else, be constrained by the rules that inhibit unnecessary verbal interaction (1980: 96).

Karp provides a useful description of the strategies he used to overcome the problem of access in public places.

Successful entry often depends on learning which suitable tactic is appropriate given particular situations or people. Hoffman, for example, provides a detailed account of the tactics she used to gain access to hospital boards.

> I began to choose my subjects on the basis of social ties, seeking interviews with all those board members who personally knew me or a member of my family. I usually wrote a letter first, outlining my interests in a formal, businesslike fashion consistent with the customary approach to executives. Most of these people must cope with large volumes of correspondence, much of which is non-business in nature, soliciting time, money, cooper-

> ation, information, or whatever. Unless something attracts their attention as they skim through the daily mail, executives are quick to refer correspondence to the waste basket or a subordinate. In order to catch attention or to compete with other requests, I included personal references in my letter (such as, 'I hope you might have the time between fishing trips . . .,' where I knew the board member often went fishing with a member of my family) and made certain my surname was written largely and legibly for them to recognise. In the letter, I usually stated that I would telephone to make an appointment (1980: 47).

The important point to remember is that the personal log captures the full details of the methods used to gain permission, as well as a reflection of whether such strategies failed or were successful.

The log also contains a detailed description and reflection on issues associated with 'learning the ropes' and 'maintaining relations' (Shaffir et al. 1980). 'Learning the ropes' involves attaining an intimate familiarity with the setting and its participants. Understanding people demands that the researcher learns to interact with informants on their own terms. 'Maintaining relations' is about establishing rapport and trust with informants.

You may think that learning about people, their setting and habits are of little scientific interest. This is far from true. Establishing a good rapport with subjects increases your chances of hearing the 'true' story. For example, Miller and Humphreys (1980) show how they were able to maintain ties with former informants involved in Humphreys' St Louis study of impersonal sexual encounters in public restrooms. The rapport he established with informants over the years allowed him to conduct further research on new questions that emerged in subsequent interpretations of the data and to gain an honest insight into the private sexual practices of men. Rapport is established slowly and with time. Much discussion and activities proceed it. In the example of the personal log (Figure 11.4), four previous contacts were required before Allison felt comfortable to formally interview Peter. A record of the interaction and activities which have taken place during these contacts should be discussed. As the personal log shows, important information can be disclosed during these contacts.

The log also illustrates your reflection on the role you played within particular situations or settings. One of the authors quickly learned not to interview aged residents living in a nursing home before morning or afternoon tea. He found that residents became agitated if they were interviewed before their tea time. These interviews were shorter. The researcher quickly understood that residents considered tea time to be their most important social activity.

Learning the ropes enhances the researcher's chances of becoming more familiar with the informant's views. Researchers who have studied deviant groups have reported in their notes how important it was for them to learn the informal language of these groups (Schwartz & Jacobs 1979). This special vocabulary provides clues about the group's basic assumptions about themselves and others. Familiarity with this knowledge provides a solid basis for becoming attuned to the informant's life style. McCall (1980) discusses how the artists' terminology helped to explain the organisation of their social world. The categories she describes in her study—'professionals' and 'amateurs'—were derived from the expressions used by the artists themselves—'serious' and 'dedicated'.

Finally, the log includes details of how the researcher orchestrated his or her departure from the field. Was it a gradual or quick exit? Were the promises made at the beginning of the study kept? How did you negotiate the possibility of returning to reinterview participants? Will you maintain contact with the informant? An example of how this information can be presented in your notes is illustrated below. Altheide explains why he decided to make a quick exit from his study of newsrooms.

> One reason I did not engage in a long and formal farewell was that I doubted it would be final. Also, however, I did not want to define a situation in which the news director could again demand that drafts of all written work be submitted to him for approval. He had insisted at one point in the study that he had veto rights over any report that came out of the research, even though we had never agreed to this unreasonable and unsatisfactory condition at the outset. So, in a manner of speaking, I had to slip out of the setting, noticed by several friends, but not in an eventful way that would have called forth the news director's wrath (1980: 308).

Methodological Issues

Decisions made about the study's design are also presented in the personal log. Which informants were selected? Why were they selected? Who has been left out of the sampling frame? Your answers to these questions (as it was explained in chapter 9) can have important implications for data analysis and theory building. Cases are selected because they represent specific types of a given phenomenon. The researcher searches for contrasts that are required to clarify the analysis and obtain saturation of emergent categories through a process of constant comparison. This allows for the possibility of testing for falsification of propositions. The researcher should make explicit the rationale for selecting cases and its relevance to theory building.

The personal log is also the place where you include comments on methodological problems encountered in the study. Did informants object to the use of the tape recorder? Were your questions too long? Did you interrupt? Were you being reflective? Did the interview follow the format of the recursive interview model? What ethical issues did you confront and what action did you take? Can you use an alternative method design? Your reflections on these issues will help you to think through the methodological problems you face and to make decisions about them. If you keep a systematic account of your research experience, these notes can be used to write the methodological section of the research report.

Analytical Log

The **analytical log** includes reflective notes on the questions asked in the course of the research and ideas emerging from the data. The notes are entered in a notebook. The analytical log can be organised around several topic areas.

First, analytical notes can include an outline of topics discussed in each interview. This will help you maintain a record of what issues were covered in the interviews, to identify issues which were not included and to follow up something that the informant said. Notes like this will assist in guiding future interviews.

Secondly, notes include a critical examination of what research questions are being asked, and how these changed as data were collected. Qualitative researchers enter the field with general questions. As the researcher collects and studies the data, he or she follows leads contained within it. Slowly, the research question becomes more focussed. The researcher learns what is feasible and what is of interest to the study. As the research question becomes narrower in scope, so does the information collected. The notes include a discussion about the preliminary questions asked, propositions developed and ideas that emerge gradually as the research winds down. You should put down on paper your reason for deciding what facts are relevant, what facts to collect and how you identified concepts.

Writing an Analytical Log

The actual process of doing research follows a different course from that which researchers report in their published papers. Researchers often give the reader the impression that the study followed a predetermined linear plan of action. This hides the fact that doing research is a creative and imaginative process which occurs throughout the course of the research. Researchers often revise their research question and change their sampling or field strategies while doing the research. For example, Macintyre notes that published reports did not contain a full account of how the research design for her study changed while she was in the field.

> In the book describing the study I simply state that I used a mixture of prospective follow-up techniques and cross-sectional interview and observational techniques to obtain more information about certain points and key events. This implies, I suppose, that this was the original intention; from what I have said above I hope it is clear that this was not so, and in fact I initially approached the supplementary strategies with a distinct feeling of 'second-best-ism'. In retrospect, however, were I to do a similar study again, I would include such strategies as an integral part of the design from the beginning (1979: 766).

In qualitative research, data are collected in light of what you have found in previous observations. The journal should include a discussion of how past knowledge is influencing what you are thinking about and what data will be next collected. You should be asking questions such as, 'What is it that I know so far?', 'What do I not know?', 'What do I need to know'?, 'How do I collect this information?'.

An analytical log should be written with the view that this represents an opportunity for the researcher to reflect on issues raised in the data and to examine how these issues relate to larger theoretical issues. A number of strategies have been suggested to facilitate this process. Bogdan and Taylor (1975) recommend writing 'story lines' (see chapter 11) and using these to guide the analysis. The story line attempts to identify the main threads running through the data. It answers the question 'What conclusions can I reach from the information I have at hand? The second example of an analytical log, presented in Figure 11.5, shows how the researcher constructed a story line to identify the major themes in people's stories about entering nursing homes. Strauss (1987) suggests scrutinising the data by asking the following questions to 'open up' the inquiry. These are, 'What study are these data pertinent to?', 'What is the main story here, and why?, 'What category or property of a category, or what part of the emerging theory, does this incident indicate?'. The purpose of asking these questions is to force the generation of categories which allow you to develop propositions. (Chapter 12 will discuss the importance of classifying data into categories.)

Of course, the analytical log becomes denser in information as the study progresses. The aim is to collect information that will generate insightful propositions relevant to the study, and to develop, refine and reformulate the questions asked. As tentative propositions are identified and modified, the researcher begins to focus on key issues and test the validity and reliability of the emerging propositions. Thus, the early days allow for the discovery of concepts and themes, while latter interviews focus on building, testing and establishing links between concepts. The two analytical logs presented in the chapter were chosen to highlight the difference between a log written after the first interview and one written after several interviews. At first, the entries will be general and descriptive. However, as propositions are developed, revised and expanded, the notes become more focussed and centre around interpreting data and theorising.

A central feature of this work involves developing concepts. Concepts are abstract ideas generalised from empirical facts. Concepts are constructed to illuminate social processes and phenomena which are not readily apparent through descriptions of specific instances. You should maintain a record of concepts and themes emerging from the data. Every time a theme or concept is identified, include it in the notes. It is important that you remember that there are many styles of writing your analytical log. The notes included in Figure 11.5 are offered as an example of one approach.

Speculation is an important aspect of any research. It plays a central role in developing ideas. Feel free to include in the notes any ideas that come to mind, and as long as they are plausible, write them down. You will have the opportunity to test the ideas as the data are collected. Too often researchers do not bother to write their ideas down because they have not collected all the data. The danger of being too cautious and overconcerned with having all the facts in front of you is that you may lose good ideas. As Bogdan and Biklen (1982) note, facts are important but they are not the end. They should be seen as a means to clear thinking and the generation of ideas. Facts can always be retrieved, ideas cannot!

Concluding Remarks on Notetaking

We have reviewed how notes are made, what format is used and what types of fieldnotes are produced. Fieldnotes can be organised into different types of files: transcript file, personal log and analytical log. These files assist the researcher to organise and reflect upon the information he or she is collecting and the strategies used.

Data recording is an essential component of the research process. It is a basic building block which permits the researcher to make sense of the information that is being assembled. Regardless of how interesting and rich the data are, they are of no use to anyone unless they are recorded accurately and systematically. For this reason, data recording needs to be carefully programmed into the research timetable. However, producing fieldnotes and transcriptions from interviews is but one part of the research process.We need to consider the interrelationship between producing fieldnotes and data analysis. This topic will be pursued in chapter 12.

Figure 11.5 Two examples of analytical logs.

Example 1—Graduate Student Project: Perception of Love.

3/5/89. Later after I had completed my interview with Peter, I listened to the tape. I was surprised at the poor quality of the interview. I had not tested the sound quality from various distances and realised that I was to be left with a product that was barely audible. My implicit trust in modern technology could have left me in a frustrated heap. I have made a mental note to test the recorder prior to each interview and to be thoroughly familiar with my machine before entering the field. Had I done so I could have placed the recorder in a better position so that I could obtain a good product. This will make my life easier when I have to transcribe the tape.

I started to listen to the tape when I realised that I had gone into the interview with a set of assumptions. I switched off the tape and made a few scruffy notes of the assumptions I held. I had knowledge of Peter, even before spending the intense weekend with him and Sue. I knew, for example, that he was strongly supportive of his wife and sensitive to her need for self-expression. This was apparent because he told me how important it was for Sue to give birth in her own home, even though he did not see what was so bad about going to a hospital. I knew that Peter had a strong feeling of 'mateship' toward his friends in the bike club. Sue had joked when she was in labour; she said, 'It was a good thing it was not Tuesday night' (Peter's 'club' night). When I rang to arrange an appointment for the interview, Sue said that any day was fine expect [*sic*] for Tuesday nights. I had seen Peter in one of the most stressful times in his life—when his son was born. I had seen him express his love for Sue on that day and his son when he held him so tenderly. I knew his religion, his occupation and background. I knew that he had experienced a gunshot wound and spent some weeks in hospital. He was involved in some sort of gang fight and capable of protecting himself. I had noticed that he always carried a knife on his belt.

I also had the impression that Peter was a very private person. But the way he openly spoke about his grief and life was not consistent with my first impressions of him (as a bikie). I think I was influenced by my preconception of bikies. I had read and heard that bikies were protective of their mates, bikes and their 'old ladies' in that order. I realised that my belief in this popular image was totally untrue as far as Peter was concerned. Thinking about this allowed me to realise that I, of course, had assumptions about bikies and what love was, and that these assumptions would affect how I heard and made sense of Peter's words.

I switched on the tape again after reflecting about my own assumptions and their influence on the interview. I was now much more aware of how I was listening to what he had to say. Peter was busy throughout the interview trying to define what love meant to him. He reflected on his childhood a great deal and talked about how, when he was young, he had a love for objects; in particular his teddy bear. The teddy bear was his favourite toy. He realised now that this was not real love; he explained that as you get older you redefine and refine your feelings and make a distinction between attraction and love.

I think Peter is explaining some developmental process, something that occurs over time and is refined and shaped through experience. The unsolicited example that he provided was his experience of 'love' with his pet dogs as a young boy. He learned that when he became too attached to his pet and, something happened to them, he would feel 'really bad inside'. As a result of this feeling he made the decision not to become too attached to them. I suppose this is an example of bonding and detachment. Just how conscious is this decision at the time?

Peter also explained that it was important to him that he received feedback or reciprocation. He described it as love having to be 'a two-way street'; he said that if you get very little back then the love is not inclined to increase in intensity. He used his dog, Sheila, as an example. She can come up to him and wag her tail. Peter could interpret this behaviour as a sign of affection, but on the other hand, Sheila may well only need to go outside to relieve her bladder, and this is her way of telling Peter. I challenged Peter's statement by asking him if this same reasoning can be applied to Jesse (his young son). I suggested that Jesse may need or want something when he smiled other than to express his love to his father. Peter, however, said that he was aware that he has different feelings towards his [late] son than he has toward the dog. The reciprocation is not evident yet with his son, but it is clearly present. Peter suggested that it was probably on a 'spiritual level'. It would have been very interesting to explore this line of reasoning further with him but I felt that pressing him to talk about his feelings towards his son was too awkward given the circumstances (the recent death of his son).

My attempt to solicit information about what Peter thought about how the experience of love changes as people grow older rather fell flat unfortunately. The mistake I made was to ask Peter about what he thought about his father's experience of love. Rather than asking him to tell me about how people's ideas about love change with time, I was asking him to tell me about how a different generation (his father's) was experiencing love.

He told me that his father and mother had been separated for a number of years. Peter mentioned that his father loved his wife more than she loved him. Peter had watched his father's love being rejected and had first-hand observation of the phenomenon he described earlier to me—in the absence of reciprocation the intensity of the love diminishes. This experience was not unproductive. By talking about Peter's perception of how his father was (or was not) experiencing love in his relationship with his wife, Peter brought to my attention the importance of the experience of love being dependent upon the person to whom the emotion is being expressed, and how that person could influence the other person's definition of love.

When I asked Peter about love between men he immediately assumed that I was asking about his views regarding homosexuality. (I made my inquiry more specific by referring to his mates; asking him if there was any expression of love between them that he recognised. My question now alerts me to the fact that there are different types of love and that I should try to identify what these are, their characteristics, and whether people conceptualise and prioritise these differently). Peter said that during the last few days the comfort and support his mates provided him in his grief made it clear to him that his mates loved him 'as a brother'. They expressed their love in the form of hugs and caring statements. I should have asked what he meant by love 'as a brother'.

The following statement captures a summary of my thoughts on love after my interview with Peter. Love is an emotion that develops and matures as time goes by and through experience. This introduces the concepts of time, developmental processes and experience with love. Peter also indicated that the expression of the emotion is dependent upon reciprocation and to whom it is being expressed. The form that the reciprocation may take is an interesting phenomena to be further explored since there may be different types of expression (e.g. verbal, non-verbal) and can be transmitted and received differently depending upon how people recognise and interpret these signals.

Peter is a middle-aged male 'bikie' who is in a relationship and has experienced the love of a husband for his wife, the love of a father for his child, the love of mateship and the love for pets (dogs). Perhaps the next person to follow up might be a bikie who is unattached. This might provide a useful comparison. I will also need to pay more attention to the following concepts: commitment/involvement/types of love.

Example 2—VM's Study: Admitting Older People into Nursing Homes.

15 June 1984—I have now interviewed 40 aged residents. I would like to reflect on the residents' stories and built [*sic*] an overall picture of the dominant themes. Specifically, I would like to write about the leading themes emerging from the residents' stories. Later, I will identify divergent themes, and examine the processes by which people participate in decision making and the circumstances that place them in different types of decision-making situations. However, I will first sketch out the aims of each chapter.

I could see the study developing chapters along the following lines. A chapter which provides an overview of how aged residents and their next-of-kin account for the decision to seek nursing home care. The purpose of this chapter would be to discover the logic behind human action. The dominant themes that emerge from the residents and next-of-kin's stories would be presented and discussed, with a further section highlighting the diversity in circumstances and outlook amongst people's stories. Following from this discussion, the next chapter could examine in detail the role the aged person, her family and health practitioners play in the decision to obtain nursing home care, and the negotiations with family and professionals. This chapter will provide explanations which account for why we find differences in who will be involved in the decision. The next chapter could present a typology of the older person's participation in the decision-making process and examine why older people vary in their involvement in decisions to enter a nursing home. Building on material presented in the earlier chapters, the discussion could centre around exploring the importance of perceptions of self-images and family support in relation to the older person's involvement in the decision-making process. Of course, the icing on the cake would be discussing the question of how clients are selected by the nursing-home staff. If the previous three chapters look [at] how the decision to seek nursing home care involves a network of consultants, ranging from the intimate and informal to the more distant and formal circles (with a major focus on the informal), then I will need a chapter that examines how directors of nursing homes select their residents. To decide that your dad needs nursing-home care does not necessary [*sic*] mean that you will be successful in obtaining the service.

I like the above chapter outline. This study is a sociological piece of research on the processes involved in older people entering and living in nursing homes. The 'entering' forms one part of the study; the 'living' the other. As such I am really pursuing two lines of inquiry. The first asks questions about the social pathways through which older people reach the doorsteps of nursing homes. What I have been doing so far in the interviews is to understand the ways in which older people and their families go about making decisions to seek nursing-home care. Together with my respondents, we have unravelled the issues associated with the decision-making process, the actors in this process, their views on what motivated the decision, and the actions and inactions of the older person vis-a-vis family members and health professionals. Just like for many of the residents, by telling me their tales, they were able to get a better grip on what happened to them (many residents expressed this to me; in particular I remember Mrs Jones words, 'Vic I am grateful for giving me the opportunity to go over how I came here because for the first time I have a better picture of what went on'), I can see more clearly where I am going with my data now that I have put on paper my ideas.

The second line of inquiry will examine the social worlds of residents after they enter nursing homes. I could explore the nature and quality of the contacts older people in nursing homes have with family and friends. As I discussed at one of the 'Ageing and the Family Project Seminars', too little attention has been paid to the question of how institutionalisation affects interaction between residents and family/friends. What changes do aged persons feel in their relationships with family and friends as a result of placement in a nursing home?

I could write two chapters; one that examines the types of contact the older person has with family and friends, the other chapter examines in more detail the processes and determinants of these visiting patterns. These chapters would allow me to mix the qualitative and quantitative data. By using the quantitative data I am collecting on visitation, I could study the interrelationship between visits and the characteristics of residents, visitors and nursing home; by using the qualitative information, I could demonstrate the processes which explain these levels of interaction and their human consequences and meaning. I must go back and reread the literature on the multi-method approach.

Back to trying to make sense of the residents' stories. There was an interesting contrast between how the residents spoke about why they came to live in a nursing home and how health professionals and policy makers generally speak about the purpose of nursing homes. Eligibility for nursing home care is defined by professionals and policy makers mostly in medical terms. For many residents, however, (I must remember that my sample is biased towards identifying and selecting residents who had been admitted predominantly for social rather than medical reasons) much of the need is social in origin. When they spoke about their reasons for moving into nursing homes, most concentrated on factors other than health (and this information was unsolicited). Very few spoke about the importance of a change in their health or a specific medical problem.

(The analytical log continues for another eight pages).

Glossary

Analytical log Contains a record of reflective notes on the question asked and ideas emerging from the data.

Analytical notes A term used by Burgess (1982) for recording ideas which led to the development and revision of themes emerging from the data.

Fieldnotes Contain a record of conversations the researcher has had with people; observations about their actions; reflections on what happened in the field and interpretations of the data.

Methodological notes A term used by Burgess (1982) for recording reflections on the researcher's field strategies and method(s) used to collect data.

Personal log An annotated chronological record of the researcher's comments on people, settings and their activities, the social expertise of doing research and methodological issues which arise in the course of the study.

Substantive notes A reproduction of the formal interview which took place between the researcher and informant, including a cover sheet that contains relevant information and brief reflective comments on the margin of the transcript.

Transcript file A reproduction of the formal interview.

References

Altheide, D. 1980. 'Leaving the field.', in W. Shaffir, R. Stebbins & A. Turowetz (eds). *Fieldwork Experiences: Qualitative Approaches to Social Research.* New York: St Martin's Press.

Bogdan, R. & Taylor, S. 1975. *Introduction to Qualitative Research Methods.* New York: Wiley.

Bogdan, R & Biklen, S. 1982. *Qualitative Research for Education.* Boston: Allyn and Bacon.

Burgess, R. 1982. 'Keeping field notes.', in R. Burgess (ed.) *Field Research: Sourcebook and Field Manual.* London: George Allen and Unwin.

Goffman, E. 1967. *Interaction Ritual.* New York: Anchor Books.

Hammersley, M. & Atkinson, P. 1983. *Ethnography: Principles in Practice.* London: Tavistock.

Hoffman, J. 1980. 'Problems of access in the study of social elites and boards of directors.', in W. Shaffir, R. Stebbins & A. Turowetz (eds.) *Fieldwork Experiences: Qualitative Approaches to Social Research.* New York: St Martin's Press.

Ives, E. 1980. *The Tape Recorded Interview.* Knoxville: University of Tennessee Press.

Karp, D. 1980. 'Observing behaviour in public places: problems and strategies.', in W. Shaffir, R. Stebbins & A. Turowetz (eds). *Fieldwork Experiences: Qualitative Approaches to Social Research.* New York: St Martin's Press.

Lofland, J. & Lofland, L. 1984. *Analysing Social Settings: A Guide to Qualitative Observations and Analysis.* Second edition. Belmont, California: Wadsworth.

Macintyre, S. 1979. 'Some issues in the study of pregnancy careers.', *Sociological Review* 27: 755–771.

McCall, M. 1980. 'Who and where are the artists.', in W. Shaffir, R. Stebbins, & A. Turowetz (eds). *Fieldwork Experiences: Qualitative Approaches Social Research.* New York: St Martin's Press.

Miles, M. & Huberman, M. 1984. *Qualitative Data Analysis.* Beverly Hills, California: Sage.

Miller, B. & Humphreys, L. 1980. 'Keeping in touch: contact with stigmatised subjects.', in W. Shaffir, R. Stebbins & A. Turowetz (eds). *Fieldwork Experiences: Qualitative Approaches to Social Research.* New York: St Martin's Press.

Schwartz, H & Jacobs, J. 1979. *Qualitative Sociology: A Method to the Madness.* New York: Free Press.

Shaffir, W., Stebbins, R. & Turowetz, A. 1980. *Fieldwork Experiences: Qualitative Approaches to Social Research.* New York: St Martin's Press.

Strauss, A. 1987. *Qualitative Analysis for Social Scientists.* Cambridge: Cambridge University Press.

Wax, R. 1971. *Doing Field Work: Warnings and Advice.* Chicago: University of Chicago Press.

Webb, B. 1982. 'The art of note-taking.', in R. Burgess (ed.). *Field Research: Sourcebook and Field Manual.* London: George Allen and Unwin.

Chapter 12
Analysing the Data and Writing It Up

The purpose of this chapter is to teach students how to analyse, interpret and report qualitative data. We will describe basic approaches to making sense of data collected through in-depth interviewing. The key issues addressed are: How are links made between the data that are recorded and subsequent theoretical writings? How are qualitative data presented in final reports? Before we address these questions, we would like to make a few general comments about issues relating to analysing qualitative data.

First, a definition of **data analysis** is required. The aim of data analysis is to find meaning in the information collected. Data analysis is the process of systematically arranging and presenting information in order to search for ideas. Data analysis can be broken down into a series of decisions. Bogdan and Taylor (1975) identify three distinct stages. The first stage involves **coding** the data, discovering themes and developing propositions. The second stage is refining one's themes and propositions. The third stage centres around reporting the findings.

Second, data analysis and data collection occur simultaneously in qualitative research. This point should not be overlooked. Unlike quantitative researchers who can employ a research assistant to collect and code the data, qualitative researchers lack a similar division of labour between data collection, coding and analysis. The ongoing analysis that takes place in qualitative research requires that the researcher develops an eye for detecting the conceptual issues while the data are collected. Without analysis occurring in the field, data has no direction.

Third, as shown in the previous chapter, the sheer size of data collected through in-depth interviewing can overload the researcher, and make qualitative data analysis an impossible task. Fortunately, there are techniques that you can use to overcome such problems. The data must be broken up into manageable units. This requires organisation so that you read and retrieve parts of the data that are relevant to the questions being addressed. It is important to remember that data analysis does not happen overnight. Many researchers read and reread their notes and fieldnotes for several weeks or even months. This allows them to discover recurring themes or events which stand out. You should not commence intensive data analysis until you are completely familiar with your data.

The remainder of this chapter will discuss techniques for analysing and reporting data, and illustrate these with examples from our own research.

Analytic Induction Method

A central feature of data analysis is conceptualising data into theory. How do we transform strings of sentences (for example, raw data) into meaningful data which contribute to knowledge? This question cannot be answered without first understanding what data are. Data collected by using in-depth interviewing includes the material the researcher has collected through talking to people. It should be obvious from our discussion in chapter 11 that people's accounts as presented in the transcript file are sentences about beliefs, feelings and state of affairs as *they* see them. These data are both the evidence and the clues from which theory can emerge. For data to become meaningful for analysis, the researcher has to identify common themes which link issues together, and ground the analysis in the informant's understandings and in scientific translations of it.

The main challenge facing qualitative researchers is how to collect and analyse data simultaneously. The **analytic induction method** uses induction not as described in chapter 2 to *justify* the theory but as a *means* of creating one. It allows for ideas to emerge from the data as they are collected. Glaser and Strauss (1967) highlight the following steps:

1 developing a general statement about a topic;
2 collecting data to gain a better understanding of the topic;
3 modifying, revising and expanding the statement as data are collected;
4 searching for cases which do not fit the explanation being formulated and revising the formulation to fit that particular case;
5 developing a satisfactory explanation.

Figure 12.1 illustrates how the principles of the analytical induction method are put into practice. Data are collected within a reflective model (Strauss 1987) where the researcher develops a general research question, conducts his or her first interview, thinks about and analyses this data, conducts another interview, then does more analysis and revision of the proposition, and so on.

The early days of the data-collection stage are often descriptive and exploratory. Let us move through the spiral displayed in Figure 12.1 and illustrate this point with an example. You want to study why older people move into nursing homes. Not all of the factors involved in the decision-making process for entering nursing homes are known. (Of course, you have reviewed the literature and this has provided some leads.) You interview your first informant—Miss Jones. After analysing the transcript of Miss Jones' interview, you develop **propositions** about why older people move into nursing homes, and refine the questions asked in subsequent interviews. On the basis of the material and analysis from the first interview, you decide that the research question

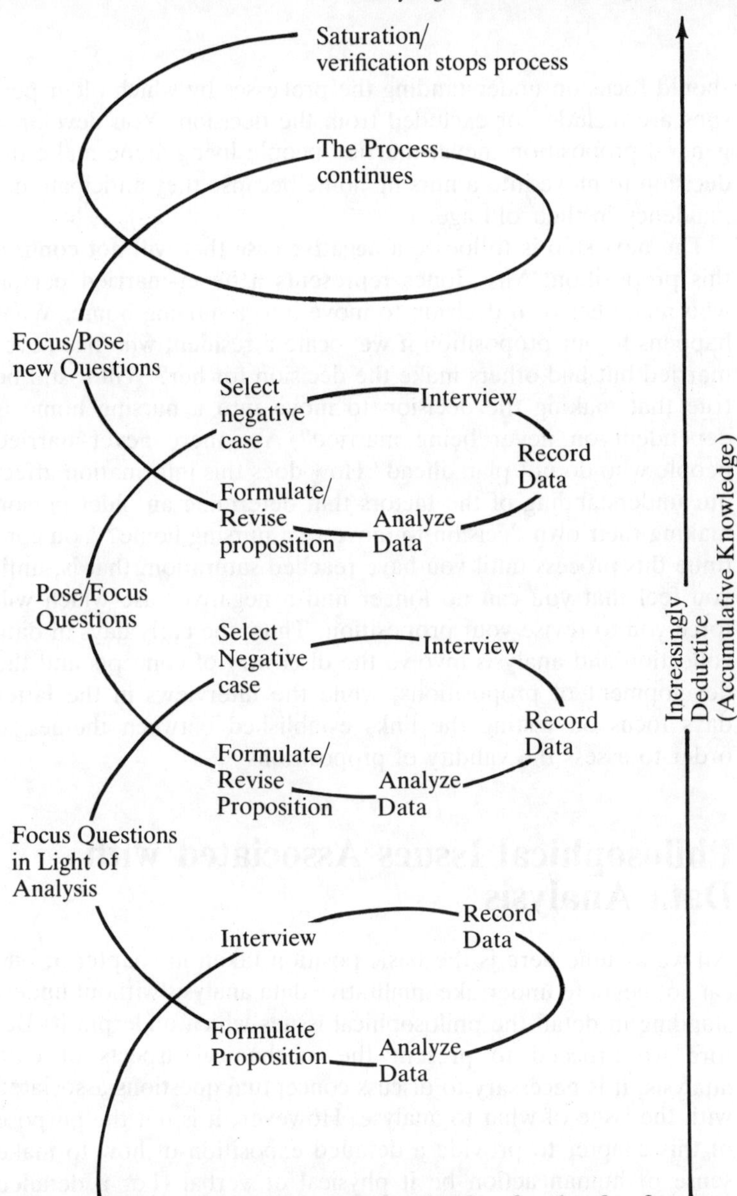

Figure 12.1 The qualitative research process

[1]Adapted from J. Eckett (1988). 'Ethnographic research on ageing', in S. Reinharz and G. Rowles (eds), *Qualitative gerontology*. New York: Springer, pp 243.

should focus on understanding the processes by which older persons are included or excluded from the decision. You develop a general proposition: never-married people living alone make the decision to move into a nursing home because they anticipate dependency in their old age.

The next step is to locate a **negative case** that will not confirm this proposition. Miss Jones represents a never-married person who made her own decision to move into a nursing home. What happens to our proposition if we locate a resident who has never married but had others make the decision for her? Will it still be true that making the decision to move into a nursing home is dependent on never being married? Are there never-married people who do not plan ahead? How does this information affect our understanding of the factors that determine an older person making their own decision to move to a nursing home? You continue this process until you have reached saturation, that is, until you feel that you can no longer find a negative case which will force you to revise your proposition. Thus, the early days of data collection and analysis involve the discovery of concepts and the development of propositions, while the interviews in the latter days focus on testing the links established between themes in order to assess the validity of propositions.

Philosophical Issues Associated with Data Analysis

All we assume here is the basic position taken in chapter 3; one cannot begin to undertake qualitative data analysis without understanding in detail the philosophical issues which underpin it. Before we proceed to present the mechanical aspects of data analysis, it is necessary to discuss conceptual questions associated with the issue of what to analyse. However, it is not the purpose of this chapter to provide a detailed exposition of how to make sense of human action be it physical or verbal (For a detailed discussion see Boudon 1982; Geertz 1973; Giddens 1979; Ricoeur 1974). As we discussed in chapters 2 and 3, there are different ways of interpreting social phenomena. The distinction between positivist and interpretative approaches ultimately depends on the distinction between causes and reasons. That distinction depends upon another, that of persons and things. Is there an absolute difference between persons and things?

Understanding a person requires a constantly shifting global assessment of his or her beliefs, utterances, actions and cultural settings. It is assumptions made about individuals and their relationship to society that gives *qualitative data* a different form from that of *quantitative data.* These assumptions direct us to ask what is to be regarded as the **unit of analysis.**

What do you Code?

The first issue is *what* gets coded? Or to put it differently, what is the unit of analysis? When you look at transcripts and notes from the interviews, are you looking for groups of words, phrases, sentences, themes or even the writing between the lines?

Some researchers suggest that the doing of **content analysis** can focus on several elements of the interview transcript or written document (letters, diaries, etc.); and that these elements are counted in terms of their frequency of appearance (Berg 1989). We, on the other hand, suggest that these elements should not only be counted in numerical terms, but should also be examined for meaning. The elements or units of analysis we consider to be useful are as follows.

Words Individual words are usually the smallest unit examined during a content analysis. Sometimes, the researcher does a frequency count—seeing how many times a word (which has been designated as *significant*) appears in the text. In other instances, the researcher also examines the way in which the word appears to be used for example, as a descriptor, as an expletive, incorrect semantic usage, in group and outgroup differentiation, and so on.

Concepts Concepts are words grouped together in clusters to indicate particular ideas. Concepts are often used in the expression of themes, that is, a group of concepts such as delinquency, fraud, etc. may be linked in the informant's discussion with the interviewer, to indicate one specific theme in that discussion. The theme would be one focussing on deviance.

Sentences Obviously, an interviewee will often explicitly say what the researcher is looking for. In addition, words, concepts and themes are all evaluated in terms of their various locations in sentences of discourse. Sentences in this way are the most fundamental and indispensable units of any analysis of qualitative data.

Themes The researcher looks for themes as expressed in the transcript. The themes can be expressed in single words, phrases, sentences, paragraphs or even entire documents. When the researcher uses themes as the unit of analysis he or she is primarily looking for the expression of an idea irrespective of its grammatical location. It is often made up of concepts which are linked together either by the informant and/or the interviewer.

These units and elements are analysed in terms of the semantics indicated by the informant's usage of them. Obviously, it is a matter of how the researcher interprets that usage. For instance, the researcher could be interpreting what Berg (1989: 107) labels the *manifest content* of the manuscript, that is, 'those elements that are physically present and countable'; or the researcher might be examining what he calls the *latent content* or 'the symbolism underlying the physically presented data', that is, the message that is written between the lines. Whenever we interpret passages of transcript, we can choose to do either manifest or latent content analysis, or both. Where we read between the lines, we must ask ourselves whether our reading is consistent with the informant's perspective. This is not an easy matter to determine and it is the point at which any mode of analysis is open to criticism. Nevertheless, all social interpretation is dependent on this latent content analysis and it is inherent in the analytic enterprise itself. Any system of analysis must label some sentences as lies, jokes and sarcasm and apply some systems (for example, Freud, Marx). Many of our beliefs and purposes are hidden from ourselves and the researcher must hope to discover these hidden beliefs and purposes by complex analytic means.

More Issues Associated with What Gets Coded

Even when you have solved the question of what gets coded by selecting the appropriate unit of analysis, the following questions remain: How do you distinguish between key issues and peripheral issues? In fact, can we legitimately use such categorisations at all? Do we take statements at their face value? Do we look for hidden meanings which are not apparent in the text but are part of our understanding of the social interaction of the interview, the informant's views and our knowledge of the informant's situation?

This last issue highlights several possibilities. First, that the researcher, in conversation with the informant, can misunderstand the meanings that the informant intends (Brown 1983). While there is debate about ways in which researchers can deal with this methodological concern, a commonly used strategy is to listen to what the informant tells us, and to use ourselves to filter what he or she says without distorting the intended meaning—this can be done by checking back with the informant. Alternatively, it is sometimes the case that the informant unintentionally provides information and expressions of attitude which he or she has not consciously examined. It is only when the researcher recognises patterns of meaning in the conversation that the discussion becomes part of the analysis.

For the researcher to act as an interpretative filter in this way, however, requires that he or she needs to go beyond the mere reporting of what was said. The researcher needs to create a picture of what might be the meaning. This is done in the context of shared symbols, language, culture and historical moments. As Brown points out, the researcher,

> . . . can not rest content with a restatement of the facts, say, about a birth weight, age of mother, parity, complications and so on. He [sic] must go on to consider their likely meaning to those involved and for this the relevance of the wider social context must be considered. Concern with meaning ultimately reflects a commitment to explore the significance of a happening or situation in terms of the lives as a whole of those involved. Fortunately, since we all spend much of our time doing just this for ourselves, the human mind is a suitable instrument for the task, even if it is only that of the investigator (1983: 35).

Thus, as was explored in chapter 3, the focus of the hermeneutic tradition is to empathetically grasp the minds of others, the subjective meaning of their behaviours, that is, using *verstehen* or *empathic understanding*.

Secondly, the researcher is operating both within the knowledge worlds of the informant and the researcher's own discipline. An important distinction made by Rose (1982) in relation to this is that between **participant concepts** and **theoretical concepts.** Participant concepts are created by informants and couched in their everyday language. Theoretical concepts are created by the researcher and not immediately recognised by the informants as part of their terminology. An example of a participant concept is the idea of 'not having a say' presented in the Minichiello (1987) study which examines the decision-making process behind moving to a nursing home. Bowers' concept of 'protective caregiving' (see chapter 1) is an example of a theoretical concept. Participants' concepts are learned by the researcher who then interprets these by giving them scientific order and meaning, and using a theoretical concept to do this translation.

But you may be asking how does the above discussion help us solve the question of what gets coded? Trivialising centuries of debate on this issue, our position can be simply summarised as follows—regardless of the choice of the unit of analysis, an important skill to master is learning to understand the logic of the informant's use of idiom, and how to translate it into a system of conceptual thought. This requires studying the whole text, not only in the context of what was said, but also in terms of what was not said, and within the boundaries of the paradigm which the researcher chooses to apply. This is an important point. The interpretation of the conversation is more than simply a quantitative content analysis of the words spoken. Williams (1981: 170) points out that the researcher makes 'claims not primarily about the dictionary meanings of words but rather about the context in which the informants' terms are used'. The researcher's aim, when doing data analysis, is to extract the essence of the informants' meanings as they are verbalised either as intended and unintended accounts.

Williams' (1981) method of logical analysis provides an example of how researchers can use **logical analysis** procedures (a method for learning the informants' language and logic) to organise informants' accounts. He uses Herzlich's (1973) concept of 'illness as an occupation' and 'illness as a destroyer' to make sense of themes arising from informants' descriptions and discussions of old age and chronic illness. The procedures involved in logical analysis, and the explanations and practical uses which arise from it, are illustrated by Williams in his application of Herzlich's concepts to the text of two case studies. Williams demonstrates how the researcher can elicit and analyse people's thinking, including making sense out of people who entertain contradictory systems of thought.

The second issue is related to recognising that there is a debate as to whether understanding is influenced by theory. According to Kuhn (1970) scientists operating in different scientific traditions with different paradigms, work in different worlds and therefore use different filters to interpret what people have said to them. In chapter 3, we quoted Quine as saying that nothing guarantees that there will be one definitive interpretation of someone's meaning. This may explain why researchers disagree with each other when interpreting the results of studies. For example, in reviewing Minichiello's (1986) study of the role families play in the decision to place an aged relative into a nursing home, Connidis states that she reached a different conclusion because

> . . . the view of the older person as victim, and family members as co-conspirators with outsiders . . . is also a function of Minichiello's fairly compelling application of Goffman's work in *Asylums* to the plight of older persons at the time of entering nursing homes (1989: 189–90).

In other words, she argues that Minichiello bases his analysis on the use of a particular theoretical framework drawn from sociology. Rather than casting family members as part of a conspiracy, she notes that family members play an advocate role and act as information sources for the elderly by informing and assisting the aged in dealing with the bureaucratic structure. She argues that the family and health-care organisations operate as a partnership with those institutions (for example, nursing homes) that control various services. Connidis reaches a different conclusion because she uses a different sociological approach.

Techniques for Doing Qualitative Data Analysis

A number of researchers have developed techniques for analysing qualitative data. These include developing coding categories, writing case summaries, typologising, and computer analysis. While these techniques are discussed separately below, researchers often employ a number of these techniques together to analyse their data.

Developing a Coding System

The main preoccupation of the researcher when doing data analysis is identifying a coding system. But what do we mean by a coding system? A coding system is a means of reorganising the data according to conceptual themes recognised by the researcher. It is used to further enhance analysis. Codes can be derived from the informant's stories, research questions and theoretical frameworks. For example, if our research question is 'Who are the decision makers behind the institutionalisation decision for older people entering nursing homes?', we might develop the following coding system: decision makers (the coding scheme) and the coding subcategories (could be) *older person, family members, friends, doctor, other professionals* and so on. Certain theoretical approaches and disciplines suggest particular coding schemes (Bogdan & Biklen 1982). For example, Wiener (1982) was interested in studying the mechanisms which patients develop for the management of pain. Using a symbolic interactionist framework (see chapter 1), Wiener developed a series of concepts which centred around the different mechanisms people use to handle pain. One concept he developed was 'pacing'. The key to developing such a coding system is to create a list of words which can be conceptualised into categories and linked into a general framework.

Why is a coding system important? Any researcher who wishes to do good qualitative research must learn to code well. 'The excellence of the research rests in large part on the excellence of the coding' (Strauss 1987: 27). Codes label and reorganise the data according to topics which open the inquiry and permit the researcher to make sense of the thousands of lines of words. They are retrieval and organising devices that cluster the relevant segment of the data relating to a particular theme or proposition (Miles & Huberman 1984). They also play an important role in the process of discovering themes or developing propositions. As you code the data, you may stumble across ideas which bring the material together in a way that you had not previously thought about. For example, you might read the transcript of Mrs Young and decide that she was excluded from the decision to enter a nursing home. However, when you read the transcript of Mrs Baker you decide that she was fully involved in the decision. You write down these two words in your analytical log. You develop the coding scheme, 'involvement in the decision-making process', and identify four types of categories, *fully involved, excluded, decision involved* and *selection involved* in concert with your decision that this coding scheme provides a conceptual model for understanding the processes by which older people enter nursing homes.

When Do You Develop Codes?

An important question you are probably asking yourself is when to start developing codes. The answer is simple. You start developing coding categories the moment you enter the field. We agree with Miles and Huberman (1984) that late coding weakens the analysis. Coding enhances the discovery of concepts and the testing of propositions as you collect the data. As Figure 12.1 illustrates, you should always code the previous set of field notes before starting the next interview.

> Coding is not just something one does to 'get the data ready' for analysis, but something that drives ongoing data collection. It is, in short, a form of continuing analysis. Qualitative fieldwork should be iterative; one pass at site leads to a reshaping of one's perspective and of one's instrumentation for the next pass (Miles & Huberman 1984: 63).

The number of codes you develop will depend on the amount of data you have collected and the complexity of your analytical scheme.

There are general principles that you should follow when constructing codes. Codes need to be conceptually based and clearly defined. There is no point developing codes simply for the sake of putting words on your list. The codes you devise should be related to the research questions asked and fit into a conceptual scheme. For example, it is important that we know what is meant by *decision makers*, and that we can distinguish it from *involvement in decision making*.

Codes should not be superimposed on the data. Some codes will not work because the way in which they describe the phenomena is not the way these phenomena appear empirically. When this happens you will need to either revise the coding scheme or get rid of it. It is important that you realise that while you might begin with a large number of coding categories, these can be pruned as you refine the focus of your study and propositions.

Strategies for Developing Codes

A strategy that is commonly used by experienced researchers to develop codes is to ask the question, 'What is this thing (or things) I have before me?' (Lofland & Lofland 1984). For example, Goffman (1961) was interested in studying mental institutions. In his attempt to answer the question, 'What is this thing I see before me?', he noted specific features of mental hospitals. By further posing the question, 'What are the general features of mental hospitals?', he developed the concept of 'total institutions'. Let us provide you with another example. Minichiello, Alexander and Jones (see Appendix A) were interested in understanding the processes by which older people enter nursing homes. In trying to answer the question, 'How do older people cross the doorsteps of nursing homes?', they developed a scheme of different levels of involvement in the decision to enter a nursing home. In addition to finding answers to the question, 'What type of unit is it?', the researcher is also searching for the conditions under which a particular type occurs; its underlying features; under what conditions it is present and under what conditions it is is absent. For example, Minichiello et al. were trying to find explanations that accounted for why some older persons were decision makers and others were not. These questions all tend to force the construction of core categories which will be at the centre of theory building and its eventual write up (Strauss 1987).

While it is an impossible task to list all the different types of codes you can construct, Bogdan and Biklen (1982) provide a useful list of categories which can be used for developing coding. These are:

1 *Setting/content codes*—general information on the setting, topic or subjects;
2 *Definitions of the situation codes*—how informants define the setting or particular topic;
3 *Perspectives held by subjects' codes*—how informants think about their situation;
4 *Process codes*—refers to activity over time and perceived change occurring in a sequence, stages, phrases, steps, careers;
5 *Event codes*—specific activities;
6 *Strategies codes*—ways people accomplish things;
7 *Relationship and social structure codes*—regular pattern of behaviour and relationships.

Coding the Data

How are the coding categories applied to the data? **Coding** the data involves learning some basic mechanical skills. This is time consuming and requires patience. To give you an appreciation of the time that it takes to code fieldnotes, Miles and Huberman estimate,

> A single-spaced page of transcribed field notes has about 45 lines. As a rough rule of thumb, it might contain 8–10 codes. (An interview) usually generates 40–80 pages, even when the researcher is disciplined. Coding each page runs about 5–10 minutes once the codes are committed to memory; in the beginning one should count 10–15 minutes. So 'inexperienced' coding of such data sets would take perhaps 2 days; later it could be done in a day or so. Taking longer than this is a signal that there are too fine units of analysis, too much dual coding, too many codes and a weak conceptual structure (1984: 64).

We will briefly discuss the steps involved in coding the data (for a detailed discussion see Bogdan & Biklen 1982; Miles & Huberman 1984; Strauss 1987).

The first step is probably the most complicated. You need to develop a list of coding categories. Once you have identified the major coding categories (which you will have entered in the analytical log), you revise your list. You may find that some categories overlap one another and can be collapsed. You then assign a number or letter to each coding category contained on the list. Our preference is to give a name to the code that is closest to the concept it is describing, and to prefix the name with numbers for distinguishing subcategories. For example, *decision* might refer to decision-making situations, while 'Decision 1' might refer to decisions made by the older person, 'Decision 2' decisions made by doctors and so on. What coding scheme you decide to use is a matter of preference (for a discussion of the advantages and disadvantages of using number or words see Miles and Huberman 1984).

The second step involves formatting the transcript file so that you can code the data. You need to make sure that all the pages in the transcript file are numbered sequentially beginning with the first interview. This is important because once you have placed information into a separate sub-file you may want to locate the original source. You should also make sure (as it was discussed in the previous chapter) that the transcript file has large enough margins which can then be used to write down the coding categories.

The third step is to read through the transcript file and code the units of data in the transcript file by placing the relevant letter and/or number corresponding to each category on the margin. By units of data, we mean the sentences or paragraphs in the interview transcript. You will notice that sometimes the same unit of data can be given different codes. This is fine. Double coding occurs when the same data set can be classified under different code categories.

After you have assigned the codes, the next step is to assemble all the data coded to each category and sort it into subfiles. There are computer packages available for this purpose, for example, NUDIST. These packages include detailed instruction manuals as will be discussed in more detail later in this chapter. Unless you are using a computer which handles the mechanical aspects of qualitative data analysis, you will have to arrange the data manually into separate sub-files. Some researchers use manila folders to sort their files, others use index cards. If you decide to arrange the data manually, we would recommend the use of index cards (For a discussion of alternative methods of sorting data see Bogdan & Taylor 1975). You will require some basic tools to sort the data. These include scissors, glue, index cards and filing boxes.

The operation of assembling your data into sub-files is not mechanically complicated. First, you will need to make sure that the top of each index card contains the following information: the identification label for each informant, the coding category, and other analytically relevant information. An example of an index card is shown in Figure 12.2. It is important that you include some means to identify where your material came from because this will enable you to go back to the original set of notes if necessary. The coding category tells you that the unit of analysis belongs to a certain coding scheme. Some researchers include relevant conceptual information that assists them in making connections between ideas. In the example reproduced in Figure 12.2, the researchers included information on older people's prior living arrangement, marital status and level of involvement in the decision-making process. These factors were identified as influencing the process of entering nursing homes.

Secondly, you cut the relevant units of analysis for each category and paste them on the index cards. (Of course, you should keep a duplicate copy of the transcript file—the original which is filed untouched, and the other for cutting and pasting.) Thirdly, you file the cards in a box. When all the units of data are in the box, you may want to regroup them according to some other part of your conceptual scheme which is relevant for the analysis.

Mrs Vurlow (No. 1; pp 6) **DECISION-MAKING PLAYERS 2**	• Widowed • Living with daughter • Little say in decision
Doctor—(When did you first think about moving into a nursing home?) Well, it was sprung on me as a sort of surprise. I didn't know I was worrying them so much, so my daughters thought they'd better see where they could get me in, and then when it was raised I cried, and I didn't want to come but the doctor explained to me how I was worrying them, you know. And they were afraid to leave me and all this business, so I just took myself in hand and said well, it's the best place for me I guess. (What did the doctor say?) He had a little talk with me and he said it would be more sensible for me to do that because the girls would know I'd be well, there'd always be somebody here and because I used to take those silly old falls, you know, and sometimes, once Patty came home and I was flat out on the bathroom floor. Well, I didn't know I was, you know, and she got me up and got me around, so that really decided things for her. (See *The Duty Chat* in Analytical Log, p. 23).	

Mr McAulay (No. 24; pp 241) **DECISION-MAKING PLAYERS 2**	• Never married • Living alone • Little say in decision
Doctor—I was living on my own after my wife died, and lately I was having blackouts, and the doctor couldn't determine what was wrong with me, but he felt it was best if I didn't stay on my own. I had war injuries and I reached the stage where I needed help, and it was really necessary for him to tell me what I should do because I knew myself that I should move into one. He helped me make up my mind sooner.	

Figure 12.2 Examples of index cards

Case Summaries

Researchers working with qualitative data are often concerned with summarizing, collapsing and reorganising data in order to discover concepts and themes contained within it. A transcript file may often be so large and complex that it may be difficult to differentiate between information relevant to the research question and information that is interesting, but peripheral to it. A strategy that is often used by researchers to condense data contained in a transcript file is to produce **case summaries** of each informant's interview, or to use Bogdan and Taylor's (1975) term, 'develop a story line'. An example of a case summary is reproduced in Figure 12.3.

There are a few general guidelines that we suggest you follow when producing case summaries. First, that you summarise your cases on index cards. Cards can be organised in such a way that comparisons between cases are easily managed. It is less difficult to pull out and sort cards than papers contained in a notebook or folder. Secondly, each card should contain material on the identity of the informant (for example, case number or fictitious name) and some major concepts which are relevant to the research question. For instance, in the example provided in Figure 12.3 the researcher included the following concept codes—prior living arrangement, marital status and level of involvement in the decision to move into a nursing home. These factors influenced the pathway residents took to enter nursing homes. Thirdly, the cards should not only contain a summary of the transcript file but also a set of general propositions arising from the researcher's understanding of the data and its relevance to the research question. Of course, these propositions are revised as the researcher collects more data.

The purpose of writing a case summary is to link the material presented in the transcript to conceptual themes and topics relevant to the research questions asked. Perhaps the best way to develop case summaries is to ask the following questions: What is going on? What are the issues raised by the informant? What are some of the possible explanations for why the informant sees the situation in a given way? For example, in writing the case summary for Mrs E, the researcher included basic information about Mrs E; her situation prior to moving into the nursing home; her involvement in the decision; how she felt about moving to a nursing home; and her possible explanations for the move. On the basis of the researcher's analysis of the interview with Mrs E who was the first informant in the study, the researcher constructed general propositions which related to how married couples entered nursing homes, and how older people decided for themselves to move into a nursing home. The researcher revised and built upon these propositions as he interviewed other residents who found themselves in a similar or different situation to Mrs E (for example, married but not fully involved in the decision, never-married resident, etc.).

Case summaries vary in the level of analytical comments they contain. The first few case summaries tend to be written in very general terms; more as mirror-like summary reports of what was said. Later, as the researcher formulates a better understanding of the topic and develops clearer analytical guidelines for analysing the data, the summary is much more interpretative and integrates knowledge gained from previous cases. As it was explained at the beginning of the chapter, the researcher develops a general picture of the informant's situation and way of seeing the social world. The researcher's understanding of this information is revised as he or she compares individual cases with other cases. This suggests that case summaries are produced not only to sort out information contained *within* the case but are used to compare *across* cases to extended the generalisability of propositions. By making comparisons between cases, the researcher is forced into confronting and explaining the similarities, differences and degress of consistency between informants' accounts. This generates an underlying uniformity which allows for concepts and themes to emerge from the data. It is possible by using this comparative method to move from examining single case studies such as life histories (chapter 7) or clinical case studies (chapter 8) to multi-case studies (chapter 5). Strauss (1987) notes that the aim of developing a theoretical commentary in interpreting the case is to give a broadened picture of the particular case. The theory puts the case within a more general context of understanding what could have happened under varying conditions, therefore [it explains] why this case happened in this particular way (1987: 221).

Figure 12.3 An example of a summary statement index card.

Mrs E. (Respondent No. 04)—Summary Index Card	Widowed Fully Involved Living with husband (1 of 6)
Mrs E. is 92 years old, and prior to moving to the nursing home, she was living with her frail 95–year–old husband whom she had nursed for the last six years. Although her two daughters helped Mrs E. with the housework and cooking 'once a week' and the 'two boys did the other things around the house', it was Mrs E. who was solely responsible for bathing, shaving and dressing Mr E. She and her husband had never once thought about 'ending up in a nursing home' until the accident. Mrs E got up to go to the toilet during the night, slipped and fell. She screamed for help, but without his wife's assistance, Mr E. could not get out of bed or to the phone. Unable to lift herself, Mrs E. remained on the floor all night long, with her husband lying helpless in bed, both 'shouting for help'. It was not until a neighbour heard their cry for help some hours later that they were rescued and rushed to the hospital.	

Mrs E (Respondent No. 04)

(2 of 6)

Upon arriving at the hospital, they jointly decided to move into a nursing home. They had never talked about moving into a home until this crisis. Mrs E. did confess to thinking about it, but she never mentioned the idea to her husband and children. She kept hoping that they would be able to manage. However, the crisis reminded both of them of how vulnerable they really had become over the years. The horror of both lying helplessly on the ground left its mark. They quickly made the decision to move into a home. (They requested that her niece, a social worker, in consultation with their daughters, search for a nursing home that would 'accept us both'. Both she and her husband were not in a position to visit nursing homes). They were emotionally very close to one another. When her husband had a stroke six years ago, Mrs E. moved into the hospital 'to be near him'. This was no time to be separated. She had to go into a hospital to recover from her fall. They were so dependent on one another that 'if one went, then the other went also'. The decision was made even before their children arrived at casualty. They [the children] had felt for some time that their parents should not have been living on their own. I was told by Mrs E.'s eldest daughter during one of her visits at the nursing home, 'We never raised the subject of moving [them] into a nursing home'. As with all of their parents' [other] decisions, 'it was going to be theirs'. However, Mrs E's children did agree with their parents' decision. 'It seemed to be the obvious choice'. Looking after both parents, the daughter explained, would have been impossible 'for any of us to handle'; they [the children] have their own families and work commitments.

Mrs E. (Respondent No. 04)

(3 of 6)

There was very little family discussion, nor the drama of a long and postponed decision. This point was confirmed by the nursing home administrator when I discussed with her the details of Mrs E.'s admission. 'They realised their situation and made the decision willingly. They simply did not believe in living with their children or in-laws'. The decision, however, was not without personal troubles. Mrs E. blames herself for leaving their home. She explains, 'I had the fall and I couldn't leave him or have him worry my children. So we had to look for a home that would take the two of us and he came with me. It was my fault that we came here really'.

Mrs E. (Respondent No. 04)

(4 of 6)

When Mrs E. recovered from her broken hip, she decided to remain at the nursing home, even though she required no assistance with any of the daily living activities. Her husband's health had deteriorated. Although capable of looking after herself, she was in no position to continue to care for [her] husband at home. Besides, it was he who now needed nursing-home care. He moved into the nursing home for her; she was not going to abandon him. Although she would rather be living at home, she is quite happy at the nursing home. She accepts the decision that she will remain at the nursing home until she dies. Her husband died a year ago and although her children tried to persuade her to move in with the family, Mrs E. prefers to live' in my new home'. Her family consists of two daughters, two sons and a total of eighteen grandchildren. She is very close to them. Mrs E. receives a daily visitor; of all her children, her eldest daughter visits most frequently. She spoke very well of her children; how proud she is of them, how close they have always been, and how caring and affectionate they are towards her. Her children also spoke described their mother in such positive terms.

Mrs E. (Respondent No. 04)

(5 of 6)

Mrs E. feels close to the other patients, and in particular to Mrs Vurlow. 'I have found a new family'. As she is getting older and frailer, she does not want to become a burden to her children. She recalls the difficulties (and embarrassments) of going to her children's homes for the day. Both she and her husband have always lived independently. When she was caring for her husband, Mrs E. would not use any of the community services. She was aware of their existence, and her entitlement to use them, but she preferred to manage without 'interference from strangers'. And she thinks she made a wise decision. She could not have continued to look after her husband for much longer at home. No one was aware of the physical burden she had carried for the last six years. She keeps her affairs private and hidden from the family. Recognising that her independent days are over, she told me, 'When you reach the stage where you feel that you are dependent on other people, the only sensible thing to do is to accept your situation and realise that you have got to be where you are and I've accepted that'. She did have the option of moving in with her eldest daughter, but she choose not to. This was in keeping with her self-image of not being a burden to others. Her health has changed greatly since admission two years ago. She is fully dependent on staff for bathing and requires assistance with going to the toilet and dressing.

Mrs E. (Respondent No. 04)

(6 of 6)

GENERAL PROPOSITIONS

- Married couples who rely on the marital dyad to meet the demands of a disability and maintain an independence from their families may find it difficult to ask or accept help from others.
- Self-images of having lead an independent life and not being a burden to others may be important factors in helping people to make the decision to move into a nursing home.
- The 'fully involved' residents can be people with family support.
- The 'fully involved' residents are not necessarily planners; they may wait until a crisis forces them to think about moving into a nursing home.

Typologising

Much attention has been focussed in this chapter on the importance of identifying themes. This is because the process of reconstructing themes drawn from sentences is the core of the analysis of qualitative data. It is through this process that 'discrete bits of information came together to make a more economical whole that, analytically speaking, is more than the sum of its parts' (Miles and Huberman 1984: 227). But you may well be asking, 'How do we accomplish this?'

Typologising is a method that researchers commonly use to understand phenomena better by grouping ideas and then forming ideal types which conceptualising situations that have similar or different characteristics. Ideal types are used to help us make sense of (and visualise) abstract and complex ideas. They are ideal in the sense that they are pure mental constructs which do not exist in reality although they help us interpret and understand reality. Ideal types themselves do not generate knowledge; rather they are a framework or tool which helps researchers to ask particular questions and formulate useful propositions. Let us provide an illustration based on the fieldnotes presented in Figure 12.4. In our attempt to make sense of the question, 'How do ministers construct eulogies?', we develop a classification system derived from the minister's personal knowledge of the deceased and the deceased next-of-kin. The classification scheme or typology presented here emerged as the study progressed. It is based on the material collected in the fieldnotes (that is, what the ministers told the interviewer) and how we, as researchers, have conceptualised this information into a paradigmatic form.

You will notice that there are four types of eulogy construction situations. Cell A a *full-knowledge eulogy* represents an ideal construction of a situation in which the minister develops the eulogy on the basis of both knowledge of the deceased and the deceased's next-of-kin or primary audience. Cell B an *audience-knowledge eulogy* represents an ideal construction of eulogies where the minister develops the eulogy on the basis of knowing the family of the deceased but having had little or no knowledge of the deceased person. Cell C a *personalised-knowledge eulogy* represents an ideal construction of eulogies given by ministers who knew the deceased but who have had little or no knowledge of their families. Cell D a *depersonalised-knowledge eulogy* represents an ideal construction of eulogies given by ministers who have had no knowledge of the deceased or their families.

There are three closely interrelated aspects associated with constructing classification schemes such as that presented in Figure 12.4. Firstly, the researcher needs to identify two or more categories (for example, knowing the deceased, knowing the next-of-kin). Secondly, these categories need to be identified as distinct and mutually exclusive (for example, *Yes/No*). Thirdly, these distinct groupings need to be given distinct names (for example, *full-knowledge eulogy*, *depersonalised eulogy*).

Looking at the data in terms of the influence of the minister's knowledge of the relevant parties at a funeral is, of course, only one way in which this information could have been organised. Any number of alternative classification schemes might have been chosen. For instance, examining the influence of the minster's training and his or her definition of the purpose of eulogies might be another avenue for devising a set of typologies. The point to remember is that whatever scheme you develop, it will allow you to draw on information which you have decided is relevant and allow the data to be categorised in theoretically meaningful ways.

		Minister knows the deceased	
		YES	***NO***
Minister knows the deceased' next-of-kin	***YES***	**CELL A** Full-knowledge eulogy	**CELL B** Audience-knowledge eulogy
	NO	**CELL C** Particularised-knowledge eulogy	**CELL D** Depersonalised-knowledge eulogy

Figure 12.4. An illustration of typology construction: types of eulogies.

The process of developing typologies is a tedious task. It is something that slowly emerges as you read and reread your fieldnotes. For this reason, it is both a frustrating and exciting task; frustrating when you are trying to develop it, exciting when the data collected begins to make sense in the categories that you have recognised as inherent to it and useful in relation to your research question.

The Use of Computers

The volume of textual data is a major stumbling block when analysing qualitative data. Indexing and coding all the data is an enormous clerical task. It is common practice for qualitative researchers to only partially classify the data. Even when the researcher codes all the data,

> . . . the task of doing something with it is too defeating. Taking indexed text and sifting, comparing, combining categories, tracking down threads of meaningful connections, finding confirmations and counter examples, simply stretches most researchers' abilities and patience too far (Richards & Richards 1988: 3).

In recent years, a number of computer packages to handle qualitative data have been developed in the United States (Drauss 1980; Gerson 1985; Seidel & Clark 1984; Shelly & Sibert 1986), and in Australia (Richards & Richards 1987). The speed and memory-storing capacity of computers have assisted researchers to explore and analyse the content of the text in ways that would be manually impossible.

Types of Computer Aids

It is important for the reader not to confuse word-processing systems with database management systems. Word-processing systems, such as MacWrite or Microsoft-Word, can be used to store qualitative data. Word processing, with its cut-paste operations, assist in indexing and ordering data. There can be no doubt that word processing is better and quicker than using the old-fashioned typewriter and photocopier. However, word-processing systems do not perform operations which classify, sort and retrieve data. When we are talking about using computers for qualitative data analysis, we are referring to using database management systems. These systems are designed to perform many of the major mechanical operations previously undertaken manually by the researcher. The programme includes operations which physically divide the data into categories and applies a set of indexing operations to retrieve relevant sections of the data.

These functions can be illustrated by describing the NUDIST program. We have selected this programme as an example because it is the most recent and only Australian package available on the market. Prior to this, the most useful programme for coding data was the American package SPSSx.

NUDIST is derived from non-numerical unstructured data indexing, searching and theorising (For a more detailed discussion of this program see Richards and Richards 1987; Richards 1987). The programme stores and formats text in a database, and the researcher then applies software analysis packages to code the data. Only the size of the allocated computer disc space limits the amount of information stored and the number of coding categories used to reorganise the data. This permits the researcher to develop a thorough categorisation and cross-filing system and to accurately apply these to the data. The important point to remember is that NUDIST, unlike a word-processor programme, not only stores and extracts data, but it reorganises and abstracts textual material to make it available for testing ideas.

A Word of Caution

While there can be little doubt that programmes such as NUDIST allow researchers to make the most of their data, the computer does not replace the analytical thinking processes underpinning qualitative research (Becker et al. 1984; Conrad & Reinharz 1984). All forms of artificial intelligence are programmed to assume that the theoretical framework is introduced by the researcher. For example, the coding categories on eulogy construction situations discussed in the previous section were not constructed by the NUDIST computer programme. The package does not have the capacity to develop the proposition that knowledge of the deceased will influence how the minister constructs the eulogy. Nor does it bring to your attention that there are different types of eulogies such as celebration, pastoral care and gospel.

The computer is an aid for data-retrieval purposes. It is a more sophisticated system for indexing and retrieving a vast mass of research material. For this reason, it complements the 'interpretive phase of data analysis to the extent that the interpretive phase relies upon the mechanical phase for the presentation of data' (Drauss 1980: 337). By using the computer, the researcher can devote more time to the interpretive phase of data analysis and perform the mechanical operations with greater efficiency, accuracy and speed.

The Connection Between Data Analysis and Writing Up

When one begins the process of 'writing up', the research analysis has not finished. In fact, the analytic and writing-up processes are totally intertwined. Good research depends on the results being communicated clearly and concisely. In this next section, we review the relationship between these processes and how the researcher can go about the writing-up process.

An experienced writer knows that he or she cannot write about everything he or she has seen or heard, and also realises that writing is a multiple-level process that begins the moment the writer enters the field and start writing fieldnotes. If you have followed our advice and recorded ideas in the personal and analytical logs, you will have started writing your research paper. The logs provide a base from which you can select material to write the substantive and methodological sections of the research paper. The rest of the chapter will examine stylistic and content issues in writing qualitative reports.

Playing the Writing Game

Two important ingredients of good writing are discipline and hard work. Experienced writers would never consider their first draft to be their final product. Becker (1985) has criticised students for being 'one-draft writers'. Many students wait to write their paper the night before the deadline. They may receive a good grade for their efforts. However, as Berg (1989) correctly points out, the submission of first drafts to editors is not likely to get the same results in the academic world. Textbooks and research articles published in journals are not written in this way. The thinking and writing stage spans several months, if not years.

The writer begins with an outline which sketches out the major themes and breaks the tasks into manageable parts. Writing seldom comes naturally. The danger of procrastination is always a reality. An outline allows you to focus on particular aspects of the massive information held in your possession. It serves as a starting point that allows you to fill in the skeleton frame of the paper. Once the writer has identified the core elements of the paper, drafts are written and rewritten. The paper is circulated among colleagues for comments. As the writer feels more confident about his or her work, the paper is submitted for publication. At this stage, the paper will go through another round of critical review. Editors and publishers will send the paper or book to anonymous reviewers. The reviewers will be asked to rank the manuscript by checking a list of such phrases as: 1 accepted for publication; 2 accepted for publications with minor changes; 3 strongly encourage author to make substantial changes and resubmit paper; 4 paper is not accepted. The reviewers' report also includes comments on the strengths and weaknesses of the paper and suggestions for improving it. Journals do not accept all submitted papers. In fact, reputable journals only publish between 20–30% of the manuscripts offered. Many are published after the authors make revisions to the original paper.

You may well be asking the question, 'What does rewriting entail?'. Does it mean merely editing for typing and spelling errors? Of course, you do not want to submit an article which contains such errors. Editing means much more than correcting typographical errors. It means rewriting substantive portions of the paper. You may decide to further develop or clarify a theme, expand or trim the analysis or reorder the sequence of ideas presented in the paper. Rewriting also involves getting rid of unnecessary 'clutter'. Zinsser uses clutter to mean 'laborious phrases which have pushed out the short word that means the same thing' (1980: 15). When writing you should simplify, prune and strive for order.

> . . . the secret of good writing is to strip every sentence to its cleanest component. Every word that serves no function, every long word that could be a short word, every adverb which carries the same meaning that is already in the verb, every passive construction that leaves the reader unsure of who is doing what—these are the thousand and one adulterants that weaken the strengths of a sentence (Zinsser, 1980: 7).

A clear and precise sentence is no accident. We seldom get this result on our first attempt. First drafts are often wordy and contain much more than a reader wants to know. Initially, it is important for the author to write everything he or she thinks is important and relevant. It is much harder to get rid of something that you have written than to add something you have not recorded. The first draft should be seen as a starting point, which contains sentences and ideas that are blurry and need to be focussed. You should examine your first draft ruthlessly for words that say nothing. A good writer is someone who is persistent, keeps looking, thinking and rewriting until all has been said in the most readable and precise manner. Figure 12.5 shows an example of the rewritten version of pages 5 and 6 of chapter 1.

The main purpose of rewriting is to ensure that what you have written is said more clearly and more precisely than in the previous draft. This process is continued until you have a 'clean' copy. When you have reached this stage you go over it once more, reading it aloud. You then ask someone else to read the paper to discover unnoticed clutter and flaws in the argument.

Like writing, **editing** cannot be completed overnight. It is advisable that you take time to withdraw from your latest draft. A few days of rest from the paper can give you a new outlook. When you return to your paper ask yourself: What am I trying to say?; Have I succeeded?; Is it clear to someone who has read it for the first time?; Have I presented the ideas in a logical order?; Is there some other way I can condense my material to make it clearer?; Is it wordy?; Are my sentences and paragraphs too long? Zinsser (1980) and Becker (1985) provide some helpful suggestions about how to write well. They recommend using active rather than passive verbs. The difference between the two is that active verbs, for instance, carry a clearer and stronger message. As Zinsser illustrates.

> Joe hit him is strong. He was hit by Joe is weak. The first is short and vivid and direct; it leaves no doubt about who did what. The second is necessarily longer and it has an insipid quality; something was done by somebody to someone else. A style which consists of mainly passive constructions, especially if the sentences are long, saps the reader's energy. He is never quite certain of what is being perpetrated by whom and on whom.

Adverbs and adjectives clutter ideas and are often unnecessary. Consider the following. Do you think there is a big difference between, 'Someone clenched his teeth *tightly*.' and 'Someone clenched his teeth.'? After all there is no other way to clench one's teeth! You should not use adverbs unless they serve a purpose. The example cited by Zinsser illustrates this point.

> If an athlete loses a game because he played badly, 'badly' gives us the helpful information that he didn't play well. But spare us the news that he moped dejectedly and that the winner grinned widely (1980: 102–03).

A number of scholars have argued that whether researchers use **qualitative** or **quantitative** is a matter of training and ideology (Denzin, 1986; Sieber, 1973; Strauss, 1988). Researchers adopt a given method because they have been trained to believe that their preferred method is superior or more scientific than others (ref). While there can be no doubt that training influences our methodological practice, this argument loses sight of the interrelationship between method and theory. As chapter 2 and 3 will discuss, the choice of method is also influenced by the assumption the researcher is making about science, people and the social world. In turn, the method used will influence what the researcher will see.

It is important that before we discuss ways to collect qualitative data through in-depth interviewing you understand some basic differences between qualitative and quantitative approaches. Qualitative research attempts to capture the quality of meanings, definitions and descriptions of things. In contrast, quantitative research aims to count and measure things (Berg, 1989). As shown in Figure 1.1. The main differences between these two approaches to research can be divided into three major characteristics. These are: 1) methodological—the handling of data; 2) conceptual—the nature of the phenomenon studied; and 3) interpretive—the expected outcomes of research (Parse et al., 1985).

Figure 12.5 An example of editing.

Paragraphs should be kept short. It is useful to limit each paragraph to one central theme or point. If you include too many themes or points in the one paragraph you risk damaging the logical flow of ideas (Becker 1985). The advantage of short paragraphs is that they look inviting. Long paragraphs can discourage the reader from starting to read.

You should make it a practice to be concise. Say what you want to say only once and write it clearly. You can master this skill by learning how to choose words that convey what you want to say. The dictionary and thesaurus are invaluable tools in the writing game. Often the difference between being clear or vague lies in the choice of a word. We suggest that you follow the advice of Bogdan and Biklen: 'If you feel that you are not saying what you want, look up the words to see if they can be replaced by something more precise' (1982: 182).

A final word of advice. You should avoid using sexist language. Feminist writers have shown us that many writers incorporate a sexist language in their writing. A common issue which confronts many writers today is what to do with the he/she pronoun. In fact, the authors of this book debated this issue. A conventional practice (and the one we decided to use in the book) is to use *or*, that is, to say *he or she.* Another common solution is to eliminate the male pronouns and substitute this with the plural pronouns *they, us, we.*

The inexperienced writer will find it useful to read well-known qualitative research articles and books. Reviewing the manuscripts that others have written may provide you with ideas on how authors present data, how they built their arguments, arrange their sentences and paragraphs, and format their papers. Some classic qualitative works are include W. Whyte's (1943) *Street Corner Society;* Thomas and Znaniecki's (1958) study of *The Polish Peasant* and Becker et al. (1961) *Boys in White.*

You may also decide to consult journals which publish qualitative studies. While this is not an exhaustive list, included are *Sociology of Health and Illness; Journal of Contemporary Ethnography; Qualitative Sociology; Human Relations; Holistics Nursing Practice; Social Problems.*

Structuring the Paper

A fundamental question is, 'Who am I writing for?'. You will remember from chapter 11 that fieldnotes are written for yourself. However, this is not the case when writing the results. You are writing for people who will be interested in what you have to say. Understanding your audience is important because this affects what you write about and how you present the information (see chapters 9 and 10). If you are interested, for example, in writing for other gerontologists, you must address issues and concerns relevant to that particular academic community. If, on the other hand, you wish to reach a more general audience such as consumers, aged people, their carers, you must place the issues in a larger and more general context. It is important to realise that the style and presentation of your argument will need to be tailored to the needs of the audience. We suggest that you compare articles which have been written in academic journals with those found in the popular press, such as *Australian Society*.

There is another reason for undertaking research—other than satisfying one's thirst for knowledge or furthering career goals. Disseminating the results of your study is an essential feature of research. Researchers have a professional responsibility to share with the scientific community to which they belong the information they have uncovered (Berg 1989). Research without a collective consciousness has little value. Also, as discussed in chapters 9 and 10, the researcher may further acknowledge a responsibility to the individual informant and/or the community to which he or she belongs.

The length and 'surface structure' of the report will vary depending on whether you are writing a book or research article. Surface structure refers to 'the number of major headings that give order to the report' (Berg 1989: 146). Books may be several hundred pages in length and may contain several interconnected themes which are organised into chapters. Articles have fewer pages (no more than 7000 words) and use subtitles to organise the flow of the argument. However, regardless of whether you are writing a book or a journal article report, the organisation requires a logical sequence. It has a beginning, a middle and an end. The beginning tells the reader what the paper intends to do and lays out the contents. The middle sections tells the story by developing, arguing and presenting the major points. The end summarises what was said and draws the reader's attention to other research questions and the implication of the results for policy and/or professional practice. These sections usually follow the sequence of steps taken in planning the research and in collecting and analysing the data. We suggest that you adopt the format used for research articles in professional journals. This format is summarised below. Obviously, there are alternative organisational strategies depending on the nature of your research and your own personal writing style.

- Introduction (What issue are you investigating and why is this relevant/important?).
- Method (What procedures did you use to obtain your information?).
- Findings/Results (What did you find? What do your findings mean?.
- Conclusion (What have you said? Why is this important? What are the implications of the study?).
- Abstract (A brief summary of the above points).
- References (A list of sources cited in the report).

The next few pages will consider in more detail the content of each of these sections.

The Introduction

The most important sentence in any article is the first one. If it fails to capture the reader's attention, he or she will not bother to read the next sentence. The first few sentences must entice the reader to want to continue reading. You should start the paragraph by presenting an interesting fact or question.

The introduction has to address several issues. First, tell the reader the nature of the problem being investigated. A reader may grow impatient if he or she has to read a few pages before finding out what it is that you are studying. Tell the reader your research question within the first few paragraphs. For example, in the introduction to the research article presented in the next chapter, the authors make it clear that they are interested in studying whether involvement in the decision to enter a nursing home influences the quality of life of residents.

Second, place your question in the context of current knowledge on the topic. This means reviewing and summarising previous literature. The analysis of the literature needs to address the following questions: What previous research has been done on this topic? What are the pertinent concepts and theories used to study this question?

You do not need to cite every study written on the topic. Nor should the analysis of the literature read like a string of summary sentences which have been written and incorporated in the introduction section. The literature should be used to substantiate major points and to justify the effort of doing the research. You should cite only those studies which are pertinent to the issues you are addressing and emphasise only their major conclusions, findings or relevant methodological issues (Kidder and Judd 1986). Avoid reporting unnecessary detail.

The cited articles should include the classic and most recent references. If you fail to include relevant studies you leave yourself open to criticism. You can use a number of reference systems for citing the source. We suggest that you consider the commonly used Harvard reference system. References in the text are cited giving the author's last name and the date of publication.

Methodology

This section should provide the reader with considerable detail about how the research was accomplished, what the data consist of and how data were collected, organised and analysed; in other words, details about the informants and data analysis techniques. A reader will carefully evaluate this information when assessing the report. Failure to report this information can weaken the report.

Who were the informants? How many were there? How were they selected? Answers to these questions will assist the reader to draw his or her conclusion on who has been left out and how this influences the conclusions drawn. The information that the researcher provides about the characteristics of informants will vary from study to study. If you were studying nursing-home residents, you may include the following information: age, gender, marital status, prior living arrangement, health status. If you were studying police officers, the following information could be relevant: age, gender, number of years in the police force, education, and social class.

The method section also provides information on how data were collected. This information includes a description of what data-collection technique was used, as well as an account of how the data were recorded and analysed. For example, if you used in-depth interviewing, the reader would like to know if the interviews were taped, the length of the interview, how you stored the data, whether you used a computer package to analyse the data and the coding system developed to classify the data. This information is important for several reasons. First, they place the results in a context that allows the reader to evaluate its merits and credibility. Second, they provide a set of procedures for others who may be interested in replicating the study.

Findings and Results

Qualitative reports differ in several ways from quantitative reports in the presentation of findings and results. First, in quantitative reports, the findings are presented in the form of numbers and tables, and these are discussed under the section heading *Findings and Results*. These two terms, as Berg points out, although often used synonymously, are quite distinct. Findings refer to what the data say. Results offer interpretations of the meaning of the data. Qualitative reports present the findings in the form of words, and are discussed under the headings of narrative labels. While particular schools of thought produce manuscripts with a distinct style (Lofland 1974), most do conform to a general principle. The organisation of findings and results are based on 'analytic logic'. It is common practice for the author to first announce the major conceptual issues or themes and to then develop these, with illustrations from the data. Two examples will be discussed to show this process.

Appendix A presents a qualitative research report. You will notice that immediately preceding the method section, the authors present their general conceptual model; a typology of decision-making situations. The typology contains four different types of decision-making situations. After presenting this general model, the authors proceed to discuss the four types of decision-making situations and use the following sub-headings—*fully involved, decision involved*, *selection involved* and *excluded*. The findings are the descriptions taken from the transcript to illustrate and substantiate claims made in the text. The results are the propositions put forward to develop an understanding of the decision making to enter nursing homes.

Another example may clarify how qualitative researchers present their findings. Glaser and Strauss (1965) undertook a classic study of the social dimensions of dying. Findings and results are arranged around the core concept of trajectory, outlining its multi-facet phases. Each section focusses on these phases which portray the movement of hospitalised sick persons toward their death and the complex interactions which take place between the sick person, staff and families. For each phase, crucial conditions and strategies associated with the different phases are identified and illustrated with data quoted from subjects.

It has been said that presenting the results of qualitative data is like writing a story (Bogdan and Taylor 1975). A good story has to be clearly and logically presented. You should ask yourself: Has the analysis been ordered clearly? Has it been said in its most effective form? Can it be presented more effectively by reordering the flow of ideas?

Conclusion

Having said that the first sentence is the most important line to write, we will now tell you that your last line is just as important. Knowing when to end an article is far more important than most writers realise. Zinsser argues,

> This may seem ridiculous. If the reader has struck with you from the beginning, trailing you around blind corners and over bumpy terrain, surely he won't leave when the end is in sight. But he will—because the end that is in sight often turns out to be a mirage. Like the minister's sermon that builds to a series of perfect conclusions which never conclude, an article that doesn't stop as its proper place is suddenly a drag and therefore, ultimately, a failure (1980: 70).

The conclusion serves two purposes. First, it reviews your argument, highlighting the central themes developed in the paper. You should write this concisely and restrict it to no more than a few paragraphs. But your conclusion should be more than a summary. It should give the reader something to think about. Rather than saying, 'In summary, this paper shows how . . .', you can provide interesting interpretations to the summary. For example, you can say that the study has illustrated the process by which older people are excluded from decisions to enter nursing homes. You may add that this provides further evidence of society preventing older people from leading autonomous lives and raises the moral question of the rights of older people.

Second, the conclusion addresses the shortcomings and implications of your study. For example, you may want to draw the reader's attention to conditions which might limit the extent to which your results can be generalised to other populations. Or you may want to discuss the implications of your results for policy development and professional practice. The Minichiello et al. study discusses, for example, strategies that can be developed to safeguard the voice of the older person in the admission decision. Many writers point out questions which remain unanswered or new questions that have been raised by the study.

Abstract

Most journals require the author to write an **abstract.** An abstract is a brief summary of the research question, methodology, findings and implications of the study. The title of the report is also part of the abstract. The title should convey the content of the paper so that the reader may decide whether or not it is of interest to him or her. A reader will grow impatient if he or she has been deceived into believing that the paper was about something that it is not. Titles can be constructed around major themes of the paper. Abstracts appear at the very beginning of the paper, and include no more than 100–150 words. Here is an example of an abstracts.

> Theory-generating methodologies can be used to add to our knowledge in areas that are already well researched in addition to areas that have not been extensively studied. The study presented here demonstrates how the grounded-theory method was used to generate a new theory of intergenerational caregiving. Analysis revealed five conceptually distinct, overlapping categories of caregiving. Only one of these includes what is generally considered to be caregiving, that is, hands-on caregiving behaviours or tasks. The other four types are not observable behaviours but are processes crucial to intergenerational caregiving and to an understanding of the experience of intergenerational caregiving (Bowers 1987: 20).

Abstracts provide the reader with an opportunity to quickly glance at the major features of the paper and decide if they wish to read the entire report. It is not easy to write an abstract. You cannot summarise everything in an abstract. You must carefully decide what to highlight. For this reason, we suggest that you write your abstract after you have written the paper. You will be in a much better position to decide what is important. Specifically, you should be looking for the key issues addressed in the study; the nature of the data analysed; the major findings; and implications of the findings. These four elements provide a framework which will enable you to produce an abstract. Abstracts are the very first lines that a reader comes across. Therefore, you should write clearly and in a way that encourages the reader to continue reading.

References

The paper needs to acknowledge the use of other people's materials. All sources consulted and used in the text should be properly cited. There are two styles for documenting the books and articles you have cited. You can use superscript numerals or source references. Superscript numbers are sequentially placed halfway upwards on the line of the text and at the end of the sentence or quotation. These numbers correspond to reference notes located either at the bottom of the page or at end of the paper. The following is an example of a superscript numeral reference.

> Depression is the psychiatric disorder most likely to occur in the elderly and, thus, a major cause of distress.[1] Blaser recently reported, however, that although a larger percentage of older people show . . .[2]

The author would then cite the full reference details either at the bottom of the page or in a reference section as follows.

> [1]Hale, W. 1982. 'Correlates of depression in the elderly: sex differences?' *The Gerontologist* 27: 703–711.
> [2]Blazer, D. 1987. *The epidemiology of depression in an elderly community population. The Gerontologist* 27: 281–287.

An alternative method is cite author's name, date of publication, and in the case of a direct quote, the page(s) from which the quote has been extracted, immediately following the point in the text where a quote, paraphrase or statement is made (This is the style used in this text). The references cited in the text are listed at the end of the paper under the heading *References*. They are arranged alphabetically. An example of the source reference style is presented below:

> Depression is the psychiatric disorder most likely to occur in the elderly and, thus, a major cause of distress (Hale 1982). Blaser (1987) recently reported, however, that although a larger percentage of older people show . . .

The author would then cite the full reference details either at the bottom of the page or in a reference section as follows.

> Blazer, D. 1987. 'The epidemiology of depression in an elderly community population.' *The Gerontologist,* 27: 281–287.
> Hale, W. 1982. 'Correlates of depression in the elderly: sex differences?' *The Gerontologist,* 27: 703–711.

Whether you adopt one or the other style will depend on the requirements of the journal to which you are submitting the paper. In the social sciences, source references are more commonly used. Science journals use the superscript numerals style. For a detailed discussion of rules governing referencing see *Manual of the American Psychological Association 1983.*

Glossary

Abstract Brief summaries of the research studies; generally includes the purpose, methods and major findings of the study.
Analytical induction method A method used to make inferences from some specific observations to a more general rule. Used in constructing propositions or theory from data.
Case summaries Brief summary of each interview; generally includes information on themes and topics relevant to the research question.
Coding The general term used for conceptualising data and categorising it. Coding includes raising questions and giving provisional answers about categories and about their relations (Strauss 1987).
Content analysis A research method applied to texts for purposes of identifying specific characteristics or themes.
Data analysis The process of systematically arranging and presenting the data in order to search for ideas and to find meaning in the information collected.
Editing Rewriting what you have written in order to say it more clearly and more precisely.
Logical analysis A method used for learning the informants' language and logic as expressed in conversation.
Negative case analysis The systematic search for disconfirming instances; used to generate and revise propositions.
NUDIST An Australian computer package designed to analyse qualitative data. NUDIST is derived from Non-numerical Unstructured Data Identity, Searching and Theorising.

Participant concepts Ideas, themes, concepts expressed by informants in their own language.
Propositions A statement or assertion of the relationship between concepts. In philosophy, a proposition can be the true-or-false sentence which is expressed in a given statement.
Theoretical concepts The ideas, themes and concepts of the informant translated by the researcher using a theoretical scheme.
Typologising The process of understanding phenomena better by grouping ideas and then forming ideal types.
Unit of analysis The specific theme, word or concept being used in data analysis.

References

Becker, H., Geer, Hughes & Strauss 1961. *Boys in White.* Chicago: University of Chicago Press.

Becker, H., Gordon, A., & LeBailly, R. 1984. 'Field work with the computer: criteria for assessing systems.', *Qualitative Sociology* 7: 16–33.

Becker, H. 1985. *Writing for Social Scientists.* Berkeley, California: University of California Press.

Berg, B. 1989. *Qualitative Research Methods for the Social Sciences.* Boston: Allyn and Bacon.

Bogdan, R. & Taylor, S. 1975. *Introduction to Qualitative Research Methods.* New York: Wiley.

Bogdan, R. & Biklen, S. 1982. *Qualitative Research for Education.* Boston: Allyn and Bacon.

Boudon, R. 1982. *The Unintended Consequences of Social Action.* London: Macmillan.

Bowers, B. 1987. 'Intergenerational caregiving: adult caregivers and their ageing parents.', *Advanced in Nursing Research* 9: 20–31.

Brown, G. 1983. 'Accounts, meaning and causality.', in G. Gilbert and P. Abell (eds). *Account and Action.* Hemisphere: Gower.

Connidis, I. 1989. 'Book reviews—Ageing and the families: a support networks perspective.', *Canadian Journal on Ageing* 8: 187–191.

Conrad, P. & Reinharz, S. 1984. 'Computers and qualitative data.', *Qualitative Sociology* 7: 3–15.

Drauss, K. 1980. 'The analysis of qualitative data.', *Urban Life* 9: 332–353.

Geertz, C. 1973. *The Interpretation of Culture.* New York: Basic Books.

Gerson, E. 1985. 'Computing in qualitative sociology.', *Qualitative Sociology* 7: 194–198.

Giddens, A. 1979. *Central Problems in Social Theory: Action, Structure and Contradiction in Social Analysis.* London: Macmillan.

Glaser, B. & Strauss, A. 1965. *Awareness of Dying.* Chicago: Aldine.

Glaser, B. & Strauss, A. 1967. *The Discovery of Grounded Theory.* Chicago: Aldine.

Goffman, F. 1961. *Asylums: Essays on the Social Situation of Mental Patients and Other Inmates.* Chicago: Aldine.

Herzlich, C. 1973. *Health and illness : A Social Psychological Analysis*. London: Academic Press.
Kidder, L. & Judd, C. 1986. *Research Methods in Social Relations*. Fifth Edition. New York: CBS.
Kuhn, T. 1970. *The Structure of Scientific Revolution*. Second edition. Chicago: University of Chicago Press.
Lofland, J. 1974. 'Styles of Reporting Qualitative Field Research.', *American Sociologist* 9: 101–111.
Lofland, J. & Lofland, L. 1984. *Analysing Social Settings: A Guide to Qualitative Observations and Analysis*. Second edition. Belmont, California: Wadsworth.
Manual of the American Psychological Association. 1983. Third edition. Washington, DC: American Psychological Association.
Miles, M. & Huberman, M. 1984. *Qualitative Data Analysis*. Beverly Hills, California: Sage.
Minichiello, V. 1986. 'Social processes in entering nursing homes.' in H. Kendig (ed.). *Ageing and Families: A Support Networks Perspective*. Sydney: Allen and Unwin.
Minichiello, V. 1987. 'Someone's decision: that is how I got here.', *Australian Journal of Social Issues* 22: 345–356.
Ricoeur, P. 1974. *The Conflict of Interpretations: Essays in Hermeneutics*. Evanston: Northwestern University Press.
Richards, L. & Richards, T. 1987. 'Qualitative data analysis: can computers do it?', *Australian and New Zealand Journal of Sociology* 23: 23–35.
Richards, T. & Richards, L. 1988. *NUDIST: a System for Qualitative Data Analysis*. Paper presented at Australian Computer Society. Victorian Branch.
Richards, T. 1987. *User manual for NUDIST: a Text Analysis Program for the Social Sciences*. Second edition. Melbourne: Replee.
Rose, G. 1982. *Deciphering Sociological Research*. London: Macmillan.
Seidel, J. & Clark, J. 1984. 'The ETHNOGRAPH: A Computer Program for the Analysis of Qualitative Data.', *Qualitative Sociology* 7: 110–125.
Shelly, A. & Sibert, E. 1986. 'Using Logic Programming to Facilitate Qualitative Data Analysis.', *Qualitative Sociology* 9: 145–161.
Strauss, A. 1987. *Qualitative Analysis for Social Scientists*. Cambridge: Cambridge University Press.
Thomas, W. & Znaniecki, F. 1958. *The Polish Peasant in Europe and America*. Second edition. New York: Dover Publications.
Whyte, W. 1943. *Street Corner Society: the Social Structure of an Italian Slum*. Chicago: University of Chicago Press.
Wiener, . (1982). 'Tolerating the Uncertain.', in G. Rose (ed.). *Deciphering Sociological Research*. London: Macmillan.
Williams, R. 1981. 'Logical Analysis as a Qualitative Method 1: Themes in Old Age and Chronic Illness.', *Sociology of Health and Illness*.
Zinsser, W. 1980. *On Writing Well: An Informal Guide to Writing Nonfiction*. New York: Harper and Row.

Appendix A An Example of a Qualitative Report in Print

A Typology of Decision-making Situations for Entry to Nursing Homes

V. Minichiello, L. Alexander and D. Jones

Introduction

The notion of control is central to theories of human behaviour. Control usually refers to the extent to which people see their situation as being contingent upon their own decisions as opposed to its being determined by others. The need to control one's destiny has been described as 'an intrinsic necessity of life itself' (Adler 1930: 398). People strive to be 'causal agents, to be the primary locus of control of, causation for, or the origin of their behaviour' (De Charms 1968: 269). Experimental studies dealing with the perception of control have found that exercising personal choice has a definite and positive role in improving quality of life (Langer, Janis and Wolfer 1975). Reviewing the psychosocial research on control and ageing, and in particular the intervention studies which examine the effect of the control of nursing-home residents, Rowe and Kahn (1987: 146) note that 'the extent to which autonomy and control are encouraged or denied may be a major determinant of whether ageing is usual or successful on a number of physiologic and behavioural dimensions'.

Entering a nursing home represents a major life transition for elderly people. Some degree of stress is felt although it may not be experienced in the same manner by all residents (Lazarus and Folkman 1984; Minichiello 1986; Tobin and Lieberman 1976). For most older people, the nursing home will be their 'last stop' (Howe 1983). There are two major stages in the process of entry to a nursing home: first, the question of making the decision to seek nursing-home care; and second, that of selecting the home.

It has been argued that a person's control over the decision to enter a home might cushion the effects of institutional living (Thomas 1986). Of equal importance is the person's involvement in selection of the nursing home. Choice of where one will live may also affect acceptance of such a change in environment. Residents who have no opportunity to visit a nursing home or to assess the environment prior to placement may not like or accept the selection. While a number of researchers have addressed issues of personal autonomy (Cohen 1988; Collopy 1988), patient responsibility in long-term care facilities (Jameton 1988; Wetle et al. 1988), and competence of aged persons to participate in decision making (Stanley et al. 1988), the literature is virtually silent on the actual processes by which older people are included or excluded in decision making to enter nursing homes. The few studies that have systematically examined *who* the decision makers are, and the role they play, have found the aged to be minor participants in the decision to enter a nursing home (Clough 1981; Minichiello 1987).

This paper will present a typology of decision-making situations based on different levels of engagement in the process of entry. The discussion will focus on the identification of factors associated with decision making and examine variations in decision-making involvement. Using case studies, the paper examines the way in which social and personal situations affect participation and how this influences the resident's outlook after admission to the nursing home.

Method

Data for this study consisted of in-depth interviews with ninety residents in eight nursing homes and their next-of-kin. Eligible aged respondents who were capable of hearing and comprehending questions were the comparatively less disabled residents as assessed by the professional nursing-home staff. At the time of their admission, 26% patients were able to perform all of Katz and Akpon's six activities of daily living, and 53% were limited in two or fewer activities. This represents 19% of the total number of 474 patients in the nursing homes and excludes patients whose admission was necessitated by a mental or physical disability. In comparison to the 1981 Australian Bureau of

Statistics' Handicapped Survey (1982), the sample did not differ markedly with respect to the basic social demographic variables of sex, age, marital status, prior living arrangement and length of stay at the nursing home. However, the present sample is biased towards the less disabled residents. The typical resident in this study can be identified as *female, aged 80 to 89, widowed, admitted directly from a private household, and living at the nursing home for between one and four years*.

Nursing homes of various types and sizes were selected because of likely differences in their resident population and admission policies. While many nursing homes in Australia are privately owned, there are also voluntary institutions run by charitable or religious organisations, and government-managed nursing homes (Howe 1990). The sample covered the range of non-government nursing homes. Of the eight homes, four are privately owned and four are in the voluntary sector. The size of the homes varied from thirty to 130 beds.

Nursing homes and informants were not selected to meet the criteria of representative sampling. The focus of the study is to identify and describe a typology of decision making. For this reason, the criteria for selecting nursing homes and informants centred on obtaining a range of processes likely to be influenced by the personal situations of informants and the kinds of nursing home which they entered. The sample size of ninety for the in-depth study was sufficient to ensure that the variations that existed in the experiences of individuals have been maximised.

The next-of-kin to be interviewed was the individual *identified by the aged resident* as having been an important participant in the decision to move. A total of seventy-nine next-of-kin were interviewed. In eight cases, the patient had no family, and in the remaining three, permission to contact a relative or friend was refused by the patient. None of the relatives who were contacted refused to be interviewed. Of the seventy-nine next-of-kin interviews conducted forty-two were with the children, eleven were with a spouse, and the remaining twenty-six were with nieces, nephews, grandchildren, cousins and friends.

The interview schedule consisted of both open-ended and closed questions. Aged residents and their next-of-kin were administered a similar set of questions on the admission decision history. When the residents' responses were compared with those of their next-of-kin, a 92% congruency rate was recorded. Next-of-kin members were slightly more likely to identify health practitioners as participants in the decision-making process, and to include health factors in their stories, than were the aged participants. Conversational questions were also asked, with the purpose of collecting qualitative data. All interviews were tape recorded. The interviews were conducted at the nursing home with the aged participants and on the telephone with the next-of-kin (For further details see Minichiello 1986).

A Typology of Decision-making Situations

The typology presented in Figure A1 shows that residents differed in their level of involvement in the decision-making process. The upper left-hand cell shows that a minority of residents were involved in decisions made both to enter a nursing home and its choice. The lower right-hand cell shows that a majority of residents were totally excluded from decision making. The other two cells represent the small numbers of residents who felt that they were involved in either the decision to enter a nursing home, or in its selection, but not in both stages. Residents in different typological categories displayed very different levels of acceptance and adjustment to the nursing-home situation. Of the four groups, the fully involved residents reported being most happy (see Table 1). While a number of factors can influence subject well being (Connor et al. 1979), a person's perception of involvement in decision making can affect willingness to live with the outcome. Residents who made their own decision and selection of nursing home, as illustrated by the case studies of Miss Barker and Mr Hamilton presented below, entered the nursing home with a positive attitude because this was their own chosen living arrangement. In contrast, residents for whom others had made both the decision and selection—like Mrs Earl, Mrs Young and Mr Barclay—found it difficult to accept and adjust to living in a nursing home because it was not their choice. They perceived that their fate had been determined by others. Their first few months in the home were spent coming to terms with the decision of another person. The extent of the residents' involvement in the decision-making process affected their relationship with others and their willingness to participate in activities organised by the nursing home.

Involvement in selecting nursing home

		YES	*NO*
Involvement in the decision to move into nursing home	*YES*	Fully involved 19	Decision involved 10
	NO	Selection involved 8	Excluded 53

Figure A1 A typology of the aged person's degree of involvement in seeking nursing-home care and number of residents in each cell (N=90).[a]

[a] To determine their involvement in the decision-making process, residents were asked two questions: 'How much say did you have in the decision to move to a nursing home?' and 'How much say did you have in selecting the nursing home?'. The residents' replies to these questions were then compared to those of their next-of-kin. In only two cases were the replies from residents and their next-of-kin in conflict with one another. In both cases, the resident reported having some say in the decision to enter a home while their next-of-kin reported that the older person had no involvement. In order to overcome this discrepancy, the director of the nursing home was asked her opinion as to whether the older person was involved in the decisions to enter and select the nursing home. Discussions with the director confirmed the relative's view that the older person had been excluded from the decision. When further clarification of their role in the decision-making process was sought, both residents changed their stories about their involvement.

Those residents who were involved with the decision but not the selection, like Mr Payne and Mrs Hays, were often forced to decide because of a health crisis. However, accepting the decision, like those fully involved residents, they were able to engage happily with life in the home. Residents who were involved only with selection—like Mr Hollier—were much less satisfied and well adjusted to their new lives.

Fully-involved Residents

The influence of gender, marital status, living arrangement and health on the ageing experience has been explored in a number of studies (Troll et al. 1979; Russell & Schofield 1986). These factors have an interactive influence on each other and lead to different types of negotiations between the older person and their family about the management of old age (Kendig 1986). These factors have also been cited (Day 1985) to explain the attitudes of older persons and their expectations of the use of formal care (contracted community care) and informal care (care provided by family and friends). Kendig (1986) and Day (1985) suggest that those that have never married are more likely to demonstrate independence and to plan ahead for protection in old age. While there can be no doubt that these factors can influence care options, individual action is not solely determined by them. People possessing similar personal characteristics can and do display different attitudes towards the use of formal and informal care. This may partly explain why studies have found these factors to be poor predictors of the use of community and institutional services (Coulton & Frost 1982; McAuley & Arling 1984). Obviously, other aspects of a person's personal situation and their perception of reality affect the interpretation and assessment of their situation. Thus, as in the case study of Miss Barber and Mr Hollier described below, it is possible for people of similar characteristics, for example having no children, to respond differently because of different perceptions of the situation.

Residents who were responsible for seeking and arranging their own admission are classified as *fully involved*. Of the ninety residents interviewed, nineteen were responsible for their own admission. These residents were nominated by themselves and their next-of-kin as the most important player in the decision-making process. They also took the initiative of contacting the nursing-home director to make arrangements for admission. Figure A2 shows some of the key personal characteristics of residents in different decision-making situations. Of the nineteen residents who themselves decided to move into a home, five were never married, four were married and ten widowed. While for some of these residents the absence of children was the underlying factor which forced them to consider institutional care, seven residents had the potential support of children and other family members which they chose not to accept. Although the majority of those fully involved in decision making were living alone, eight were living with family members or friends. It is notable that the absence of offspring is not a necessary factor in the decision to move into a home. Of the fifty-three residents in the excluded category, seventeen were without children but they nevertheless did not anticipate or choose living in a nursing home as a viable option.

There are clear differences between people involved in and excluded from decision making. Not only were the fully involved more likely to be in better health prior to admission, independent and self-supporting (according to nursing assessment), but their orientation towards self-management and (negative) attitude to the acceptance of informal care differed markedly from that of the excluded group. Yet obviously a factor beyond good health prevented these people from relying on others to help them with household and personal tasks. Self-perception was important in shaping acceptance of care arrangements. They held strong views about not accepting help from others. The following quotes highlight the determination to remain independent in old age.

> I would not go and live with my daughter. I have always preferred to be on my own, to be independent and make decisions for myself. The thought that I could become dependent on my people, like my mother was on us, scares me. This is why I decided to come here (Mrs Hodges, widowed, 89 years old).

The majority of these residents had been living alone. They preferred this living arrangement to avoid the mutual obligations placed on people when sharing households.

> When my wife died my daughter asked me to go and live with her. I did not want to give up my little ways of doing things because when you go and live with your children you have to change. And I was not prepared to give up my independence. Well I gave it a good battle for three years and then I decided to move into a nursing home when I felt a little tired (Mr Greenwood, widowed, 70 years old).

Of the involved group who had been living with others, none was living in what was described as a 'dependent relationship'. Help was reciprocally and voluntarily given and received.

> I was not a burden. We all shared the work. We never asked our neighbours to help because between us we could manage (Miss Kaye, never married, 84 years old).

Many of these residents were living with people of a similar age. Shared living was seen to be a way of combating the dependency brought about by old age.

Profile characteristics	Fully involved (Decision and selection)	Partial decision makers Decision involved	Selection involved	Excluded
Number of respondents	19	10	8	53
Gender				
Male	4	4	2	13
Female	15	6	6	40
Marital Status				
Never married	5	2	—	12
Widowed	10	4	8	29
Married	4	4	—	6
Divorced/separated	—	—	—	6
Living arrangement				
Alone	11	6	4	25
With others	8	4	4	28
Source of help[a]				
Self	13	—	—	19
Informal	4	6	8	21
Formal	2	4	—	13
Mean Age	85	83	83	79
Mean functional health[b]	22	36	24	27
Mean happy score[c]	1.7	2.0	2.4	2.5

FigureA2 A profile of the residents with different levels of involvement in the decision-making process by age, gender, marital status, health, living arrangement, source of help when living in the community and subjective well-being.

[a] Respondents were asked to nominate the person who did most of the shopping, meal preparation and housework when living in the community. The informal sector includes family members, friends and neighbours while the formal sector includes paid help, and community and government agencies.
[b] This score represents the person's ability to perform eighteen activities of daily living. A score of eighteen indicates that the person was capable of performing all of the activities of daily living, while a score of seventy-two indicates that the person was not capable of performing any of the activities when living in the community.
[c] Subjective well being was measured by asking the residents the following question, 'Taking things altogether, how would you say things are these days? Would you say that you're happy, fairly happy, or not happy?'. A score of 1 indicates that the resident is very happy while a score of 3 indicates that the resident is not too happy. Significant differences in the level of happiness were found between the four groups ($F = 12.8$ $p < .001$).

These residents spoke about their self-sufficiency. When they were asked to nominate the person who did the major household and personal tasks just prior to admission, all but three of the eight residents who lived with others stated that they were responsible for or jointly shared these tasks. The three residents who relied on outside help were married men whose wives were in hospital. Their wives had always done 'such chores'. Lacking the necessary skills, they relied on female family members to assist them with cooking, shopping and house cleaning. Although grateful for the help, they interpreted it as an intrusion into their personal lives. When their partners entered a nursing home they voluntarily admitted themselves.

> I did not like my daughter coming in and helping me. My wife and I have always been very independent. We never asked our children for help. The doctor asked me if I would consider getting Meals-on-Wheels when my wife was in the hospital. I refused. I wouldn't want other people coming into my house. When someone is helping you, there is a sense of owing them something. My daughter would prepare a meal when it was convenient for her. And although it was not when I wanted to eat, I felt that I had to because it was a big effort on her part (Mr Jukic, married, 93 years old).

Two case studies are presented to highlight how the residents' personal orientation and perception of their social circumstances influenced involvement in the decision to enter a nursing home.

Miss Barber

Miss Barber was 78 years old and never married. She lived with her sister for twenty years. When her sister died, Miss Barber moved into a flat. She lived alone for the next ten years.

At this stage, becoming aware of her increasing age, she began to plan although she was still capable of independent living and did not yet require help with any of the household and personal-care tasks of daily living. Because she did not have any children 'to look after her' she considered moving into a nursing home. She selected the nursing home and then consulted a physician, because she required an admission referral.

Selection involved visiting a total of ten nursing homes, and waiting eight months for a vacancy in *Nursing Home A* chosen because of the friendly staff, the cleanliness of the home and its close proximity to her brother's residence.

The number of nursing homes Miss Barber visited and her reason for selecting the nursing home are consistent with the experiences of other residents who were fully involved in the decision to seek nursing home care. In the search for a nursing home, residents who were fully involved contacted a mean of nine homes. After lodging their application, they waited a mean of three months before placement. The most frequent reason for selecting the home was the availability of a single room, the friendliness of staff and the homely features of the home.

When Miss Barber was asked the question, 'What did you think of moving into a nursing home?', she replied, like the other eighteen residents who fully participated in the decision, that she 'was very much in favour of the move'. A crisis would remove any opportunity to determine her own fate. She had time to think about and come to terms with institutional living.

Mr Hamilton

Couples who have lived together for fifty or so years often turn to each other for personal support. When they are separated, however, they face a kind of vulnerability that those who have long lived alone have either faced or adjusted to much earlier in their lives (Day 1985). Older males are particularly vulnerable to change in their living arrangement when their partner dies or moves to a nursing home.

Mr Hamilton, 87 years old, found himself in this situation when his wife moved into a nursing home after suffering a stroke. Although he tried to live alone for 'almost a year' he decided that it would be easier to live in the same nursing home. Two factors were important; his strong bond with his wife, and his reluctance to be a burden to his children.

Mr Hamilton has a close emotional bond with his three children; a son who lives in Sydney, and a daughter and older son who both live interstate. Although he relies on his children to make him feel needed and appreciated, he and his wife have never been dependent on them for instrumental support. Throughout the years, it was they who were providing help to their children. When his wife had the stroke, there was no uncertainty about what they should do. The choice was obvious. Nursing-home care would allow them to continue enjoying their independence from the family.

When Mr Hamilton lived alone he did most of his own cooking, shopping and house cleaning. He would only reluctantly agree to accept help with the housework from his daughter-in-law, or help with the gardening from his son and grandsons. His sister and children often invited him to 'stay with them on weekends'. However, it was only on 'very special occasions' that he would accept their hospitality. When asked why he did not use community services, he replied that he preferred not to use them.

Mr Hamilton decided to move into the nursing home when the senior nurse and doctor informed him that his wife would not live for much longer. He wanted to be close to his wife when she died. It was his own decision. He discussed the subject with his children and inquired about a vacancy.

He accepted the house rules of bed planning, and spent most of his time caring for his wife. When his wife died six months after his admission, he was able to accept her death. He remained in the home because of his involvement with the nursing-home community which gave him satisfaction and enjoyment. Foremost on his mind was that he did not want to be a burden to his children.

Common Themes in the Stories of Fully Involved Residents

Common factors in the stories of residents fully involved in decision making were their good health on entry to a nursing home and their life-long independence. Good health makes it possible for the older person to travel to the nursing-home and be involved in the organisational arrangements for nursing home entry. It also reduces the chances of being placed in a situation of dependency prior to admission which forces a decision without choice. A dependent person seeking help from others is under pressure to comply with the advice given by helpers. This requires the surrender of self-determination. None of the fully involved residents were in situations where they had given others the right to determine their fate, nor were any of them prepared to be placed in such a situation. Realising that 'time' would create dependency upon family or friends, they made the entry decision while they were still 'in the driver's seat'.

Forward planning or *crisis decision making* typifies the nursing home decisions. Forward planning, as illustrated by Miss Barber, can involve the conscious decision by the older person to find 'a home', but not all the fully involved residents were planners. Of these nineteen residents, ten made a forward-planning decision. The others had not thought of moving into a nursing home until a crisis forced them to consider institutional living. Involved entrants admitted in a time of crisis differed from the excluded entrants admitted under the same conditions in that they maintained a strong determination to remain independent. For this reason, they took the initiative to move into a nursing home.

Forward planners appraised their social situation in terms of family support, or lack of family support, and their own self-care abilities. A striking feature of the forward planners was their perception that admission to a nursing home gave rather than deprived them of independence. They were also aware of having limited family support available to them.

Four of the ten forward planners were never married, four were married without children and two were childless widows. They recognised clues that helped them determine 'when the time had come'.

> I lost my motor car and I thought, well this is a sign that it is time to go into a home. I never wanted to worry my grandsons so I decided not to tell them about my plans. (Mrs Alkins, widowed, 88 years old).

They obtained nursing-home care as security. Many of these people did not initially require the extent of care provided by the nursing home, but limited by their options, they had no choice.

> I was quite able to look after myself but I decided to put my name down. Because I had no children I thought that when I got old it would be nice to be looked after. I was 85 years old and I put my name down. I did not think I would get in for years but I was accepted in six months (Mrs Bennett, widowed, 87 years old).

Involved residents who made a crisis decision varied in the circumstances that led to moving into a nursing home. The illness of a spouse, the onset of an acute illness or a change in living arrangement initiated thoughts of nursing home entry. All had given attention to this option because they wanted to avoid dependency upon family members or friends. Family support was an option for most, but nursing-home care was the choice made.

> I felt that moving into a nursing home was loyal to my family. I can't see now. I couldn't put that responsibility on my children. They have families of their own (Mrs McCoppin, widowed, 72 years old).

The family had never assumed the constant burden of the care-giver role because the older person had made plans to ensure that this was avoided.

They entered the nursing home voluntarily and this made it easier for them to accept institutional life. When these residents were asked about their feelings regarding the move, none spoke of the apprehension and fears that characterised the stories of residents who were excluded from the decisions. All nineteen residents selected words such as *accepting* and *security*, which suggests that they had come to terms with their decision—*No regrets, no point looking back*.

Because these residents held the view that they were selecting a home, all were concerned about locating 'the right place'. For most, this involved a number of visits to nursing homes. For some, the search had begun many years earlier. Planners were more likely than the other residents to 'take their time' searching for a home as they were not restricted by a crisis situation.

Excluded Residents

The *excluded* were those residents who were not involved in decisions to seek institutional care or to choose the nursing home. Of the ninety residents, fifty-three saw themselves as silent parties in the decision-making process. When asked who made the decisions, these residents nominated people other than themselves.

None had visited the nursing home prior to admission neither were they were able to recall the administrative details of the application. The following quote is representative of the level of knowledge these residents had about who had contacted the director of the nursing home and whether applications to other nursing homes had been lodged.

> *Interviewer:* Could we now talk about your application to the nursing home?
> *Mr Osborne:* Well I never applied to go to any nursing home. I really don't know anything about that. My son would have done all of that.
> *Interviewer:* Do you know why he selected this nursing home?
> *Mr Osborne:* I can't answer that truthfully. The only thing I know is that he came in one day and said I was coming here (Mr Osborne, widowed; 75 years old)

Figure A2 shows that excluded residents differ in many ways from the involved residents. The excluded residents had decisions made for them at a time when deteriorating health forced dependence on others. They generally were in much poorer physical health than the involved residents. Excluded residents waited until their health situation deteriorated or their caregivers could no longer manage.

> *Mrs Newman:* My husband died and I lived alone for twelve months. I had been living alone for some time and I wasn't really feeling well. My daughter had been helping me with the housework. I had an asthma attack and the ambulance took me to the hospital. It was while I was in the hospital that I was told by my daughter that I was moving into a home (widowed, 83 years old).
>
> *Mrs Newman's daughter:* Even before my father died I was worried about her. I helped her nurse my father. But she also needed help. I used to spend a lot of my time running to her place. I am an only child but our house is not big enough to have her live with us. When she went into the hospital I made the decision (married, 50 years old).

The majority of excluded residents had been dependent on informal and/or formal support to complete the tasks of daily living. Over two-thirds relied on either family members or community services for shopping, meal preparation and housework. They used formal services for an average of twelve months, and informal services on the average for the last twenty-three months prior to admission. Not only had they become dependent on formal or informal help, but they were also more likely than the involved residents to have been living with others, generally offspring, prior to admission. Once a person enters into a dependency relationship, 'both they and those responsible for their care see the drift into greater dependency as irreversible' (Day 1985: 112). Family members spoke about nursing homes as the only alternative to home care after family support had failed (Minichiello 1986).

Another distinguishing feature of the involved and excluded groups was their attitude to future care plans. While the involved residents had ruled out reliance on family support, excluded residents were more likely to expect families to provide long-term support. Many had cared for their own parents at home and had seen them die in an acute hospital. Based on their past care experiences, they expected a similar fate.

> I never thought I would end up in a nursing home. Just like my father and mother, I thought I was one of these people that would go on doing things for myself or have my family look after me (Mrs Cocke, widowed, 89 years old).

They believed that it was not necessary to make plans because their families would look after them if 'there was a need'. Day refers to these people as 'counters on family support'.

> . . . not only did [they] believe that their children would be available to give personal care when needed, but they accepted the appropriateness of this filial obligation. These parents apparently welcomed without shame, fear or ambivalence their children's offers to provide the last-ditch custodial care (1985: 120).

Formal services were not seen as a substitute for family care. They held the expectation that between themselves and their families, they could manage until 'the end'. Few ever expected to live their remaining lives in a nursing home.

> I never thought I would end up in a nursing home. I feel my children have let me down. I would never have put my parents in a nursing home—people just didn't think of doing that and I know of other younger people who are looking after their aged parents (Mrs Telling, widowed, 72 years old).

Many of these residents spoke about how the 'family has changed' and that the younger generation was less willing to care for an aged parent. On the other hand, family members often wanted to provide care, however, they found it difficult because of the effects of social change on their own lives.

With the increase in life expectancy in the second half of the twentieth century, greater demand for care of ageing parents has been placed upon families. Uhlenberg (1980) shows that the number of people who experienced the death of a parent before the age of fifteen dropped from one in four to one in twenty, while the number of middle-aged couples with two or more living parents increased from 10% to 47 per cent. Not only do we now have more people in their late fifties with surviving parents, but there has also been a change in the nature and duration of care. Death following chronic illness has replaced death from acute disease. As a result families are required to offer more care for longer periods of time. Many of these residents failed to understand that current lifestyle and economic demands made it difficult for families to provide long-term care as was possible in the 'good old days'. Whereas family members came to grips with the difficulty of providing long-term care, the older person held on to the view that ‘everything would work out’. Holding contradictory views on what the family should and could do, and finding it difficult to raise the topic of nursing homes with their aged relative, family members excluded the older person from the decision-making process.

> *Mrs Askin:* I thought I was managing quite well. I used to get my cleaning done and my daughters and meals-on-wheels would help me with the cooking. But my daughters did not think it was wise for me to stay home alone. They told me I had to come here. When I first came here I used to cry and go to see matron and tell her that I wanted to return home, and matron would say I can’t unless the daughters gave their consent (widowed, 91 years old).
>
> *Mrs Askin’s daughter:* My mother is 91 years old and she was losing her eyesight. She used to say she was all right but she wasn’t. She would not eat properly. At the time, my sister and I both worked and we would call by to see her every day. But the situation was getting worse and we could not continue the pace. We couldn’t talk to her because she thought everything was fine. So we decided to put her in a home. We did not think it was safe for her to live alone (married, 60 years old).

Caregivers and families often waited for a major crisis before making the decision to seek nursing-home care for their relatives. Of the fifty-three residents in the excluded category, thirty-two were admitted after an illness placed them in an institutional setting, and six were admitted after they had experienced a change in living arrangement, such as the death of a spouse or eviction from housing. Hospitalisation for an acute illness was for some residents the final signal for a change in care arrangement. The remaining eight residents were admitted after family members were no longer willing to continue providing support. It is interesting to note that many family members had tried hard to maintain their older person at home. Most waited until the situation required some drastic measure to be taken. The decision to institutionalise an aged parent is not an easy one.

The crisis placed the older person in a position where their future was governed by forces beyond their control. When a health crisis occurred family members and health professionals took it upon themselves to act on behalf of the older person, making a decision which had been postponed many times in the past. Health professionals reinforced the decision, making the only recommendation they thought was possible given the failure of community and/or family care.

As illustrated by the next three case studies, residents who were totally excluded from the decision to enter a home had different attitudes to entering a nursing home from those of the involved groups.

Mrs Young

Mrs Young had been living with her daughter for more than three years before entering the nursing home. When her husband died she had asked her daughter, who was going through a separation from her husband, if she could live with her. She sold her family home and looked forward to living with her daughter, but the experience was unhappy for both. Her daughter worked, was seldom home, and resented feeling guilty about leaving her mother alone. She felt her mother was not trying 'hard enough' to lead an independent life. Mrs Young felt that her daughter was not very supportive. She expected her daughter to give her more companionship and attention.

It was not Mrs Young's decision to move into a home. 'It all happened so quickly. I did not even know she was thinking along those lines.' One day Mrs Young's daughter announced that she had spoken to a director of a nursing home and lodged an application. 'She told me I had to go.' Mrs Young was devastated. She could not understand her daughter's actions. She would never have considered putting her own parents into a home.

Mrs Young did not think she was a nuisance. She required very little help from her daughter. Other children were looking after parents much more dependent than she. And her daughter had no family of her own.

A week later she moved into the nursing home and found it very difficult to cope. She had never thought about the possibility, and could not forgive her only daughter for doing this to her. She feared that dying would take a long time. Visits from her daughter are marred by demands to return home. 'When I visit mum we mostly argue so I do not go as often as I should.'

Mrs Earl

Mrs Earl, a widow of fifteen years standing, became a diabetic. She was not eating properly or taking her medication regularly. She often had dizzy spells and fell. Her consequent poor health alarmed the family and her personality and past family history ruled out caring for her in her own home or the homes of either of her sons. While she had not thought about living in a nursing home, her sons and the doctor made the decision for her. When it was first suggested that she move into a nursing home Mrs Earl cried and told her sons that she would not 'abandon' her home.

> I don't mean to complain about her but she has many problems; too many for one single person. We have too little patience to tolerate her (daughter-in-law, married, 50 years old).

They searched for a nursing home bed, but were not selective. Mrs Earl was admitted to the first home that offered a place. She had no involvement with decision or selection.

Mrs Earl found it difficult to accept living in a home. She did not get along with the other patients or participate in any of the activities. Her relationship with her family worsened. Her daughter-in-law said that the last 'six months have been hell'. They visit only when 'it is necessary'.

Mr Barclay

Mr Barclay was 70 years old and had never married. A loner throughout his life, he drifted from one boarding house to another. He had few friends. Although he has two brothers and three sisters, he had not kept in touch with them 'for years'. He lost contact when his mother died twenty years ago. He said he feels close to no one.

For Mr Barclay, life after retirement was different from expectations. Without a job to go to, he no longer felt useful. With failing eyesight, he could not read the newspaper or watch television. Eye surgery was refused by his doctor unless Mr Barclay moved into a nursing home.

Mr Barclay had never thought about living in a nursing home. In fact, he held some very negative views about nursing homes.

> Some of them are like hovels. All they are interested in is taking old people's money. The government has closed some of them down because of abuses to patients, for ill treatment, neglect and all that ugly business. Well I was very wary of them.

Without consultation, the social worker announced the decision. Mr Barclay 'was not given a choice'. He was unhappy, had no knowledge of nursing homes, nor had he the opportunity to visit the home selected for him, prior to his admission.

> You just do not walk into places like this. You go to the doctor and he makes enquiries. It works just like going into a hospital. You just do not arrive at their doorsteps and say you want a bed. I did not choose to come here. They sent me here. If I had my way I would still be living in a boarding home.

Common Themes in the Stories of Excluded Residents

Exclusion from the decision-making process resulted in feelings of powerlessness and helplessness.

> *Interviewer:* Who told you about . . . (the nursing home)?
> *Mrs Yates:* Well no one. I had never heard of the place until my son brought me here.
> *Interviewer:* How did you feel about this?
> *Mrs Yates:* I never thought my only child would ever suggest such a thing. But what was I to do? I was living in their house and he was telling me I had to go. I did not have a choice. I was heartbroken (widowed, 68 years old).

Unlike the residents who were totally involved with the decision, none of the excluded residents had ever considered institutional living. They held a derogatory view of nursing homes. 'Such places' were not for them but for other 'poor souls', who had no family or who had been abandoned by their families. Like Mrs Earl, many of these residents did not recognise that they were not managing and had become a burden to others. However, there were differences in how people defined 'burden'. Mrs Earl was 'a burden' to her family because they could not 'get along with her'. This was the reason why they did not offer help. Other family members, like Mrs Young's daughter, felt their parents were 'a burden' because they were asking for more support than was available at home.

There were also differences in perception of the older person's capacity to cope with independent living. While the elderly person believed that they could continue current living arrangements until they died, family members felt that they were no longer capable of living at home. Family members found it difficult to raise the topic of nursing homes. Many waited for a crisis before taking action. When the opportunity arose, the decision was made quickly and excluded the older person. Often nursing homes were selected on the basis of the bed availability rather than on an assessment of the suitability of the services and environment. The older person was 'surprised' and unwilling to move. None of these residents said they favoured the move.

Some residents excluded from the decision (like Mr Barclay, without family ties) were also admitted in crisis. Although they may have given some thought to nursing-home care, they postponed making the decision. Without the support of an informal network, and in the midst of a crisis, they felt that they had no choice but to accept the decision of a health professional who usually referred them to a nursing home. When asked how they felt about the move, they all experienced mixed feelings about the decision. On one hand, they had never wanted to move into a home. On the other hand, they accepted the decision because they had no family. In many ways, they held similar views towards planning for their own care, as did people whom Day (1985) refers to as *fatalists*. Fatalists, in her view, did not believe in planning ahead and avoided thinking about what their needs would be when they could no longer manage. They believed that the 'future is governed by forces beyond their control' (Day 1985: 117). They preferred to continue living as they had always done but were forced by circumstances to allow others to make plans on their behalf.

Partial Decision Makers

The involved and excluded situations represent the extreme ends of the older person's involvement in the decision-making process. Some residents, as shown in Figure A1, played a partial role in decisions. They were directly involved in making the decision either to enter a home (decision involved) or to select a home (selection involved), but not in both decisions. Figure A2 provides a profile of these residents. In general, they were widowed and dependent on family or friends to assist them with the activities of daily living prior to their admission. However, these figures mask a number of differences found between these two types of partial decision makers.

Figure A2 shows that the ten decision-involved residents were in poorer health than the eight residents who were selection involved. All decision-involved residents were admitted from a hospital. Their poor health and the fact that they had not made prior plans to move into a nursing home forced them to entrust selection to others.

> *Interviewer:* Why did you not visit the nursing home before moving into it?
> *Mrs Davies:* I would have but I was in hospital and it was not possible. So I asked my daughter to make all of the arrangements. But it was not her decision. I made the decision to go into a nursing home. She just helped me find one (widowed, 84 years old).

Decision-involved residents expressed views about self-care and family support which were similar to those of the involved residents; whereas selection-involved residents made statements about family care and nursing-home care which were similar to those of totally excluded residents. Some differences, however, exist between those residents who played a partial role in the decision and selection, and those residents who were either totally involved or totally excluded from decisions. While the involved residents had ruled out receiving support from their family members, decision-involved residents were more ambivalent about the type of care they expected in old age. Prior to their admission, six of these residents relied on family members to do most of their cooking, house cleaning and shopping, and four relied on formal services. These residents were very similar to the 'procrastinators' that Day describes in her study.

> . . .(they) were all people in frail health who knew it would be wise for them to make contingency plans, who were aware of various services for the aged, but who had made no move to adopt any of the possible alternatives (1985: 116).

They preferred to hold out and adopt a 'wait-and-see' attitude (Day 1985). Although they had not committed themselves to institutional care while they were in good health, with the onset of further dependency on others, they took the initiative by involving themselves in the planning process.

> I was getting old and couldn't do the things I used to do. I became very dependent on my children. My sons were worried about me. They wanted me to go and live with them. I wasn't happy about that. I went into hospital and my son was going to convert his house for me. But I decided it was not what I wanted. I thought, well the best of friends get a bit cross with each other at times so I decided that I was going to a home (Mrs Jones, widowed, 87 years old).

While the suggestion of nursing-home care may have been raised by others, these residents made a clear choice in maintaining self-determination in the decision. They spoke about the problems they were creating for others.

> The most important reason for making the decision was because I was a lot of trouble to my wife. When I discussed it with her we both agreed that this was the best solution (Mr Kirby, married, 78 years old).

It was recognition of the fact that they may be 'trouble' that led these residents to discuss nursing-home care with their family members. Because of their involvement in these discussions they saw the decision as resting largely in their hands. They spoke about being 'very much in favour' of the move and saw its necessity. They delegated the task of selecting a home to someone they trusted. None complained about the nursing home chosen on their behalf.

> I was in hospital but my sister searched for a nursing home. I had total confidence in her judgment. She is a fussy person and if she thought the place was fine then I knew it would be okay. And she couldn't have chosen a better place (Mr Smith, never married, 90 years old).

Residents who had others make the decision for them but weɪe involved in the selection of the home had no perception of the difficulties they were creating for others.

> When my wife died my daughters helped me with the cooking and housework. I did not think I was too much of a trouble. They helped me one day a week. They would come to the house and clean the place, do the washing and all that sort of thing. During the week I managed on my own. I was surprised when my oldest daughter told me that I had to move into a home (Mr Hollier, widowed, 86 years old).

In all eight cases, family members were doing most of their cooking, house cleaning and shopping and four of these residents had been living with a family member. They relied on family members to look after them and had no conception that others were thinking about nursing-home care. It also was clear that they themselves were not considering nursing-home care.

> I never thought about nursing homes before my daughter suggested to me that I come to one (Mr Hollier, widowed, 86 years old).

There was a certain amount of trauma when they were told about the decision. However, in return for agreeing to move into the home, the older person was permitted to negotiate with family members in the selection process. Some family members gave the older person this opportunity to lessen their guilt. Others were concerned that the older person approved of the nursing home into which they moved.

> I was afraid of her being left on her own. She insisted that she could cope on her own and that my brother and I give her another chance. She was nearly blind and she would fall or run into things. We explained to her that sooner or later she would have to move and that it was best if she did it now while she was able to select a nursing home she liked. She agreed and we saw several places before she decided on 'Nursing Home A' (Mrs Brown's son, never married, 50 years old).

Mr Payne and Mrs Hays represent the views and situation of those residents who made their own decision to enter into a home but left the selection of the nursing home in the hands of others. Mr Hollier's story captures the situation of residents who had the decision made by others but who selected the nursing home.

Mr Payne

Mr Payne was 81 years old. He lived alone following the death of his wife eight years ago. He had no children. He engaged home help and ate at the RSL Club.

After having blackouts he was hospitalised for several weeks. While in hospital, the doctor suggested that he move into a nursing home. Mr Payne accepted the advice.

As he was too weak to search for a nursing home he asked his sister and nephew to locate 'a decent place'. His sister was an active member of the Anglican Church and knew of a 'good home'. She lodged an application on his behalf and because of her longstanding membership of the congregation, a vacancy was made available within a few weeks. He was discharged from the hospital to the nursing home. When asked whether he was worried about entering a home which he had not visited, he replied that he trusted his sister's judgment, and she could not have 'picked a better place'.

Mrs Hays

Mrs Hays was 84 years old. Her husband died ten years ago. Although her offspring had each invited Mrs Hays to live with them, she decided to live alone. With some assistance from her daughters and daughters-in-law, Mrs Hays managed her shopping and housework. She was forced to think about moving into a nursing home only when she found herself in hospital.

> I had a virus, Bell's palsy and shingles and it left me so very ill. And they have stitched my eyelids together which they do after Bell's palsy. I have very little sight. I am handicapped that way.

Her daughter and son-in-law first raised the subject of moving into a nursing home. She had several views about not moving in 'with the family'.

> I was well aware that I couldn't look after myself. And I didn't want to put myself on my family. I can't see now or just barely. I couldn't put that responsibility on my children. They have families of their own and their own lives to live. And I feel that it is not my place to intrude on their privacy. To be honest I prayed I would have died when I was in hospital. I have lived my life. My ill health came at a bad time. While I was in hospital my daughter died of cancer and my son was in a bad car accident. They did not want to put me here, and I never thought about living in a home, but what else were we to do?

After discussions with family and doctor, Mrs Hays asked her daughter to look 'for a nice home'. Following a number of enquiries, her daughter located a nursing home that had a single room and 'felt homely'. Three weeks later Mrs Hays 'jumped from the hospital to the nursing home'. She went peacefully and willingly. Although she had 'no idea' of what to expect, she does not feel the nursing home has robbed her of any freedom. Given her poor health she feels that she could not cope on her own.

Mr Hollier

Mr Hollier was 86 years old. When his wife died, he lived alone for three months. He had two daughters who regularly helped him. He was also receiving meals-on-wheels. The burden of worrying about their father was disruptive. Mr Hollier's children decided that 'some other arrangement had to be found'. Seeing their father as 'an old man' and 'helpless' they decided to turn to nursing-home care.

Mr Hollier was unhappy about moving to a nursing home. But under 'great pressure' from his daughters, he agreed. He felt he had no choice. His wife was dead. However, he did stress that he would not move into 'any home'. He would have to choose it. He and his daughters visited several homes. Although he did not 'like any of them' he chose a home with a garden and a single room. However, being involved in the selection of the home has not made it easier to accept his daughters' decision. The nursing home provided him with 'plenty of blankets to keep me warm and that sort of thing', but he could not get used to institutional living. He was 'shocked' by the lack of privacy. 'Everything is public here.'

Common Themes in the Stories of Partial Decision Makers

Elderly people do not necessarily anticipate moving into a nursing home when they can no longer manage independent living. The separation of residents into categories of being either totally involved or excluded from the decision-making process fails to capture the myriad of alternatives in the spectrum. There are a number of older people who have never thought about moving into a nursing home until a crisis had forced them to think of an alternative living arrangement. Unlike the planners, these people have made no contingency plans. They did not place themselves on a nursing-home waiting list. However, given their preference for not wishing to be a burden on others, they made the only decision possible. Their health situation prevented them from selecting the nursing home. This selection process was left to others.

Other residents who were either counting on family support or had not thought that they would require nursing-home care had others tell them that they should move into a home. Nevertheless, these residents had the good fortune of being asked to participate in the decision of selecting a home. They were fortunate in that their good health enabled them to travel and that family members gave them the opportunity to participate in the decision-making process. While some of these residents may not have been happy about the prospect of living in a home, their control over where they were going to live made the decision more acceptable. The older person's involvement in the decision to enter a home can have some influence on the older person's subjective well being. Indeed, Figure A2 shows that of the four groups, excluded residents reported being least happy. While a number of factors can influence subjective well being (Connor et al. 1979) a person's perception of their involvement in any decision can affect their willingness to live with their fate. As the case studies have shown, residents who made their own decision to move, like Miss Barber and Mr Hamilton, entered the nursing home with a positive attitude because this was the preferred choice of living arrangement. In contrast, residents who had others make the decision for them, like Mrs Earl, found it difficult to accept and adjust to living in a nursing home because it was not their choice. Their fate had been determined by others. Their first few months in the home were spent coming to terms with someone else's decision.

Conclusion

There was a marked difference in perception of autonomy and independence between those fully involved and those excluded from decision making to enter a nursing home. For the involved group, entry to a nursing home expressed their desire to protect others by not being a burden, while the excluded group expected others to meet their demands, without understanding the level of burden which this imposed. Both had strong justification for their positions. Using Kelley's (1955) personal construct theory, it could be argued that those who chose to enter a nursing home did so because their personal construct of a nursing home incorporated the notion of personal autonomy. For them, the nursing home would support areas of present or perceived future needs for health support and protect them from the loss of control and autonomy that would occur should a health crisis require decisions to be made by others. While they accepted that they may become physically dependent on others in a nursing home, they would still retain their autonomy in terms of control of their own situation. In contrast, those excluded from decisions confused autonomy with independence. To be physically dependent on others was acceptable, and in fact expected, from family and friends, but, it was not acceptable to be dependent on staff in nursing homes. They interpreted being placed in a home as loss of autonomy and rejection.

The recent collection of papers published in *The Gerontologist* supplementary issue (June 1988) on autonomy and long-term care illustrate that aged clients are entitled to maximum self- determination. In practice, however, others often tend to make decisions for the elderly. Nursing-home residents are frequently perceived by staff and family members to be unable or unwilling to participate in care decisions (Wetle et al. 1988). While the good intention of those who act on behalf of the elderly is not in question, the paternalistic rationale for acting in this way leads to constraints on the automomy of aged persons (Cohen 1988). An important goal of educators and policy makers should be to 'change what seems to be the commonly held view that disability in old age marks the point at which resignation, disengagement, and acquiescence in the authority exercised by others is appropriate behaviour' (Cohen 1988: 30). Nursing-home administrators need to ensure that competent residents are fully informed of the admission procedures and told which professionals and family members are parties to the negotiating process. Planners of services should establish mechanisms which empower older persons in the decision-making processes thus enabling them to maintain control of their own lives. For example, resources using brochures, video film, or visits from other residents could be provided. Of the two groups who chose to enter a nursing home, the partially involved who were not involved in selection, were precluded by lack of access. While recognising that some applicants because of diminished capability cannot become fully involved with the decision-making process, the principle of automony should be regarded not only as valid but also as an important goal to achieve. Moody's (1988) concept of 'negotiated consent' provides a model by which we can uphold the values of personal automony and individual dignity in those situations in which decisions are made on behalf of another person.

The findings of this study have significance for the recent restructuring in admission policy to nursing homes taking place in Australia and other western countries (Minichiello 1988). The government has established regional geriatric team-assessment procedures to ensure that only the most dependent are selected for admission. Residents admitted under these policy procedures are often in crisis situations and less physically able to become involved in the selection process. As a consequence of this, fewer residents will have the opportunity to enter a home of their own choice. The supply of beds outstrips the demand, and this leads to placement wherever a bed is available. Whether or not persons have control over decisions to enter and select a nursing home impinge on their consequent acceptance and adjustment. Policymakers will have to develop safeguards which protect personal choice and freedom for those who become residents. This is an issue which will require further attention if the quality of care/life standards established by government policy statements are to be met.

References

Adler, A. 1930. 'Individual psychology.', in C. Murchinson (ed.). *Psychologies of 1930*. Worchester, Massachusetts: Clark University Press.

Australian Bureau of Statistics 1982. *Survey of Handicapped Persons, Australia*. Canberra: Australian Bureau of Statistics.

Cohen, E. 1988. 'The elderly mystique: constraints on the autonomy of the elderly with disabilities.', *The Gerontologist* 28: (Suppl) 24–31.

Collopy, B. 1988. 'Autonomy in long-term care: some crucial distinctions.', *The Gerontologist* 28: (Sup.) 10–23.

Connor, K.A., Powers, E.A. & Bultena, G.L. 1979. 'Social interaction and life satisfaction: an empirical assessment of late-life patterns.', *Journal of Gerontology* 34: 116–121.

Coulton, C. & Frost, A.K. 1982. 'Use of social and health services by the elderly.', *Journal of Health and Social Behaviour* 23: 330–339.

Day, A. 1985. *We Can Manage: Expectations About Care and Varieties of Family Support Among People 75 Years of Age and Over*. Melbourne: Institute of Family Studies.

De Charms, R. 1968. *Personal Causation*. New York: Academic.

Howe, A. 1983. 'How Long is Long-Term Care?' *Community Health Studies* 2: 149–154.

Howe, A. 1990. 'Policy for the Provision of Nursing-Home Care.', in H. Kendig, J. McCallum (eds). *Ageing and Public Policies: The Australian Case*. Sydney: Allen and Unwin.

Jameton, A. 1988. 'In the borderlands of autonomy: responsibility in long-term care facilities.', *The Gerontologist* 28: (Sup.) 18–23.

Kelley, G. 1955. *The Psychology of Personal Constructs*. New York: Norton.

Kendig, H.L. 1986. *Ageing and Families: A Social Network Perspective*. Sydney: Allen and Unwin.

Langer, E.J., Janis, I.L. & Wolfer, J.A. 1975. 'Reduction of psychological stress in surgical patients.', *Journal of Experimental Social Psychology* 11: 155–165.

Lazarus, R. & Folkman, S. 1984. *Stress, Appraisal and Coping*. New York: Springer.

Minichiello, V. 1986. 'Social factors in entering nursing homes.', in H. Kendig (ed.). *Ageing and Families: A Support Networks Perspective*. Sydney: Allen and Unwin.

Minichiello, V. 1987. 'Someone's decision: that is how I got here.' *Australian Journal of Social Issues* 22: 345–356.

Minichiello, V. 1988. *Beyond the Medical Admission: Social Pathways Into Nursing Homes*. Unpublished PhD Thesis, Canberra, ACT: Australian National University.

Rowe, J.W. & Kahn, R. 1987. *Human Ageing: Usual and Successful Science* 257: 143–149.

Russell, C. & Schofield, T. 1986. *Where I Hurts: An Introduction to Sociology for Health Workers*. Sydney: Allen and Unwin.

Sarkissian, W. & Perlgut, D. 1986. *Retirement Housing in Australia: Guidelines for Planning and Design*. Roseville, NSW C.4: Impacts Press.

Stanley, B. Stanley, M., Guido, J. & Garvin, L. 1988. 'The functional competency of elderly at risk.', *The Gerontologist* 28: (Sup.) 53–58.

Thomas, T. 1986. 'The psychological well-being of elderly women entering long-term-care residencies.', *Australian Journal on Ageing* 5: 18–23.

Tobin, S. & Lieberman, M. 1976. *Last Homes for the Aged*. San Francisco: Jossey Bass.

Troll, L.E., Miller, S.J. & Atchley, R.C. 1979. *Families in Later Life*. Belmont, California: Wadsworth.

Uhlenberg, P. 1980. 'Death and the family.', *Journal of Family History* 5: 313–320.

Wetle, T., Levkoff, I., Cwikel, J. & Rosen, A. 1988. 'Nursing-home resident participation in medical decisions: perceptions and preferences.', *The Gerontologist* 28: (Sup.) 32–38.

Wingard, D., Jones, D. & Kaplan, R. 1987. 'Institutionalisation care utilisation by the elderly: a critical review.', *The Gerontologist* 27: 156–163.

Index

Entries giving definitions or glossary entries are given in **bold**. Those words given in the text in **bold** usually refer to an entry in the glossary at the end of each chapter.